Losing Work, Moving On

International Perspectives on Worker Displacement

Losing Work, Moving On

International Perspectives on Worker Displacement

Peter J. Kuhn
Editor

2002

W.E. Upjohn Institute for Employment Research
Kalamazoo, Michigan

Library of Congress Cataloging-in-Publication Data

Losing work, moving on : international perspectives on worker displacement / Peter J. Kuhn, editor.

p. cm.

Includes bibliographical references and index.

ISBN 0-88099-233-6 (pbk. : alk. paper) — ISBN 0-88099-234-4 (cloth : alk. paper)

1. Displaced workers—Case studies. 2. Unemployment—Case studies. 3. Unemployed—Case studies. I. Kuhn, Peter Joseph.

HF5549.5.D55 L67 2002
331.13'7—dc21

2002069190

W.E. Upjohn Institute for Employment Research
300 S. Westnedge Avenue
Kalamazoo, Michigan 49007–4686

Cover design by J.R. Underhill.
Index prepared by Leoni McVey.
Printed in the United States of America.

Contents

Figures

Tables

Preface

The inspiration for this project dates to a number of conversations I had with colleagues in the United Kingdom, Australia, and Germany in the early and mid 1990s. Typically, after I would discuss some of my own research on displaced workers, these colleagues would point out how little was known about displaced workers anywhere except in the United States. One reason for this, it turned out, was the availability of data: until recently, the kinds of panel data needed for an analysis of labor market transitions were simply not available in countries outside the United States. Another reason was an absence of policy interest: with Japanese and many European unemployment rates below U.S. levels and with very high levels of job security among older workers in those countries, not many non-US economists were interested in the effects of displacement on workers.

By the mid 1990s, however, both these things had changed dramatically. Panel data sets in countries like Germany, the Netherlands, and the United Kingdom had reached a level of maturity that made analysis of transitions feasible; important longitudinal administrative databases were being made available for research purposes for the first time. In addition, European and Japanese unemployment rose while that in the United States began dropping to levels not seen in decades. Thus, a research project was born.

From the beginning this research project had two key questions at its heart. First, are the experiences of U.S. displaced workers, and the patterns of experiences among workers, typical of other developed countries too? Second, what can we learn from both the similarities and the differences among countries? Do commonalities in displaced workers' experiences among all countries reveal fundamental features of modern industrialized economies? Are international differences informative about the efficacy of different public policy approaches to worker displacement? These are "big" questions, and while the prospect of shedding even a little light on them was tantalizing, the prospect of coming away with very little of general value from such an untouched area of research was distressingly real as well.

From the beginning it was obvious that this project could not be a one-person task. While the World Wide Web has greatly facilitated access to microdata and policy information in many countries other than one's own, there remains no substitute for a lifetime of expertise in understanding how a country's laws and institutions really work and for having a working knowledge of the details and pitfalls of each country's labor market microdata. Ultimately, therefore, the 10 countries examined in this volume consist of those industrialized countries for which I was able to identify a combination of adequate panel data and the human expertise required to analyze it. All authors involved in the project either live in or have spent much of their lives in the countries they are writing about, and all are accomplished labor economists with whom I have been honored to work. While it would be interesting to consider worker displacement in less-developed countries as well, our attention in this volume is focused on developed countries, whose similarity on at least this dimension maximizes the amount those countries might be able to learn from each others' experiences.

Collaborative work on the project began in October 1997,with a planning meeting in the autumn woods of Ancaster, Ontario, where authors met to discuss data comparability, definitions of displacement, and research methodologies. Preliminary drafts of research papers were produced and then circulated among the research group between March 1998 and the following summer. Semifinal versions of all five comparative chapters were presented at a conference in Burlington, Ontario on September 27–28, 1998. Participating authors acted as formal discussants for each others' papers, and all then participated in a round-table discussion on the overall meaning of the results. Based on the discussion and comments in that meeting, the authors prepared final drafts by mid 1999. Finally, I attempted to summarize and synthesize the results of the various chapters. The hard-won results of this exercise constitute Chapter 1 of this volume.

The United States and the Netherlands? Canada and Japan? Why these odd couples? Certainly a much easier volume to write and edit would have contained ten chapters, each covering a single country, each written by an expert in that country's data and institutions. At our planning meeting in October 1997, however, two decisions were made which, for better or worse, determined the structure of this book. First, given the long list of sampling and data decisions involved in doing careful labor market analysis, and given the different methods of data collection used in different countries, it soon became clear that a "one-chapter-per-country" volume ran a high risk of generating no internationally comparable results. To guarantee that at least some comparisons could be made, we decided to pair countries, yielding five chapters on two countries each. Second, while it was appealing to base these pairings on intrinsic research interest, the very limited comparative knowledge about displaced workers that was available at the outset of this project meant that it was not at all clear just what these matches should be. Thus, again to maximize the prospect of producing genuinely comparable results, these "arranged marriages" were based largely, but not exclusively, on similarity of the underlying data sources used to identify displaced workers. While this similarity is far from complete in the pairings ultimately chosen, it dictated certain choices: that analyses based on administrative data be placed with like analyses—for example Belgium and Denmark—and the same for analyses based on survey data—the United Kingdom and Australia).

In the end, Belgium was paired with Denmark because both use administrative data on employers, the countries are of similar size, and they both trade mainly with Germany. They provide an informative comparison because of the differences between their employment-protection laws, as well. France and Germany also use administrative employer-based data, and they are similar in size. Canada and Japan both collect data on displaced workers using a flow sample of job separations. The United States is the only country in the volume that collects data on displaced workers primarily via a retrospective survey; we decided to pair it with the Netherlands (which exploits three different data sets) because that offered an opportunity to focus on the effects of displacement on early-retirement decisions. This is an issue of considerable policy interest in the Netherlands and a surprisingly underresearched issue in the United States. Finally, the United Kingdom and Australia have similar survey-based data and afford an interesting contrast of systems similar in many dimensions, but different in the degree to which wages are regulated—highly regulated in one (Australia) and essentially unregulated in the other.

While pairwise comparisons are interesting, broader ones are, of course, better. To maximize a reader's ability to make broader comparisons, the authors also agreed at the organizational meeting on a common structure and a common set of topics to cover for each country. Roughly, each chapter begins with a description of the institutions likely to affect displacement in the countries under study; these institutions include employment protection law, unemployment insurance and other forms of income support for unemployed workers, and institutions affecting the country's overall wage structure. After describing the data used and the general economic conditions prevailing in the countries at the time the data were collected, each chapter then analyzes the frequency of displacement, the effects of displacement on employment and unemployment, and the effects of displacement on wages.

After some discussion, one thing we quite consciously decided *not* to agree on was a common definition of displacement. Primarily, this was ruled out by differences in the underlying methods of data collection among the countries. Typically, data based on administrative records provide large sample sizes and match workers to firms, but they supply little or no information on why any given firm-worker separation occurred. In countries in which the main data source is administrative, displaced workers are thus defined as all workers who separate from a dying or shrinking employer in a certain period around the closure or shrinkage. Household surveys, on the other hand, tend to have smaller samples but more detail on (reported) separation reasons. The small samples typically make it impractical to focus only on workers involved in plant closures or mass layoffs, but these data do allow the analyst to restrict attention to separations that the worker saw as involuntary. Thus, two distinct definitions of displacement pervade the chapters in this volume.

A second issue in the definition of displaced workers was whether to restrict attention only to workers with relatively high levels of tenure on the lost job. Workers with very short tenures typically lose very little from displacement, to the point where some studies, such as Jacobson, Lalonde, and Sullivan (1993), exclude them from their analysis altogether. While some chapters in this volume restrict most of their attention to workers with more than three or four years of tenure, most adopt a broader definition that does not automatically exclude short-tenure workers. Those chapters which use a broader definition, however, provide separate results for high- and low-tenure workers wherever possible.

Many people and organizations deserve thanks for their help in making this project happen. Foremost are the contributing authors themselves, who put up with several long flights, e-mailed questions, and requests for revisions, some of which involved substantial changes to the analysis. Thank you all! Malik Ljutic did a splendid job of organizing the initial meeting of authors and the major conference in September 1998 at which the five comparative chapters were presented. My wife, Barbara, and sons, Michael and Jonathan, did without their husband and dad for too many evenings. Both the authors and Randy Eberts of Upjohn have been particularly understanding about some delays which resulted from my moving, in the middle of the editing process, from Canada to California. Finally, of course, the two funding organizations—the Social Sciences and Humanities Research Council of Canada (SSHRCC) through its generous support of the Canadian International Labour Network (CILN) and the W.E. Upjohn Institute for Employment Research—made it all possible.

Santa Barbara, California
July 2000

1
Summary and Synthesis

Peter J. Kuhn
University of California, Santa Barbara

Almost every day, we are told that innovation and change are the chief sources of prosperity in advanced industrial economies. Innovation and change, however, often involve abandoning the production of goods and services which are technologically superseded or relocating their production to lower-wage countries. All modern economies thus face the problem of how to move workers out of outmoded activities and into more productive ones.

What is the best way to achieve this? In some situations, a combination of voluntary practices, including workforce attrition, reductions in overtime and in regular weekly work hours, cuts in bonuses and wages, and adoption of new products and lines of business can be used to adjust to declines in business without permanent layoffs. Sometimes, however, worker displacement, i.e., the involuntary, permanent termination of long-term employees, is unavoidable. In the United States, displacement is fairly common, affecting about 5 percent of all employed workers each year, and 2.5 percent of those with more than 10 years of service.[1] Furthermore, at least for workers with high levels of tenure in the lost job, the lifetime consequences of displacement can be both severe and permanent (Ruhm 1991).

Do countries other than the United States rely more or less on worker displacement as a method of industrial adjustment? Are the consequences of displacement, when it occurs, more or less severe, and does this differ for employment versus wages? Do international differences in labor market policy, including employment-protection laws, unemployment insurance systems, and wage-setting regimes play a role in explaining differences in the incidence and effects of displacement? Are international differences in the experiences of displaced workers informative about important structural features of labor markets, such as the wage returns to tenure or the amount of firm-specific training?

To date, questions like these have been difficult to answer. Because displacement involves a change in individuals' labor market status, its statistical analysis requires panel data (in other words, data on individuals at more than one point in time). Such data have only recently become publicly available in many countries other than the United States, paving the way for a first examination of worker displacement there. The purpose of this volume is to conduct such an analysis, with an aim to answering as many of the above research questions as we can.

The insights gained from the research in this volume fall into four main categories. The first concerns the tremendous variation in the institutions that regulate and affect displacement in different countries. Institutions that affect displaced workers include employment-protection laws (such as advance notice, consultation requirements, and severance-pay requirements surrounding layoffs and plant closures), income support and retraining programs aimed at the unemployed (especially unemployment insurance), and the broader set of institutions involved in the setting of wages (which may have significant effects on the distribution of wage changes experienced by displaced workers).

The second set of lessons from this volume concern methodology. Because this volume has been a first foray into cross-national research on displacement, one of its most important outcomes is a list of methodological desiderata and pitfalls that future analyses of displaced workers, and future international labor market comparisons, would do well to take into account.

Third are substantive results concerning within-country patterns of displacement and its consequences: is displacement, for example, always more common among men than women? Are the consequences of displacement always more severe for older workers? In a search for "universal" patterns in displacement, we have uncovered a few probable universals, as well as some fascinating exceptions, which are worthy of study precisely because of their exceptionality.

Finally, the most difficult kind of results to generate, but potentially the most rewarding, are those which make cross-national comparisons in the levels of key variables (such as the frequency of displacement or the duration of postdisplacement unemployment) and which associate these with international differences in labor market structure and policy. In this area, our conclusions are less firmly held than in other areas, but in equal measure more tantalizing.

In the remainder of this chapter, I discuss the four main categories of lessons learned from our analysis in turn.

INSTITUTIONS AFFECTING DISPLACED WORKERS

The main institutional differences among the 10 labor markets studied in this volume are summarized in Tables 1.1–1.3. These tables are derived from the much more detailed descriptions in Chapters 2 through 6, and they refer to the situation prevailing at the time for which the statistical analyses in those chapters was conducted. In four cases (Belgium, Denmark, France, and Germany) this is the mid to late 1980s. In the remaining six cases it is the mid 1990s. I begin this section by briefly summarizing the main features of employment protection laws, income support, and wage-setting policies in all these countries in turn. I then discuss a number of observations concerning the variation in institutions among countries and the ways in which this variation affects our analysis of displaced workers.

Employment Protection Laws

As Table 1.1 shows, there is dramatic variation among our 10 countries in the scope and stringency of their employment protection laws (EPLs). For example, suppose a firm wanted to lay some workers off permanently in response to a decline in sales. United States employers—like those in several other countries—would find the notion that they would need to explain and justify such layoffs to some external authority quite alien. Yet this is precisely the law in four of the countries under study here. In Japan, France, and Germany, economic necessity and/or social acceptability must be demonstrated to a point where the decision could be defended in a court of law. In Germany, for example, social acceptability is defined by a considerable body of case law and often involves detailed seniority rules for layoffs, consideration of economic need—such as family size and the number of dependents—in choosing whom to lay off, and extensive relocation assistance. In the Netherlands, a firm needs to obtain a permit from a regional employment institution before it can lay off any workers.

Much more common than justification requirements for economic layoffs are mandatory notice laws covering layoffs of individual workers. Indeed, consistent with the emphasis on employment at will in the United States, individual notice requirements are present in all of the countries under study except the United States.[2] These requirements generally index the statutory amount of notice to a worker's tenure on the lost job (the Netherlands, in an interesting exception, ties it to the worker's age). In addition, several European countries (in particular Germany, Belgium, and Denmark) draw quite dramatic distinctions between blue-collar and white-collar workers, with the latter entitled to more notice. For example, in Belgium, a white-collar worker with 20 years' service is entitled to a year of notice, while an identical blue-collar worker is entitled to only two months; in Denmark, blue-collar workers are not entitled to any notice at all. Finally, comparing the level of individual notice at similar tenure levels reveals very large differences among countries, especially at high tenure levels. Inspection of the table reveals, for example, legislated notice levels for a white-collar worker with 20 years of service include zero notice in the United States, one week in Australia, one month in Japan, two months in Canada and France, three months in the United Kingdom, six months in Germany and Denmark, and—as already noted—one year in Belgium. This tendency of Belgium to stand out as an extreme case of EPL is discussed and analyzed much more thoroughly in Chapter 6 of this volume.

Many U.S. readers will be familiar with the United States' advance notice requirement for mass layoffs, passed into law in 1988. The Worker Adjustment and Retraining Notification Act (WARN) mandates two months of notice for workers involved in layoffs of a large fraction of an establishment's workforce. Are such group notice laws even more stringent in other countries (as we might expect from the previous discussion)? Perhaps surprisingly, the answer here is "no." While group notice levels can be higher for very large layoffs in the United Kingdom (up to three months) and Canada (up to four months), none of the remaining countries have group notice periods distinct from the individual requirements summarized above. One reason for this, of course, is the relatively high levels of individual notice already required in those cases. Equally important, however, in three cases (Denmark, France, and Germany), the absence of extra legislated notice for mass layoffs is explained by the use of a different, consultative process for managing mass layoffs. This process involves mandated, case-by-case negotiations of notice, severance, and other downsizing procedures with the works council, union, and/or local government authorities. The resulting "social plan" can involve many forms of assistance to displaced workers, including job search assistance and direct outplacement with other firms.

Aside from mandated advance notice and in-kind job search/placement assistance, the other main form taken by EPLs involves cash payments to laid-off workers. In our sample of countries, mandated severance pay is totally absent in the United States, Japan, and Denmark. It is rare in Australia (applying to "model" awards only) and the Netherlands (applying only when a case goes to court). In some other countries it is limited in scope; for example, it applies only to a single (albeit populous) province in Canada, and only to mass layoffs in Belgium and Germany (in Germany's case it is negotiated in the social plan). These qualifications aside, however, mandated severance payments can be very substantial in some countries and situations. In the United Kingdom, France, and in parts of Canada, they can amount to a half year or more of pay for individual terminations; in Belgium they can add up to several years' wages when a plant is closed.

Finally, in a number of countries, the state's involvement in layoffs takes forms that are harder to quantify but not without potentially great effect. Extensive procedural requirements such as those in Japan and France can lead to long, uncertain, and costly delays in implementing mass layoffs, but it is hard to specify their cost equivalent in terms of weeks of legislated notice or dollars of severance pay. Consultative requirements, including mandated negotiations with a union and/or works council, determine the main dimensions of assistance provided to mass-layoff victims in Germany and France. These can be very generous but will vary on a case-by-case basis depending on the outcomes of negotiations. Analyses that ignore these dimensions of EPL can seriously mismeasure the strength of EPL in some countries.

In sum, looking across countries, it is clear that restrictions on firms' abilities to dismiss workers vary dramatically. Along almost all dimensions, the United States appears at one end of the spectrum with the least-stringent regulations, and Belgium at the other end with the most stringent. Between these extremes, however, there is no consistent ranking: countries can be high on some dimensions of EPL and low on others. Canada, for example, has relatively high statutory notice and severance provisions, but relatively few consultative and other procedural impediments to layoffs. At the other extreme, Japan requires no severance pay and only a month of notice, but has extensive and complex procedural requirements for layoffs. Nor is "Europe" a high-EPL monolith: compare restrictive Belgium with *laissez-faire* Denmark. One important implication of this kind of heterogeneity is that any overall ranking of EPL among countries (including the several that are commonly used in cross-country regression studies) will not be invariant to the weights assigned to different EPL components.[3] Another implication is that research opportunities clearly exist comparing European countries, a prime example of which is Chapter 6 of this volume.

Income Support Programs

As for employment protection laws, the countries in our sample differ substantially in their approaches to providing income support to unemployed workers (Table 1.2). For example, while most countries require some work history in the year preceding a claim, some—notably Australia and Belgium—do not. The most common qualifying periods amount to about six months of work in the year preceding the unemployment insurance (UI) claim (the United States, the Netherlands, Japan, and Denmark). Some are more restrictive (two years of continuous employment in the United Kingdom); others are less (as few as 10 weeks in high-unemployment regions of Canada). Benefits are unlimited in duration in Australia, Belgium, and Denmark; they can last up to five years in the Netherlands and almost three years in France and Germany. Maximum benefit durations in the United States, Japan, Canada, and the United Kingdom are all under one year.

Seven of the 10 countries under study set UI benefits as a fraction of predisplacement earnings; of these, 4 (the United States, Japan, Canada, and Denmark) have either a maximum benefit level or a sliding benefit scale that reduces the actual replacement rates well below the "statutory" rate for workers with higher levels of predisplacement earnings. Three do not, offering *actual* replacement rates of 70 percent (the Netherlands), 57–75 percent (France) and 60–67 percent (Germany), which are much higher than U.S. levels. Three countries (the United Kingdom, Australia, and Belgium) do not index benefits to previous earnings at all, instead providing a fixed needs-based amount depending on family size and structure. Finally, the countries with limited UI duration all have some sort of fallback source of income support (such as "Unemployment Assistance" (UA) in the United Kingdom and *Arbeitslosenhilfe* (AH) in Germany). These programs can sometimes be quite generous (including a full rent and property-tax subsidy in the United Kingdom, and income support equal to 57 percent of the previous wage in Germany), but they are extremely limited in the United States.

Other noteworthy elements of the cross-country variation in income support systems include the fact that, in several cases (including the United States, the Netherlands, and the United Kingdom), disability or early-retirement benefits offer an attractive alternative to either unemployment insurance or general welfare. Also, with the exception of France, all countries impose some restrictions on UI payments to persons who voluntarily quit their jobs. Interestingly, however, France disentitles *seasonal* workers from UI, while in Canada they are among the system's most politically influential beneficiaries. In Denmark, the trade unions rather than the state administer the unemployment insurance system(s). Finally, in addition to UI, some countries have income support and retraining programs targeted specifically at displaced workers or at workers who are displaced for specific reasons, such as changes in international trade. Best known here is the Trade Adjustment Assistance (TAA) program in the United States. Similar programs exist on a more ad hoc basis in Canada. The most formalized system of this kind, however, is Japan's system of "employment maintenance and adjustment subsidies." These programs make payments to laid-off workers in a (periodically updated) list of industries deemed to be in serious decline. They also subsidize retraining; and most interestingly, they pay wage subsidies to employers who hire workers displaced *from* the targeted industries.

Wage-Setting Institutions

Countries also differ dramatically in their regulation of the wage-setting process (Table 1.3). Union coverage rates vary from 14 percent in the United States to 90 percent in France, Germany, and Belgium. In many countries (especially the Netherlands, Australia, France, Germany, and Belgium) coverage is much higher than membership because of the mandatory extension of union contracts to nonmembers. Some nations, like Britain and Germany, have no minimum wage regulations at all; some (like the United States and Japan) set minima that are a very small fraction (30 to 40 percent) of the average manufacturing wage. This contrasts with France's minimum of over 80 percent of the mean industrial wage. Wage minima can be set on the national level (France), national and state levels (United States), province level only (Canada), industry and industry-by-prefecture level (Japan), and even nationally by occupation (Australia), with fascinating (but largely unexplored) implications for wage structure.

Some Observations on Institutions

In this subsection I discuss three main features of displacement-related institutions that are particularly relevant to the comparative study of the effects of labor market institutions on labor market outcomes, including the experiences of displaced workers.

First, although the various subdimensions of the institutional environment are correlated among countries, these correlations are highly imperfect. Still, it is probably a useful descriptive device to group the 10 countries examined here into two groups. In the United States, Canada, the United Kingdom, Australia, and to some extent Denmark, it strikes one that the primary focus of displacement-related institutions is a "palliative" one. At least in their public policy, these countries seem to place most of their emphasis on assisting impacted workers after the fact of displacement, via unemployment insurance and state-financed retraining programs. They seem much more reluctant to intervene in the displacement process itself than those European and Japanese governments, who—while also adopting some palliative measures—take what might be called a "preventative" stance. Preventative policies aim to prevent the layoff in the first place or, if that is unavoidable, to prevent a spell of unemployment as a consequence of the layoff. The idea (presumably) is that unemployment can lead to a negative feedback cycle involving loss of skills, health, and self-esteem, which is best avoided completely.[4] The challenge—and the source of much current debate in Europe and Japan—is how to do this without reducing firms' incentives to hire new workers, especially in times or industries where demand uncertainty is high. One option, used in Japan, might be the payment of subsidies to firms which hire workers *formerly employed* in industries the government believes should be shut down.

Concerning the imperfection of the above correlations, a number of examples illustrate the point. First, within the palliative group, during our sample period Australia had a highly centralized wage-setting system, while Britain had no minimum wages at all. Canada and the United Kingdom had fairly stringent advance-notice requirements while the United States and Australia had almost none. Within the preventative group, Japan has very modest notice requirements compared to some countries (such as Canada) in the palliative group. (Japan's preventative institutions take other forms.) While Denmark has generous unemployment insurance and centralized wage-setting, employment-protection laws differ so dramatically between Belgium and Denmark that Albæk, Van Audenrode, and Browning conclude in Chapter 6 that this is the most likely explanation for the large differences in displaced workers' unemployment durations between these countries.

It is common in current public discussions to refer to the problem of high European unemployment or to attribute non-European differences in labor market performance to rigid European laws and institutions. As our discussion here makes clear, however, many differences exist within these two groups of countries. Furthermore, comparing broadly similar countries that differ substantially in only one or two relevant dimensions—such as the comparisons between Belgium and Denmark and between the United Kingdom and Australia in the current volume, and that between Canada and the United States in Card and Freeman (1993)—may be the most informative way to explore the effects of labor market institutions on labor market outcomes.

My second observation about institutions is simply that they are multidimensional. In particular, even legislation bearing on a very specific action (e.g., a firm's ability to initiate a layoff) can have several components, some of which are not easily quantified. Thus, as noted, in addition to severance pay and notice provisions, some countries (for example, Japan and Germany) prohibit layoffs unless they are "socially acceptable" or "economically necessary" and require them to be conducted according to appropriate procedures. In Italy, mandated notice periods are minimal but dismissals must be pre-approved by state officials with highly variable decision lags (Garibaldi and Brixiova 1997). The main implication of multidimensionality is that simple measures of a law's most-easily quantified aspects (such as weeks of notice) can be very poor proxies for its overall stringency. Japan has very lenient advance-notice laws, for example, but this does not mean it is easy to lay off a worker there. Both this and future studies would do well to pay close attention to procedural and other details when comparing legislation among countries.

My third observation is that not all institutions constraining individual firms and workers take the form of legislation. At least four main forms of nonlegislated institutions affect displaced workers, the most obvious of which are restrictions contained in union contracts. In many cases, collective bargaining agreements, especially those negotiated on national levels, and sometimes extended to unorganized workers, set binding constraints on minimum wages, dismissal procedures, and other elements of the employment contract. For example, in France, statutory advance-notice provisions are usually superseded by collectively bargained provisions, which cover 90 percent of the workforce.

A second set of nonlegislated institutions that are directly relevant to displaced workers are the mechanisms of exchange in industrial labor markets. An important case in point is the construction industry. In North America this industry has a very high separation and displacement rate because it is organized along craft lines: workers have long-run attachments to their craft, but not to any particular firm, and move with great frequency from one firm to another as projects are completed. Furthermore, while displacement in this industry is relatively inconsequential in its effect on wages, it is sufficiently frequent (and the industry is sufficiently large) to have a significant effect on the average *national* displacement rate. In Britain, construction labor markets are organized differently, and the construction industry has a lower displacement rate than manufacturing. Whether or not construction is included in the statistics also affects comparisons of Canada's and Japan's displacement rates (see Chapter 3).

Just as the organization of labor markets can differ across industries, countries have different national mechanisms of worker termination. Among other things this necessitates great care in defining roughly comparable measures of displacement. In North American economies, for example, where temporary layoffs are common, the precise point at which any given worker makes a permanent break with his or her firm is often quite unclear. Workers on temporary layoff often look for other jobs and may or may not eventually be recalled to their former employer. They may even return after starting a job with another firm. The whole permanent separation process can thus be very drawn out, and results using *ex post* versus *ex ante* definitions of permanent layoffs can differ substantially. In some other countries (such as Germany or the Netherlands), displacement constitutes a sharper, more well-defined event. Still other countries have institutional mechanisms, such as the *shukko* system in Japan—involving outplacements with other firms within an association, or *keiretsu*—where workers can be involuntarily moved out of the firm without any spell of unemployment or any uncertainty regarding their new wage rate. As the next section illustrates, it matters whether we count such workers as displaced or not.

It is of course possible that these national termination styles are simply the *result* of long-standing differences in legislation among countries (see Burdett and Wright 1989; Van Audenrode 1994). The hypothesis that they are caused by legislation is, however, not always consistent with historical evidence, as Huberman (1997) argues. In several cases, differences in national adjustment practices predate the legislative differences that are supposed to have caused them. These long-standing practices may therefore be the more "primitive" of the institutions affecting displacement. Long traditions, as well as historical accident, thus play a role in any complete analysis of institutions' effects.

A final kind of nonlegislated institution is the generally accepted standard of relocation assistance that is "voluntarily" provided by firms to workers who are permanently laid off. In different countries and industries, certain amounts of help are simply considered normal and fair treatment; sometimes (as in Canada and Belgium) these accepted practices are explicitly recognized in the common law regulating terminations. In some countries, like the United States, this may be quite minimal, but even there, significant amounts of advance notice were voluntarily provided by firms before any legislated standard existed.[5] Another example is outplacement services, provided by many former employers, that directly secure jobs for workers at other firms. Such services, especially in some European countries, can make unemployment following plant closures the exception rather than the rule, unlike the case in North America. Voluntary relocation assistance is often ignored in existing analyses of displacement, to some extent surely because the U.S. Displaced Worker Survey contains no information on these activities. As some recent Canadian research (Riddell 1999) indicates, however, it can be substantial even when not required by any legislation.

Summary

In sum, the 10 countries studied in this volume can be roughly categorized into two groups. The first, consisting of the United States, Canada, the United Kingdom, Australia, and (to some extent) Denmark, confine their market interventions largely to palliative measures aimed at workers after the fact of displacement. The remainder (the Netherlands, Japan, France, Germany, and Belgium), while adopting (sometimes very generous) palliative measures, also take a preventative stance, adopting a number of policies designed to prevent layoffs in the event of plant closures or, if layoffs are inevitable, to prevent unemployment in the event of layoffs.

Within these very broad patterns, tremendous and often quite unexpected institutional heterogeneity remains. Policies affecting displacement are multidimensional, and some of the dimensions in which variation occurs (such as consultation requirements and approval procedures for layoff permits) can be hard to quantify. In some countries, collectively bargained provisions supersede legislated requirements as the main binding constraints on employers, not just in wage-setting decisions but in worker termination and plant shutdown procedures as well. Voluntarily provided assistance from firms in many cases constitutes the most important part of a worker's severance package. Sometimes the institution with the greatest effect on a statistic like the displacement rate is simply the organization of labor markets on the industry level: industries which are organized on a craft or hiring-hall basis, like construction in North America, will have very high displacement rates (and relatively small consequences of displacement) because of the methods by which labor is exchanged. National mechanisms of displacement differ too, ranging from the temporary-to-permanent transition common in North America, to the much sharper breaks which are traditional in some other countries. No analysis of international differences in displacement is complete without reference to these less formal (but no less fundamental) institutional differences between countries.

METHODOLOGICAL LESSONS FOR THE STUDY OF DISPLACED WORKERS AND FOR CROSS-NATIONAL LABOR MARKET RESEARCH

Because cross-national research on displacement—and on labor market dynamics more generally—is very new, one of the most useful things a volume like this can do is to alert future researchers to a number of key methodological issues that naturally arise in this context. That is the role of this section. Its main intended audience, therefore, is labor economists, especially those actively engaged in cross-national research and, most especially, that on labor market dynamics. Readers interested primarily in substantive results may wish to skip or skim this section and move right on to the next section of this chapter (p. 22).

One methodological lesson of this volume has already been discussed: the importance of getting the institutions right, i.e., taking care in measuring all aspects, including the nonlegislated ones, of the institutional environment in all countries. Aside from this, the main methodological lessons I believe we learned, as a group of 22 authors, are the following.

Defining Displaced Workers

Definitional issues arise in all comparative studies of labor markets. For example, studies of wage structure need to decide whether to define the annual bonuses paid to workers in countries like Japan and Germany as part of wages. These bonuses can be a large (and in Japan's case, a highly variable) fraction of compensation, and their treatment can change one's most basic conclusions.[6] In the current volume, however, definitions matter in an even more fundamental way, because they concern membership in the population under study. At the very outset, we are confronted with the question of who *is* a displaced worker, in a group of countries with different institutional mechanisms of labor adjustment, each with its own nomenclature for worker-firm separations.

As noted already, two working definitions of displaced workers are used in this volume. One of these, used in administrative databases, consists of separations surrounding a firm or plant closure (or a large reduction in firm or plant size). This definition does not make use of the reported reason for a separation, either by the worker or the firm. The other definition consists of self-reported layoffs in surveys of individual workers.

Both the administrative-data-based and the survey-based definitions of displaced workers used here have their advantages and disadvantages. An advantage of the administrative definition is that it will include early leavers in the sample of displaced workers (*early leavers* are individuals who start searching for new jobs in response to information about an impending shutdown and who quit to take such jobs even before the plant closes). Presumably we would wish to include these very successful adaptees in our count of the displaced. Another advantage is the notion, common in the displacement literature, that plant closure constitutes a better "natural experiment" with which to analyze broader labor market phenomena, because involvement in a shutdown is more likely to be orthogonal to an individual's unobserved ability than involvement in a person-specific layoff. A disadvantage is that a large majority of involuntary worker terminations occur on an individual basis; thus a study of plant closure victims alone would be unrepresentative of the whole population of displaced workers.[7] Another disadvantage of the plant-closure-based definition, especially if the "window" around the plant shutdown is relatively wide, is that such definitions can include a considerable amount of normal workforce turnover, i.e., workers who would have voluntarily left the firm even in the absence of an impending shutdown. A final disadvantage, the "false firm death" problem, is discussed in more detail below.

Consider now the survey-based definition of displaced workers, consisting of all separations labeled as involuntary (from the worker's point of view). As argued above, this has the advantage of greater representativeness, but has the disadvantage—especially in an international context—of relying on workers' (and/or firms') self-reported reasons for why a separation occurred. Relying on reported separation reasons can give rise to three kinds of problems, especially in international studies. First, there may be simple, or "classical," measurement error. Some evidence for this is available in the chapter on Canada and Japan, which presents data from a Canadian survey in which both firms and workers reported a separation reason. Interestingly, while the marginal totals in these cross-tabulations are roughly similar (for example, workers and firms both labeled about the same fraction of separations as firm-initiated), there are substantial off-diagonal elements (workers and firms often disagree on the cause of any given separation). Second, rather than reflecting fundamental differences in the source of the shock giving rise to the separation (see McLaughlin 1991), the labeling of separations as worker- versus firm-initiated may be an endogenous response to a nation's labor market institutions. For example, the high share of layoffs relative to quits in the Canadian economy may reflect employers' willingness, in the absence of experience rating, to label workers' separations as layoffs in order to qualify them for employment insurance benefits (e.g., Kuhn and Sweetman 1988b). On the other hand, Bender, Dustmann, Margolis, and Meghir claim in Chapter 5 that in some European countries, "true" layoffs are relabeled as quits (presumably with some means of ensuring the worker's cooperation) to avoid the many administrative complications involved in laying workers off. In Japan, a larger share of separations is labeled as voluntary than in any other OECD country (OECD 1997, Table 5.12). Abe, Higuchi, Kuhn, Nakamura, and Sweetman suggest in Chapter 3 that this may, in part, reflect a cultural reluctance to admit to a kind of "failure" on the worker's part.

Third, languages, survey instruments, and the actual mix of mechanisms via which labor moves between firms all differ among countries. At a mundane level, perhaps because layoffs often give rise to discomfort in conversation—at least when they affect us personally—they encourage both slang and euphemism. The variety of such expressions, even among English-speaking countries, is remarkable: consider "getting the sack," "getting canned," "downsized," "right-sized," "outplaced," "fired," "dismissed," "discharged," "dislocated," getting the "pink slip," "redundancy" (common in the United Kingdom), and "retrenchment" (common in Australia). Japan has "forced vacations" and "*kata tataki*" (literally, "shoulder-tapping," referring to the common method by which employees are informed of their layoffs). More to the point, "firing" or "dismissal" in North America typically means a worker has not performed his or her job duties adequately; thus we would not typically count workers reporting these separation reasons as displaced. In Europe it is much more common to use "firing" and "dismissal" to refer to employment adjustments for purely economic reasons. For example, a worker with less than enough job tenure to qualify for statutory redundancy pay in Britain—typically two years—might very plausibly report that he or she had been dismissed if the firm reduced employment due to a shortage of demand. Analyses that do not take account of such semantic differences may not be comparing similar classes of workers. Furthermore, international comparisons need to decide how to compare certain methods of shedding labor which only exist in some countries (such as U.S.-style temporary layoffs or Japanese *shukko*) with other kinds of displacements used in other countries.

Aside from nomenclature, there are a number of other issues involved in the definition of displaced workers that, if not carefully accounted for, can change the main results of a one-country study or reverse the sign of international comparisons. One, already mentioned, is whether to condition on tenure: are workers who lose very short jobs really "displaced"? In this volume we usually focus on high-tenure workers, but for all countries we also provide some results—especially for displacement *rates*—that do not condition on tenure in the job lost.

Related to the issue of very short jobs, how should we treat separations due to the end of a seasonal job or the expiration of a fixed-term contract? The treatment of contract expirations is particularly difficult in the United States, as its Displaced Worker Survey does not include this as a possible separation reason. Presumably some of these workers classify themselves as layoffs (i.e., separated due to a "shortage of work"), and some choose the "other" category. As Farber (1997) has shown, this can substantially affect estimates of displacement and its consequences in the United States. In Chapter 4, Borland, Gregg, Knight, and Wadsworth document very different wage-change patterns in the United Kingdom for temporary contract expirations versus other involuntary separations. Because contract expirations constitute a substantial fraction of involuntary separations in Japan, the statistical picture of displacement rates in that country (see Chapter 3) is quite different depending on whether these workers are classified as "displaced" or not. When contract expirations are not separately identified in the data, presumably restricting attention to jobs with longer tenures will eliminate most of them from the sample. To our knowledge, however, no hard evidence on this point exists.

One response to uncertainty regarding the usefulness of survey reports of separation reasons is to use *ex post* criteria to identify separations we truly believe are involuntary. One option, used for some countries in this volume (for example, the United Kingdom), is to ask how the results change when we restrict attention to individuals who experienced a positive unemployment spell. While this, to some extent, conflates initial conditions with outcomes, it can be a useful descriptive device and sensitivity check. A more extreme version of this strategy is adopted in the Canada/Japan chapter, which experiments with the idea of defining displacements by their wage consequences. This is of course tautological when measuring the effects of displacement on wages but can be useful when making international comparisons of displacement rates. Specifically, by defining *displacement* as a separation which leads to a large decline in hourly wages, one can compare displacement rates among countries in a manner which is unaffected by any labeling conventions—whether these are induced by survey instruments, "cultural" predispositions against admitting a separation was involuntary, opportunistic relabelling to avoid or take advantage of government regulations, or semantic differences. Future comparative studies of employment dynamics might do well to document the resulting statistic—the frequency of "substantial separation-induced wage losses"—in a greater number of countries.

Other definitions

Clearly, how one defines the population of interest is a major consideration in any international study of displaced workers. A number of other definitions can also have pivotal impacts in such studies, however, and deserve close scrutiny. One of these is the distinction between *establishments* and *firms*: when the definition of displacement involves closure or substantial shrinkage of one's workplace, it can matter a lot if the workplace is defined as an establishment or a firm. In two of the four longitudinal employer databases used in this volume, the unit of analysis is the firm; in the other two, it is the establishment. Because a common practice, especially in European plant closures, involves the relocation of large numbers of employees to other branches of the same firm, this can substantially affect estimates of the consequences of displacement in addition to the overall displacement rate. Close attention to the firm/establishment distinction is therefore required in any comparative study of displacement or of labor market dynamics more generally.

In analyzing the employment and wage consequences of displacement, three more definitions can have major impacts on the results. One is the distinction between *jobless durations* and *unemployment durations*. Because most data sets do not make careful distinctions between the unemployed and those who respond to displacement by leaving the labor force, most existing studies of displacement are careful to label their findings as applying to total jobless durations. Clearly, however, the mean jobless spell in a sample can substantially exceed the mean unemployment spell, especially among populations, such as women and older workers, for whom labor-force withdrawal is more common. A second key distinction is between the *mean unconditional jobless duration* and *mean duration conditional on experiencing a positive spell*. In the existing literature, both are commonly reported without further modifiers as "jobless durations." Especially in some European countries, where fewer than half of displaced workers experience any unemployment at all, this distinction can be crucial, and all the chapters in this volume pay it close attention.

Finally, there is the distinction between *wages* and *earnings*. Due to data limitations, many studies of the financial implications of displacement limit their attention to total earnings in a month, quarter, or year. (For example, Jacobson, Lalonde and Sullivan's influential 1993 study confined its attention to quarterly earnings.) Even though the earnings declines in these studies consist of a mixture of unemployment, involuntary part-time work, and hourly wage declines, they are often discussed as if they are directly informative about hourly wage rates.[8] Yet, as Stevens (1997) showed, making this distinction can change one's results considerably. The chapters in this volume are particularly careful in this regard, and future comparative work on displaced workers would do well to repeat that care.

Control Groups

A third methodological lesson concerns the use of control groups. While it is not obvious how relevant control groups would be to the analysis of displacement incidence or postdisplacement unemployment durations, they have been advocated and used by a number of authors for the study of displacement-induced wage and earnings losses. It has been argued, for example, that simple before-after wage changes experienced by displaced workers will understate the wage losses caused by displacement because they fail to account for any predisplacement wage losses,[9] or for any foregone postdisplacement wage growth experienced by displaced workers, relative to their nondisplaced peers. The use of a control group of nondisplaced workers, it is argued, can address both these problems.

Some of the analyses in this volume have access to a nondisplaced control group; others do not. What does the experience of the authors who *can* use controls indicate for the rest? Our analysis shows that, in most cases, simple "difference" estimates do indeed underestimate wage losses, though exceptions exist. In particular, because real wages of Belgian nondisplaced workers fell during the sample period (Chapter 6), their "difference in difference" wage loss estimates are smaller than the simple difference estimates. That said, however, in most cases the use of a control group does not substantially change the results unless (as is the case for Australia in this volume) the population under study consists largely of young workers, who tend to be in a high-wage-growth life-cycle stage.[10] One reason for this is our focus in this volume on wage changes over a one- or two-year period bracketing the displacement date. During this relatively short period, wage or earnings growth among continuously employed workers is not sufficient to make a large difference in most of the estimates. Second, we cannot detect any predisplacement wage losses in countries outside the United States. We conjecture that this is largely due to the fact that wage-setting institutions in those countries are more centralized: as both Bertola and Rogerson (1997) and Teulings and Hartog (1998) have argued, there is simply less room for downward wage adjustments at the firm level in many non-U.S. economies.

There are also some drawbacks to using control groups. One is that, unless the data allow one to separate the two effects, the analysis may conflate temporary layoffs and/or hours cuts before the layoff with wage reductions, thus yielding a less accurate estimate of, say, the amount of firm-specific capital lost due to displacement. Finally, unless one has a very large sample of displaced workers, regression specifications—such as Jacobson, LaLonde, and Sullivan's—which estimate completely separate earnings paths for displaced workers and controls, do not easily allow one to estimate a large number of interaction effects with observable characteristics, like age, tenure, or gender.

False Firm Deaths

False firm deaths is a methodological problem that is specific to administrative-data-based studies of displaced workers. In such databases, firm (or plant) closures are typically identified by the disappearance of a firm (or plant) identification number from the data. This could of course involve the shutdown of a plant or firm, but the possibility also exists that such changes result from simple reorganizations, in which a plant, together with its entire workforce, is simply subsumed into a new firm and continues producing as before.

The administrative-data-based chapters in this volume make diverse attempts to deal with the false-deaths problem, as discussed in detail in later chapters. A common approach is to exclude from the analysis large groups of workers who move together from one dying firm and into the same new firm.[11] This will, of course, eliminate simple takeovers, but it will also eliminate cases in which the displacing firm has gone through extraordinary efforts to secure reemployment of its workers at other firms (or, in the case of plant closures, relocated them to another of its plants). While such efforts may be uncommon in North America, they are more frequent elsewhere, especially in those jurisdictions where a "social plan" must be implemented for all mass layoffs. In the research conducted for this volume, the results for some countries changed dramatically after corrections for false firm deaths were introduced. Future research on displacement using administrative data sources would be well advised to take great care in addressing this issue.

Alternative Destinations for Displaced Workers

Our collective experience in this volume strongly suggests that more attention should be given to several possible "destination" states for displaced workers besides reemployment. The possibility of labor-force withdrawal has already been mentioned, but further disaggregation of this state, as well as of the reemployment state, is needed. For example, in Chapter 2, Abbring, van den Berg, Gautier, van Lomwel, van Ours, and Ruhm show that both early retirement and official "disability" are important consequences of displacement. Farber (1999) recently pointed out the importance of nontraditional forms of employment as transitional states in the adjustment to displacement.

In addition to painting a more complete picture of displaced workers' experiences, consideration of alternative destinations has several key implications for research on displaced workers. One is a better understanding of existing empirical regularities; for example, how much of the observed effects of age and gender on jobless durations can be explained by induced early retirement or by labor-force withdrawal? Another is a clarification of the welfare impacts of displacement; I argue below that the *direction* of the effect of displacement on retirement is informative about the *size* of its effects on lifetime utility. Research on these aspects of displacement, whether in the United States or elsewhere, has only just begun.

Comparability and Regression Design in Cross-National Research

Finally, an interesting consensus emerged among the authors around the broader issue of how to design regression-based studies in the context of comparative labor market research. A common temptation in the quest for comparability between countries is to choose a set of covariates that constitutes the lowest common denominator, in other words, the subset of control variables that is 1) available, and 2) measured in roughly the same way in both countries.[12] While most chapters in this volume provide this kind of comparison, they also make a point of providing less-comparable results based on fuller, more theoretically appropriate specifications of unemployment or earnings-loss regressions in each country. For example, just because Japan does not include a tenure variable in the relevant survey does not mean we should present no Canadian results that control for tenure. Sometimes, ancillary information from other data sources (such as age-tenure distributions in the Canada/Japan case) can be used to provide supplementary insights into what the results would be if the fuller set of covariates were indeed available. International studies of labor markets, in general, should not focus only on lowest-common-denominator regression specifications.

WITHIN-COUNTRY PATTERNS: EXCEPTIONS AND UNIVERSALS

Some economic phenomena are so deeply rooted in human tastes or technologies that they are observed in all cultures or countries that have been examined.[13] Are there any such universal patterns in the incidence and effects of displacement? In this section I examine the variation in three displacement-related phenomena—the incidence of displacement, the unemployment effects of displacement, and the wage effects of displacement—across four basic demographic attributes (gender, age, predisplacement job tenure, and skill level) in all 10 countries studied in this volume. I identify some "universals," as well as some fascinating and significant exceptions, and speculate on the meaning of both.

It is worth emphasizing at the outset that my focus in this section is on the patterns of covariation, within countries, between demographic attributes and economic outcomes. Unlike the following section, which tries to describe and explain differences in levels among countries, this exercise is not affected by international noncomparabilities in data, as long as these noncomparabilities affect only outcome *levels*. In that sense, the results—because they implicitly difference out a fixed effect for each country—are more robust to differences in data collection techniques among countries than the results in the following section.

The patterns of displacement-related outcomes across gender, age, tenure, and skill groups found in this volume are summarized in Tables 1.4–1.15. The tables display both raw correlations and regression-adjusted correlations, together with a list of all the characteristics held constant in each regression. To facilitate access to other details underlying the results, I also list the source table from which each result is drawn. The absence of a country from any one of these tables, or "n.d." in a cell in any of them, means the corresponding results are not available for that country. For each table, I pose a question for which the majority answer—if any—is "yes." If there is no majority answer, I choose what seems to me the most likely *ex ante* hypothesis. In the summaries of regression results, "insignif." means the coefficient was not significant at the 5 percent level; "no" means the coefficient was significant but opposite in sign to the question posed.

Who Is Displaced?

Patterns in the incidence of displacement are summarized in Tables 1.4 through 1.7. Looking first at Tables 1.4 and 1.5, it is immediately clear that displacement disproportionately affects men, and unskilled workers, in essentially all countries.[14] To some extent this is surely a consequence of the greater cyclicality of industries, such as construction and manufacturing, where unskilled men are overrepresented. As noted, the craft-based organization of the construction labor market also plays a role in some countries. Also related to industry effects, men are disproportionately employed in "old economy" sectors which are in long-term secular decline in all advanced economies. Not all of the disproportionate incidence of displacement among men is attributable to industry mix, however: this result persists in the two countries (the Netherlands and the United Kingdom) for which the authors can add industry controls to displacement-rate regressions. The higher level of unskilled male displacement, to some extent, may thus also reflect the continuing erosion of men's traditional advantages in the labor market and the increase in demand for skill that appears to pervade all industrialized labor markets.

Tables 1.6 and 1.7 shed additional light on the incidence of displacement by focusing on age and tenure effects. With one important exception—Japan—the message of these tables is essentially the same for all countries. First, simply comparing means for different age categories, young workers are more likely to be displaced than older workers.[15] As the rest of Table 1.6, and all of Table 1.7 make clear, however, this is *not* a genuine age effect: when tenure is held constant, displacement rates are no longer correlated with age. Tenure, however, continues to affect displacement when age is held constant. Thus, for all countries except Japan, the probability of being displaced from a job declines with the amount of time one has spent in it. Precise causes of this phenomenon are unclear—it could reflect institutions such as inverse-seniority (last-in, first-out, or LIFO) layoff rules, or simply the likelihood that high-tenure workers are, on average, better matched to their current jobs—but the phenomenon itself appears to be universal outside Japan.

And what of the Japanese exception? This phenomenon is analyzed in considerable detail in Chapter 3. All the evidence suggests that 1) it is largely confined to men, and 2) it reflects a practice, dominant among large Japanese employers, of offering essentially total job security to newly hired young men. Japanese workforce adjustment, when required, then takes a number of forms, all of which disproportionately affect senior workers: a variable age of mandatory retirement, an essentially mandatory form of outplacement called *shukko*, and (especially in the last few years) simple layoffs.

Thus, with one exception—Japan—displacement is most common among young, unskilled men. Furthermore, the greater prevalence of displacement among the young outside Japan is wholly explained by their lower tenure levels.

Joblessness Following Displacement

According to Table 1.8, women experience more joblessness than men after displacement. This phenomenon is essentially universal among developed countries, and—as is the case for the skill, age, and tenure patterns discussed below as well—holds irrespective of whether we measure joblessness as the occurrence of a positive spell, as duration conditional on a positive spell, as unconditional duration, or as non-employment at a particular (postdisplacement) survey date. Whatever causes women's postdisplacement joblessness to be higher in all countries is very likely related to the factors that cause women's overall labor force participation rate to be lower than men's in all countries. Among these are greater participation in child-rearing (thus a higher opportunity cost of working) and—of particular relevance to displaced women—greater geographic constraints on married women's job search.

According to Table 1.9, unskilled workers experience more joblessness than skilled workers, with one statistically significant exception (Germany). The most likely cause of this almost-universal phenomenon is unemployment insurance, which in most cases provides much higher benefit replacement rates to low-wage workers. (Absent something like unemployment insurance, one might expect skilled workers to have higher durations as they tend to operate in more specialized labor markets.) In this regard, it is intriguing to note that Germany is one of only three countries in our sample where UI benefits are a fixed fraction of the predisplacement wage with no maximum, and is the *only* country where the "second-tier" benefit system that takes over when UI expires (in Germany's case, *Arbeitslosenhilfe*; see Table 1.2) has the same feature.

Although (as we have seen) older workers are less likely to be displaced, Table 1.10 shows clearly that they suffer longer jobless spells when displacement does occur. Further, Tables 1.10 and 1.11 together show that, unlike our incidence results, this is *not* simply a tenure effect. For one thing, tenure does not have a uniform effect on durations when age is held constant; the effect is significant in five of the seven countries where we can run these regressions, but the coefficient is negative in two of these five cases. Second, age remains significant when tenure is held constant. Thus there does appear to be a "pure" age effect on postdisplacement unemployment that is essentially universal among countries with very different labor market institutions and conditions.

What explains the universal effect of age on postdisplacement joblessness? On one hand, this could reflect something as basic as the biology of aging, making older workers, on average, less adaptable to change than younger workers. On the other hand, it could reflect the fact that a greater fraction of older workers' skills are specific to an occupation and industry,[16] thus exposing them to a much "thinner" labor market. An older worker's optimal response to what are presumably lower offer-arrival rates in such markets might well be to spend longer searching for a job.[17] Alternatively, since these results are for jobless durations (rather than unemployment durations), they could simply reflect greater labor-force withdrawal for older workers. Indeed, Abbring et al. demonstrate in Chapter 2 that displacement hastens retirement in the United States. At the same time, however, a number of analyses find higher jobless durations among older workers even when workers who leave the labor market are dropped from the sample. Thus, labor-force withdrawal cannot be the only explanation for this phenomenon.[18] Finally, longer unemployment durations could be caused by the greater average wealth (and therefore higher reservation wages) of older workers, though if this were the case one might expect older displaced workers to experience smaller wage losses (see below).

What explains the very different correlations between predisplacement job tenure and postdisplacement unemployment among countries as noted above? This correlation can be calculated for 7 of the 10 countries under study and is positive or insignificant in the United States, Canada, the United Kingdom, and Denmark—all countries with relatively weak employment-protection laws (EPL), by international standards. In contrast, the correlation is negative and significant in Germany, Belgium, and France[19]—all countries with strong employment-protection systems. Notably, this correlation is positive *even when age is not held constant*: even though older on average, high-tenure displaced workers in these high-EPL countries experience less unemployment than low-tenure displaced workers.

It is tempting to see the effects of employment-protection systems in these statistics: by requiring lengthy notice periods and detailed adjustment plans, German-style employment-protection systems appear to continue to shield high-tenure "insiders" from market forces even if their firm or plant closes down. (Low-tenure workers in general qualify for less job protection than high-tenure workers.) This interpretation is supported by a comparison of the overall incidence of unemployment of displaced workers among countries: in high-EPL countries, displaced workers are much more likely to avoid a spell of unemployment altogether than, for example, in the United States or Canada. We discuss the effects of EPL on unemployment further in the section on "Patterns among Countries" (p. 34).

In sum, looking at postdisplacement jobless durations, a number of very consistent patterns emerge among all the countries in our sample. In particular, the demographic groups which are most likely to be displaced are not always those who suffer the least, or the most, from displacement. In particular, young, low-tenure men are more likely to be displaced, but they experience less joblessness if they are displaced. The one group that suffers disproportionately on both dimensions is the unskilled: unskilled workers are more likely to be displaced and take longer to become reemployed after displacement than other workers. Unlike with older workers, who also have longer durations, this seems unlikely to be caused by a disproportionate level of industry- and occupation-specific skill. More likely, this is caused—at least in part—by the greater relative attractiveness of income-support programs available to unemployed low-wage workers: as noted earlier, in most countries, the UI benefit replacement ratio declines precipitously with predisplacement earnings.[20] Another contributing factor may be the ongoing decline in demand for unskilled workers throughout the industrialized world, though it is unclear why—in the absence of a social safety net income "floor"—this would be reflected in unemployment durations, rather than simply in lower wages.

Displacement-Induced Wage Losses

In the United States, much discussion has centered around the widely observed positive correlation between tenure and displaced workers' wage losses (see, for example, Kletzer 1989; Ruhm 1991; and Topel 1990). It is now broadly recognized that this phenomenon could reflect either a causal effect of tenure (such as specific human-capital accumulation or seniority-related implicit contracts) or simply differences in average match quality between low- and high-tenure workers.[21] Less well known, however, is the fact that in the simplest of dynamic matching models where workers move to better matches as they age, the expected correlation between average match quality and tenure (holding age constant) is negative.[22] Thus, under very reasonable assumptions, a positive partial correlation between tenure and wages implies a positive causal effect of tenure on wages. As Topel (1991) argued, we can thus be fairly sure that firm-specific skills (or some similar causal mechanism such as seniority-based implicit contracts or industry-specific skills)[23] is an important feature of the U.S. labor market.

Is this also true in other countries? According to Table 1.12, the answer is a qualified "yes." Reasonably strong and statistically significant tenure effects are found in the United States, Canada, and the United Kingdom, but tenure effects are generally insignificant in the Netherlands, Belgium, and Denmark—the only other countries where results are available.[24] In the Netherlands and Denmark, this can quite plausibly be attributed to the very small samples of displaced workers for whom reemployment wages are observed. In Belgium, however, sample size is not a plausible explanation: estimates of tenure effects on wage losses are tightly bounded near zero. As noted in Chapter 6, this may reflect two features of Belgian wage-setting institutions. One feature is the relatively high level of union coverage and the centralized nature of wage bargaining: most workers are covered by industry-level wage contracts that affect all Belgian firms in their industry. The second feature is the portability of seniority across firms in the same union bargaining unit, i.e., covered workers changing jobs within an industry retain their seniority in the new firm. Both of these factors make it harder for individual Belgian workers to accept a wage cut in order to become reemployed and may contribute to their very low reemployment rates.

In sum, the positive correlation between tenure and wage losses observed in the United States is also seen in two other countries (Canada and the United Kingdom) with similar wage-setting institutions. It is not seen in a country (Belgium) with very different, much more centralized wage-setting institutions, which also happens to be the only other country with enough data to estimate a tenure effect with reasonable precision in this volume. This does not, of course, negate the possibility of firm-specific capital accumulation in countries like Belgium, but it does imply that the effects of firm-specific capital on wages are, in general, mediated by a country's system of wage-setting institutions. It also reinforces the notion, pursued further below, that a substantial fraction of the large wage losses observed among high-tenure displaced workers in the United States. may be directly associated with two features of its decentralized wage-setting institutions: 1) partial union coverage and 2) a high level of overall wage inequality in the labor market as a whole.[25] Both these features are less characteristic of most European countries.

The effect of age on displaced workers' wage losses is summarized in Table 1.13. Compared with the tenure effects just discussed, these are much more robust and uniform across countries: *in all countries for which we have data, older workers experience greater wage losses.* Furthermore, with one exception (Denmark), this effect persists when we hold tenure constant. Like the results for unemployment, these results suggest a pure effect of age, perhaps working through changes in workers' adaptability.[26] Given the strength and robustness of these results, it is in a way surprising that pure age effects on displaced workers' wage losses have not received more attention in the economic literature. If adaptability is a function of age, there may be important, but as yet largely unexplored, effects of an economy's (or firm's) age structure on its ability to adapt to change. An exceptionally old workforce might, for example, help explain Japan's current difficulties in restructuring its economy. Counterbalancing this, however, Japan's FIFO layoff system may promote the survival and recovery of ailing firms by keeping them relatively young during sustained periods of downsizing.

Do men or women experience larger wage losses when they are displaced? Outside Japan, Table 1.14 shows either no gender difference in wage losses, or a larger (percentage) fall for women. The latter result echoes a finding in Crossley, Jones, and Kuhn (1994), who found larger losses for displaced women (at all tenure levels) in Canada and who argued that this might be caused by tighter geographic constraints on women's job-search activities. This geographical mobility hypothesis is supported by Gladden's (1999) research, which quantified the effect of differential geographic mobility on the gender wage gap in the United States. The exceptional Japanese result may reflect its peculiar institution of FIFO layoffs, which—being largely confined to men—may make the pool of displaced men and women very different. One simple way in which this might be true involves age: laid-off Japanese men might be, on average, considerably older than laid-off Japanese women, who do not appear to participate in the FIFO layoff system. Since we have no regression results that control for age and gender simultaneously in Japan, we cannot rule this out as an explanation of this particular Japanese exception.

Table 1.15 examines the association between education and wage losses among countries. Unlike the case of jobless durations, there is no consistent or significant association. The presence of an education/joblessness link, but the absence of an education/wage loss link, is consistent with the notion that income-support programs play an important role in the jobless durations of less-skilled workers: while lengthening jobless spells, these programs should not depress reemployment wages and may, in fact, raise them if more job offers are sampled during the jobless spell.

Summing up, our analysis of tenure patterns in displacement-induced wage losses cannot rule out the notion that substantial losses of firm- or industry-specific human capital occur among high-tenure displaced workers in all countries. However, the analysis strongly suggests that other factors, in particular labor market institutions, also play a role in determining the wage losses experienced by displaced workers. In particular, it appears that predisplacement tenure affects displaced workers' wage losses *only* in countries with decentralized wage bargaining and high overall wage inequality. In different institutional environments (such as Belgium's), the wage-loss pattern seen in the United States, Canada, and the United Kingdom is not present. Our analysis also suggests that gender differences in job search play a role in the gender differential in wage losses due to displacement, though this effect can also be overridden by institutional factors, as in Japan. Finally, we document a universal positive correlation between wage losses and age in all countries examined. Given its ubiquity, it is surprising that this relationship has not received more attention in the literature. Further attention to the potential causes of this pure "aging" effect would seem to be warranted in future analyses.

Summing Up: Who Loses Most?

Pulling together the three outcome measures (frequency of displacement, unemployment effects of displacement, and wage effects of displacement) and the four dimensions of demographic variation (gender, age, tenure, and skill level), is there any one demographic group that is hurt most on all dimensions in all countries examined? Our answer to this question is summarized in Table 1.16, which distills the results of Tables 1.4–1.15 into one 4 x 3 table. In almost all cases, the patterns reported in Table 1.16 apply both to zero-order correlations (not holding any other characteristics constant) and to correlations that hold the other characteristics constant in a regression framework. Cases where a distinction needs to be drawn are highlighted below.

Overall, none of the demographic groups examined in Table 1.16 fares unambiguously worse on all dimensions in all countries examined, though unskilled workers come close: they experience more frequent displacement, more postdisplacement joblessness, and about the same (percentage) wage loss from displacement as do skilled workers. Thus, as Farber (1997) has pointed out, while displacement among skilled workers is increasing and is attracting more public attention in the United States, displacement both in the United States and in all other developed countries where evidence exists remains a phenomenon that disproportionately hurts the unskilled.

Older workers fare worse than younger workers after displacement in all countries, but they are less likely to be displaced in the first place in all countries except Japan. Thus, Japan—perhaps paradoxically a culture reputed to place exceptional value on respect for one's elders—is the only country in which older workers fare worse on all three displacement-related outcomes examined here.

Tenure effects are more complex than age effects. First, as for age, in all countries but Japan, high-tenure workers are less likely to be displaced than low-tenure workers. The effect of tenure on postdisplacement joblessness, however, appears to vary with the strength of the employment-protection legislation in a country: high-tenure displaced workers seem to have shorter durations in high-EPL countries and longer durations elsewhere. As expected, in the United States and other countries with broadly similar institutions, senior workers are less likely to be displaced but experience larger wage losses if they are.

In this volume, however, we have not been able to document seniority-related wage losses in countries with more centralized wage-setting institutions, and in one country (Belgium) we can rule out this phenomenon quite convincingly.

In all countries, men are more likely to be displaced than women, but (with the exception of Japan) women lose equal amounts or more when displaced. Overall, the most consistent patterns that emerge from Table 1.16 are that older workers, and unskilled workers, bear the main costs of displacement.

Other Within-Country Patterns

A careful reading of the chapters in this volume reveals four other cross-sectional patterns that, while not fitting neatly into the above framework of incidence, unemployment, and wages, nonetheless appear to be universal among countries.[27] One of these is negative duration dependence in the reemployment hazard. For all countries in which this statistic is available (the United States, the Netherlands, Canada, Japan, the United Kingdom, Australia, and France), workers who have been unemployed a longer time have a smaller chance of becoming reemployed than workers closer to the start of their unemployment spell. As is well known, this could be either a direct causal effect of unemployment (for example, skills may atrophy with time out of work, or workers may become depressed, discouraged, or ill) or a pure composition effect: workers who are most attractive to employers (on dimensions not measured by the econometrician) tend to be hired out of the pool of unemployed workers sooner than others. What the data firmly reject, however, is a model in which the predominant factor affecting durations is liquidity constraints: in such a model, unemployed workers become increasingly likely to accept jobs as their assets or UI benefit entitlements are used up during an unemployment spell. Increasing hazard rates are not seen in any country in any econometric specification in this volume.

Related to the declining-hazard phenomenon, the authors for four of the countries under study in this book (the Netherlands, France, Germany, and the United Kingdom) examined the correlation between (completed) unemployment durations and wages upon reemployment. In all four cases, this correlation is negative, even when we use the predisplacement wage to control for unobserved heterogeneity in workers' abilities. While consistent with a story in which longer unemployment durations cause workers' skills to atrophy, this pattern could, of course, also be explained by selection effects. Indeed, as noted below, the low reemployment wages of German, French, Belgian, and Danish displaced workers who have been unemployed for more than a year appear to constitute the only observable gap in the safety net protecting displaced workers from adverse outcomes in those countries. The authors for the same four countries also compared the unemployment durations of displaced workers to those of workers experiencing other kinds of separations, such as voluntary quits. In a finding reminiscent of Gibbons and Katz's (1991) "layoffs and lemons" result (workers displaced *en masse* fare better than those displaced individually), it appears that—at least in the Netherlands, France and Germany—displaced workers fare *better* than other separators. This finding is particularly striking in the Netherlands, where displaced workers receive higher unemployment benefits than other separators and thus have a lower incentive to become reemployed. In the case of the Netherlands, the authors speculate that, once again, employment-protection laws may play a role; nondisplaced workers do not benefit from nearly as much relocation assistance as displaced workers. Further exploration of this distinction in countries such as the Netherlands with very generous EPL certainly seems warranted.

Finally, in only two countries did the authors pose the question, "Does displacement hasten retirement?" Before considering their answers, it is worth noting that, theoretically, the answer to this question is not obvious. While the wage loss associated with displacement among older workers creates a substitution effect away from continued work, an income effect could encourage later retirement: at a lower wage, people need to work longer to finance the same level of retirement income. Despite the possibility of these income effects, however, in both the Netherlands and the United States, displacement appears to hasten, not to delay, retirement. Either the income effects of displacement are unimportant for workers who are displaced late in life, or a combination of generous severance payments and social programs makes these income effects unimportant. The retirement-inducing effect of displacement thus offers some insight into the long-term effects of displacement-related wage losses on workers' well being. If such effects were very severe, we would expect older displaced workers to delay, rather than to hasten, their retirement plans.[28]

PATTERNS AMONG COUNTRIES

In this section I discuss what can be learned from patterns in the levels of various displacement-related phenomena among countries. As noted, these conclusions are more sensitive to differences in data collection methods among countries than those discussed in the previous section. Nonetheless, as I hope the discussion will show, attention to detail does allow some broad conclusions to be drawn.

Displacement Rates

Estimates of annual displacement rates taken from Chapters 2 through 6 are presented in Table 1.17. Because two alternative definitions of displacement are used in those chapters, these rates should be considered in two groups. In the first six countries (the United States, the Netherlands, Japan, Canada, the United Kingdom, and Australia) the statistics refer to total displacement rates—displacements of individual workers as well as mass layoffs and plant closures. In the remaining four countries (France, Germany, Belgium, and Denmark) they refer to persons displaced due to the closure of a firm or establishment, only.

Examination of the first six countries in Table 1.17 yields a result that some readers might find surprising: overall, total displacement rates are very similar among countries with very different labor market institutions. In fact, the annual rates for the United States, the Netherlands, Canada, the United Kingdom., and Australia are all between 4 and 5 percent per annum.[29] In Japan, if we restrict attention to "Western-style" layoffs only, its estimated displacement rate is much lower than all the other countries, at 1.2 percent. However, if we include in the count of Japanese displaced workers one source of job loss that is much more common in Japan than elsewhere (temporary contract expirations) plus another that is largely unique to Japan (mandatory retirements for which the timing is totally at the firm's discretion), the estimated displacement rate rises to 3.5 percent. This is not that different from the other five countries for which total displacement rates are available.

The remainder of Table 1.17 presents estimates of mass displacement rates for France, Germany, Belgium, and Denmark. Restricting attention to firm closures and to employees with more than three or four years of tenure yields annual displacement rates of 2.8 and 1.6 percent in France and Belgium, respectively.[30] Comparable estimates for plant closures are 1.0 and 0.6 percent for Germany and Denmark, respectively. In the United States, a little over a third of all displacements are due to plant closures.[31] Given that high-tenure workers tend to have lower displacement rates (see Table 1.6), these figures seem roughly consistent with a 4- to 5-percent overall displacement rate as well (with the exception of France). While we remain unsure of the precise explanation for this French exception, we note that France is probably the country in which the false-firm-deaths problem is most severe. Individuals moving "together" into the same new firm can only be identified from sample information (rather than a census of the firm's employees). Thus it is possible that the value of 2.8 percent per annum substantially overestimates France's mass layoff rate.

How do we reconcile the rough similarity in displacement rates among countries with the popular notion that jobs are, on average, much less secure in the United States than in countries with strong employment-protection laws, like the Netherlands, or with a tradition of lifetime employment, like Japan? One point has already been made: at least in Japan, displacement is much more common than traditional statistics suggest if we account for the peculiar institutional features of involuntary workforce adjustment in that country. Two other considerations are also relevant to the Japanese case: first, displacement in Japan is concentrated among older workers, and women generally do not participate in the lifetime employment system. The former phenomenon makes the jobs of younger Japanese men much more secure than in the United States, and contributes to Japanese men's very high age-specific mean tenure levels (see Chapter 3, Table 3.17), without necessarily reducing the total displacement rate. The latter raises Japan's displacement rate substantially when women are included in the statistics.

Another point concerns the relationship between the displacement rates computed here and widely cited comparative estimates of unemployment inflows, such as those in Layard, Nickell and Jackman (1991, Chap. 5, Table 1) or OECD (1995, Table 1.9). These unemployment inflow rates are much higher in the United States than in most other OECD countries, but they differ from displacement rates for two very important reasons. First, unemployment inflow statistics generally include workers starting a temporary layoff spell. Temporary layoffs are much more common in the United States than most other countries and do not constitute displacements since the worker returns to his or her previous job. Second, as is shown below, when displacement occurs in the United States, it almost always results in an unemployment spell. The same is not true in a number of European countries, where a substantial majority of displaced workers never enter unemployment. As a result, similar European and U.S. displacement rates are quite consistent with a much lower unemployment inflow rate in Europe.[32]

A final point regarding the perceived relative insecurity of U.S. jobs is that popular perceptions are influenced by the severity of displacement's effects, as well as by its frequency. As I shall argue below, the consequences of displacement do differ substantially among countries, and—at least for the case of wage losses— these are considerably more severe in the United States than most other countries.

What, if anything, does the international similarity in displacement rates imply about the relation between labor market institutions and outcomes? Perhaps, as noted, institutions can affect the precise *form* that displacement takes (for example, the distinction between "pure" layoffs and mandatory outplacements such as *shukko*). Perhaps, as I shall argue below, they can also have important effects on the *consequences* of displacement by providing generous outplacement assistance. But it may be that overall displacement rates are relatively immune to policy interventions. There could simply be a relatively fixed amount of labor reallocation that must occur in any dynamic capitalist economy.[33] At a minimum, we have yet to see convincing evidence of a modern capitalist economy with a total displacement rate very different from 4 to 5 percent per annum.

Incidence of Joblessness

International differences in the amount of joblessness experienced by displaced workers are summarized in Table 1.18. In sharp contrast to the evidence for displacement rates, there is wide variation among countries in the probability that a displaced worker experiences any joblessness. While U.S. analysts tend to assume (correctly, for their country) that involuntary termination almost always results in a jobless spell, this is not the case in some other countries. For example, Abbring et al. draw attention to the large difference in incidence of joblessness between U.S. and Dutch displaced workers. Using very similar samples and definitions, they calculate that only 30 percent of displaced workers in the Netherlands actually experience any joblessness, compared with 85 percent in the United States. A very low incidence of joblessness among displaced workers is also observed among workers involved in plant closures in Germany (39 percent) and in plant closures or shrinkages in Denmark (31 percent).[34]

As is argued in several chapters of this volume, the most likely explanation for the low incidence of joblessness among displaced workers in some European countries is employment-protection legislation. This should not be surprising, since in many cases the intent of European EPL is to prevent displacement-induced joblessness. As Table 1.18 suggests, these apparent effects of EPL are most visible in the case of plant, rather than firm, closures (the French and Belgian statistics refer to firm closures and are not so low). It is in the case of plant closures that EPL is both strongest—involving all the provisions associated with mass layoffs such as a "social plan"—and most enforceable (enforcement problems naturally arise when the legal entity responsible for complying with the law ceases to exist). While further research is certainly warranted, the chapters in this volume strongly suggest that joblessness is *not* an inevitable consequence of displacement, and that—for better or worse—it is possible to design a system of employment-protection laws that makes joblessness the exception rather than the rule among workers displaced from dying plants.

Conditional Jobless Durations

Now suppose a displaced Dutch, German, or Japanese worker is unlucky enough to start a jobless spell. Is he or she likely to be jobless much longer than a U.S. worker in the same situation? Perhaps surprisingly, given the prevailing view of these labor markets as low-turnover and "sclerotic," Table 1.18 provides only mixed support for this hypothesis. The conditional probability of long-term joblessness is substantially higher in Germany and France than in the United States. Given the much higher unemployment rates in these countries during the sample period, this is not surprising. More surprisingly, in the Netherlands, 28 percent of jobless spells experienced by displaced workers last more than a year, a fraction which is identical to that in the United States. Even more surprisingly, conditional durations in the United Kingdom are below those in the United States.

Why are U.S. displaced workers' unemployment durations so unexpectedly high when viewed in an international context? To understand this phenomenon, at least three definitional and statistical points are relevant. First, recall again that the statistics in Table 1.18 exclude temporary layoff spells—which tend to be short—from the sample of jobless durations in all countries where they are a significant phenomenon (especially the United States and Canada, but also France). These short spells *are* included in most published estimates of comparative unemployment durations, which tend to show much shorter average spells in the United States. Second, note that Table 1.18 reports actual survivor rates (the fraction of displaced persons actually reemployed within 6 and 12 months of displacement) rather than, for example, estimated mean durations extrapolated from a sample of incomplete spells (as in Layard, Nickell, and Jackman 1991, Chapter 5, Table 1). As jobless durations tend to be very skewed, means tend to be much higher than the median; i.e., than the duration experienced by a typical individual, especially in European countries where the distribution has a long right tail. Even more importantly (in contrast to extrapolated means), our survivor function estimates do not depend on assumptions about the distribution of spells beyond the censoring point or on the assumption of a steady state.

Third, note that our numbers also differ from relatively well known statistics on the fraction of the stock of unemployed workers who have been employed for over a year (e.g., OECD 1995, Table 1.8). These "stock" statistics vary much more among countries than ours do, but are unrepresentative of the experiences of a typical displaced worker in each country for a different reason. Stock statistics refer to the population of workers who are unemployed at a point in time. In contrast, our "flow" statistics refer to a random sample of new unemployment spells. Because long spells will (by definition) be overrepresented in a stock sample, such samples overstate the duration of unemployment a newly unemployed worker is likely to experience.

Aside from the above statistical issues, there may be a potentially important substantive reason why U.S. unemployment durations are so high. Consider a North American worker who is (*ex post*) permanently displaced. Compared to, say, a laid-off worker in Japan who has no prospect of returning to his or her original job, the North American worker may not search as intensively for a new job near the start of his or her spell because recall remains a possibility. Clearly, the effects of the North American temporary layoff system on the jobless durations of workers who are, ultimately, permanently displaced warrant further research.

Unconditional Jobless Durations

Combining incidence and duration, in which countries do displaced workers experience the most joblessness? This statistic is examined in the final three columns of Table 1.18 for the seven countries for which it is available. Three features stand out. First are the very low total jobless durations in Japan and the United Kingdom. Contrary to many popular discussions about the "thinness" of non-entry-level labor markets in Japan, by international standards displaced Japanese workers do *not* have long jobless durations, even when we exclude from the calculations those displacements taking place via mandatory outplacements (*shukko*) and even in 1995, when Japan was in a deep and prolonged recession. Furthermore, when we exclude temporary layoffs from the U.S. statistics, U.S. displaced workers in fact experience *more* joblessness than do the British. The second feature is the fact that total jobless durations in Canada, France, and Germany *do* exceed those in the United States. Among other factors, this could reflect a much more generous unemployment insurance system.

The third feature is the large gap between Belgian and Danish jobless durations, which is thoroughly documented and analyzed in Chapter 6 by Albæk et al. According to these authors, the only factor that can plausibly explain this differential between otherwise very similar countries is a negative effect of Belgium's very stringent employment-protection laws on the rate of new job creation. Certainly, Belgium has the most stringent advance-notice laws of the countries considered in this volume; it also has the highest total jobless durations among its displaced workers. Thus, despite their direct effect in reducing the incidence of jobless spells, it appears that very high EPLs can be counterproductive in combatting unemployment among displaced workers: their negative equilibrium effects on new job offer arrival rates can outweigh these direct effects.

In sum, rather than being at the low end of the scale, the United States is in the middle of the pack when it comes to the total amount of joblessness experienced by displaced workers. One reason for this is definitional: previous estimates of comparative unemployment durations underestimate the amount of unemployment experienced by U.S. displaced workers because they include the short durations of the many U.S. workers who are not displaced but are just on temporary layoff. Another may be a detrimental causal effect of the North American temporary layoff system on the jobless durations of workers who ultimately are permanently displaced: an expectation of recall might reduce search intensity. A third factor explaining the unexpectedly good unemployment "performance" of displaced workers in some European countries is related to the relatively large fractions of displaced workers who avoid unemployment altogether: strict EPLs prevent the inception of unemployment spells, raising the number of spells with an unconditional duration of zero. At the same time, however, EPLs—especially when they are very strict and legalistic, as in Belgium—may also play a detrimental role in the high conditional jobless durations experienced by displaced workers by reducing the equilibrium offer arrival rate.[35]

Wage Changes

Table 1.19 presents estimates of mean percentage wage changes experienced by displaced workers, drawn from Chapters 2 through 6 of this volume. In all cases these estimates are formulated to correspond as closely as possible to changes in the wage earned per hour of work (rather than total earnings during periods that could contain jobless spells) before and after displacement. Because—at least in some countries—displaced workers' wage losses vary substantially with predisplacement tenure, the table presents disaggregated results by individual years of tenure. (Where the only available results combine multiple years of tenure, I simply repeat the estimates in adjacent cells of the table.) Most estimates in the table consist of simple before/after mean wage changes for workers reemployed within a year or two of displacement. Where available, however, estimates of wage losses relative to a control group of continuously employed workers are also shown.

Even though Chapter 2 reports some estimates of wage losses for the Netherlands (see the discussion of Table 2.22), these are not included in Table 1.19. As the authors of that chapter indicate, their wage-change results are based on a very small sample, resulting in standard errors so high that no remotely plausible sizes of wage changes can be ruled out. Estimates from Australia (Table 4.17) are also excluded because they apply to a sample of very young workers and are thus not comparable with any of the other countries in Table 1.19. Because wage changes can differ between individual and mass layoffs, throughout the table I note whether the statistics refer to mass layoffs only or to the population of all displaced workers. To ensure that any conclusions involving wage changes in the United States are robust as to whether a sample of mass layoffs from administrative data or survey-based samples of individual layoffs are used, Table 1.19 also reports estimates from the well-known administrative-data-based study of U.S. displaced workers by Jacobson, LaLonde, and Sullivan (1993).

Among the broad patterns that emerge from an examination of Table 1.19, one has already been noted (see Table 1.14): real-wage changes associated with displacement become more negative (or less positive) with tenure on the lost job. Two other observations are primarily of methodological interest. First, in all countries but Belgium (and at all tenure levels within those countries), wage-change estimates that utilize a control group of continuously employed workers are more negative (or less positive) than estimates that do not use a control group. Evidently, in all those countries (even the United States, where aggregate real wages had stagnated for decades) the typical nondisplaced worker experienced real wage growth during the sample period.[36] Displaced workers' own wage declines thus understate their losses relative to comparable workers who are not displaced. The exception is Belgium, where during our sample period continuously employed workers experienced real wage declines; here simple "difference" estimates *overstate* the wage losses "caused" by displacement. Second, in most cases—and especially in Germany, France, and Belgium—the disparity between the simple "difference" estimates and the "difference in differences" estimator is not large. Disparities of more than 5 percentage points are confined to the U.S. results of Jacobson, LaLonde, and Sullivan (1993)—where they are small relative to the size of the losses incurred—and the United Kingdom. Among the countries examined, the United Kingdom appears to be the only country where 1) continuously employed workers experience high rates of real wage growth during the sample period (of over 7 percent per year for continuously employed low-tenure workers and 3.5 percent for high-tenure workers), *and* 2) displaced workers experience measurable real wage declines. In general, however, because of real wage growth among continuously employed workers, simple "difference" estimates usually understate the amount workers lose as a result of displacement. However, because real wage growth in most economies during our sample period is not very large, they usually don't understate it by very much.

Turning to more substantive conclusions, consider first the wage changes experienced either by displaced workers with low levels of predisplacement tenure (say, under two years) or those experienced by displaced workers of all tenure levels combined. With one exception—again, the United Kingdom—the wage changes experienced by both these groups are either positive (as for short-tenure workers in the United States and Canada) or close to zero (as for the United States, Japan, and Canada overall). The small loss (or the gain) among short-tenure workers requires no explanation: most reasons displaced workers might experience substantial wage losses do not apply to very short-tenure workers. The small overall loss stems from a simple composition effect: because displacement rates decline sharply with job tenure (see Table 1.6), low-tenure workers will dominate in any representative sample of involuntary separations.

What of the British exception to this pattern? A closer examination of Table 1.19 shows that the British exception stems entirely from relatively large wage losses experienced by workers with under a year of tenure. Workers with between one and two years of tenure do fit the pattern noted above; furthermore, the inverted U-shaped relation between wage changes and predisplacement tenure observed for Britain is not found in any other country. Given this, I suspect that the real wage changes in the lowest tenure category in Britain may be related to the difficulties in measuring tenure in the British Household Panel Survey and to the resulting large number of missing observations on tenure there. I shall treat them as anomalous here and in what follows. If further research shows, instead, that they are genuine, it will be fascinating to try to understand what explains these high losses among a group for whom they are very rarely seen.

Next, it is hard not to notice the large number of positive entries in Table 1.19: U.S. displaced workers with tenure of under four years, Canadian displaced workers with tenure under one year, and apparently all German and French displaced workers experience a *mean* wage change that is positive. Apparently the large losses documented by Jacobson, LaLonde, and Sullivan (1993) for Pennsylvania workers are not universal; their focus on high-tenure workers (and, as I shall argue below, on workers in highly unionized industries in a relatively nonunionized, high-wage-inequality country, plus focus on quarterly earnings rather than on wage rates) explains much of their results.

Finally, consider high-tenure displaced workers. In contrast to the wage increases observed for many low-tenure workers, Table 1.19 indicates (as expected) that large mean wage losses *are* seen in some countries, in particular the United States, Canada, and—to a lesser extent—the United Kingdom. They are not observed in other countries, however.[37] What, then, is distinctive about the United States, the United Kingdom, and Canada? Recalling the discussion of labor market institutions earlier in this chapter, these are clearly the three countries with the most decentralized wage-setting institutions.[38] The likely effects of wage structure on displaced workers' wage losses are addressed most directly in Chapter 3 by Abe et al. Using very similar surveys and definitions, they document a much higher *variance* of displacement-induced wage changes in Canada than in Japan. This higher variance has dramatic implications for the amount of lifetime wage security experienced by workers in both countries. For example, Table 3.21 indicates that an average 20- to 24-year-old employed Canadian man has a 4.7 percent chance of experiencing a separation that will cut his hourly wage rate by 30 percent or more. The comparable statistic in Japan is 0.8 percent. For men aged 35–39, the Canadian and Japanese probabilities are 1.7 percent and 0.2 percent, respectively. The much higher level of Japanese wage security cannot be primarily attributed to a lower permanent separation rate (Table 3.5). A substantial fraction of Japanese men's wage security thus derives from the much more compressed structure of wage changes they experience when they are displaced.

It is also well known that Germany, France, Belgium, and Denmark have much more compressed wage structures than the United States and Canada. This is in part due to higher collective bargaining coverage; in France's case the very high national minimum wage also plays a role. And according to Table 1.19, high-tenure displaced workers in these countries do not experience significant wage losses, either unconditionally or relative to continuously employed workers. Further, the fact that Jacobson, LaLonde, and Sullivan (1993) found large wage losses in the United States using administrative data on workers involved in mass layoffs implies that the low losses found in the above European countries are not just an artifact of a different data-collection scheme and displacement definition.[39]

Blau and Kahn (1996b) convincingly demonstrated that international differences in overall wage inequality play a major role in explaining international differences in the gender pay gap. Overall, our findings in this section suggest that a similar mechanism may be at work for displaced workers: in countries with high wage inequality, senior displaced workers appear to experience larger wage losses. Relatedly—since partial union coverage in a nation contributes to high levels of wage inequality—both Jacobson, LaLonde, and Sullivan (1993, p. 703) and Kuhn and Sweetman (1988a) observed that a substantial portion of U.S. displaced workers' wage losses may in fact be attributable to the loss of union coverage upon displacement. Naturally, this is much less of a factor in countries where union coverage is almost universal.

Before leaving the subject of wage changes it is worth drawing attention to two exceptions to the phenomenon of small wage losses in countries with compressed wage structures. In some sense, these are exceptions which, because of the special circumstances in which they occur, "prove" the rule. First, as Bender et al. point out, larger wage losses are observed in France and Germany when attention is restricted to the small minority of displaced workers who become unemployed and remain so for over a year. These workers appear to fall out of the protective net provided both by EPL and the compressed national wage structure. Second are Japanese men over the age of 50 or 55. These men essentially leave the "primary" labor market where jobs and wages are protected and take new "post-retirement" jobs in a very different sector of the labor market. They experience large wage losses because they switch from a primary to a secondary segment of the labor market, much like displaced Pennsylvania steelworkers who become reemployed in a nonunion, service-sector job.

Summary

In comparing the levels of displacement rates, postdisplacement unemployment, and displacement-induced wage losses among the countries under study in this volume, the following main conclusions emerge:

1) Although some difficulties remain in reconciling displacement counts from firm-based versus worker-based data, comparable worker-based data yields estimated displacement rates, which are surprisingly similar in all countries where they are available, of between 4 and 5 percent of the employed population each year. This occurs despite substantial differences in labor market institutions among countries. This phenomenon is *not* inconsistent with previous statistics showing very large differences in unemployment inflows among countries, and it is consistent with statistics showing similar rates of sectoral labor reallocation (Bertola and Rogerson 1997). Perhaps a certain rate of displacement is simply a necessary feature of a dynamic capitalist economy.

2) Given that a worker is displaced, the probability that he or she will experience any joblessness at all varies a great deal among countries. While over 80 percent of U.S. displaced workers

experience some joblessness immediately following displacement, experiencing a spell of joblessness is the exception rather than the rule in such countries as the Netherlands, Denmark, and Germany. The most likely explanations of this low incidence of unemployment are employment-protection laws and union negotiations of the terms surrounding layoffs, both of which employ a variety of means to forestall the inception of an unemployment spell.

Supporting evidence for the EPL explanation of low unemployment incidence among some European displaced workers comes from two sources. One is the effect of predisplacement tenure on postdisplacement unemployment, examined in Table 1.11: as noted, in France, Germany, and Belgium (no Dutch data on this question are available), high-tenure displaced workers actually experience less unemployment than low-tenure workers. In France and Germany this is true even if age is *not* held constant, even though older workers tend to have both higher tenures and longer unemployment spells otherwise. This is strongly suggestive of greater advance notice and reemployment assistance provided to high-tenure "insiders" in these economies. A second source of corroborating evidence is the observation that, in the Netherlands, displaced workers actually get reemployed faster than workers who voluntarily quit their jobs, even though quitters face unemployment insurance penalties. As Abbring et al. suggest, this may be attributable to extensive reemployment assistance required for displaced workers but not in the case of quits.

3) Given that a spell of joblessness has begun, its expected length also varies substantially across countries. Perhaps unexpectedly, these conditional durations are not lowest in the United States: the United States is in the middle of the pack. One reason for the unexpectedly high unemployment durations of U.S. workers is that previous comparisons may have been contaminated by the inclusion of temporary layoffs, which tend to have short durations, in the U.S. statistics. Also, the fact that many (*ex post*) displaced workers in the United States have a prospect of being recalled to their former firm may reduce their search intensity

relative to workers in countries where displacement is a more discrete phenomenon.

4) In all countries, the mean wage change experienced by a low-tenure displaced worker is close to zero or positive. Small losses are also observed when we consider all displaced workers as a group, not conditioning on tenure. In essence, this reflects the fact that all the countries under study have a casual labor market, in which displacement is frequent but relatively inconsequential for current wages. Displacements from such jobs tend to dominate flow samples of involuntary separations everywhere.

5) Large percentage wage losses are observed only for workers with high tenure levels, and only in countries (the United States, Canada, and the United Kingdom.) with relatively high levels of wage inequality and low rates of union coverage. Just as a compressed wage structure may reduce the size of gender-wage differentials (Blau and Kahn 1996b), it may also reduce the magnitude of the wage changes experienced by displaced workers. Relatedly, displaced workers in a partially unionized economy such as these may be more likely to experience wage losses due to the loss of union coverage upon displacement.

Overall, the cross-national experience suggests that—with the possible exception of Belgium and its especially inflexible employment-protection system—it is hard to pinpoint any large negative effects of the highly regulated labor markets of Europe and Japan on displaced workers. Instead, employment-protection laws appear to dramatically reduce the incidence of an unemployment spell among workers who lose their jobs involuntarily. Compressed national wage structures also appear to reduce the frequency of large, displacement-induced wage losses experienced by a country's labor force. And while jobless durations, conditional on starting a spell, do tend to be higher outside the United States, they are not dramatically so, especially when temporary layoffs are removed from the statistics.

Of course, this does not necessarily mean that strong EPLs, for example, are good for any country. It does mean, however—and again with the probable exception of Belgium—that researchers looking for evidence of major EPL-induced costs need to look somewhere other than at displaced workers, perhaps at the labor market for new entrants, including immigrants, women, and students.[40] There is a sense in which, in some European labor markets, once one becomes an insider, one is always an insider. Even permanent job loss and the closure of one's workplace do not undermine the strong employment rights given to incumbents in these labor markets. This may harm new entrants, but that is one subject that is beyond the scope of this volume.

FUTURE DIRECTIONS

Clearly, much has been learned from the research in this volume, both about displaced workers and about comparative labor markets. Just as clearly, however, much more remains to be learned. Indeed, as was noted, and as is to be expected in a first attempt at international research on displacement, some of the key lessons from our work are methodological ones, which we hope will speed up and improve the work of others on these topics. Just what should future researchers in this area focus on, and how should they approach this subject matter? I consider these two questions in turn below.

One very worthwhile goal for future research would be to understand the "universals" uncovered in this volume. For example, pure age effects on wage losses and on unemployment following displacement are observed in every country under study. What is it about older workers that causes these larger losses? Can one disentangle "thinner" labor markets from shorter time horizons, higher wealth, or declining adaptability to change? Why are women's jobless durations almost always longer? Is it simply greater labor-force withdrawal connected with family responsibilities or are other factors (like geographical search constraints) at work? Careful studies, which pay close attention to empirical implications that distinguish these simple hypotheses from each other, can add a lot to our understanding of labor markets worldwide.

Another universal that could benefit from greater scrutiny is the finding of very small, or zero wage losses for the entire population of displaced workers in all countries. The contrast between this result and Jacobson, LaLonde, and Sullivan's could not be more stark, emphasizing the point that their workers may be a very special case: they are high-tenure workers, in distressed, high-rent, highly unionized industries in a relatively nonunionized country, displaced during a major recession. Further research needs to carefully distinguish these special cases from the experiences of typical job losers, whose situations are not nearly as severe. Just when and where do large wage losses occur, and when do they not?

Second are the exceptions, especially Japan. In particular, what drives the apparent Japanese exception to the age profile of displacement? Can a FIFO layoff system be directly observed in Japanese firms? In what industries is it the strongest? How does it affect declining firms (does it keep them younger, thus helping to forestall their decline)? As the relative displacement rates of older workers in North America are beginning to increase, an examination of this Japanese practice might yield insights of relevance to North America as well.

Third is a deeper understanding of displaced workers' flows into labor market states other than reemployment: what is the role of early retirement, discouragement, disability, retraining, and other forms of nonparticipation? Not only are these flows interesting in their own right, they also yield insights into the welfare effects of displacement. Retirement behavior, for example, like consumption behavior, provides clues to the severity of displacement's effects on workers' permanent incomes.

Fourth is the need to draw closer links between labor market institutions and outcomes, links which, while highly suggestive, are of necessity drawn on a relatively preliminary and impressionistic basis in this volume. One key institution that deserves more comparative attention is the system of temporary layoffs in the United States and Canada. Does the prospect of recall reduce search? During a layoff spell with some (*ex ante*) probability of recall, how do workers update their priors about recall probabilities and adjust their search strategies? How does this system compare with one in which the break with the predisplacement employer is a sharper, more well-defined event? Other key institutions appear to be the level of union coverage and the degree of centralization in wage bargaining. This volume provides highly suggestive, though not yet conclusive, evidence that loss of union coverage and a decentralized wage-setting system explain much of the large wage losses experienced by senior workers in the United States.

Fifth, more needs to be known about voluntary reemployment assistance provided by firms even in the absence of, or in excess of legislated benefits. Such help can take the form of arranging employee transfers, setting up interviews, providing outplacement consultants, and so forth. Is this more, or less common in jurisdictions with strong EPLs? If less common, then EPLs could simply be displacing voluntary assistance with little net effect. If more common, EPLs effects may be magnified by changes in assistance voluntarily provided by firms.

Most important, however, is the effect of employment-protection laws and compressed national wage structures on workers who are not displaced—who, after all, at least in any particular year constitute the vast majority of a nation's labor force. Of particular interest here are new entrants to the labor force, including young school-leavers, women reentering after childbirth or child-rearing, and immigrants. We have already shown, I believe quite convincingly, that for the most part, displaced workers benefit from strong EPLs and compressed wage structures. Demonstrating whether or not new labor market entrants are harmed by these practices—which may also make it more difficult to break into the labor market and become a protected "insider"—is a much harder question to answer. This is because the effects are indirect, working through changes in market prices and search frictions rather than directly on the groups specifically targeted by these laws. It is, however, the most important question left unanswered by this volume.

How should future studies conduct the above analyses? As our collective experience makes clear, such studies will need to pay close attention to institutional details, and not just those embodied in legislation and regulations. These nonlegislated institutions include labor unions, the organization of industrial labor markets, and accepted mechanisms of worker termination that differ among countries for apparently historical reasons. Future studies also need to pay excruciatingly close attention to definitional and, perhaps less expected, to linguistic issues. This is hard work, but, as this volume shows, it can be done. The results not only test existing hypotheses and preconceptions about how labor markets work, but they also yield new hypotheses to be assessed in future work. It is my sincere hope that this volume will encourage others to embark on the difficult but rewarding path of comparative labor market research.

Notes

1. In this volume, Chapter 2, Table 2.3.
2. The United States imposes notice requirements only for *mass* layoffs, as defined in the Worker Adjustment and Retraining Notification Act (WARN).
3. For a recent example of such a study and a summary of various recent attempts to derive one-dimensional measures of the overall "strictness" of EPL across countries, see Heckman and Pages (2000).
4. For a recent example of the effects of displacement on health, see Gallo et al. (2000).
5. See, for example, Addison and Blackburn (1994).
6. See, for example, Tachibanaki (1996).
7. One might think a plant-closure-based sample would overestimate the severity of the consequences of displacement, as congestion effects in local labor markets might make it harder for each individual worker to become reemployed. As is now well known, however, Gibbons and Katz (1991) found the opposite: persons displaced individually fare worse. They attribute this to a "lemons" phenomenon in which individual layoffs serve as adverse signals about an employee's productivity.
8. Any discussion of losses in firm- or industry-specific skills as a possible cause of displacement-induced wage losses implicitly makes this assumption.
9. See de la Rica (1995).
10. See also Kletzer and Fairlie's 1999 study of displacement among young U.S. workers.
11. This is typically only possible in data sets where one has access to the full population of workers at each plant before it disappears. Identifying the size of a group of workers who move together when one only has a sample of workers raises some difficult sampling issues. This is the case with the data from France and is discussed in detail in Chapter 5.
12. A similar comment applies to the way in which variables are measured themselves; e.g., the number of occupational categories used or the time units in which wages are measured.
13. One example appears to be the effect of children on women's labor-force participation rates. See, for example, Duleep and Sanders (1994).
14. The only exception to the gender pattern in incidence is in the simple means for Belgium; this applies to mass displacements only, and reverses sign when standard covariates are added to the regression. Some minor exceptions affect the education patterns (a U-shaped effect in France and a positive effect of job com-

plexity in the Netherlands, when both education and the predisplacement wage are held constant).

15. There is a tendency for displacement rates to rise a small amount after age 50 or 55 in some countries, but no other country exhibits anything like the monotonic increase in age, starting at age 20, that is observed very clearly in Japan.
16. Skills that are specific to a firm should be captured by the tenure coefficient.
17. See van den Berg (1994).
18. For example, these results hold for Dutch reemployment hazards in Chapter 2, where the sample consists only of workers engaged in active search; they also hold in Crossley, Jones, and Kuhn (1994), who remove workers who leave the labor market from their sample.
19. In France, this is only the case for the probability of experiencing a positive spell of unemployment.
20. Evidence in favor of this interpretation comes from a number of less-developed countries without a meaningful social safety net. Unlike the United States and Western Europe, unemployment rates are higher in these countries among skilled workers, perhaps because only they can afford to spend time in this activity. For further discussion, see Dickens and Lang (1995).
21. Any differences in general ability that might exist between high- and low-tenure workers in a cross-section sample are "differenced out" when looking at wage changes experienced by displaced workers.
22. See Topel (1991, p. 152). The intuition is that, while good matches last, it is also the case that (especially among more experienced workers) new matches will not be consummated unless they are especially good. Whenever the true causal effect of tenure is positive, the latter effect outweighs the former.
23. Neal (1995) has noted that the tenure effect also captures industry-specific skills when (as is usually the case) tenure in the industry is not in the list of regressors.
24. Hashimoto and Raisian (1985) presented estimates of stronger tenure effects on wages in Japan than in the United States. Teulings and Hartog (1998, chap. 1) presented estimates for 11 countries that are consistent with the patterns noted below (higher tenure effects in "noncorporatist" countries). Unlike the displacement-based estimates in this volume, however, all these estimates are based on cross-section data only, and thus do not correct for unobserved ability differences between workers of different tenure levels.
25. See Teulings and Hartog (1998), Table 1 of the synopsis, and Chapter 5.
26. If anything, human-capital theory predicts the opposite: older workers should invest less in new skills; to the extent they pay their own training costs, this should *raise* their starting wages on their postdisplacement jobs. As discussed for unemployment durations, however, older workers may have more specialized industry- or occupation-specific skills that are not completely captured by the tenure variables used here. Another explanation might be a composition effect related to induced retirement. For this to explain the age effect, however, it would have to be the case that among older workers, those with *low* reemployment wage

prospects (relative to their previous job) are more likely to return to work. This seems unlikely.

27. At least this is true in the sense that, for every country in which the given correlation is reported in this volume, it has the same sign.
28. This question has recently been addressed using consumption data by Stephens (1999) and by Browning and Crossley (2000).
29. This assumes the Australian average for men (3.9) and women (5.2) together is between 4 and 5 percent.
30. I focus on closures rather than substantial shrinkage of a firm's or plant's workforce for two reasons. One is comparability among all four countries: in France and Germany, the statistics on closures are the only ones reported. The more important reason is conceptual: estimated displacement rates due to firm or plant shrinkage in Belgium and Denmark may be substantially inflated by voluntary turnover during the window period, especially in small firms and plants.
31. See, for example, Kuhn and Sweetman (1999, Table 1).
32. Consistent with our interpretation, Bertola and Rogerson (1997) also noted a broad uniformity among countries in job turnover rates, despite large differences in unemployment inflows. They also made reference to employment-protection laws as an explanation for this pattern because they allow worker reallocation to occur without an intervening unemployment spell.
33. One could counter, of course, that even if the total amount of labor reallocation is fixed, the share of such reallocation that is involuntary (from the worker's point of view) may not be. Bertola and Rogerson (1997), however, reported similar rates of labor reallocation (as measured by job turnover) among countries, and present theoretical arguments—related to wage compression—for why most reallocation is involuntary from the worker's point of view.
34. It may be worth recalling (see Note 30) that the Danish data could be contaminated by normal turnover during the "window" period, especially in small plants. This is of much less concern in the German data, which restrict attention to plant closures only.
35. Other European countries tend to have more flexible EPL provisions, which may be more sensitive to the circumstances surrounding each mass layoff or plant closure, because they involve case-by-case negotiations in the construction of a "social plan."
36. Recall that the control group wage-growth rates that are relevant here occur within cohorts, while most aggregate wage-growth statistics make comparisons among cohorts.
37. The six percent loss (relative to controls) among Danish workers with three or more years of tenure is the most negative point estimate, but—due in part to the small sample size—the 95 percent confidence interval stretches from about –2 to –10 percent (see Chapter 6, Table 6.10B).
38. These countries also tend to have the highest measured earnings inequality, especially at the low end of the earnings distribution—which is most relevant to the losses experienced by displaced workers. See, for example, the statistics on the

ratio between the 50th and 10th percentiles of the earnings distribution in OECD 1993, Table 5.2.

39. Another possible manifestation of the relation between wage-setting institutions and displaced workers' wage losses is alluded to in Chapter 4 by Borland et al. In many respects, the United Kingdom and Australia have similar labor markets, with low levels of employment protection and moderate levels of union membership. One big difference, however, is the very centralized system of wage-setting institutions embodied in Australia's awards system. Noting that they found substantial wage losses in Britain but not Australia, these authors speculated that wage-setting institutions may play a role. As they pointed out, however, the fact that their Australian sample was much younger could also have accounted for some, or all, of this difference.
40. These issues have recently been addressed for a sample of Latin American countries by Heckman and Pages (2000).

Table 1.1 Institutions Affecting Displacement: Employment-Protection Laws

Country	Justification for "economic" layoffs needed?	Mandatory advance notice: individual terminations	Mandatory advance notice: mass terminations	Mandatory severance pay	Consultation and other requirements
U.S.A.	No	None	2 Months	None	Inform local government of mass layoffs
Netherlands	Yes[a]—layoffs are by permit only	Workers under age 45: 0.25 month per year service Over age 45: 0.5 months per year service, up to 6 months Notice begins after permit issued	No special provision	Only in court cases	No special provisions
Japan	Yes—firms must demonstrate economic necessity and correct procedure	One month	No special provision	None	Extensive procedural requirements, including use of all reasonable alternatives (early retirements, cutting temporary and part-time employment) before layoffs of "regular" employees
Canada[b]	No	0.25 Month per year service, up to 2 months	Up to 4 months for layoffs of over 500 workers	0.25 Months per year of service, up to 6 months[c]	Notify local authorities of mass layoffs

U.K.	No	0.25 Month per year service, up to 3 months.	1 Month for layoffs of 20–100 workers 3 Months for layoffs of over 100 workers	0.25 Month per year of service between ages 22–40 0.375 Months per year of service between ages 41–60[d]	No special provisions
Australia	No	0.25 Month in "typical" pre-1984 award "As soon as practicable" in TCR test-case award[e]	No special provision	0.5 Months per year service, up to 2 mo. (in TCR-test case awards only)	Restrictions on terminations specified in award settlements, which vary by occupation, industry, and state.
France	Yes—must demonstrate economic necessity to works council	0.5–2 Years service: 1 month >2 Years service: 2 months However, legal procedures *before* notice can be issued take from 1 to 2.5 months.	Same as for individual terminations	>2 Years service: 0.1 month salary per year of service >10 Years service: 0.17 month salary per year of service	Employer must offer a retraining option Workers have priority in future hiring for one year Must share accounting information with works council In larger layoffs, a "social plan" must be devised

(continued)

Table 1.1 (continued)

Country	Justification for "economic" layoffs needed?	Mandatory advance notice: individual terminations	Mandatory advance notice: mass terminations	Mandatory severance pay	Consultation and other requirements
Germany	Yes—layoffs of workers with > 6 months tenure prohibited unless shown to be "socially acceptable"[f]	Blue-collar workers: 1 month after 5 years 3 months after 10 years White collar workers: 3 months after 5 years 6 months after 10 years	No special legislation; may be negotiated in social plan	Generally negotiated in social plan	Works council must be consulted for all layoffs For large layoffs, council can demand a "social plan" For large layoffs, must inform local employment office
Belgium	No	Blue-collar workers: <20 years service: 1 month >20 years service: 2 months White-collar workers: <5 years service: 3 months 5-9 years: 6 months 10-15 years: 9 months, etc. (courts often award even longer notice periods for white-collar workers)	None	One month's pay per year service in plant closures (less in mass layoffs)	In addition to statutory minima, notice periods for white-collar workers are affected by an extensive body of case law. Typical periods depend on age, specialization, tenure and wage, ranging up to 36 months

Denmark	No	White-collar workers only: increases with tenure to a maximum of 6 months	None	None	For mass layoffs: required to notify regional labor market board and negotiate with union

NOTE: For comparability, any notice or severance requirements legislated in weeks have been converted to monthly amounts, at 0.25 months per week (exception: 26 weeks is converted as 6 months).

[a] Employees on fixed-term contracts are exempt from these requirements.

[b] Canadian legislation varies by province. Figures are for Ontario, which is the largest province and fairly typical (except for severance pay).

[c] Only applies to Ontario (Canada's most populous province). Ontario has about 40% of the national population.

[d] The maximum period of service for which severance is paid is 20 years. Statutory redundancy payments are free of income tax.

[e] The TCR (Termination, Change, and Redundancy) test case award incorporated stronger restrictions on dismissals for the first time; its provisions have been adopted by only a minority of awards since 1984.

[f] Since the 1985 Employment Promotion Act, nonrenewable limited-duration contracts of up to 18 months have been exempt from these requirements.

Table 1.2 Institutions Affecting Displacement: Unemployment Insurance Systems

Country	Qualifying period	Duration of benefits	Replacement rate	"Fallback" program	Comments
U.S.A.[a]	26 Weeks of work in past year	26 Weeks (plus 13 weeks extended benefits in years or states with high unemployment)	50–70% to a maximum Actual average replacement rate 30–40%	Means-tested welfare benefits available to single parents only Lifetime limit of 5 years	Very low takeup rate Quitters disqualified Benefits taxed as income
Netherlands	26 Weeks of work in past year	6 Months to 5 years, depending on employment history	70%	Universal social assistance; unlimited duration Disability insurance an attractive alternative to UI	Quitters disqualified High takeup Long-term unemployed must accept jobs below their previous "skill" level
Japan	26 Weeks of work in past year	90–300 Days; increases with age, years worked, and full time status	50–80%, depending on age and rate of pay, to a maximum	Universal welfare, unlimited duration	Some restrictions on quitters
Canada	10–20 Weeks of work in past year (decreases with local unemployment rate)	14–50 Weeks, increases with weeks worked and local unemployment rate	55%, to a maximum	Universal welfare, unlimited duration	Quitters disqualified Easy to requalify in successive years based on seasonal work. Higher takeup than U.S.A.

U.K.	2 Years continuous employment[b]	6 Months	Flat rate cash benefit (£48.25 in 1996)	UA (means-tested unemployment assistance), based on household income; unlimited duration Long-term sickness benefit an attractive alternative to both UA and UI	UA is often more generous than UI, especially if no other earners in the household. UA can include full rent and property tax subsidy.
Australia	None	Unlimited	Flat amounts based on family income, family size, and home ownership	Unemployment benefit itself acts as "the" welfare system.	Benefits low relative to average earnings
France	5 Alternative ways to qualify for different benefit durations, depending on work history in last 3 years	4 Months to 33 months, depending on employment history and age	57–75% of previous earnings (no maximum); benefit rate falls after an initial jobless period	RMI (Minimum Insertion Allowance): means-tested program	Seasonal workers disqualified

(continued)

Table 1.2 (continued)

Country	Qualifying period	Duration of benefits	Replacement rate	"Fallback" program	Comments
Germany	12 months in last 3 years (for AG or *Arbeitslosengeld*)	156–832 Days, depending on age and employment history	67% of previous net wage (60% for workers without children)	AH (*Arbeitslosenhilfe*) 57% of previous net wage (50% without children) Means-tested; unlimited duration.	12-Week waiting period for quitters
Belgium	None	Unlimited, though benefits reduced after one year of unemployment	Effectively, benefits are flat amounts based on family status and current income[c]	UI functions as the main social safety net	Search requirement rarely enforced
Denmark	6 Months work in previous year[d]	Essentially unlimited[e]	Up to 90% Declines with previous wage; Average replacement rate is 65%	Means-tested "social assistance" program (*bistandsydelse*) provides unlimited-duration benefits	UI funds administered by trade union; very wide coverage

[a] Provisions vary by state. Typical parameters are presented.

[b] Before 1988, insurance contributions could be credited during unemployment spells to maintain eligibility.

[c] Official replacement rates are 60% in the first year of unemployment and 40% after that. In most cases these are made irrelevant by a higher flat benefit amount based on the family's "needs."

[d] Some new entrants can qualify for UI based on apprenticeship training periods.

[e] Throughout the sample period in this volume (until the early 1990s) unemployed workers could requalify for UI by participating in a public employment scheme.

Table 1.3 Institutions Affecting Displacement: Unions and Minimum Wages

Country	Union density and coverage	Bargaining level(s), contract extension	Minimum wages: jurisdict. and coverage	Minimum wages: levels
U.S.A.	Density 14.5% (1996) (10% in private sector) Coverage rates similar to membership	Firm-level bargaining No extension	State and federal; federal supersedes state if higher	$5.15/hr (1997) (40% of average production worker wage)
Netherlands	Membership 26% (1990)[a] Coverage 75% (1998)	Industry-level bargaining, extensions common	National	14.01 Guilders (US$7)/hr
Japan	Membership 24% (1998) Coverage similar	Firm-level bargaining, no extension	Prefectural minima, plus some industry minima within prefectures	4868 Yen/day (weighted regional minimum, 1995); 36% of mean contract wage
Canada	Membership 31% Coverage 34% (1997)	Firm-level bargaining, no extension	Provincial (with a small federal sector)	38% of mean manufacturing wage, 1994
U.K.	Membership about 30% Coverage 37% (1996)	Firm-level bargaining, no extension	None: wages councils were abolished in 1993	None
Australia	Membership 31% (1996) Coverage 80% ((1990)[a]	Industrial tribunals, with union and firm representation; set wage "awards" by occup. and industry	Awards pervasive; no other wage minima	Set by awards
France	Membership 10% (1996) Coverage 90% (1985)[a]	Industry-level bargaining, extension pervasive	National minimum wage	84% of mean industrial wage (1995)

Germany	Membership 32% Coverage 90% (1992)[a]	Industry- and regional-level bargaining, extension is pervasive	No minimum wage apart from (extended) union contracts	None
Belgium	Membership 51% Coverage 90% (1990)[a]	National-, industry-, and firm-level bargaining (pyramidal)	National minimum wage	Low national minimum, generally superseded by extended union contracts
Denmark	Membership 80–90% Coverage 75%	National bargaining, supplemented by firm-level agreements	No minimum wage apart from (extended) union contracts	None

[a] Figures from OECD 1994, chart 5.1.

Table 1.4 Displacement and Gender: Are Men More Likely to Be Displaced?

	Comparing means		Using regressions		
Country	Result	Source (table no.)	Result	Source (table no.)	Variables held constant
U.S.A.	Yes	2.2	n.d.[a]	—	—
Netherlands	Yes	2.7	Yes	2.9	Age, tenure, educ., part-time, industry, firm size, wage, occup., job complexity
Japan	Yes, but small difference	3.8	n.d.	—	—
Canada	Yes, very much	3.8	n.d.	—	—
U.K.	yes	4.2	Yes[b]	4.3	Age, tenure, educ., part-time, industry, firm size, marital status, children
Australia	Yes	4.11	n.d.	—	—
Belgium	No, women more likely	6.4	Yes	6.5	Age, tenure, blue-collar, wage
Denmark	No difference	6.4	Yes	6.2	Age, tenure, blue-collar, wage

NOTE: The chapter on France and Germany presents results for men only and thus is excluded from this table.

[a] n.d. = no data available.

[b] But significant only for temporary contract expirations.

Table 1.5 Displacement and Skills: Are Unskilled Workers More Likely to Be Displaced?

		Comparing means		Using regressions		
Country	Skill measure	Result	Source (table no.)	Result	Source (table no.)	Variables held constant
Netherlands	Job complexity	Yes	2.7	No,[a] lower rates in less complex jobs	2.8, 2.9	Gender, age, tenure, educ., part-time, industry, firm size, wage, occup.
	Wage	n.d.[b]	—	Yes	2.8, 2.9	Gender, age, tenure, educ., part-time, industry, firm size, occup., job complexity
	Education	Yes (weak effect)	2.7	Insignif.[c]	2.8, 2.9	Gender, age, tenure, part-time, industry, firm size, wage, occup., job complexity
U.K.	Education	Nonmonotonic: lowest disp. in middle groups	4.2	Yes	4.3	Gender, age, tenure, part-time, industry, firm size, marital status, children

(continued)

Table 1.5 (continued)

		Comparing means		Using regressions		
Country	Skill measure	Result	Source (table no.)	Result	Source (table no.)	Variables held constant
France	Education	n.d.	—	Lowest disp. in middle groups	5.3	Gender,[d] age, tenure
Belgium	B/W collar	Yes	6.4	Yes	6.5	Gender, age, tenure, wage
	Wage	Yes	6.4	Yes	6.5	Gender, age, tenure, blue-collar
Denmark	B/W collar	Yes	6.4	Yes	6.5	Gender, age, tenure, wage
	Wage	Yes	6.4	Yes	6.5	Gender, age, tenure, blue-collar

NOTE: Recall that France, Germany, Belgium, and Denmark focus on mass displacements only; others combine individual and mass displacements. No results on skills and displacement rates are available in this volume for the U.S.A., Australia, Japan, Canada, or Germany. For the United States, Farber (1997) showed that educated workers are much less likely to be displaced than other workers, though the relative displacement rates of these groups increased in the 1990s. For Canada, Picot, Lin, and Pyper (1997) showed that Canadians earning high wages are much less likely to be displaced than other Canadians.

[a] No = coefficient significant at 5% level but opposite in size to question posed.

[b] n.d. = no data available.

[c] Insignif. = not significant at the 5% level.

[d] Regressions run for men only.

Table 1.6 Displacement and Age: Are Younger Workers More Likely to Be Displaced?

	Comparing means		Using regressions		
Country	Result	Source (table no.)	Result	Source (table no.)	Variables held constant
U.S.A.	Yes	2.4	n.d.[a]	—	—
Netherlands	Yes	2.7	Small, nonmonotonic effect	2.9	Gender, tenure, educ., part-time, industry, firm size, wage, occup., job complexity
Japan	No, less likely	3.8	n.d.	—	—
Canada	Yes, but disp. rates rise after 55	3.8	n.d.	—	—
U.K.	Yes, but disp. rates rise after 55	4.2	Yes[b]	4.3	Gender, tenure, educ., part-time, industry, firm size, marital status, children
Australia	No effect	4.13	n.d.	—	—
France	Yes, but disp. rates rise after 50	5.2	No	5.3	Gender,[c] tenure, educ.
Germany	Yes, but disp. rates rise after 50	5.4	No	5.5	Gender,[c] tenure, educ., industry

(continued)

Table 1.6 (continued)

	Comparing means		Using regressions		
Country	Result	Source (table no.)	Result	Source (table no.)	Variables held constant
Belgium	Yes, but not strongly	6.4	Yes, within displacing firms, otherwise no[d]	6.5	Gender, tenure, blue-collar, wage (but the tenure variable groups together all those with 6 or more years)
Denmark	No effect	6.4	Yes	6.5	Gender, tenure, blue-collar, wage (but the tenure variable groups together all those with 6 or more years)

NOTE: Recall that France, Germany, Belgium, and Denmark focus on mass displacements only; others combine individual and mass displacements.

[a] n.d. = no data available.

[b] But significant only for temporary contract expirations.

[c] Regressions run for men only.

[d] In a sample of all employed workers, displacement is correlated to age between ages 20 and 59. Teens have lower displacement rates and workers over 60 have higher rates than those 20–59.

Table 1.7 Displacement and Tenure: Are Low-Tenure Workers More Likely to Be Displaced?

	Comparing means		Using regressions		
Country	Result	Source (table no.)	Result	Source (table no.)	Variables held constant
U.S.A.	Yes, strongly	2.3	n.d.[a]	—	—
Netherlands	Yes, strongly	2.6	Yes	2.9	Gender, age, educ., part-time, industry, firm size, wage, occ., job complexity
Canada	Yes[b]	—	n.d.	—	—
U.K.	Yes, strongly	4.2	Yes	4.3	Gender, age, educ., part-time, industry, firm size, marital status, children
Australia	Yes	4.12, 4.13	n.d.	—	—
France	Yes, not strongly	5.2	Yes	5.3	Gender,[c] age, educ.
Germany	Yes	5.4	Yes	5.5	Gender, age, educ., industry
Belgium	Yes	6.4	Yes	6.5	Gender, age, blue-collar, wage
Denmark	Yes	6.4	Yes	6.5	Gender, age, blue-collar, wage

NOTE: Recall that France, Germany, Belgium, and Denmark focus on mass displacements only; others combine individual and mass displacements.

[a] n.d. = no data available.

[b] No results are reported in this volume for Japan or Canada. However, when jobs lasting under a year were excluded from the Canadian displacement counts, displacement rates fell dramatically.

[c] Regressions run for men only.

Table 1.8 Joblessness and Gender: Do Displaced Women Experience More Joblessness?

		Comparing means		Using regressions		
Country	Jobless measure	Result	Source (table no.)	Result	Source (table no.)	Variables held constant
U.S.A.	Prob. (positive spell)	n.d.[a]	—	Insignif.[b]	2.12	Age, tenure, educ., married, nonwhite, immig., closure, notice
	Duration of positive spells	Yes	2.10	Yes	2.12	Age, tenure, educ., married, nonwhite, immig., closure, notice
	Unconditional duration	Yes	2.10	Yes	2.12	Age, tenure, educ., married, nonwhite, immig., closure, notice
Netherlands	Duration of positive spells (insured unemployment)	Yes	2.16	Yes	2.17	Age, wage, married, urban, part-time, UI sanction
Japan[c]	Unconditional duration	Yes	3.11	n.d.	—	—
Canada	Unconditional duration	Yes	3.11	n.d.	—	—
U.K.	Duration of positive spells	n.d.	—	Insignif.	4.6	Age, tenure, qualif., married, children, part-time, occup., industry, industry declining, firm size

	Unconditional duration	n.d.	—	Insignif.	4.6	Age, tenure, qualif., married, children, part-time, occup., industry, industry declining, firm size
Australia	Survey date reemployment	Yes	4.12, 4.13	Yes	4.16	Age, educ., math and reading aptitude, unempl. rate in last occup.
Belgium	Duration of positive spells (insured unemployment)	n.d.	—	Yes	6.8	Age, tenure, last wage, white-collar
Denmark	Duration of positive spells (insured unemployment)	n.d.	—	Insignif.	6.8	Age, tenure, last wage, white-collar (very small sample)

NOTE: The chapter on France and Germany presents results for men only. Except where noted, durations refer to total joblessness following displacement, whether due to unemployment or labor-force withdrawal.

[a] n.d. = no data available.

[b] Insignif. = not significant at the 5% level.

[c] For Japan and Canada, separate duration regressions were run for women and men, but no predictions at common values of the regressors were performed.

Table 1.9 Joblessness and Skills: Do Skilled Displaced Workers Experience Less Joblessness?

		Comparing means		Using regressions		
Country (skill measure)	Jobless measure	Result	Source (table no.)	Result	Source (table no.)	Variables held constant
U.S.A. (education)	Prob. (positive spell)	n.d.[a]	—	Yes	2.12	Gender, age, tenure, married, nonwhite, immig., closure, notice
	Duration of positive spells	n.d.	—	Yes	2.12	Gender, age, tenure, married, nonwhite, immig., closure, notice
	Unconditional duration	n.d.	—	Yes	2.12	Gender, age, tenure, married, nonwhite, immig., closure, notice
Netherlands (predisp. wage)	Duration of positive (insured UI) spells	n.d.	—	Yes	2.17	Gender, age, married, urban, part-time, UI sanction
Japan (education)	Unconditional duration	n.d.	—	Insignif.	3.12	Gender,[c] age, firm size, part-time, industry, age-sex specific U/V ratio.
Canada (education, predisp. wage)	Unconditional duration	n.d.	—	Yes	3.13	Gender,[c] age, tenure, firm size, part-time, industry, region (only the predisp. wage is signif. for men; only education is signif. for women)
U.K. (qualifications)	Duration of positive spells	n.d.	—	Insignif.	4.6	Gender, age, tenure, occup., married, children, part-time, industry, industry declining, firm size
	Unconditional duration	n.d.	—	Insignif.	4.6	Gender, age, tenure, occupation, married, children, part-time, industry, industry declining, firm size

Australia (education)	Survey date reemployment	Yes	4.13	Yes	4.16	Gender, age, math and reading aptitude, unempl. rate in last occup. (aptitude scores are *not* significant)
France (education)	Duration of positive spells	n.d.	—	Yes	5.7	Gender,[d] age, tenure, year
Germany (education)	Duration of positive spells	n.d.	—	No[e]—educated workers have *longer* durations	5.9	Gender,[d] age, tenure, year
Belgium (predisp. wage)	Duration of positive (insured UI) spells	n.d.	—	Yes	6.8	Gender, age, tenure, white-collar
Denmark (predisp. wage)	Duration of positive (insured UI) spells	n.d.	—	Insignif.	6.8	Gender, age, tenure, white-collar (*very* small sample; positive point estimate)

NOTE: Recall that France, Germany, Belgium, and Denmark focus on mass displacements only; others combine individual and mass displacements.

[a] n.d. = no data available.

[b] Insignif. = not significant at the 5% level.

[c] Separate regressions were run for women and men.

[d] Regressions were run for men only.

[e] No = coefficient significant at 5% level but opposite in sign to question posed.

Table 1.10 Joblessness and Age: Do Older Displaced Workers Experience More Joblessness?

		Comparing means		Using regressions		
Country	Jobless measure[a]	Result	Source (table no.)	Result	Source (table no.)	Variables held constant
U.S.A.	Prob. (positive spell)	n.d.[b]	—	Yes (borderline significant)	2.12	Gender, tenure, educ., married, nonwhite, immig., closure, notice
	Duration of positive spells	Yes	2.10	Yes	2.12	Gender, tenure, educ., married, nonwhite, immig., closure, notice
	Unconditional duration	Yes	2.10	Yes	2.12	Gender, tenure, educ, married, nonwhite, immig., closure, notice
Netherlands	Duration of positive spells (insured unemployment)	Yes	2.16	Yes	2.17	Gender, wage, married, urban, part-time, UI sanction
Japan	Unconditional duration	n.d.	—	Insignif.	3.12	Gender,[c] educ., firm size, part-time, industry, age-sex specific U/V ratio.
Canada	Unconditional duration	n.d.	—	U-shaped effect	3.13	Gender,[c] educ., firm size, part-time, industry, region (result also holds when tenure, union and wage are included)
U.K.	Duration of positive spells	n.d.	—	Yes	4.6	Gender, tenure, qualif., occup., married, children, part-time, industry, industry declining, firm size

	Unconditional duration	n.d.	—	Yes	4.6	Gender, tenure, qualif., occup., married, children, part-time, industry, industry declining, firm size
Australia	Survey date reemployment	Yes (mostly age 55–64)	4.13	Yes	4.16	Gender, educ., math and reading aptitude, unempl. rate in last occupation [becomes insignif. when year dummies included]
France	Duration of positive spells	n.d.	—	Insignif.	5.7	Gender,[d] tenure, educ., year
Germany	Duration of positive spells	n.d.	—	Yes	5.9	Gender,[d] tenure, educ., year
Belgium	Duration of positive spells (insured unemployment)	n.d.	—	Yes	6.8	Gender, tenure, last wage, white-collar
Denmark	Duration of positive spells (insured unemployment)	n.d.	—	Insignif.	6.8	Gender, tenure, last wage, white-collar (very small sample; point estimates suggest older workers do have longer durations)

[a] Except where noted, durations refer to total joblessness following displacement, whether due to unemployment or labor-force withdrawal.
[b] n.d. = no data available.
[c] Separate regressions were run for women and men.
[d] Regressions were run for men only.

Table 1.11 Joblessness and Tenure: Do High-Tenure Displaced Workers Experience More Joblessness?

		Comparing means		Using regressions		
Country	Jobless measure	Result	Source (table no.)	Result	Source (table no.)	Variables held constant
U.S.A.	Prob. (positive spell)	n.d.[a]	—	Insignif.	2.12	Gender, age, educ., married, nonwhite, immig., closure, notice
	Duration of positive spells	Yes	12.0	Insignif.	2.12	Gender, age, educ., married, nonwhite, immig., closure, notice
	Unconditional duration	Yes	2.10	Insignif.	2.12	Gender, age, educ, married, nonwhite, immig., closure, notice
Canada	Unconditional duration	n.d.	—	Yes	3.13	Gender,[c] age, educ., firm size, part-time, industry, region (result also holds when union and wage are included)
U.K.	Duration of positive spells	n.d.	—	Yes	4.6	Gender, age, qualif., occup., married, children, part-time, industry, industry declining, firm size (but age controls are coarse and the only signif. effect is for tenure < 1 year)
	Unconditional duration	n.d.	—	Yes	4.6	Gender, age, qualif., occup., married, children, part-time, industry, industry declining, firm size (see comment above)

Australia	Survey date reemployment	Yes, but largely for tenure >10 years	4.12, 4.13	n.d.	—	—
France	Prob. (positive spell)	No[d]—unemployment spells *less* likely	5.6	n.d.	—	—
	Duration of positive spells	n.d.	—	Yes	5.7	Gender,[e] age, educ., year
Germany	Prob. (positive spell)	No[d]—unemployment spells *less* likely	5.8	n.d.	—	—
	Duration of positive spells	n.d.	—	No—senior workers have *shorter* durations	5.9	Gender,[b] age, educ., year
Belgium	Duration of positive spells (insured unemployment)	n.d.	—	No—senior workers have *shorter* durations	6.8	Gender, age, last wage, white-collar

(continued)

Table 1.11 (continued)

		Comparing means		Using regressions		
Country	Jobless measure	Result	Source (table no.)	Result	Source (table no.)	Variables held constant
Denmark	Duration of positive spells (insured unemployment)	n.d.	—	Insignif.	6.8	Gender, age, last wage, white-collar (very small sample; point estimates suggest senior workers have *shorter* durations)

NOTE: No information on tenure is available in the Netherlands or Japan. Recall that France, Germany, Belgium, and Denmark focus on mass displacements only; others combine individual and mass displacements.

[a] n.d. = no data available.

[b] Insignif. = not significant at the 5% level.

[c] Separate regressions were run for women and men.

[d] In a sample of all employed workers, displacement is correlated to age between ages 20 and 59. Teens have lower displacement rates and workers over 60 have higher rates than those 20–59.

Table 1.12 Wage Loss and Tenure: Do High-Tenure Displaced Workers Experience Larger Wage Losses?

		Comparing means		Using regressions		
Country	Wage loss measure[a]	Result	Source (table no.)	Result	Source (table no.)	Variables held constant
U.S.A.	Weekly earnings	Yes	2.19	Yes	2.21	Gender, age, educ., married, nonwhite, immig., closure, notice, union
Netherlands	Monthly earnings, within an employment spell	n.d.[b]	—	Yes, though significant only for tenure under vs. over 1 year	2.22	Gender, age, educ., married, immig., spell length, type of displacement
Canada	Hourly wage rate	Yes	3.16	Yes	3.20	Gender,[c] age, educ., firm size (pre and post), industry change, visible minority, union (pre and post), province
U.K.	Weekly earnings	Yes, except lowest tenure category	4.8a	Yes, but signif. only in Table 4.10 (which includes all separation reasons)	4.9, 4.10	Gender, age, educ., change in firm size, industry decline, unempl. duration, part-time predispl., part-time postdispl.
	Weekly earnings, full-time–full-time only	Yes	4.8b	Yes, but signif. only in Table 4.10 (which includes all separation reasons)	4.9, 4.10	Gender, age, educ., change in firm size, industry decline, unempl. duration

(continued)

Table 1.12 (continued)

		Comparing means		Using regressions		
Country	Wage loss measure[a]	Result	Source (table no.)	Result	Source (table no.)	Variables held constant
Belgium	Daily wage rate	n.d.	—	Insignif., point estimates consistently show higher losses though	16.11	Gender, age, blue-collar, predispl. firm size, closure, region, occup.[d]
Denmark	Hourly wage rate	n.d.	—	Insignif.; point estimates consistently show higher losses though	6.11	Gender, age, blue-collar, predispl. firm size, closure, region, occup.[d]

NOTE: Data on predisplacement tenure are unavailable for Australia or Japan. Wage regressions for France and Germany do not interact wage losses with demographic characteristics.

In all cases the dependent variable is a wage measure (pay per unit of time worked), not an earnings measure. Details are as follows:

U.S.: Change in log wages, up to three years after displacement

Netherlands: Change in log wages, up to four months after displacement

Japan: Worker's self-reported percentage change in wages, within a year of displacement

Canada: (calculated) percentage change in wages, from actual pre- and postdisplacement wages up to 16 months apart

U.K. Change in log wages, one year after displacement

[a] Australia: Change in log wages, one to two years after displacement
Belgium: Log hourly wage rate two years after displacement
Denmark: Log hourly wage rate two years after displacement

[b] n.d. = no data available.

[c] Separate regressions were run for women and men.

[d] Regression is for postdisplacement wage, controlling for predisplacement wage.

Table 1.13 Wage Loss and Age: Do Older Displaced Workers Experience Larger Wage Losses?

		Comparing means		Using regressions		
Country	Wage loss measure[a]	Result	Source (table no.)	Result	Source (table no.)	Variables held constant
U.S.A.	Weekly wages	Yes (except for oldest group)	2.19	Yes	2.21	Gender, tenure, educ., married, nonwhite, immig., closure, notice, union
Netherlands	Monthly earnings, within an employment spell	n.d.[b]	—	Insignif.[c]	2.22	Gender, tenure, educ., married, immig., spell length, type of displacement
Japan	Wage rate per month, excluding bonuses	Yes, though primarily among men	3.14	Yes	3.18, 3.19	Gender,[d] educ., firm size (pre and post), type of displacement (*shukko* vs. layoff), industry change, year

Canada	Hourly wage rate	Yes (both men and women)	3.15	Yes	3.20	Gender,[d] educ., firm size (pre and post), industry change, visible minority (result is robust to additional controls for tenure and union)
U.K.	Weekly wages	Yes	4.8[a]	Insignif.	4.9	Gender, tenure, educ., change in firm size, industry decline, unempl. duration, part-time
	Weekly wages, full-time–full-time only	Yes	4.8[b]	Yes	4.9	Gender, tenure, educ., change in firm size, industry decline, unempl. duration
Australia	Average weekly earnings	n.d.	—	Yes	4.19	Sex, educ., immigrant, full-time–part-time changes, unempl. rate in predisp. occup.[e]

(continued)

Table 1.13 (continued)

Country	Wage loss measure[a]	Comparing means: Result	Comparing means: Source (table no.)	Using regressions: Result	Using regressions: Source (table no.)	Using regressions: Variables held constant
Belgium	Daily wage rate	n.d.	—	Yes, but only over age 60	6.11	Gender, tenure, blue-collar, predispl. firm size, closure, region, occup.[f]
Denmark	Hourly wage rate	n.d.	—	Yes, but only over age 60	6.11	Gender, tenure, blue-collar, predispl. firm size, closure, region, occup.[f]

NOTE: Wage regressions for France and Germany do not interact wage losses with demographic characteristics.
[a] See notes to Table 1.12 for more detail on the dependent variables.
[b] n.d. = no data available.
[c] Insignif. = not significant at the 5% level.
[d] Separate regressions were run for women and men.
[e] Sample includes quitters, with a dummy for displaced.
[f] Regression is for postdisplacement wage, controlling for predisplacement wage.

Table 1.14 Wage Loss and Gender: Do Displaced Women Experience Larger Wage Losses?

		Comparing means		Using regressions		
Country	Wage loss measure[a]	Result	Source (table no.)	Result	Source (table no.)	Variables held constant
U.S.A.	Weekly wages	Yes[b]	2.19	Insignif.	2.21 (col. 3)	Age, tenure, educ, married, nonwhite, immig., closure, notice, union
Netherlands	Monthly earnings, within an employment spell	n.d.	—	Insignif.	2.22	Age, tenure, educ, married, immig., type of displacement
Japan	Wage rate per month, excluding bonuses	No[c]—men have bigger losses	3.14	n.d.	—	—
Canada	Hourly wage rate	Yes, but difference is small	3.15	n.d.	—	—
U.K.	Weekly wages	Yes	4.8a	Insignif.	4.9	Age, tenure, educ., change in firm size, industry decline, unemp. duration, part-time predisp., part-time postdisp.
	Weekly wages, full-time–full-time only	Yes	4.8b	Insignif.	4.9	Age, tenure, educ., change in firm size, industry decline, unempl. duration

(continued)

Table 1.14 (continued)

		Comparing means		Using regressions		
Country	Wage loss measure[a]	Result	Source (table no.)	Result	Source (table no.)	Variables held constant
Australia	Average weekly earnings	No difference	4.18	Insignif.	4.19	Age, educ., immigrant, full-time-part-time changes, unempl. rate in predispl. occup. (sample includes quitters)
Belgium	Daily wage rate	n.d.	—	Yes	6.11	Age, tenure, blue-collar, predispl. firm size, closure, region, occup.[d]
Denmark	Hourly wage rate	n.d.	—	Yes	6.11	Age, tenure, blue-collar, predispl. firm size, closure, region, occup.[d]

NOTE: Wage regressions for France and Germany do not interact wage losses with demographic characteristics. For Japan and Canada, separate duration regressions were run for women and men, but no predictions at common values of the regressors were performed.

[a] See notes to Table 1.12 for more detail on the dependent variables.

[b] Men experience a small wage gain; women, a small loss.

[c] n.d. = no data available.

[d] Regression is for postdisplacement wage, controlling for predisplacement wage.

Table 1.15 Wage Loss and Skills: Do Skilled Displaced Workers Experience Smaller Wage Losses?

		Comparing means		Using regressions		
Country and skill measure	Wage loss measure[a]	Result	Source (table no.)	Result	Source (table no.)	Variables held constant
U.S.A. (education)	Weekly wages	n.d.[b]	—	Insignif.[c]	2.21	Gender, tenure, age, married, nonwhite, immig., closure, notice, union
Netherlands (education)	Monthly earnings, within an employment spell	n.d.	—	Insignif.	2.22	Gender, tenure, age, married, immig., spell length, type of displacement
Japan (education)	Wage rate per month, excluding bonuses	n.d.	—	No—educated workers have *larger* losses	3.18, 3.19	Gender,[d] age, firm size (pre and post), type of displacement (*shukko* vs. layoff), industry change, year

(continued)

Table 1.15 (continued)

		Comparing means		Using regressions		
Country and skill measure	Wage loss measure[a]	Result	Source (table no.)	Result	Source (table no.)	Variables held constant
Canada (education)	Hourly wage rate	n.d.	—	No real pattern, mostly insignif.	3.20	Gender,[d] age, firm size (pre and post), industry change, visible minority (result is robust to additional controls for tenure and union)
U.K. (education)	Weekly wages	Yes, though small effect	4.8a	Insignif.	4.9	Gender, tenure, educ., change in firm size, industry decline, unempl. duration, part-time predispl., part-time postdispl.
	Weekly wages, full-time–full-time only	Yes, large effect	4.8b	Insignif.	4.9	Gender, tenure, age, change in firm size, industry decline, unempl. duration

Australia (education)	Average weekly earnings	n.d.	—	Insignif.	4.19	Gender, age, immigrant, full-time–part-time changes, unemployment rate in predispl. occup.[e]
Belgium (white-collar)	Daily wage rate	n.d.	—	Yes	6.11	Gender, age, tenure, predispl. firm size, closure, region, occup.[f]
Denmark (white-collar)	Hourly wage rate	n.d.	—	Insignif.	6.11	Gender, age, tenure, predispl. firm size, closure, region, occup.[f]

NOTE: Wage regressions for France and Germany do not interact wage losses with demographic characteristics.

[a] See notes to Table 1.12 for more detail on the dependent variables.

[b] n.d. = no data available.

[c] Insignif. = not significant at the 5% level.

[d] Separate regressions were run for women and men.

[e] Sample includes quitters, with a dummy for displaced.

[f] Regression is for postdisplacement wage, controlling for predisplacement wage.

Table 1.16 Who Loses Most from Displacement across Countries? The Effects of Gender, Age, Tenure, and Skill Level

Attribute \ Outcome measure	Frequency of displacement	Postdisplacement joblessness	Displacement-induced wage losses
Gender	Men	Women	Either no difference, or women lose more (except Japan)
Age	Young (except Japan[a])	Old	Old
Tenure	Junior[a]	Varies	Senior (in U.S.A., U.K., and Canada)
Skill level	Unskilled	Unskilled	No consistent difference

[a] In Japan, no tenure information is available. Thus, we cannot say whether the observed age effect is purely due to lower tenure among the young, or what the "true" tenure effect is.

Table 1.17 Annual Displacement Rates: International Comparisons

	Data source	Displacement definition	Period	Population	Rate (annual)	Source (table no.)	Comments
U.S.A.	Retrospective survey of persons	Self reports of permanent job loss due to plant closing, slack work, position or shift abolished (includes individual *and* mass layoffs)	1993–95	Tenure greater than 1 year, age 20–64	4.9 (M) 4.3 (F) 4.6 (A)	2.3	
				All tenure levels, age 20–64	5.3 (M) 4.5 (F) 4.9 (A)	2.3	
Netherlands	Panel survey of firms	Firms' reported layoffs, *plus*: workers moving into new jobs, early retirement, or disability insurance from firms shrinking 30% or more	1993–95	All tenure levels, age 60 and under	4.2 (M) 4.0 (F) 4.1 (A)	2.6	Layoffs during probationary periods excluded
Japan	Panel survey of firms	Firms' reports of separations due to "management convenience" only	1995	Establishments with more than 5 employees, tenure one month or more, age 15 and over	1.3 (M) 1.1 (F) 1.2 (A)	3.8	—

(continued)

Table 1.17 (continued)

	Data source	Displacement definition	Period	Population	Rate (annual)	Source (table no.)	Comments
		"Management convenience," plus "contract finished," plus mandatory retirement	1995	Establishments with more than 5 employees, tenure one month or more, age 15 and over	3.7 (M) 3.2 (F) 3.5 (A)	3.8	
Canada	Administrative data on separations (from Employment Insurance system)	Firms' reports of layoffs (separations due to "short work," excluding workers who return to the original firm within a year)	1995	Establishments with more than 5 employees, tenure one month or more, age 15 and over	6.1 (M) 3.4 (F) 4.9 (A)	3.8	Same list of industries as Japan May include a small number of fixed-term contract expirations
U.K.	Household panel survey	Workers' reported job loss due to redundancy or dismissal	1990–96	Age 18 to pensionable age	6.4 (M) 2.9 (F) 4.7 (A)	4.1, 4.2	Includes a small number of dismissals for cause
Australia	Labor mobility survey, 1995	Workers ceasing a job due to retrenchment, ill health, seasonal or temporary job ended.	1995	Employed workers	5.2 (M) 3.9 (F)	4.12	

France	Panel of administrative social security records	Workers separating from dying *firms*, in the calendar year of "death" and the preceding calendar year Adjustments made for "false firm deaths" Excludes workers who return to original firm within a year	1984	Age 25–50, tenure at least 4 years	2.8 (M)	5.2	
Germany	Panel of administrative social security records	Workers separating from dying *plants*, in the calendar year of "death" and the preceding calendar year Adjustments made for "false firm deaths"	1984–90	Age 25–50, tenure at least 4 years	1.0 (M)	5.4	Value is calculated by dividing the 7-year displacement rate in Table 5.4 (for 1984–1990) by 7
Belgium	Panel of administrative social security records	Workers separating from dying *firms* in the calendar year of death (firms with at least 5 employees)	1983	Tenure at least 3 years	1.6 (A)	6.3	Adjustments made for "false firm deaths," excludes public sector
				All tenures	2.1(A)		

(continued)

Table 1.17 (continued)

	Data source	Displacement definition	Period	Population	Rate (annual)	Source (table no.)	Comments
Denmark	Panel of administrative records	Workers separating from dying *plants* with at least 5 employees in the calendar year of death	1988	Tenure at least 3 years	0.6 (A)	6.3	Adjustments made for "false firm deaths," excludes public sector
				All tenures	1.6 (A)		

NOTE: (M) denotes "men"; (F), "women"; and (A), "all workers."

Table 1.18 Postdisplacement Unemployment: International Comparisons

Country (displacement type)	Population	Probability of a positive jobless spell		Jobless durations conditional on a positive spell		Unconditional jobless durations		Source for durations
		Result	Source (table no.)	Prob.[a] jobless after 6 months	Prob. jobless after 12 months	Prob. jobless after 6 months	Prob. jobless after 12 months	
U.S.A. (all layoffs)	All tenure levels	0.84	2.3	n.d.	n.d.	n.d.	n.d.	—
	Tenure greater than 1 year	.0.85	2.3	0.39	0.28	0.33	0.24	Tab. 2.10
	Tenure 3 years or more[b]	n.d.	—	0.41	0.30	0.34	0.25	Tab. 2.10
Netherlands (all layoffs)	All tenure levels	0.30	2.13	0.45	0.27	n.d.	n.d.	Tab. 2.18
	Tenure greater than 1 year	0.30	2.13	n.d.	n.d.	n.d.	n.d.	—
Japan (all "layoffs"[c])	All tenure levels	n.d.	—	n.d.	n.d.	0.23 (M)[d] 0.25 (F)	0.14 (M) 0.11 (F)	Tab. 3.11
Canada (all layoffs)	All tenure levels	n.d.	—	n.d.	n.d.	0.47 (M) 0.68 (F)	0.0 (M) 0.41 (F)	Tab. 3.11[e]
U.K. (all layoffs)	All tenure levels	0.63	4.5	0.32	0.19[f]	0.20	0.12[f]	Tab. 4.5

(continued)

Table 1.18 (continued)

Country (displacement type)	Population	Probability of a positive jobless spell		Jobless durations conditional on a positive spell		Unconditional jobless durations		Source for durations
		Result	Source (table no.)	Prob.[a] jobless after 6 months	Prob. jobless after 12 months	Prob. jobless after 6 months	Prob. jobless after 12 months	
Australia (all layoffs)	All tenure levels, young workers only	n.d.	—	0.27	0.15	n.d.	n.d.	Tab. 4.14
France (firm closures only)	Tenure at least 4 years	0.78 (M)	5:6	0.62 (M)	0.45 (M)	n.d.	n.d.	Fig. 5.1[g]
Germany (plant closures only)	Tenure at least 4 years	0.39 (M)	5:8	0.52 (M)	0.40 (M)	n.d.	n.d.	Fig. 5.2[g]
Belgium (firm shrinkage and closures only)	Tenure at least 3 years	0.65[h]	6:6	n.d.	0.63 (M)	0.72 (M)		Tab. 6.7
Denmark (plant shrinkage and closures only)	Tenure at least 3 years	0.31[h]	6:6	n.d.	0.28 (M)	0.37 (M)	n.d.	Tab. 6.7

[a] n.d. = no data available.
[b] Simple average of the proportions for 3–4, 5–9, and more than 10 years, respectively (these do not differ markedly).
[c] Includes mandatory retirement and contract expirations; does not include *shukko*.
[d] M = men; F = women.
[e] Simple average of the "Canada A" and "Canada B" figures (these do not differ markedly).
[f] After 10 months.
[g] Numerical estimates based on figure.
[h] Percent experiencing *any* unemployment in the three years after displacement.

Table 1.19 Displacement-Induced Percentage Wage Changes: International Comparisons

Country (displace-ment type)	Relative to controls?[a]	Tenure on the predisplacement job (years)[b] <1	1	2	3	4	5	6	7	8	9	10+	All	Source
U.S.A. (all displacements)	No		+11	+11	5	5	0	0	0	0	0	–19	0	Tab. 2.19
U.S.A. (mass, from Jacobson, LaLonde, and Sullivan 1993)[c]	No							–23	–23	–23	–23	–23		Fig. 1[c]
	Yes							–30	–30	–30	–30	–30		
Japan (all)[d]	No												–4(M)[e] 0(F)	Tab. 3.14
Canada (all)	No	3(M) 1(F)	0(M) 1(F)		–5(M) –8(F)		–5(M) –4(F)	–5(M) –4(F)	–5(M) –4(F)	–5(M) –4(F)	–5(M) –4(F)	–11(M) –7(F)	–1(M) –2(F)	Tab. 3.16
U.K. (all)[f]	No	–6	1	–5			–6						–4	Tab. 4.7, 4.8b
					–5	–5		–6	–6	–6	–6	–6		
	Yes	–13	–7	–11	–11	–11	–10	–10	–10	–10	–10	–10	–10	
France (mass)	No					17	17	12	12	14	14	10	10	Tab. 5.10
	Yes					12	2	8	8	10	10	7	7	
Germany (mass)	No					2	2	6	6	6		2	2	Tab. 5.11
	Yes					–1	–1	2	2	–3	–3	–1	–1	

(continued)

Table 1.19 (continued)

Country (displacement type)	Relative to controls?[a]	Tenure on the predisplacement job (years)[b] <1	1	2	3	4	5	6	7	8	9	10+	All	Source
Belgium	No				–6	–6	–5	–6	–6	–6	–6	–6	–6	Tab. 6.10b,
	Yes				–3	–3	–2	–3	–3	–3	–3	–3	–3	6. 11[g]
Denmark	No				–1	–1	–1	–1	–1	–1	–1	–1	–1	Tab. 6.10,
(mass)	Yes				–6	–6	–6	–6	–6	–6	–6	–6	–6	6.11[g]

NOTE: In all cases, percentage change estimates condition on reemployment and measure rates of pay per unit of time worked.

[a] In all cases where a control group is used, it is continuously employed workers (not necessarily in the same plants as the displaced workers).

[b] <1 = less than 1 yr.; 1 = at least a year but less than two years; 2 = at least 2 yrs. but less than 3 yrs; and so forth.

[c] Estimates are from Jacobson, LaLonde, and Sullivan (1993) for 3 years after displacement, for workers with positive earnings in each year after displacement. Percentage changes are based on the following estimates taken from their Figure 1: mean (quarterly) predisplacement earnings of $6,000 for both displaced workers and controls; mean quarterly earnings six years after displacement of $4,600 for displaced workers and $6,600 for controls.

[d] Excluding *shukko*.

[e] M and F indicate statistics for men and women respectively. Wage-change statistics for Australia (Chapter 4, Table 4.17) are not included because they apply to a sample of very young workers only and are not directly comparable. Wage-change statistics for the Netherlands (provided in the discussion of Table 2.22, Chapter 2) are not included because they are based on a very small sample. While some of their estimates are large in magnitude, none are significantly different from zero.

[f] Full time in both the predisplacement and postdisplacement job.

[g] Figures calculated from sample means in Table 6.10b (for wages two years after displacement) in combination with regression coefficients in Table 6.11. The estimates with controls simply subtract off the two-year earnings growth of continuously employed workers reported in Table 6.10b. Due to the very small sample size and the resulting high standard errors on Table 6.11 tenure coefficients, I report here only the totals for all workers in their sample for Denmark.

References

Addison, J., and M. Blackburn. 1994. "The Worker Adjustment and Retraining Notification Act: Effects on Notice Provision." *Industrial and Labor Relations Review* 47(4): 650–662.

Bertola, G., and R. Rogerson. 1997. "Institutions and Labor Reallocation." *European Economic Review* 41(6): 937–957.

Blau, F., and L. Kahn. 1996a. "International Differences in Male Wage Inequality: Institutions versus Market Forces." *Journal of Political Economy* 104(4): 791–836.

———. 1996b. "Wage Structure and Gender Earnings Differentials: An International Comparison." *Economica* 63(250): S29–S62.

Browning, M., and T. Crossley. 2000. "The Long Run Costs of Job Loss as Measured by Consumption Changes." Unpublished paper, York University, Toronto, Canada.

Burdett, K., and R. Wright. 1989. "Unemployment Insurance and Short-Time Compensation: The Effects on Layoffs, Hours per Worker, and Wages." *Journal of Political Economy* 97(6): 1479–1496.

Card, D., and R. Freeman, eds. 1993. *Small Differences that Matter: Labor Markets and Income Maintenance in Canada and the United States.* Chicago: University of Chicago Press.

Crossley, T., S. Jones, and P. Kuhn. 1994. "Gender Differences in Displacement Costs: Evidence and Implications." *Journal of Human Resources* 29 (Spring): 461–480.

de la Rica, Sara. 1995. "Evidence of Preseparation Earnings Losses in the Displaced Worker Survey." *Journal of Human Resources* 30(3): 610–621.

Dickens, W.T., and K. Lang. 1995. "An Analysis of the Nature of Unemployment in Sri Lanka." *Journal of Development Studies* 31(4): 620–636.

DiNardo, J., N. Fortin, and T. Lemieux. 1996. "Labor Market Institutions and the Distribution of Wages, 1973–1992: A Semiparametric Approach." *Econometrica* 64(5): 1001–1044.

Duleep, H.O., and S. Sanders. 1994. "Empirical Regularities across Cultures: The Effect of Children on Woman's Work." *Journal of Human Resources* 29(2): 328–347.

Farber, H. 1997. "The Changing Face of Job Loss in the United States, 1981–1995." *Brookings Papers on Economic Activity, Microeconomics*, pp. 55–128.

———. 1999. "Alternative and Part-Time Employment Arrangements as a Response to Job Loss." *Journal of Labor Economics* 17(4), Part 2: S142–S169.

Gallo, W., E. Bradley, M. Siegel, and S. Kasl. 2000. "Health Effects of Involuntary Job Loss among Older Workers: Findings from the Health and Retirement Survey." *Journal of Gerontology* 55B(3): S131–S139.

Garibaldi, P., and Z. Brixiova. 1997. "Labor Market Institutions and Unemployment Dynamics in Transition Economies." Working paper WP/97/137, International Monetary Fund, Washington, D.C.

Gibbons, R., and L. Katz. 1991. "Layoffs and Lemons." *Journal of Labor Economics* 9(4): 351–380.

Gladden, T. 1999. "Labor Market Effects of Family Ties and Migration." Unpublished paper, Northwestern University, Evanston, Illinois.

Hashimoto, M., and J. Raisian. 1985. "Employment Tenure and Earnings Profiles in Japan and the United States." *American Economic Review* 75(4): 721–735.

Heckman, J., and C. Pages. 2000. *The Cost of Job Security Regulation: Evidence from Latin American Labor Markets.* Working paper no. W7773, National Bureau of Economic Research, Cambridge, Massachusetts.

Huberman, M. 1997. "An Economic and Business History of Worksharing: The Bell Canada and Volkswagen Experiences." *Business and Economic History* 26(2): 404–415.

Jacobson, L., R. Lalonde, and D. Sullivan. 1993. "Earnings Losss of Displaced Workers." *American Economic Review* 83(4): 685–709.

Kletzer, L. 1989. "Returns to Seniority after Permanent Job Loss." *American Economic Review* 79(3): 536–543.

Kletzer, L.G., and R. Fairlie. 1999. "The Long-Term Costs of Job Displacement among Young Workers." Unpublished paper, University of California, Santa Cruz.

Kuhn, P., and A. Sweetman. 1988a. "Wage Loss Following Displacement: The Role of Union Coverage." *Industrial and Labor Relations Review* 51(3): 384–400.

———. 1988b. "Unemployment Insurance and Quits in Canada." *Canadian Journal of Economics* 31(3): 549–572.

———. 1999. "Vulnerable Seniors: Unions, Tenure, and Wages Following Permanent Job Loss." *Journal of Labor Economics* 17(October): 671–693.

Layard, R., S. Nickell, and R. Jackman. 1991. *Unemployment: Macroeconomic Performance and the Labour Market.* Oxford: Oxford University Press.

McLaughlin, K. 1991. "A Theory of Quits and Layoffs with Efficient Turnover." *Journal of Political Economy* 99(1): 1–29.

Neal, D. 1995. "Industry-Specific Human Capital: Evidence from Displaced Workers." *Journal of Labor Economics* 13(October): 653–677.

OECD. Various years. *Employment Outlook.* Paris: OECD.

Picot, G., Z. Lin, and W. Pyper. 1997. *Permanent Layoffs in Canada: Overview and Longitudinal Analysis.* Working paper no. 382, Statistics Canada Analytical Studies Branch, Ottawa.

Riddell, Chris. 1999. "The Role of Firms and Unions in Mass Layoffs." Unpublished manuscript, University of British Columbia. Vancouver, Canada.

———. 1990. "Do Earnings Increase with Job Seniority?" *Review of Economics and Statistics* 72(1): 143–147.

Ruhm, C. 1991. "Are Workers Permanently Scarred by Job Displacements?" *American Economic Review* 81(1): 319–324.

Stephens, M., Jr. 1999. "The Long-Run Consumption Effects of Earnings Shocks." Unpublished paper, University of Michigan, Ann Arbor.

Stevens, Ann Huff. 1997. "Persistent Effects of Job Displacement: The Importance of Multiple Job Losses." *Journal of Labor Economics* 15(1): 165–188.

Tachibanaki, T. 1996. *Wage Determination and Distribution in Japan.* Oxford: Clarendon Press.

Teulings, Coen, and Joop Hartog. 1998. *Corporatism or Competition? Labour Contracts, Institutions and Wage Structures in International Comparison.* Cambridge: Cambridge University Press.

Topel, R. 1990. "Specific Capital and Unemployment: Measuring the Costs and Consequences of Job Loss." *Carnegie-Rochester Conference Series on Public Policy* 33: 181–214.

———. 1991. "Specific Capital, Mobility, and Wages: Wages Rise with Job Seniority." *Journal of Political Economy* 99(February): 145–176.

Van Audenrode, M. 1994. "Short-Time Compensation, Job Security, and Employment Contracts: Evidence from Selected OECD Countries." *Journal of Political Economy* 102(1): 76–102.

van den Berg, G.J. 1994. "The Effects of Changes in the Job Offer Arrival Rate on the Duration of Unemployment." *Journal of Labor Economics* 12(3): 478–498.

2
Displaced Workers in the United States and the Netherlands

Jaap H. Abbring
Gerard J. van den Berg
Pieter A. Gautier
Vrije Universiteit, Amsterdam

A. Gijsbert C. van Lomwel
Jan C. van Ours
Tilburg University

Christopher J. Ruhm
University of North Carolina, Greensboro

In this chapter, we analyze worker displacement (permanent job separations initiated by employers because of adverse economic conditions) in the United States and the Netherlands. Labor displacement has been widely studied in the U.S. context, where adequate data have been available for a considerably longer period than in most other countries. No similar literature exists for the Netherlands, even though displacement is an increasingly important phenomenon there.[1] We discuss the relevant institutions and provide an empirical analysis of the incidence of displacement and the labor market transitions and earnings changes induced by displacement in both countries.

Our analysis of worker displacement generally identifies displacement as permanent (rather than temporary) layoffs, controlling to varying extents for the cause of job termination. In much of the analysis, we focus on workers with substantial tenure or compare their experiences to those of dislocated persons with less tenure. Restricting our analysis to permanent layoffs is almost irrelevant in the Netherlands because temporary layoffs with recall are rarely observed there. In fact, Dutch institutions work against them. Arrangements for providing unemployment insurance (UI) to workers who are laid off temporarily, for instance, are restricted to very specific activities.[2]

This chapter also provides new information on the relationship between displacement and retirement. In the 1970s and the 1980s, disability insurance (DI) was allegedly used as a convenient alternative to unemployment insurance for the separation of workers in the Netherlands. Early retirement arrangements may also have facilitated the displacement of older workers. Although the data for the Netherlands provide some information on transitions from employment into these alternative destinations, this information is not as rich as for other issues addressed below. Therefore, we mainly discuss the relevant institutional arrangements and findings from existing empirical work in order to clarify the role of DI and early retirement in the Netherlands. Surprisingly, despite richer data, there has been little previous analysis of the relationship between displacement and retirement in the United States. A preliminary investigation of that relationship is also provided in this chapter.

Our discussion of displacement in the United States frequently refers to the results of an extensive North American literature on displacement. These data are well known and were designed specifically for the study of displaced workers. As a result, this chapter provides only a modest updating of prior U.S. analyses. In contrast, our Dutch analyses require data from various sources, none explicitly addressing displacement, and represent the first substantive study of these issues. Our discussions of the Dutch data and results, therefore, usually need to be more extensive than those for the United States.

The plan of this chapter is as follows. First we discuss institutions that are relevant to displacement (such as wage formation, employment protection, and social security) and the data sets used in the analyses. We continue by discussing time-series and cross-sectional properties of displacement rates. Then we analyze labor market transitions following displacement and wage or earnings changes induced by displacement. We finish by discussing the role of early retirement and DI.

INSTITUTIONAL ENVIRONMENT

United States

Minimum wages

Compared with most other industrialized nations, U.S. labor markets are highly flexible.[3] Few workers are unionized and minimum wages are low as a fraction of average earnings. In 1996, for example, union members accounted for only 14.5 percent of total wage and salary employment and 10.0 percent of private wage and salary workers (U.S. Bureau of the Census 1997, Table 688). Effective September 1, 1997, the minimum wage was raised to $5.15 per hour. Even after this increase, however, it was only about 40 percent of the average hourly earnings of production workers.[4]

Employment protection

Employees in most European nations have considerable protection against "unjust" dismissals. In contrast, the U.S. "employment-at-will" doctrine provides U.S. employers with wide latitude to terminate workers for almost any reason. There are important exceptions, however, for unionized workers and for individuals with contracts containing provisions governing discharges. Some state courts have also recognized exceptions that limit dismissals when employees perform acts serving the interests of public policy (such as jury duty) or when an implied contract exists due to written or oral statements made by employers. Some courts have upheld "good faith" provisions requiring employers to treat workers in a "fair and reasonable" manner in all employment relationships, including terminations.[5] Since the Worker Retraining and Notification Act (WARN) took effect in 1989, employers with more than 100 full-time workers have been required to provide 60 days' written advance notice of plant closings or mass layoffs. However, the law contains numerous exemptions, and a preliminary analysis by Addison and Blackburn (1994) suggested that the legislation has had little effect on the provision of notice.

Programs to assist displaced workers

The United States provides limited support to workers who lose jobs. By far the most important assistance comes from unemployment insurance. The UI program is overseen by the U.S. Department of Labor but administered by the individual states, resulting in variation in program eligibility and benefits among geographic locations. Workers with qualified employment histories are eligible for benefits if they are available for work and have become unemployed due to involuntary separation from their jobs (without good cause) or voluntary separation with good cause.[6] Benefit duration is generally restricted to 26 weeks, although up to 13 additional weeks can be obtained under the Extended Benefits Program, if the state unemployment rate is sufficiently high.[7] Almost all wage and salary workers are covered by the UI system, but only a fraction of the unemployed actually receive benefits (36 percent in 1995).[8] Wage replacement rates are also relatively low, generally ranging from 50 to 70 percent of the individual's average weekly pretax wage up to a state-determined maximum, and these funds are taxable as normal income. Due to the ceiling, benefits are somewhat progressive and typically average between 30 and 40 percent of previous earnings.

Other programs assist job losers more directly. Trade Assistance Adjustment (TAA), originally enacted in 1962, targets persons displaced from industries adversely affected by import competition. Qualifying workers can receive up to 52 weeks of combined UI and Trade Readjustment Allowance (TRA) benefits, 76 weeks if enrolled in an approved training program, with TRA generally paid at the same rate as UI. TRA is a limited program, however; only 31,000 workers were supported in 1994, at a cost of $120 million.[9] Some assistance is also provided to dislocated workers under the North American Free Trade Agreement (NAFTA) Worker Security Act and the Employment Dislocation and Worker Adjustment Assistance Program. In addition, a variety of demonstration programs have been implemented to test the efficacy of particular assistance strategies for displaced workers.[10] The relatively small size of these efforts implies that most displaced workers receive relatively limited support from the government beyond that available to persons who are jobless for other reasons.[11]

The Netherlands

Wage formation

Minimum wages in the Netherlands are higher than those in the United States. As of July 1998, the minimum wage has been set at 14.01 Dutch guilders (f.; U.S.$7) per hour before taxes and social security premium payments.[12] In contrast to the United States, 75 percent of all employees are covered by collective agreements, which are negotiated by central bargaining between large firms or employer organizations and unions. The resulting agreements, called *Collectieve Arbeids Overeenkomsten* (CAOs), are usually, but not always, put in terms of lower bounds on the terms of employment, notably the wage. Since 1927 central agreements reached by worker unions have, by law, also been applicable to nonunion employees. Another law, passed in 1937, enabled the Minister of Social Affairs and Employment to declare collective agreements binding for entire sectors. Such extensions of the scope of CAOs, called *Algemeen Verbindend Verklaring* (AVVs) are indeed common practice.[13]

Employment protection

Although there is currently a tendency toward more flexible employment relations, employment protection is stronger in the Netherlands than in the United States. Employment relationships are arranged by either fixed-term or permanent contracts.[14] Fixed-term contracts allow employers to lay workers off at the end of the contracted period without either prior notice or a permit, therefore offering no employment protection to the employee. If the employee is allowed to continue to work after the contracted period, however, or if a new fixed-term contract is written within 31 days of the end date of the first contract, the employee is considered to be working on a "continued contract," and is basically provided the protection of a permanent contract.[15]

As long as workers and firms are bound by a contract, they can separate only after a permit has been granted by a regional employment institution, although this rule is generally applied only to firm-initiated separations. Employers always need a permit for dismissal or layoff of workers unless there is mutual agreement between the employer and the employee, severe misconduct by the employee (like stealing), bankruptcy of the employer, or unless the employment contract is dissolved by a court. Permits are usually granted for dismissal based on low employee performance and for layoffs necessitated by economic circumstances (displacement). Dismissal because of illness, marriage, pregnancy, or military service is prohibited. Court cases and permits are frequently used to dissolve labor contracts.

Both employers and employees who want to end their employment relationship are bound by mandatory advance-notice requirements. Advance-notice periods are always shorter than six months. Exact durations depend on age, tenure, and the type of contract involved.[16] Severance pay is generally provided only in cases where the contract is dissolved by a court and the employee is not declared responsible. In these cases, severance pay is typically between one and two months' salary per year of tenure.

Public pensions and other programs assisting displaced workers

Assistance to unemployed displaced workers is far more generous in the Netherlands than in the United States. The most important source of income for workers displaced from private sector jobs is unemployment insurance, which is set according to the Unemployment Law.[17] A worker in the Netherlands is entitled to UI benefits if he or she has been employed for at least 26 of the prior 52 weeks, faces a sufficiently large, unpaid, reduction in working hours, and is willing to accept a new job.[18] Benefits equal 70 percent of the gross wage in the last job before unemployment to a maximum (as of January 1999) of 217 f. (U.S.$105) per day and are subject to income tax. The maximum duration of these benefits ranges from six months to five years, depending on the employment history of the unemployed workers.[19] Some unemployed workers are entitled to an extension of these benefits at a level related to the mandatory minimum wage.[20] If, after the expiration of UI benefits, the unemployed individual has not found a job, he may receive subsistence benefits (social assistance), which are means-tested (by household income) and related to what is considered to be the social minimum income.[21] The Unemployment Law provides some arrangements for "short-time unemployment" due to weather conditions, but none for temporary layoffs. This may be the reason that temporary layoffs are not an important phenomenon in the Netherlands (see Emerson 1988).

According to the Unemployment Law, a worker has to prevent unnecessary job loss in order to be entitled to UI. The administrators of the unemployment benefits system, mainly organized at the level of the industry, are authorized to impose sanctions on unemployed workers who have violated this rule.[22] Thus, to the extent that they do not immediately move into new jobs, most displaced workers in the private sector can be identified as workers flowing into UI and not receiving sanctions for unnecessary job loss. Because of the institutional arrangements, this definition restricts attention both to longer service workers, although not necessarily workers with long tenure in their last jobs, and to layoffs due to economic conditions. In this context, it is relevant that UI premiums are not experience rated at the level of the individual firm.[23]

Other social security schemes have also served as destinations for displaced workers during some periods in recent history, disability insurance being a well-known alleged escape route for displacement.[24] In the 1970s and 1980s, DI was more attractive than UI for both employers and employees in terms of replacement rates and, perhaps, less negative stigma effects. In 1990, there were in fact 139 DI claimants for every 1,000 workers in the Netherlands, while there were only 78 in Sweden and 43 in Germany (Aarts, Dercksen, and de Jong 1993). Since Dutch workers are not likely to run much higher health risks than workers in Sweden and Germany, this suggests that Dutch DI serves more goals than just disability insurance.[25] Policy changes in the late 1980s and the 1990s have been directed at preventing abuse of DI. First, DI replacement rates were reduced in 1985 and 1987. Stricter rules concerning disability, and more extensive monitoring, were introduced in the 1993 law. As a consequence, the DI rate has now reduced, after increasing continuously until 1985 (CTSV 1997).

Another possible escape route for displaced workers is early retirement. Since the late 1970s there have been arrangements for retirement before the standard retirement age (65 years), which were formally established by law in 1981. There is some circumstantial evidence that early retirement may be relevant to worker displacement: labor-force participation rates of Dutch men over age 50 decrease relatively quickly with age compared to other OECD countries (Thio

1997). The use of early retirement to avoid layoff costs in case of displacement is clearly restricted, however, by specific age requirements. Also, early retirement schemes have recently been incorporated in private so-called flexible pension plans, which may reduce the scope for abuse of this scheme. Additional information on the role of DI and early retirement is provided at the end of this chapter.

DATA

United States

Significant improvements in data availability have led to an explosion of analysis on U.S. displaced workers during the last decade. The majority of this research has used information available from the Displaced Worker Supplements (DWS) to the Current Population Survey (CPS). The first DWS was conducted in January 1984, with new supplements released at two-year intervals since that time. Until recently, the surveys collected information for workers losing jobs in the five calendar years prior to the interview date. Beginning in 1994, the surveys were switched from January to February and the period over which job loss was measured was cut from five to three years. Information is collected on pre- and postdisplacement job characteristics and on the intervening period of joblessness.[26] Sample sizes are reasonably large, the DWS data can be supplemented with the information contained in the normal monthly CPS, and the information is fairly easy to analyze.[27] The new analysis of displacement contained in this chapter uses data from the February 1996 DWS and CPS and focuses on 20- to 64-year-old workers (at the survey date) losing jobs due to a plant closing, slack work, or position or shift abolishment. In order to make the investigation more comparable with that conducted for the Netherlands, many of the results focus on persons losing jobs that have lasted at least one year. Special attention is also paid to those who are out of work for some time following the termination.

For all its strengths, the DWS has a variety of disadvantages. First, the data are retrospective and subject to recall bias. Second, information is available for only one lost job, and data on company characteristics or the situation prior to displacement are limited. Most importantly, it is difficult to construct a comparison group of nondisplaced workers.[28] This has led some researchers to use longitudinal data sets (such as the Panel Study of Income Dynamics) or administrative data (such as payroll or unemployment insurance records) to analyze the incidence or consequences of displacement.[29] These alternate sources have advantages, particularly the availability of a comparison group, but they also have problems. For instance, sample sizes of displaced workers are typically quite small in panel data, and the reason for job change often cannot be identified from administrative sources.

The Netherlands

There is no equivalent to the DWS for the Netherlands. We have access, however, to three microdata sets that contain information on various aspects of displacement: the Firm Employment (FE) data set, an administrative longitudinal UI data set of the Dutch Social Security Council (*Sociale Verzekeringsraad* or SVr), and the Labor Force Survey (LFS) of the Netherlands Organization for Strategic Labor Market Research (OSA). Unlike the DWS these data allow, to some extent, for the construction of comparison groups of nondisplaced workers. For some of the analyses, however, sample sizes are small compared to the DWS.

The FE data set is constructed by sampling individuals from administrative records of firms covering the period 1992–1996. It provides information on tenure and separation, reasons for separation, and a variety of individual and job characteristics. The data provide very useful information on the incidence of displacement and shed some light on labor market transitions immediately following displacement. However, the FE data are silent about subsequent labor market transitions and earnings losses.

The UI data set provides information on unemployment spells of all workers entering UI in 1992. Because all unemployed workers in the market sector with sufficiently long employment records end up in UI, and the data reveal worker-initiated separations, these data can be used to study reemployment durations after displacement, conditional on a positive non-employment spell. Since these data show the entire inflow into UI by sector, municipality, and month, we can also construct indicators of excessive inflow into UI in local labor markets, which can be used as indicators of excessive, or even mass, layoffs. Earnings losses, however, are not observed in this data set either: for this we require the LFS data, a labor-force panel survey covering the period 1985–1990. The LFS data set provides extensive information on labor market transitions and earnings, but suffers from small numbers of displaced workers.

Table 2.1 summarizes the main features of the data. Because the Dutch data sets have not been used to study displacement before, we will discuss these in more detail. The appendix provides additional information.

The Firm Employment Data

The Firm Employment data (or *Arbeidsvoorwaardenonderzoek* in Dutch) are firm-worker data collected by civil servants (of the Labor Inspection Service, or *Arbeidinspectie*) of the Ministry of Social Affairs and Employment (*Ministerie van Sociale Zaker en Werkgelenheid*). These data provide information on the incidence of displacement over the period 1992–1996. The data are collected yearly (in October 1993–1996) as repeated cross sections from administrative wage records of a sample of firms by means of a stratified two-step sampling procedure.[30]

In the first step a sample of firms is drawn (about 2,000 in each year) from the Ministry's own database (which is roughly similar to the database of firms of Statistics Netherlands, CBS). In the second step, a sample of workers (about 26,000 per year) is drawn from the records of the firms selected in the first step. The workers are sampled from administrative records of two moments in time, one year before the sampling date and at the sampling date. A distinction is made among employees who are present in both years ("stayers"), workers who are present only in the first year ("leavers"), and workers who are present only in the second year ("entrants"). More than 75 percent of the workers are stayers. Information obtained on the way leavers separate from firms is later used to distinguish between displacement and other separations.

The data set includes additional information on wages, hours worked, days worked, and a number of other variables, including age, gender, education, job complexity, occupation, SIC industry code, firm size, and type of wage contract.

The UI Data Set

The UI data, which are provided by the SVr, are administrative data from the sectoral organizations that implement the unemployment insurance system. The data cover all individuals who started collecting UI benefits in 1992. Individuals are followed up to September 1993, if necessary. Note that for a given individual the date of inflow into UI as a rule coincides with the date of inflow into unemployment. For each individual we know the duration of UI benefit receipt, except when it is right-censored by the end of the observation period (late 1993); that occurs in 17 percent of all cases. If the UI duration is completed we know the exit state, which is usually either employment (67 percent of the completed spells) or continued unemployment after completion of UI entitlement (14 percent). Only 8 percent of the spells end because of transitions into DI, and hardly any UI spells in our sample end in retirement.[31] Apart from this, we do not have information on events occurring after individuals leave UI.

We observe whether individuals have had a sanction imposed right at the start of the UI spell. These sanctions are punitive benefit reductions that are applied if the UI applicant is considered to bear at least some responsibility for his job loss. Thus, this variable can be used to control for worker-initiated separations, as far as these are not excluded by restricting attention to UI inflow. Otherwise, the number of explanatory variables is limited by the character of the data set. The data do not contain the exact magnitude of the individual UI benefit level. The magnitude is a direct function of the wage earned before entering unemployment, however, affected by personal and household characteristics. Both the wage and these characteristics can be observed, but the data provide only limited information on individual maximum UI entitlement, except of course when the individual is seen to complete entitlement.

The Labor Force Survey of the OSA

The OSA Labor Supply Panel Survey, or just LFS, is a panel which started in 1985. Presently four waves are available (April–May 1985, August–October 1986, August–October 1988, and August–November 1990). In the LFS a random sample of households in the Netherlands is followed over time. Because the study concentrates on individuals between 15 and 61 years of age who are not full-time students, only households with at least one person in this category are included. For households chosen, all individuals in this category (and in all cases the head of the household) are interviewed. The first wave consists of 4,020 individuals (in 2,132 households). The four waves together contain information on 8,121 individuals.

In every interview, retrospective questions are asked to elicit information on possible labor market transitions made by the respondent during the period between the prior and current interviews.[32] This process allows us to reconstruct the sequence of labor market states experienced by 8,075 respondents, with the sojourn times and income levels in all these states.[33] The LFS data identify employment, self-employment, unemployment, not-in-labor-force, military service, and full-time education as labor market states.[34] The respondent is asked to provide a motive or cause for each transition between any two of these labor market states and to indicate whether the transition was made voluntarily.[35] This information enables us to distinguish displacement from other separations. We will come back to this issue when we discuss the analysis of labor market transitions following displacement.

DISPLACEMENT RATES

Incidence of Displacement

United States

Farber (1997) estimated displacement probabilities, over three-year periods, using information from all the available Displaced Worker Supplements. A crude estimate of annual job loss due to plant closing, slack work, or position or shift abolishment is obtained by dividing his estimated values by three.[36] These results, displayed in Table 2.2, reveal displacement rates of between 2 and 4 percent per year, with higher probabilities for men than women. Displacements are somewhat countercyclical—e.g., notice the high rates during the recessionary period in the early 1980s and the low rates during the economic expansion at the end of the decade—but there is little indication of a time trend.[37]

There are at least two reasons why these estimates understate displacement probabilities. First, the DWS records a maximum of one job loss during the three-year period, thus missing multiple separations.[38] Second, the surveys suffer from recall bias, whereby terminations occurring further in the past are more likely to be forgotten (Topel 1990; Evans and Leighton 1995). Table 2.3 provides estimates of annual displacement rates for the 1993–1995 period, with an attempt made to correct for both sources of bias. The top section shows estimates for all types of displacements, whereas the second is limited to job loss resulting in an initial period of joblessness. This is done to make the results more comparable to those of the Netherlands and some of the countries analyzed in other chapters of this volume, where data limitations restrict the analysis to displacements that lead to unemployment.

The first row of each section shows estimated displacement rates both for all workers and separately by gender. The "correction" involves two parts. First, it is assumed that an equal number of persons are displaced in all three years. Second, it is assumed that in each of the next two years 10 percent of the workers displaced in any given year experience a second job loss.[39] Using these assumptions, persons losing jobs in 1995 should account for 29.9 percent of the displacements observed in the 1996 DWS.[40] Instead, 47.5 percent of displaced workers in the 1996 DWS report losing their jobs in 1995, suggesting that the number of displacements is understated by around 59 percent (0.475/0.299 = 1.589) and that the corrected annual displacement probability is 4.9 percent (0.031 × 1.589 = 0.049). A similar procedure yields a 5.3 percent estimated rate of annual job loss for men and 4.5 percent probability for women.[41] The corresponding entry in the bottom section deflates the displacement probability by the percentage of job losers who obtain new employment without an intervening spell of non-employment. For instance, 14.4 percent of displaced individuals do not experience any initial joblessness, implying that 3.8 percent (0.049 × 0.856 = 0.042) are expected to lose positions and become jobless.

The remainder of the table provides estimates of annual displacement rates as a function of tenure in the predisplacement job. Since Farber (1997) did not break down his statistics by tenure, additional steps are required to obtain these estimates. First, the predisplacement tenure distribution of workers losing jobs between 1993 and 1995 is calculated from the 1996 DWS. Second, the job tenure of all 20- to 64-year-old workers in February 1996 is estimated using data from the monthly CPS. Third, a relative risk of displacement is calculated by dividing the share of displaced workers in a tenure group by the corresponding share for all workers. Finally, this relative risk is multiplied by the aggregate displacement rate to arrive at a probability of job loss for each tenure category. For example, persons with 1–2 years of preseparation tenure accounted for 26.8 percent of displaced workers but just 13.2 percent of the nondisplaced, implying a relative risk of 2.03 (0.268/0.132) and an estimated annual displacement rate of 9.9 percent (2.03 × 0.049). This procedure is performed separately for men and women, as well as for both together.

Table 2.3 shows an almost monotonic negative relationship between job tenure and the probability of job loss. Persons holding jobs for ten or more years are only about one-fourth as likely to be displaced as those in positions that have lasted for just a year or two. The one exception to this pattern is that persons in the first year of the job appear to have somewhat lower displacement rates than those with one to two years of tenure. This result is probably erroneous, for two reasons. First, recall bias is probably most severe for very short-tenure workers, since these persons may incur few adjustment problems when their positions end.[42] Second, information on predisplacement tenure is missing for 11 percent of the displaced workers; these individuals are excluded from the calculations in the table. If, as is likely, data are missing relatively frequently for very brief employment spells, the share of displacements and the corresponding risk of job loss will be understated for this group. Overall, the evidence strongly suggests that displacement rates fall with job tenure.[43]

The age pattern of displacement rates over the 1993–1995 period is shown in Table 2.4. These estimates adjust the overall displacement probabilities in Table 2.3 by the age-specific relative probabilities of job loss calculated by Farber (1997). For example, the probability of displacement is 11.6 percent higher for 20- to 24-year-olds than for all workers, implying an estimated displacement rate of 5.5 percent (0.049 × 1.116 = 0.055). The table shows clear evidence that probabilities of job loss decline with age, but the profile is not nearly as steep as for job tenure. For instance, 55- to 64-year-olds are roughly three-quarters as likely to be permanently laid off as 20- to 24-year-olds.

The lack of a comparison group in the DWS makes it difficult to perform a regression analysis of the determinants of displacement. However, Farber (1997) estimated a series of probit models where the dependent variable indicated whether or not a job loss had occurred over a three-year period and the regressors were limited to characteristics observed at the survey date. His analysis confirmed that displacement probabilities decline with age and indicated lower rates of job loss for educated workers, women, and whites.

The Netherlands

Reasonably long displacement-rate time series can be constructed from aggregate UI data, giving the yearly numbers of new UI cases and data on the number of employed individuals at risk. The merits of the first series as a measure of displacement have been discussed in the institutions and data sections. Although it provides only an imperfect measure of displacement, it is the only measure for which we can construct time series over several business cycles.[44] Ideally, one would like to measure the number of individuals at risk as the number of employed individuals who would be eligible for UI benefits in case of displacement. Unfortunately, we have to approximate this series by the number of employed individuals paying UI premiums. Because this number includes individuals with employment histories insufficient for UI eligibility, it provides an upper bound to the number of individuals at risk. As a consequence, the rate computed is a lower bound on the true rate of displacement leading to positive unemployment spells.

Figure 2.1 graphs the annual displacement-rate time series constructed in this manner, together with real Gross Domestic Product (GDP) growth in the Netherlands (percentage change from previous year) for the period 1970–1993. The rate of displacement is clearly an

Figure 2.1 Netherlands: The Annual Rate of Displacement

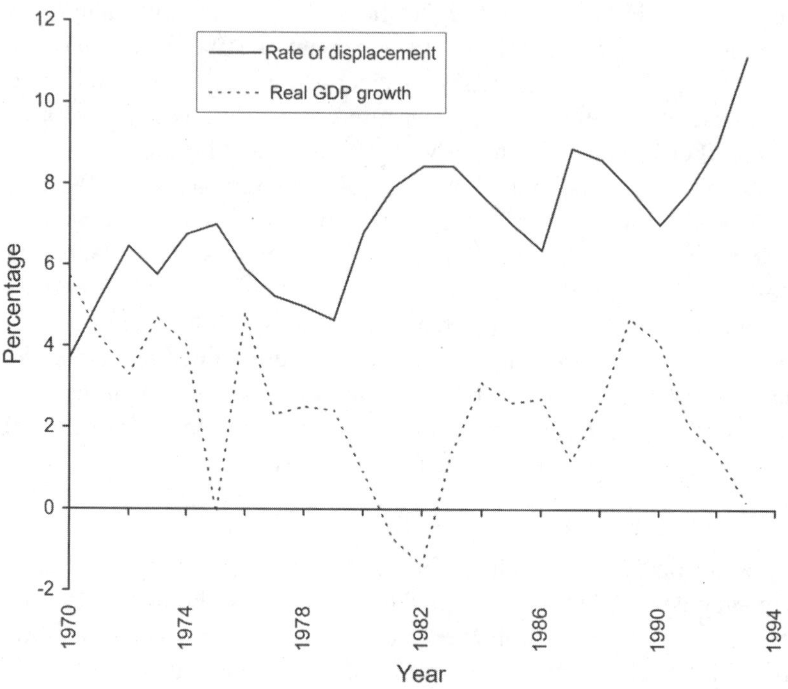

upward trend over the data period, rising from around 4 percent in 1970 to 11 percent in 1993.[45] As is to be expected, we also observe strong fluctuations over the business cycle, with steep increases in 1970–1972, 1973–1975, 1979–1982, 1986–1987, and 1990–1993. Comparing this to the superimposed macro indicator, real GDP growth, we see that displacement rates are countercyclical. Notable exceptions are 1976–1977, 1984–1985, and 1989–1990, which are all years with decreasing growth and displacement rates. A simple explanation could be that the downturns of the business cycle led to worker displacement, although this seems not to be true for the early 1970s. However, the correlation between the two series is –0.58. A regression of displacement on GDP growth and time shows that displacement changes –0.33 (s.e. 0.12) percentage points for each percentage-point increase in real GDP growth, and 0.15 (s.e. 0.03) percentage points per year (R^2 = 0.69). We do not find significant coefficients for one- and two-year lagged GDP growth.

The FE data can be used to study the variation of displacement over groups of workers.[46] For each separation, information is available that is helpful in identifying displacement. Among other things, the data distinguish layoffs, separations because of the expiration of fixed-term contracts, and transitions into other jobs, DI, and early and normal retirement.[47] It should be understood that this information comes from administrative records of the firm and is therefore limited by the observational scope of the firm's administration. For instance, a worker who is given notice of layoff in the near future may quit immediately to go to another job (before the date of layoff) in order to avoid unemployment. In such a case, the worker would most likely be recorded as a job-to-job mover, without any reference to the layoff. A worker who stays with the firm until the date of layoff, however, is most likely to be recorded as a laid-off worker. For the latter worker the data do not provide information on the labor market state occupied just after displacement. Similar arguments can be made for workers moving into DI or early retirement. For a worker observed to move into early retirement, for instance, we do not have independent information on the circumstances leading to early retirement. Thus, the causes of separations and destinations of labor market transitions following separations are intertwined in the data, and we have to decide on an appropriate way to identify displacement.

We have opted for the following method. For all firms, workers under age 60 with tenure of at least one year who are recorded to be laid off are considered to be displaced. As argued above, some displaced workers who immediately find a new job, or move into DI or early retirement, will be excluded by this definition of displacement. To include at least some of these cases, we will label leavers moving into new jobs, DI, or early retirement from "strongly shrinking" firms to be displaced as well. Since there is no *a priori* reason to pick any particular threshold employment-loss level, we have experimented with a number of different criteria. The results can be found in Table 2.5, which gives the contributions to the annual displacement rate over the period 1993–1996 of separations from strongly shrinking firms by type of separation for six different criteria. The first question is whether we should focus on net or gross employment (outflow) changes. Using the latter, we will overestimate displacement rates in high turnover sectors, where high simultaneous employment inflow and outflow rates are no exception, whereas using the former we will underestimate displacement at restructuring firms.[48] The weakest criterion in Table 2.5 results in an aggregate annual displacement rate of 7.2 percent, while the strongest criterion results in an aggregate displacement rate of 3.5 percent, over the 1993–1996 period. With all criteria, we find that most workers displaced from strongly shrinking firms are labeled as moving directly into new jobs, with almost as many labeled as being laid off. Early retirement and, in particular, DI seem of minor importance. Note again, however, that some of the workers labeled as being laid off could have moved into new jobs, early retirement, or DI. We will return to this issue later. In what follows we use the net employment criterion, with a –30 percent threshold, mainly because other authors in this volume (Denmark, Belgium) do so.

First, we will give a short description of the variation in displacement rates over time and among different categories of workers. Table 2.6 shows that displacement rates are somewhat higher for men than for women and that displacement rates are much lower for workers with high tenure. Note that, despite the institutional differences, the results are very similar to those for the United States shown in Table 2.3.[49] In both countries, low-tenure men have higher displacement rates than low-tenure women, whereas at the highest tenure levels women have higher displacement rates than men. Table 2.7 shows that displacement rates are highest in 1993 and lowest in 1996. Since 1993 was the year in which the Netherlands had its lowest net employment growth (it was even negative) and the Dutch economy has strongly recovered since 1995, this result is consistent with countercyclical displacement rates. The table also shows that workers covered by a collective agreement (CAO) have lower displacement rates than both workers whose wage contract is required to follow CAO contracts of other firms in the same sector (AVV) and workers with only individual contracts.[50] The finding that displacement rates are highest for AVV workers could reflect the fact that firms are bound to pay such workers wages that are agreed upon by other firms. These wages may not reflect the business conditions of AVV firms. It is also interesting to see that displacement rates for workers at simple jobs, for workers with little formal training, and for young workers are relatively high. This is in line with standard labor hoarding and human-capital theories. Finally, we see that displacement rates decline with age.

We continue to investigate the results by estimating a logit model for the incidence of displacement (Table 2.8). As the net marginal benefits of displacing a worker will typically be influenced by macroeconomic conditions, we not only include firm and worker characteristics, but sets of calendar-time and sectoral dummies, too. It is important to point out that some of the variables that are used as explanatory variables may well be endogenous. Employed workers who have been relatively successful at avoiding displacement in the past may have both a high current tenure and a low current probability of displacement. Employed workers who have been promoted by accident to a job with fringe benefits that exceed what they can get from other employers may have both a high current tenure and a high current probability of displacement. This potential endogeneity hampers straightforward interpretation of the parameter estimates. Table 2.8 gives the corresponding estimates. The displacement probability decreases with tenure (up to some level), and with gross hourly wages, and it increases with educational and job-complexity level. It is also relatively high for workers without collective contracts and workers employed at large firms.

Using these estimates, we compute displacement probabilities for different types of workers. We evaluate these probabilities at the estimated parameter values and the mean observed characteristics. Table 2.9 illustrates the partial effects of the different worker and firm characteristics. We see some differences from the exploratory results in Table 2.7. Controlling for other characteristics, the displacement probability no longer decreases with education and job complexity level. Furthermore, displacement probabilities differ very little as a result of the type of contract. It appears that low-wage and low-tenure workers have a particularly high probability of being displaced. According to the logit model, a worker with average characteristics who earns 15 f. an hour faces a 4.3 percent chance of being displaced, whereas this probability is only 1.1 percent for a worker who earns 50 f. an hour. This is not a surprising result if wages are determined by a surplus sharing rule, in which case matches with the highest surplus have the lowest probability of ending.

Finally, note that displacement rates calculated with the FE data set are lower than the UI inflow time-series figures because we observe very few firm closings in the FE data. Furthermore, we include individuals who lose only part of their job (those whose hours of work are reduced) in the UI data, and we do not exclude individuals with sanctions.[51]

TRANSITIONS

Labor Market Transitions after Displacement

United States

Job loss increases the risk that an individual will be out of work for some period. Swaim and Podgursky (1991) estimated that the median worker is jobless for 25 to 30 weeks following a permanent layoff, and Farber (1993) found that 29 to 38 percent of men displaced during the previous two years were unemployed at the DWS interview date, compared to 4 to 5 percent of the nondisplaced.[52] Much of the employment reduction is temporary, however. Ruhm (1991a) estimated that unemployment increases by around eight weeks in the year of the permanent layoff, four weeks in the next year, but only around one week four years after the event.

The patterns of postdisplacement joblessness and labor-force status for 1996 DWS respondents losing jobs that had lasted at least one year are shown in Tables 2.10 and 2.11. Table 2.10 shows the probability that workers obtain new jobs within either six months or one year after displacement. By European standards, non-employment spells in the United States are brief, with around two-thirds reemployed in six months or less and three-quarters within a year. Over 60 percent of those with an initial spell of joblessness are working again within six months and 72 percent in less than a year. Men and short-tenure workers obtain new jobs somewhat faster than women and those with longer tenure. The age differences in reemployment are fairly small through the workers' late forties, but workers beyond that age are much more likely to have extended spells of joblessness. This may represent greater adjustment difficulties following displacement, but it could also confound the effects of job loss and retirement. We return to this point below. Groups obtaining new jobs rapidly generally have rather high rates of survey date employment. The patterns of unemployment and labor-force participation, however, are more divergent, as is shown in Table 2.11. In particular, the relatively low employment rates of mature adults and women are explained by high rates of labor-force withdrawal, rather than elevated unemployment.

Econometric estimates of the determinants of postdisplacement joblessness are summarized in Table 2.12. The first column shows results of a probit equation where the dependent variable equals one for persons finding new jobs without any intervening joblessness and zero for those who are out of work for at least one week. The second shows results of a Cox proportional hazard model where the dependent variable is weeks of joblessness and the sample is restricted to those out of work for at least one week. The third shows corresponding hazard estimates for the full sample, where the dependent variable is weeks of joblessness plus one-half. Thus, the second column indicates hazard rates, conditional on a positive spell, while the third shows results for the unconditional model (that includes both zero- and positive-week spells). The excluded reference category is a white, unmarried, female, high school dropout, born outside the United States, with one to two years of predisplacement tenure, age 20 to 29, who loses a job due to a position or shift abolishment, and receives no written advance notice. A higher hazard rate implies faster exit from joblessness and shorter spells.

The results are generally consistent with those in earlier research. Non-employment declines with education, increases with age, and is higher for nonwhites than whites. Men are just as likely as women to experience some joblessness but transition into employment more quickly. Conversely, married and native-born persons are more likely than their counterparts to move directly into new jobs but once out-of-work show little evidence of faster reemployment. Long-tenure workers have relatively high probabilities of avoiding joblessness but may have modestly lower reemployment hazard rates, conditional on a positive spell. Persons involved in plant closings are more likely to move directly into new positions than those losing jobs due to a position or shift abolishment and have elevated reemployment hazards relative to both this group and those displaced by slack work.[53] Individuals receiving lengthy written notice are more likely than the non-notified to avoid joblessness, but the notice does not appear to have any effect on reemployment hazard rates. Furthermore, the exit probabilities for those with brief notice are, if anything, actually lower than for those not receiving any written warnings.[54]

The Netherlands

Both the LFS and the FE data provide some information on the labor market states occupied by workers just after displacement. In the LFS, we are able to distinguish job-to-job transitions (E-E), transitions from employment to unemployment (E-U), and transitions from employment to not-in-the-labor-force (E-N) in each individual labor market history. We use the self-reported motive or cause for each transition and the information on whether or not transitions are made voluntarily to distinguish displacement from other types of separations in each case. Details are provided in the appendix.

Table 2.13 shows the number of displaced workers in our sample by transition and motivation. In total we observe 327 displacements. The large majority, 70 percent, involve job-to-job transitions. In contrast, in the United States many more workers experience a positive non-employment spell. As for motivations, in most cases (68 percent) displacement is indicated by the most clear-cut motivation, "reorganization or plant closure" (of which 73 percent involve no joblessness). Only a small share is due to DI (17 percent) or early retirement (1 percent). If we restrict attention to workers with tenure of at least one year, only 162 displacements are left. However, qualitatively similar results hold for this subsample.

As we stated before, the FE data also give some information on the labor market state just after displacement. Although this data set does not indicate the labor market state for those displaced workers labeled as being laid off, firms may be involved in arranging DI and, in particular, early retirement if these destinations are really used as convenient ways to displace workers. In such a case we may expect these transitions actually to be recorded. Similarly, because of employment protection regulation, we may expect firms to be involved in reemploying displaced workers, and so at least some job-to-job transitions of displaced workers will be recorded. In any case, the share of layoffs in overall displacement provides only an upper bound to the share of displaced workers ending up in unemployment right after being displaced.

Table 2.14 compares the FE layoff rates, job-to-job transition rates, DI inflow rates, and early retirement rates between firms shrinking by 30 percent or more and other firms. We see that not only the layoff rates but also the other separation probabilities are higher at the 30-percent-shrinking firms. This seems to indicate that at least some displaced workers enter DI or early retirement, or move directly into another job. The second column for each type of firms shows, however, that a relatively high share of separations from shrinking firms are labeled as layoffs, and relatively few as job-to-job transitions. So, most of the displacement seems to be captured by layoffs.

The LFS data also provide information on the labor market states occupied by displaced workers 12 months after displacement. Table 2.15 gives the number of individuals in the different labor market states, by type of transition made just after displacement.[55] The table shows that most individuals remain in the same state as they were when they became displaced. We cannot derive strong results on E-U and E-N transitions because of the limited number of individuals in these categories, but it seems that the job-to-job movers do not have problems finding steady employment after being displaced.

Finally, we can analyze reemployment durations following displacement using the 1992 UI inflow data set. We distinguish individuals who have been sanctioned for responsibility for job loss from individuals who have not been sanctioned. Only the latter are considered to be displaced. The sanctioned individuals may then serve as a "control" group, where we should acknowledge that this group contains only individuals who are eligible for UI benefits and no individuals who have, for instance, also quit their jobs or who have been dismissed for severe misconduct. The groups may also differ for two reasons other than cause of separation. First, the "nondisplaced" individuals have been sanctioned, which implies that they face reduced benefits for some period of time. Second, workers are likely to be nonrandomly selected into both states, for which we will not directly control.

Table 2.16 presents summary statistics of reemployment durations by demographic group. Because 44 percent of the durations are right-censored, we compute median durations, in particular median residual durations at 0 and 26 weeks. From the upper segment we learn that the median reemployment duration of all spells is 20.8 weeks. For displaced workers, the median duration is 3.5 weeks shorter than for sanctioned workers. The median residual durations at 26 weeks are 4–5 times larger, implying strong negative duration dependence of the corresponding reemployment hazard rates. It is well known that this can be explained by both "genuine" duration dependence at the individual level (because of stigma effects or atrophy of skills), and dynamic sorting because of exit-rate heterogeneity.[56] The lower panel restricts attention to displaced workers and gives median durations for various demographic groups. One feature worth noting is the strong increase in median durations with age. This may be due to the institutional structure of UI, which is more generous for older unemployed and unemployed with longer employment histories. In addition, search rules are less strict for older individuals.

We also develop a measure of excess layoffs in the local labor market of each individual. From the UI inflow census we can compute the size of the inflow in UI in each month of 1992 in each Dutch municipality by sector. Thus, we can distinguish local labor markets by municipality and sector, and define excess UI inflow in a local labor market to be the inflow into UI in that market net of the overall average inflow over time, municipality, and sector. More formally, if C_{mst} is the inflow in UI in municipality m in sector s in month t, then data on C_{mst} for all municipalities, sectors, and months in 1992 are regressed on municipality, sector, and time dummies, yielding both predicted counts C_{mst} and residual counts $\hat{\varepsilon}_{mst} = C_{mst} - \hat{C}_{mst}$ for each cell or (m,s,t). Now, each combination (m,s) represents a local labor market, and the $\hat{\varepsilon}_{mst}$ is an indicator of excess layoffs in local labor market (m,s) in month t. We can assign each individual to a local labor market, and use $\hat{\varepsilon}$ as a regressor in an analysis of reemployment durations. Because we will include province indicators instead of municipality indicators in the duration analysis (for computational reasons), it is useful to also include C as a regressor.

The duration model for reemployment durations is specified as a single-risk mixed proportional hazard (MPH) model, with the log hazard for reemployment given by $\ln \theta(t|\boldsymbol{x}, v) = \lambda(t) + \boldsymbol{x}' \beta = v$, where λ is a piecewise constant log baseline hazard, and β is the regressor parameter vector. The vector $\boldsymbol{x}$ is a regressor vector containing the sanction indicator, the cell or local labor market indicators, and other individual characteristics. The variable v is an unobserved component which is assumed to be discretely distributed so that, with n points of support, $\Pr(v = v_i) = p_i$, for $i = 1, \ldots n$, and $p_n = 1 - \sum_{i=1}^{n-1} p_i$.[57] We fix the number of mass points at $n = 2$ and perform sensitivity analysis by reestimating the model for higher values of n. Finally, we treat destinations different from reemployment as randomly right-censoring the reemployment durations. We have right-censoring because of the fact that individuals are followed only until late 1993.

Table 2.17 shows results from maximum likelihood estimation. The most important finding is that individuals who are displaced according to the sanction indicator, in other words, those who do not have sanctions imposed, have approximately 20 percent higher reemployment rates than sanctioned individuals. Considering the fact that sanctions are likely to increase reemployment rates if they have any direct effect, this figure provides a lower bound on the difference between displaced and nondisplaced workers, given a similar benefits level.[58] This result is consistent with the work of Gibbons and Katz (1991) for the United States, who find that workers displaced because of plant closings have shorter reemployment durations than workers laid off because of slack work or elimination of a position or shift. It is also interesting to note that the predicted size of the local labor market has a significantly negative effect on reemployment rates, which could be a symptom of congestion effects in local labor markets. It should be noted that this variable is identified only from variation between municipalities, as the model contains full sets of time and sector dummies. The wage has a significantly positive effect on reemployment rates, and age a significantly negative effect (from age 16 onwards). Wald-test statistics for the joint significance of the three sets of dummy variables show that there is significant variation (at the 5 percent level) among sectors, months of inflow, and provinces. Most of the variation in reemployment rates between cells or local labor markets is caused by sectoral heterogeneity. Finally, we find significant unobserved heterogeneity and negative individual duration dependence of reemployment rates.[59]

Table 2.18 gives reemployment probabilities computed with the estimated model, by fixing the unobserved heterogeneity component at its estimated mean and the regressors at the sample mean, and considering one-by-one deviations of regressors from this mean. Of the displaced workers, 55 percent are reemployed within 26 weeks, 73 percent within 52 weeks. For sanctioned individuals these probabilities are slightly lower. We still find strong negative effects of age on reemployment probabilities. Wages have positive effects on reemployment probabilities, *ceteris paribus*, a finding which overturns the results from the raw median estimates.

Earnings and Wage Changes

United States

In addition to transitory increases in joblessness, labor displacement in the United States is frequently accompanied by substantial and lasting wage reductions. Several studies have examined these earnings losses in detail, using longitudinal or administrative data to allow a comparison group of nondisplaced workers. Using the Panel Study of Income Dynamics, Ruhm (1991a) found that job loss reduces weekly wages by 14 to 18 percent in the following year and 11 to 15 percent four years later, with little evidence of recovery beyond this point. A more recent study of the same data source by Stevens (1997) indicated average decreases of roughly the same magnitude and pattern but further highlighted that large losses are concentrated among persons experiencing repeated turnover. Jacobson, LaLonde, and Sullivan's 1993 analysis of administrative data for Pennsylvania workers with six or more years of tenure on the predisplacement job uncovered a similar time profile and even larger losses—quarterly earnings declined by 30 to 40 percent initially, with persistent losses of 20 to 30 percent. The variance of wage changes is also large, however. Early studies by Ruhm (1987) or Kletzer (1991), for example, pointed out that many workers earn more after job loss than before it. Storer and Van Audenrode (1997) suggested that uncertainty over potential wage changes is a major source of the utility losses resulting from displacement, far outweighing the comparatively modest reduction in average wages.

Table 2.19 displays changes in average real weekly earnings occurring between the time of a job loss and the survey date for respondents to the 1996 DWS who have been displaced from jobs lasting at least one year.[60] The first column shows results for the subsample who are working at the survey date; the second presents averages for the full sample, using a zero value for weekly wages for those not employed in February 1996. Average real weekly wages of reemployed sample members do not change between the displacement and interview dates, with gains observed for persons avoiding joblessness, men, and those with little seniority on the lost job.

These relatively favorable results may partially reflect the robust economic conditions in the United States during the time period analyzed.[61] The findings are not inconsistent with the large earnings losses mentioned above, however, for at least three reasons. First, persons who are not working at the survey date (and so are excluded from these calculations) may have relatively low earnings potential. Second, the "before" versus "after" comparison does not account for changes that would have occurred in the absence of the job loss (young workers, for example, have steep age–wage profiles, suggesting that losses could result from foregone growth in wages). Third, pay frequently begins to decline prior to the actual displacement (Hamermesh 1991; Ruhm 1991b; Jacobson, LaLonde, and Sullivan 1993), implying that the earnings reduction is understated by these estimates. In addition, the median displaced worker does considerably worse than the mean individual—median weekly wages decline by 6 percent conditional on reemployment and 30 percent for all job losers—demonstrating the importance of considering the variance of wage outcomes.

The distribution of earnings changes is displayed in Table 2.20. As above, the analysis is restricted to those losing jobs that have lasted at least one year. The conditional estimates restrict the sample to reemployed workers, whereas the unconditional results assume zero wages for those not working in February of 1996. The last two columns restrict the sample to 25- to 49-year-old men in order to focus on a group with particularly strong labor-force attachments. The table highlights the substantial dispersion of postdisplacement outcomes. Over one-quarter of the reemployed workers earn at least 10 percent more than before being displaced, and the pay of 18 percent increases by at least 25 percent. Even when persons not working at the survey date are included and treated as having a zero wage, 20 percent receive a wage premium exceeding 10 percent in the new job while 13 percent earn at least 25 percent more. Conversely, weekly earnings fall 25 percent or more for 52 percent of all displaced individuals and for 32 percent of those working at the survey date. Interestingly, the results are quite similar for 25- to 49-year-old men, with the main exception being that their higher rates of reemployment imply somewhat lower unconditional probabilities of large wage losses.

Table 2.21 summarizes the results of a series of earnings regressions for workers displaced from jobs lasting at least one year. The dependent variable in the first two columns is the natural log of weekly wages in February 1996. The second column includes predisplacement wages as a regressor, whereas the first does not. The outcome in column 3 is the change in weekly (ln) earnings. Effectively, this specification constrains the coefficient on previous wages to one, whereas column 2 allows it to vary freely.[62]

Wage levels and changes could be affected by different factors. Postdisplacement earnings will primarily reflect the general human capital possessed by the individual, whereas reductions in pay can occur from losses of firm-specific human capital, job or industry rents, or idiosyncratic residuals (luck). For instance, survey-date earnings are positively related with predisplacement tenure but wage reductions also increase with previous seniority, suggesting that the preseparation tenure differential reflects a combination of specific and general human capital.[63] In contrast, education is positively correlated with earnings on both jobs, suggesting that it provides general human capital.[64] Men and married individuals also earn more on both jobs. Conversely, persons 55 and over experience very large wage reductions. There is little evidence of race or advance-notice effects, once the other regressors are controlled for. Interestingly, there is also an indication, albeit only a modest one, that unionized workers suffer relatively large losses following displacements. Somewhat surprisingly, those displaced due to slack work gain relative to those losing jobs because of position or shift abolishment.[65] Finally, the coefficient on the predisplacement wage, in column 2, suggests that slightly over half of any earnings residual received on the old job is transferred to the new position.

The Netherlands

To analyze possible earnings losses between pre- and postdisplacement jobs, we use data on transitions between jobs, either with or without intervening non-employment spells, from the LFS. Thus, we consider E-N-E, E-U-E, and E-E transitions, of which we have 1,719 observations in our sample, including both displacement and other types of separation from the first employment spell. Only one income level is reported for each labor market spell. However, under the assumption that earnings do not vary within employment spells, the change in earnings between pre- and postseparation jobs equals the change of earnings between the date of separation and the date of entering the first new job. To correct these earnings differentials for inflation, we have used the monthly all-item Consumer Price Index (CPI).[66] After this inflation correction, 1,551 observations remain.[67] If we restrict our sample to workers with tenure of at least one year in the first employment spell, we have 668 observations.[68]

The average post- to preseparation earnings ratio in this sample is 1.24, with a standard error (of the mean) equal to 0.02. For the subsample of displaced individuals (232 observations) this average equals 1.18, with a standard error equal to 0.04. For our subsample of workers with sufficient tenure we find an average earnings ratio of 1.24 (0.02) for all workers and of 1.14 (0.03) for displaced workers (116 observations). In either case, real earnings rise significantly between two consecutive employment spells. Because there is no significant difference between the ratio for all workers and that for displaced workers (their 95 percent confidence intervals are overlapping), this indicates that displacement has no significant effect on future earnings. To investigate this further, we have regressed the log real earnings ratio on tenure in the first employment spell, the duration of the intervening non-employment spell (defined to be 0 for E-E cases), a dummy variable indicating whether the separation involves displacement, and some additional controls. The estimation results are reported in Table 2.22.

The results confirm the preliminary conclusions from the comparison of the averages. Displacement does not have a significant effect on earnings after a separation. Moreover, the first column shows that the effect of displacement is very small if we do not include the tenure criterion in the displacement definition. In the second column, we find some evidence of a negative effect of displacement if we restrict the displacement indicator to separations of workers with at least one year of tenure. This is confirmed by estimates for the tenure-restricted sample in the third column. Also, in all cases we find a significantly negative effect of the length of the spell of intervening joblessness. Thus, workers who have been without work longer experience smaller earnings gains. This can be explained by either stigma effects or loss of skills. Log tenure is generally insignificant, but the results in the second column indicate that workers with tenure below one year face significantly smaller earnings gains.

Retirement and Disability

United States

As discussed, compared with younger individuals, older persons obtain new jobs more slowly following displacements and suffer relatively larger wage reductions when they do. Rather than indicating a causal effect, however, it is possible that the effects of aging and displacement may be confounded. This possibility is particularly important given that labor-force participation rates fall rapidly once individuals reach their late fifties; previous research provides little insight, however, into the relationship between job loss and retirement.[69]

Table 2.23 supplies information on labor-force participation and retirement or disability status in February 1996 of displaced workers with more than one year on the preseparation job. The missing category is "other" reasons for being out of the labor force. Retirement and disability status are combined because these are likely to be close substitutes for at least some older workers. The table shows that retirement or disability probabilities rise and labor-force participation rates decline with age. However, as discussed, this may represent the normal process of aging rather than any unique consequence of job loss. To examine this possibility, we compare the labor-force status of displaced and nondisplaced men (Table 2.24). Displacement again includes job loss in 1993, 1994, or 1995 due to plant closing, slack work, or position or shift abolishment. We focus on men because women are much more likely to report being out of the labor force for ambiguous "other" reasons. Data are from the February 1996 Current Population Survey and Displaced Worker Supplement.

The table shows that male job losers are more likely than their nondisplaced peers to participate in the labor force but less likely to report being retired or disabled. Taken at face value, this suggests that permanent layoffs delay rather than promote retirement. This could be the result of reduced wages (and a dominant income effect) or of other financial losses (such as reductions in housing equity) that follow displacement. However, there is an important qualification to this interpretation. The participation and retirement rates of nondisplaced individuals do not condition on labor-force status in previous years. To the contrary, one must be working to be at risk of displacement. Therefore, the probabilities for displaced men in Table 2.24 are dependent on recent labor-force participation, whereas those for nondisplaced men are not. This distinction becomes increasingly important with age. For example, 62 percent of 62- to 64-year-old male job losers participated in the labor force in February 1996, compared to 46 percent of men not terminated. Many of the latter group were likely to have left the labor force several years earlier, however, implying that the conditional participation probabilities are much higher.[70]

The following procedure was used to provide more comparable estimates of survey-date labor-force status. First, age-specific probabilities of being in each labor-force state were calculated.[71] Second, lagged labor-force participation was estimated as the participation rate of workers two years younger than the specified age. A two-year lag was chosen roughly to correspond to the average amount of time since job loss for displaced workers. Third, conditional labor-force participation rates for nondisplaced men were calculated as the difference between current and lagged labor-force participation divided by the lagged rate. Similarly, conditional retirement or disability rates were estimated as the difference between current and lagged values of retirement or disability probabilities, divided by the lagged participation rates.[72]

Figures 2.2 and 2.3 display the age-specific labor-force participation and retirement or disability probabilities for displaced and nondisplaced men. The unconditional estimates for nondisplaced men correspond to those in Table 2.24; the conditional estimates were obtained using the procedure described above. As mentioned, nondisplaced men have uniformly lower probabilities of participating in the labor force and higher rates of retirement or disability. Conditional on being in the labor force two years earlier, however, men in their middle fifties and older who have not lost jobs are more likely to participate and less likely to classify themselves as retired or disabled than those who have lost jobs. For example, the conditional retirement or disabil-

Figure 2.2 United States: Labor Force Participation Rates of Displaced and Nondisplaced Males

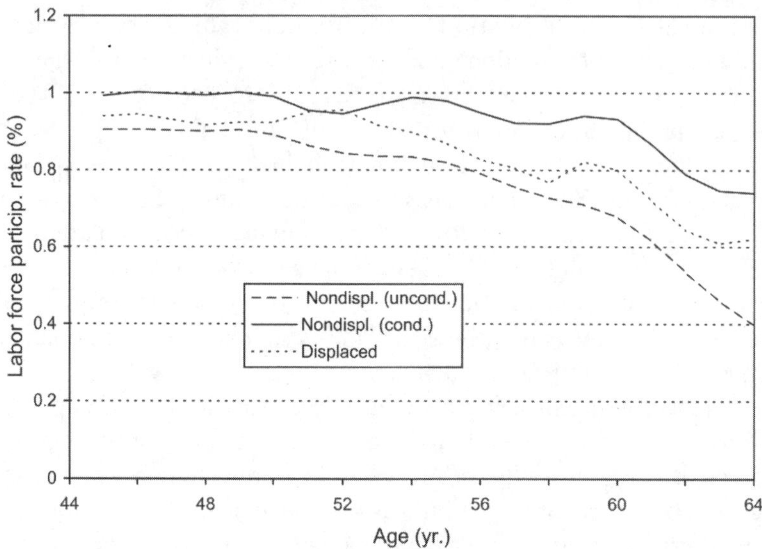

Figure 2.3 United States: Retirement/Disability Rates of Displaced and Nondisplaced Males

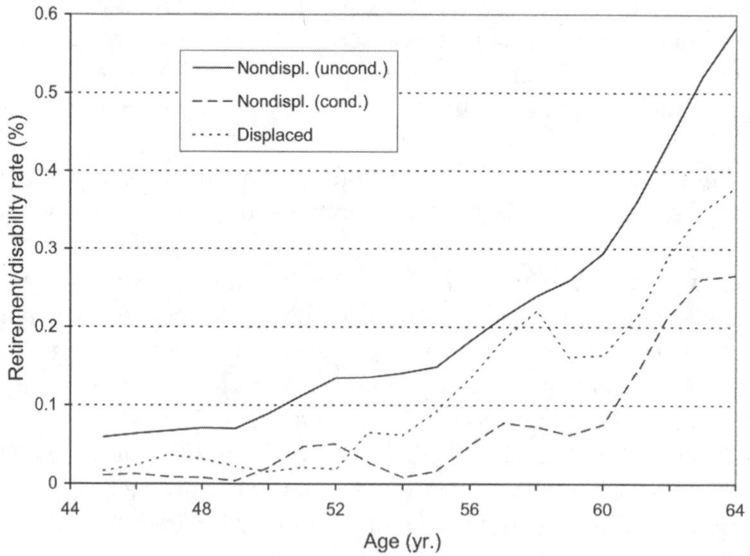

ity probabilities of 55-, 60-, and 64-year-old nondisplaced men are 2, 8, and 27 percent, compared to 9, 16, and 38 percent for displaced men.[73] These results suggest that job loss may hasten retirement. Further analysis is needed before this conclusion can be asserted with confidence, however.

The Netherlands

The results from the analyses of labor market transitions following displacement suggest that early retirement and DI have been used to facilitate displacement in the Netherlands. Recall, for example, that in the LFS data (Tables 2.13 and 2.15) at least some displaced workers withdrew from the labor force, either by early retirement or in DI, in the 1985–1990 period. The tables also indicate that this concerns at most 10 percent of all displaced workers. More surprisingly, the FE data (Table 2.14) attribute some role to both early retirement and DI in the 1993–1996 period, even though DI legislation had already undergone major changes to avoid improper use (see the institutional details provided earlier).

The improper use of DI and the role of early retirement have received ample attention in the Dutch policy debate, and numerous empirical studies on these issues exist. Although these usually do not focus on displaced workers per se, some of these papers offer insights that are useful in the context of displacement.

A series of papers has sought to explain the relatively high DI caseload in the Netherlands (see Hassink, van Ours, and Ridder 1997 for an overview). The data suggest that before the reforms in the late 1980s up to 50 percent of the DI inflow was related to "redundancy of workers" and not to actual health problems. This conclusion may appear rather extreme, but it is consistent with the relatively high DI rates in the Netherlands (see the earlier discussion of Dutch institutions). Hassink, van Ours, and Ridder, using an OSA panel survey of *firms,* estimated that in the late 1980s (after the 1980s reforms) there was still 10 percent of the DI inflow that was related to redundancy. Although these authors did not investigate DI in the 1990s, one can expect that the 1993 reforms have reduced this number even further.

Thio (1997) used data from a 1993 survey among elderly heads of households and their partners, conducted by the Centre for Economic Research on Retirement and Ageing, to sample heads of household,

53- to 63-year-olds, who were not working (were "retired") at the time of the interview, had been working at least up to age 40, and had been working for at least three months with their last employer. The data distinguish various self-reported reasons for retiring from their last job. One group of explanation corresponds to layoffs for economic reasons (displacement). Other categories are quits, health-related separations, separations related to working conditions, and separations for family reasons. The data also distinguish various exit routes for retirement, including early retirement and DI. In the sample of retired heads of households used, 37 percent were on DI and 43 percent were in early retirement. The average retirement age was 54 years.

In 96 percent of the DI cases, health was reported as a reason for retirement, and in 86 percent as the primary reason. In 24 percent of the DI cases, layoff was reported as a reason, but in only 8 percent as the primary reason. This seems consistent with the results found by Hassink, van Ours, and Ridder (1997): the average time between retirement and the survey was five years, implying that the results were roughly applicable to the late 1980s. Furthermore, since the data applied to the period before the major DI reform of 1993, the results were again likely to overestimate the current role of DI in facilitating adjustment to displacement. Of individuals in early retirement, 37 percent reported layoff as a reason for retirement, and 26 percent reported layoff as the primary reason. Thus, it seems that a significant share of the inflow into early retirement was related to displacement. Finally, it was shown that 60 percent of retirement due to layoffs, including those retired in UI and other schemes, was concentrated among 54- to 59-year-olds, and only 9 percent concerned individuals of age 60 and up.[74]

CONCLUSION

Discussion

This chapter analyzes the incidence and consequences of displacement in the United States and the Netherlands. For the United States, we provide an illustrative investigation using data from the February 1996 Current Population Survey and attached Displaced Worker Supplement. For the Netherlands, no equivalent to the Displaced Worker Supplements exists, and so displacement is studied using three longitudinal data sets: an administrative firm-worker data set, an administrative UI data set, and a labor-force panel survey.

Although the scope for direct comparisons between the United States and the Netherlands is limited by differences in the available data, several interesting comparisons can be drawn. First, the evidence indicates that displacement is a common event and occurs with roughly the same frequency in both countries: during the 1993–1995 period, between 3 and 4 percent of persons holding jobs lasting more than one year were estimated to have been permanently laid off and to have experienced at least some unemployment. Displacement probabilities are also lower for women than men and decline with job tenure in both nations. Termination rates are estimated to fall with age and education in each country. These effects may reflect other factors, however, and do not persist in the regression analysis provided for the Netherlands. Employment terminations also appear to hasten retirement or transition into disability status in both the United States and the Netherlands, and there is reason to believe that the consequences of displacement were less severe in the booming U.S. labor market of the mid 1990s than in earlier years. In contrast, displacement in the Netherlands seems to have been more frequent in the 1990s than in the 1970s and 1980s.

Patterns of non-employment following displacement exhibit intriguing differences and similarities for the two countries. As might be expected, terminated workers in the Netherlands are out of work for a much longer period of time, conditional on experiencing some joblessness. A much larger share of displaced workers move into alternative employment directly, however, without experiencing unemployment.[75] The lower Dutch reemployment hazard rates are consistent with the possibility that greater labor market rigidity and support during periods of joblessness reduce both the opportunity and the incentive to obtain new positions. The higher frequency of direct transitions into new jobs is harder to explain. Possibly the data are inadequate to make this comparison (the DWS data in the United States, for example, may miss many displacements that result in direct transitions to new employment). Alternatively, the employment protection provisions in the Netherlands may be more likely to restrict displacements to cases in which new jobs have already been obtained or are readily available.

Despite the aforementioned differences, there are many common patterns of post-termination joblessness in the two countries. For example, reemployment hazard rates decline with age and are lower for women (compared to men) in both nations. The data also suggest negative duration dependence in the United States and the Netherlands. Finally, the overall probabilities that displaced workers are reemployed within six months or one year are surprisingly similar in the two countries. These similarities suggest that there may be adjustment patterns following job loss that are common among many countries, and perhaps even universal, despite substantial differences in institutional arrangements.

It is difficult to compare the wage changes that follow job loss in the two countries. As already mentioned, one problem is that patterns of reemployment are so different in the United States and the Netherlands.[76] In the Netherlands, displaced workers experiencing positive non-employment spells are likely to be out of work for sufficiently lengthy periods to have sorting and stigma effects and loss of skills that significantly affect their labor market position per se (see Andersen 1997). This hampers the interpretation of empirical results on this wage difference.[77] Also, given the difficulties in getting a job once unemployed, workers in the Netherlands who expect displacement may have particularly strong incentives to search actively for another job while still employed. Consequently, some job-to-job transitions may be the result of anticipated displacement. Indeed, if unemployment durations are long, employment may be an even more important destination state following displacement.[78] Again, this suggests that issues like sorting are important and that workers moving directly into other jobs in the Netherlands may be quite different from their U.S. counterparts. Another problem is that only the data analyzed for the Netherlands allow for a comparison of displaced and nondisplaced workers. On the other hand, since sample sizes are small for the Netherlands, it is not possible to say much about how the experiences differ among groups.

This notwithstanding, it is noteworthy that there is no evidence that mean wages decline following displacement in either country. The point estimates actually show significantly higher subsequent earnings in the Netherlands and no change in the United States. This suggests that the losses in average earnings of reemployed workers should take the form of slower wage growth than for workers avoiding displacement, rather than of outright reductions in compensation (as is shown in the Dutch data). The variance of outcomes is substantial, however. For example, the U.S. evidence indicates that substantial earnings losses are experienced by older workers, those displaced from long-tenure jobs, and those whose earnings were originally relatively high compared to others with similar observable characteristics. Finally, the results suggest two important sources of risk beyond any expected changes in wages for reemployed workers. The first relates to uncertainty regarding duration of the spell of joblessness and the second to the substantial variance of subsequent earnings experienced by workers on their new jobs. These risks and the institutional arrangements for dealing with them are also related to the experiences of displaced individuals. For instance, Dutch workers who experience unemployment following displacement may have longer spells than their U.S. counterparts precisely because the Dutch social protections reduce the size of loss during periods of unemployment. This could result in reduced dispersion of postdisplacement wage changes, conditional on reemployment, because workers have less incentive to obtain new jobs that pay substantially less than their old ones.

Notes

We thank Peter Kuhn and Christian Dustmann for useful comments on earlier drafts of this chapter.

1. Displacement rates increased from about 4 percent in 1970 to 11 percent in 1993, according to a rough estimate based on the unemployment insurance (UI). Displacement rates are lower in 1994–1996, however, than in 1993. See the section on incidence for details.
2. Temporary layoffs may occur in less organized ways, however. Seasonally unemployed workers, for instance, can sometimes receive UI. Institutional details and a discussion of the consequences for our analysis are provided in later sections. Emerson (1988) discussed the role of temporary layoffs in various industrialized countries.
3. See Siebert (1997) and Nickell (1997) for recent, and somewhat conflicting, discussions of the role of labor market rigidities in explaining the disparate employment experiences of the United States and Europe.
4. Production workers averaged $12.39 per hour in September 1997 (U.S. Bureau of Labor Statistics 1998).
5. More detailed discussion of these issues are provided in Krueger (1991) and Dertouzos and Karoly (1993).
6. Generally individuals must have worked at least two quarters and earned a minimum amount (typically between $500 and $3000, depending on the state) during the year prior to the immediately completed calendar quarter. The claimant must also be available for, and able to, work if a "suitable" offer is received.
7. Most of the information in this and the next paragraph comes from the Committee on Ways and Means (1996).
8. For displaced workers, a somewhat larger fraction probably qualify for benefits. Data from the 1996 Displaced Worker Supplement indicates, for instance, that 44 percent of the 25- to 64-year olds losing jobs due to plant closings, slack work, or position or shift abolishment between 1993 and 1995 received UI.
9. Payments under TAA were much larger in earlier years, peaking at 532,000 persons and $1.6 billion in 1980.
10. Leigh (1995) and Kodrzycki (1997) provided useful summaries of these programs and their effectiveness.
11. The total budget for dislocated worker programs funded through the Employment and Training Administration of the Department of Labor was $1.1 billion in fiscal year 1996 (Office of Management and Budget 1998).
12. Minimum wages in the Netherlands are actually set as monthly wages. They can be transformed to hourly minimum wages by dividing the sector-specific normal working hours. The reported hourly minimum wage is valid for a 38 hour/week sector. For young workers up to 23 years of age, minimum wages are lower.

13. One of the data sets used in our analyses distinguishes between individuals employed under CAO contracts or AVVs and employees who are not covered by either of these. See the data section.
14. In recent years, so-called flexible contracts have been used increasingly. Such contracts do not specify working hours and correspond more closely to U.S. employment-at-will arrangements. In 1996, however, only 6 percent of all working hours were controlled by such flexible contracts (CBS 1998).
15. Note that employers have to avoid such "continued contracts" in several ways, by only offering new contracts after slightly more than 31 days. Although such contracts are not formally "continued contracts," employees have been successful in fighting such contracting behavior in court. Also note that, currently, laws are proposed that allow for more flexible fixed-term contracting, offering less protection to the employee.
16. In case of separation, advance-notice periods start after a permit has been granted and, if not specified otherwise in the contract, generally equal the time between two subsequent wage payments, as a base. This period is usually one month. In addition, however, the employer must give one week's notice for each year of the employee's tenure, up to a maximum of 13 weeks, with one additional week per year of tenure for employees of age 45–65, up to a maximum of 26 weeks. Advance-notice periods can be contracted, instead. However, such periods can never be excluded, nor can they exceed six months.
17. Actually, there are two laws, of 1949 and 1987, which were both revised in the 1990s.
18. We use administrative UI data for 1992–1993 in this chapter. To qualify as unemployed, the individual has to face a reduction of at least five hours of work per week or half of his original hours if he worked fewer than 10 hours per week.
19. For example, to get an initial benefit-entitlement period of five years, the unemployed worker has to have had jobs for at least 40 months, including at least three of the five years just prior to the start of the unemployment spell.
20. The extended benefits are equal to 70 percent of the gross minimum wage or 70 percent of the gross wage in the last job before unemployment, whichever is lower, and are again subject to income tax. Unemployed who have had jobs in the last three of the last five years are eligible for extended benefits, for a maximum duration of one year, or sometimes longer for older workers.
21. In general, welfare is applicable to all jobless not covered by UI, DI, or other schemes, and provides benefits at the subsistence level (currently around $500 after taxes per month for singles without children).
22. A UI recipient should 1) take actions to avoid staying unemployed—to search for a job and accept appropriate job offers, register as a job searcher at the public employment office, participate in education and training, etc., and 2) keep the administration informed about everything that is relevant to the payment of his UI benefits. For more details and references see Abbring, van den Berg, and van Ours (1997).

23. A small part of the cost of UI—roughly 50 percent of the costs induced by UI benefits paid during the first 13 weeks of unemployment—is covered by premiums related to sectoral unemployment risk.
24. DI is arranged by a variety of laws from 1967 (referring to a law from 1930), 1976, and 1993, and is revised throughout. Also, DI actually consists of two separate arrangements, one for the first 52 weeks of DI, and one for the remaining DI spell. In this chapter, we simply label both arrangements as DI. See CTSV (1997) for details.
25. It should be noted that Dutch DI also covers disability that is not work related, however.
26. Analysis of DWS data typically focuses on joblessness, rather than unemployment, since information on labor-force participation is not available.
27. For additional information on the Displaced Worker Supplements, as well as excellent reviews of research using these and other data sources, see Fallick 1996 or Kletzer 1998.
28. Researchers have used a variety of strategies in an attempt to surmount this shortcoming. For instance, displacement probabilities are sometimes calculated by assuming that the number of persons at risk of permanent layoff (the denominator of the displacement rate) is equal to the number employed at the survey date. Similarly, the quasi-longitudinal nature of the Current Population Survey Outgoing Rotation Group data has been used to construct estimates of the earnings changes of nondisplaced workers, which can then be compared to those of job losers. Farber (1993) is an example of a study using several of these techniques.
29. Studies using longitudinal data include Topel (1990); Ruhm (1991a); and Stevens (1997). Administrative data have been utilized by Jacobson, Lalonde, and Sullivan (1993) and Schoeni and Dardia (1996), among others.
30. Note that the structure of the FE data is similar to that of the Japanese data used in this volume.
31. The remaining spells are completed for quantitatively less important reasons like death, military service, self-employment, or permanent 100 percent benefit reductions because, for instance, of noncompliance with eligibility rules.
32. Thus, we do not miss transitions made between two consecutive interview dates, assuming recall errors are absent.
33. We exclude 46 individuals whose interviews are not successive. This reconstruction covers at most the five-year period 1985 until the end of 1990 for respondents who participated in all waves, and some retrospective information on the state occupied at the date of the first interview. See van den Berg, Lindeboom, and Ridder (1994) for an analysis of attrition using these data. They found that the effects of attrition on estimates of transition models are unimportant.
34. Unemployment and not-in-the-labor-force are differentiated by requiring those who are unemployed to actively search for a job.
35. Job-to-job changes are recorded. The motive or cause is selected from an extensive list.

36. Farber (1997) included in this category job loss for "other" reasons in his analysis. We have deleted persons in this category from our calculations. In a recent analysis of additional data collected on respondents to the 1996 DWS who report being displaced for "other" reasons, Farber (1998) concluded that fewer than one-quarter of persons giving this response had "involuntary" job losses (and some of these may have left temporary or seasonal jobs). It is also worth noting that workers whose contracts expire do not fit neatly into any of the DWS categories. These individuals might classify themselves as displaced for "other" reasons or, alternatively, say that their position has been abolished or that they have concluded a temporary job.
37. Using data from the Panel Study of Income Dynamics, Hall (1995) estimated the rate of permanent layoffs to be around 1.8 percent per quarter or roughly 7 percent per year. Using the same data source, Stevens (1997) estimates, however, that annual displacement rates are only around half as large. On the other hand, Hamermesh (1989) indicated that displacement rates were 20 to 40 percent higher in the 1980s than the 1970s.
38. The issue of multiple turnover was discussed in Ruhm (1987) and played a key role in the analysis made by Stevens (1997).
39. Farber (1997) estimated that 30 percent of persons losing jobs in a given year are again displaced at some point during the next three. Stevens (1997) estimated annual displacement rates of between 10 and 12 percent in the two years following an initial job loss.
40. Assume that 100 individuals are displaced in each year between 1993 and 1995. Under the second assumption above, 10 persons terminating jobs in 1994 will also have been displaced in 1993 and so only 90 of the job losses will be recorded in the 1996 DWS. Similarly, 10 of those terminated in 1995 will have had a 1993 job loss and 9 of them a 1994 displacement. Therefore, workers identified as displaced in 1995 will constitute 81 out of 271 sample members.
41. Men and women losing jobs in 1995 account for 46.2 and 48.5 percent of the 1996 DWS samples, implying inflation factors of 1.545 (0.462/0.299) and 1.622 (0.485/0.299) respectively. In the absence of recall bias, observed displacements might be concentrated in the later years if the rate of job loss actually increased over time. Given that the economy was improving, however (unemployment fell from 6.9 percent in 1993 to 5.6 percent in 1995), this seems unlikely.
42. A common inflation factor is used to account for the effects of recall bias, with no attempt made to differentiate as a function of job seniority. In fact, 58 percent of observed displacements involving those with less than one year of tenure occur in 1995, suggesting that recall bias is particularly severe for this group.
43. A multivariate analysis by Farber (1993) indicated a strong monotonic decline in the risk of job loss with tenure. Fallick (1996) summarized evidence suggesting that the protective effect of tenure decreases over time.
44. A more complete measure of aggregate displacement can be computed from the FE data on a much shorter time interval. This measure and its differences from the UI measure will be discussed later.

45. Note that we will show later that displacement rates are lower again in 1994–1996.
46. Analyses based on the FE data draw on results from a project on crowding out of low-skilled workers, in which three of the authors of this chapter are involved at the CPB Netherlands Bureau for Economic Policy Analysis in The Hague.
47. Note that we observe that workers are on a fixed-term contract only once they separate for that reason; so we cannot exclude these workers from the data set. This is not a serious problem, however, as we condition on tenure, which seems more relevant as a determinant of the risk set for displacement.
48. If, for example, Philips displaces all workers at its computer division and at the same time expands its audio and video divisions, we will underestimate the true displacement rate when we use the net employment criterion.
49. The relatively low displacement rate of the lowest tenure group could be an artifact of the FE sampling procedure, which undersamples workers who separate within a year (see the data section). Note that the FE data are administrative and cannot suffer from recall bias as the DWS possibly does. On the other hand, the nonmonotonicity could be explained by a learning model along the lines of Jovanovic (1979).
50. See the institutions section for a discussion of collective agreements in the Netherlands.
51. See the discussion of the role of sanctions in the data and transitions sections. We do not exclude low-tenure individuals. However, the UI eligibility requirements would prevent most of the low-tenure workers from ending up in UI. Also note that we will conclude later that a large proportion of displaced workers in the Netherlands experience no unemployment spells at all, which implies that the UI data may well underestimate the true displacement rate.
52. Displacements are also associated with lower employment probabilities for women, although the differences are less dramatic for men.
53. This is consistent with Gibbons and Katz's evidence (1991) that workers displaced by plant closings are reemployed more quickly than those losing jobs due to slack work or position or shift abolishment. They attributed this to the possibility that plant closings affect a relatively random group of workers, whereas the other types of job loss impact those of lower average quality.
54. Finding that advance notice is associated with the lower rates of joblessness but without reductions in durations, conditional on a positive spell, is common in this literature (see Addison and Portugal 1987; or Ehrenberg and Jakubson 1988). Ruhm (1992, 1994) provided evidence that persons with short written notice have longer spells and concluded that this occurs because firms disproportionately supply voluntary notice to workers with unobserved characteristics correlated with low reemployment probabilities. Previous research has also shown that union membership, high predisplacement earnings, and depressed local labor market conditions are associated with extended joblessness (see Fallick 1996 for examples). Estimation of corresponding Weibull hazard models reveals that baseline

rates decline over time. This could reflect either observed heterogeneity (where "better" workers get reemployed first) or duration dependence.

55. The total number of observations is smaller than in Table 2.13 because information on sojourn times was missing in some cases.
56. See, for instance, Lancaster (1979). The fact that median residual durations are now longer for displaced workers can possibly be traced back to heterogeneity in terms of unobserved and other observed characteristics. Earlier analyses of the same data by Abbring, van den Berg, and van Ours (1997) indeed did show that both negative genuine duration dependence and observed and unobserved heterogeneity play a significant role in explaining the observed duration dependency pattern.
57. Because of their flexibility and computational convenience, discrete distributions for unobservables are frequently used in MPH analyses. The flexibility of discrete distributions as heterogeneity or mixture of distributions was illustrated by a result of Heckman and Singer (1984) who showed that in MPH models the nonparametric maximum likelihood estimator or the heterogeneity distribution is a discrete distribution. The estimation procedure requires the number of points of support not to be fixed in advance, however, and the estimation of standard errors is not straightforward.
58. Recall, however, that unobserved differences between the two groups of individuals may interfere with this argument. The excess layoffs indicator, the "residual size of the cell," has a significantly positive effect on reemployment rates, which could be explained as a signaling effect. Workers who are involved in excess, or even mass, layoffs, are more attractive than workers who are singled out for layoff.
59. The table includes an Information Matrix (IM) test on the unobserved heterogeneity parameters (see White 1982). Chesher (1984) has shown that this test on the equality of the score and Hessian representations of the IM can be interpreted as a test of local parameter variation. In this case, the IM test can be expected to detect additional unobserved heterogeneity, and can be shown to be distributed with two degrees of freedom. Thus, the IM is rejected at just a 5 percent significance level. Adding an additional mass point to the heterogeneity distribution does not change the results, however, two mass points converge to the same value and other parameter estimates are unaffected.
60. The DWS does not contain information on hourly earnings. Crude controls for part-time versus full-time work are available, but these are not used in the analysis below because these changes are likely to be endogenous (e.g., some displaced workers may be unable to obtain full-time jobs).
61. During the 1993–1995 period, the civilian unemployment rate averaged 6.2 percent, 62.4 percent of the civilian population were employed, and real GDP grew 2.6 percent per year. The comparable figures for the 1990–1992 time span were 6.6, 62.0, and 1.0 percent. Herz (1990) and Farber (1997), among others, showed that workers adjust more easily to displacements occurring during booming periods than when economic conditions are less favorable. In addition, many of the

earlier analyses have been restricted to groups likely to experience relatively large wage losses, such as persons with more than three years' tenure.

62. No effort is made to control for selection into employment. Therefore these results should be interpreted as providing information on the determinants of wages (or earnings changes) conditional on survey-date employment.
63. Kletzer (1989), Addison and Portugal (1989), and Ruhm (1990), among others, provided earlier related analyses.
64. Other research also suggests the usefulness of distinguishing between general and specific human capital. For example, larger losses have been found for displaced workers who switch industries than for those who do not; see Kletzer (1998) for a detailed summary of this literature.
65. Gibbons and Katz (1991) indicated smaller displacement-induced losses for those affected by plant closings than for other job losers but, as mentioned, do not distinguish between slack work and position or shift abolishment.
66. Source: CBS (1998, 1991).
67. There are several reasons for this loss of observations. First, the starting date of the initial observed labor market state can be missing. In this case the different states cannot be linked to a calendar time, a necessity for the inflation correction. Second, the starting date may be inconsistent with the reported sojourn time, given the date of the first interview. Finally, one or more sojourn times may be missing.
68. Note that most observations are lost because tenure is missing: tenure is observed for 1,069 of the 1,551 observations. Of these 1,069 cases, 168 cases concern displacement. Of the 668 observations with sufficient tenure, 116 concern displacement, which is 69 percent of 168. This number is referred to in the discussion of the UI inflow measure later on.
69. The labor-force participation rates of 45- to 54- and 55- to 64-year-old men (women) were 89 and 67 (75 and 50) percent, respectively, in 1996 (U.S. Bureau of the Census 1997). In contrast, 35- to 44-year-olds were only marginally more likely than those age 45 to 54 to participate (92 percent of the men and 78 percent of the women). The lack of research on displacement and retirement is probably due to the difficulty in using the DWS for this type of analysis. The small bit of earlier literature that is relevant to this issue uncovered little evidence that displacements have strong effects on retirement ages.
70. Workers with less than a year on the predisplacement job are retained in this portion of the analysis because the end of even a brief job has the potential of creating considerable adjustment problems for older workers. In addition, information on prior tenure is unavailable for nondisplaced workers, making it difficult to undertake the comparison procedure discussed next.
71. To reduce fluctuations due to small sample sizes (particularly for displaced workers) the probabilities are actually calculated as three-year averages centered around the specific age (for example, the retirement or disability rate for "60-year-olds" is actually the average retirement or disability rate of 59- to 61-year-olds).

72. These conditional probabilities are analogous but not identical to hazard rates. They differ in part because 1) some men who are initially nonparticipants might reenter the labor force during the compensation period; 2) "lagged" status is calculated for slightly younger workers in 1996, rather than for the same cohort of men in an earlier year; 3) there can be some movement over time between "other" reasons for nonparticipation and retirement or disability.
73. The unconditional retirement or disability probabilities for nondisplaced men are 15, 29, and 58 percent.
74. By construction of the data set, the remainder is in the 40–53 age group.
75. Layard, Nickell, and Jackman (1991, chap. 5, Table 1) provided a steady state estimate of unemployment durations of around three months for 1988 for both countries. Furthermore, their Table 2 showed that this is fairly typical of the period 1962–1989. In the Netherlands, however, mean unemployment durations are usually longer than one year: Layard, Nickell, and Jackman even gave a steady state estimate of 25 months for 1988. Also, median reemployment durations of displaced workers in our 1992 UI data set for the Netherlands (20 weeks; see Table 2.16) are substantially longer than median reemployment durations in our U.S. data set (7 weeks). This is remarkable, as our data set excludes workers entering other schemes and hardly ever returning to employment, and includes at least some short-tenure workers, who can be expected to be more mobile.
76. These problems have recently been encountered by Cohen, Lefranc, and Saint-Paul (1997), who compared the U.S. and French labor markets. Using the Enquete Emploi, collected by the INSEE, for France and the Panel Study of Income Dynamics for the United States, they found that wage discounts after displacement are roughly the same in both countries. The discussion following the paper, however, showed that it is not easy to draw and clear conclusions from this.
77. An additional empirical problem is that the postdisplacement wage will frequently be unobserved for these workers due to right-censored unemployment spells.
78. Of course, workers in the United States also have incentives to avoid unemployment and to find new jobs prior to job loss, but they are generally weaker incentives.
79. See the section on labor market transitions following displacement. We exclude individuals who are living abroad.
80. This may be due to DI legislation, however. Partly disabled workers have to find a job for their remaining work capacity because of a rule that came into effect in 1987. We cannot distinguish these cases, but the rule only affects observations in part of our observation period (see Hassink, van Ours, and Ridder 1997).

Table 2.1 Netherlands: Overview of the Data Sets

Data set	FE data	LFS	UI data
Unit of observation	Firm/worker	Household (hh.)/individ. (i.)	UI case
Type of data	Administrative	Survey	Administrative
Sampling scheme	2-yr. rotating panel 4 waves (1991–92, 1992–93, 1993–94, 1994–95)	Random panel 4 waves (1985, 1986, 1988, 1990)	Inflow sample UI inflow 1992 (spells followed up to Sept. 1993)
No. of observations	Approx. 2,000 firms/26,000 workers per year	2,132 hh./4,020 i. in the first wave	209,478 cases
Key feature	Worker transitions into and out of firms	Full individual labor market histories	Transitions into and out of UI
Displacement criterion	Separations labeled as layoffs and those from shrinking firms	Layoffs for economic reasons	UI inflow (minus sanctions responsibility for job loss)
Tenure restriction	Tenure ≥1 yr.	Tenure ≥1 yr.	Entitlement to UI
Information on			
displacement rate	Yes	No	No[a]
Transitions following displacement	Yes	No	No
Prob. positive spell joblessness	Upper bound[b]	Yes	No
Reemployment duration	No	Yes[c]	Yes

Labor market state after 1 yr.	No	Yes	No[d]
Role of early retirement or DI	Some[e]	Some[e]	No
Earnings changes induced by displacement	No	Yes	No

[a] However, the corresponding aggregate time series on UI inflow over the period 1970–93 are used to construct displacement-rate time series.

[b] Only for displacement identified by separations from shrinking firms, some job-to-job transitions are recorded; thus the probability of a positive spell of joblessness is overestimated.

[c] The LFS data are not used here, however, because of the superiority of the UI data for this purpose.

[d] We observe whether an individual leaves UI and why (i.e., to what labor market state), but not the subsequent labor market transitions made.

[e] These data can be used to construct circumstantial evidence, but we employ results from other studies using data that are better suited to analyze these issues.

Table 2.2 United States: "Lower-Bound" Estimates of Annual Displacement Rates (%)

Time period	All workers	Men	Women
1981–83	3.8	4.4	3.0
1983–85	3.0	3.4	2.5
1985–87	2.7	3.1	2.2
1987–89	2.4	2.6	2.1
1989–91	3.4	4.0	2.8
1991–93	3.2	3.6	2.7
1993–95	3.1	3.4	2.8

NOTE: The table refers to job loss among 20- to 64-year-olds (at the survey date) due to plant closing, slack work, or position or shift abolishments.

SOURCE: Estimates obtained by dividing by three the estimates for three-year displacement rates calculated by Farber (1997).

Table 2.3 United States: Estimated Annual Displacement Rates during the 1993–95 Period by Predisplacement Job Tenure (%)

Tenure (yr.)	All workers	Men	Women
All displacements[a,b]			
All	4.9	5.3	4.5
<1	5.9	6.7	5.1
>1	4.6	4.9	4.3
1–2	9.9	10.9	9.0
3–4	4.7	5.6	4.0
5–9	3.5	4.0	3.0
≥10	2.7	2.5	2.9
Displacements resulting in joblessness[c]			
All	4.2	4.5	3.9
<1	5.1	5.7	4.4
>1	3.9	4.2	3.7
1–2	8.5	9.3	7.7
3–4	4.0	4.8	3.5
5–9	3.0	3.4	2.6
≥10	2.3	2.1	2.5

NOTE: Estimates for overall and gender-specific annual displacement rates are obtained using the lower-bound displacement rates in Table 2.2 and then inflating them via the procedure discussed in the text.

[a] Tenure-specific rates are calculated by multiplying the overall displacement rate by the ratio of the fraction of displaced workers with the specified amount of tenure divided by the franction of all workers with that amount of tenure. For example, the displacement rate for persons with 1–2 years of seniority is calculated as 0.049 x 0.268/0.132 = 0.099.

[b] Results for all types of permanent job loss.

[c] Restricted to displacements resulting in an initial spell of joblessness.

Table 2.4 United States: Estimated Annual Displacement Rates during the 1993–95 Period by Age (%)

Age (yr.)	All displacements	Displacements resulting in joblessness
All	4.9	4.2
20–24	5.5	4.7
25–34	5.3	4.5
35–44	4.7	4.0
45–54	4.4	3.8
55–64	4.1	3.5

NOTE: Estimates for overall displacement rates are obtained from Table 2.3. Age-specific rates are calculated by adjusting the overall rate by the relative age-specific differences in displacement probabilities calculated by Farber (1997).

Table 2.5 Netherlands: Reported Labor Market States of Workers at Strongly Shrinking Firms, 1993–96 (% of Employment at all Firms)

Criterion		Firms (%)[a]	Layoff[b]	New job[b]	Early retirement[b]	DI[b]	Displacement[c]
Employment	–20%	16.0	0.6	0.7	0.1	0.0	4.8
(net change)	–30%	9.4	0.4	0.4	0.1	0.0	3.8
	–40%	4.7	0.2	0.3	0.0	0.0	3.5
Outflow	–20%	50.3	1.5	2.4	0.2	0.1	7.2
(gross change)	–30%	32.4	1.0	1.7	0.2	0.1	5.9
	–40%	19.5	0.7	1.2	0.1	0.0	5.1

NOTE: Workers older than 60 years are excluded, as are workers with less than one year's tenure.

[a] Firm shares are computed among firms with workers in the selected category.

[b] Separations only from strongly shrinking firms added to annual displacement rates.

[c] Total displacement as a percentage of total employment. Displacement includes "layoffs" (excluding layoffs during test periods) at all firms, plus transitions into "new jobs," "early retirement," and "DI" at strongly shrinking firms.

SOURCE: Based on weighted FE data.

Table 2.6 Annual Displacement Rates by Tenure during the 1993–95 Period (%)

Tenure (yr.)	All workers	Men	Women
All	4.1	4.2	4.0
<1	5.8	6.3	5.2
1–2	8.1	9.2	6.7
3–4	4.7	5.2	4.0
5–9	3.0	3.0	2.9
≥10	1.9	1.9	2.0

NOTE: Workers older than 60 are excluded. Displacement is identified with "layoffs" (excluding "layoffs during test periods") at any firm, plus transitions into "new jobs," "early retirement," and "DI" at firms with net employment changes < –30%.
SOURCE: Based on weighted FE data.

Table 2.7 Netherlands: Displacement and Other Separation Frequencies 1993–96 (%)

Variable	No transition	Displaced	Other outflow
All	88.3	3.8	7.8
Year			
1993	87.2	7.6	5.2
1994	89.8	2.9	7.4
1995	88.3	3.6	8.1
1996	88.1	1.7	10.2
Gender			
Female	87.0	3.6	9.4
Male	89.1	3.9	7.0
Tenure (yr.)			
<1	88.0	4.5	7.5
1–2	81.7	6.8	11.5
3–4	87.1	4.0	9.0
5–10	91.3	2.6	6.1
>10	93.9	1.7	4.4
Coll. agreement			
CAO[a]	88.8	3.6	7.7
AVV[b]	85.8	5.2	9.0
None	87.3	4.3	8.4
Job complexity level			
Low	82.6	5.7	11.8
Intermediate	89.5	3.4	7.1
High	91.3	3.3	5.4
Education (yr.)			
≤10	87.4	4.3	8.4
>10 – <15	89.9	3.1	7.1
≥15	89.6	3.3	7.1
Age (yr.)			
18–19	72.3	10.7	17.0

(continued)

Table 2.7 (continued)

Variable	No transition	Displaced	Other outflow
20–29	83.0	5.8	11.2
30–39	89.7	3.4	6.9
40–49	93.0	2.6	4.4
≥50	90.4	2.1	7.5

NOTE: Workers older than 60 are excluded, as are workers with less than one year's tenure (except in the row giving results for these workers). Displacement is identified with "layoff" (excluding "layoffs during test periods") at any firm, plus transitions into "new jobs," "early retirement," and "DI" at firms with net employment changes < –30%.

[a] Covered by a collective agreement.

[b] Covered by a mandatory extension of a CAO.

SOURCE: Based on weighted FE data.

Table 2.8 Netherlands: Logit Estimates of Probability of Displacement

Variable[a]	Estimate	(std. error)
Intercept	–11.21***	(2.58)
log Age	8.15***	(1.62)
(log Age)^2	–1.13***	(0.23)
Woman	–0.36***	(0.05)
log Tenure	–0.54***	(0.05)
(log Tenure)^2	0.02	(0.02)
log Wage	–2.52***	(0.31)
(log Wage)^2	0.20***	(0.05)
Part-time	–0.24***	(0.05)
Education (yr.)	0.00	(0.01)
Job complexity		
Low	–0.72***	(0.10)
Intermediate	–0.68***	(0.08)
Occupation		
Simple technical	0.09	(0.16)
Administrative	0.30**	(0.15)
Management	–0.06	(0.17)
Services	0.14	(0.16)
Commercial	0.20	(0.16)
Creative	0.19	(0.21)
Wage agreement[b]		
CAO	–0.00	(0.05)
AVV	–0.05	(0.08)
Sector		
Manufacturing	0.20*	(0.11)
Construction	0.44***	(0.11)
Trade	–0.16	(0.11)
Restaurants, etc.	0.39***	(0.14)
Transport, comm.	–0.03	(0.13)
Financial	0.16	(0.12)

(continued)

Table 2.8 (continued)

Variable[a]	Estimate	(std. error)
Health	–0.12	(0.11)
Firm size[c]		
10–19	–0.26***	(0.06)
20–49	–0.42***	(0.06)
50–99	–0.56***	(0.07)
100–199	–0.49***	(0.06)
200–499	–0.24***	(0.06)
≥500	0.48***	(0.05)
Year = 1993	1.46***	(0.06)
Year = 1994	0.38***	(0.06)
Year = 1995	1.07***	(0.06)
log L	–32,842.81	
N	100,908	

NOTE: Logit estimates with dependent states "displaced" and "not displaced" (reference state). Workers older than 60 or with tenure less than one year are excluded. Displacement is identified with "layoffs" (excluding "layoffs during test periods") at any firm, plus transitions into "new jobs," "early retirement," and "DI" at firms with net employment changes < –30%. Wages are real gross hourly wages (in Dutch guilders) including extra time payments, profit sharing, etc. *** = statistically significant at the 1% level; ** = statistically significant at the 5% level; * = statistically significant at the 10% level.

[a] Age and tenure are measured in years. Reference states are "male," "full-time," "high job complexity," "IT," "no collective wage agreement," "agriculture/mining," "firm with < 10 workers," and "year = 1996."

[b] "CAO" refers to coverage by a collective agreement, "AVV" to coverage by a mandatory extension of such an agreement.

[c] Firm size is measured by the number of employees.

SOURCE: Based on weighted FE data.

Table 2.9 Netherlands: Simulated Annual Displacement Probabilities (%)

Variable	Not displaced	Displaced
Total population	97.8	2.2
Year		
1993	95.3	4.7
1994	98.4	1.6
1995	96.8	3.2
1996	98.9	1.1
Gender		
Female	98.2	1.8
Male	97.4	2.5
Tenure (yr.)		
1	95.0	5.0
2	96.5	3.5
4	97.5	2.5
10	98.3	1.7
20	98.8	1.2
Wage agreement[a]		
CAO	97.8	2.2
AVV	97.9	2.1
No collective wage agreement	97.8	2.2
Job-complexity level		
Low	98.0	2.0
Intermediate	98.0	2.0
High	96.0	4.0
Age (yr.)		
20	98.1	1.8
30	97.5	2.5
40	97.4	2.6
50	97.7	2.3

(continued)

Table 2.9 (continued)

Variable	Not displaced	Displaced
Wage (guilders)		
15	95.7	4.3
20	97.0	3.0
40	98.7	1.3
50	98.9	1.1

NOTE: Based on logit estimates (see Table 2.8), evaluated at the mean characteristics of the population over the period 1993–96. Displacement is identified with "layoffs" (excluding "layoffs during test periods") at any firm, plus transitions into "new jobs," "early retirement," and "DI" at firms with net employment changes < –30%.

[a] "CAO" refers to coverage by a collective agreement, "AVV" to coverage by a mandatory extension of such an agreement.

Table 2.10 United States: Duration of Postdisplacement Joblessness

	All displacements		Displacements resulting in joblessness	
	% reemployed within		% reemployed within	
Variable	6 mo.	1 yr.	6 mo.	1 yr.
All displaced workers	67.3	76.1	61.0	71.7
Gender				
Male	69.7	77.8	63.5	73.2
Female	64.0	74.3	57.7	69.8
Age (yr.)				
20–29	70.9	78.0	66.5	75.7
30–39	72.4	79.6	66.7	75.4
40–49	67.8	79.0	61.5	74.8
50–54	58.8	68.9	50.3	62.5
55–59	52.7	63.0	42.3	54.8
60–64	44.0	53.0	34.5	45.1
Job tenure (yr.)				
1–2	70.0	77.8	65.2	74.2
3–4	66.6	76.5	61.1	72.7
5–9	67.7	74.4	60.4	68.7
≥10	64.2	76.0	55.8	70.4

NOTE: Data are weighted so as to be nationally representative.The data apply to workers who were 20 to 64 years old at the survey date and were displaced from jobs lasting more than one year in 1993 or 1994.

SOURCE: From the February 1996 Displaced Worker Supplement.

Table 2.11 United States: Labor-Force Status of Displaced Workers (%)

Variable	Employed	Unemployed	Out of labor force
All displaced workers	73.7	14.7	11.6
Gender			
Male	76.5	16.5	6.9
Female	69.9	12.3	17.8
Age (yr.)			
20–29	77.9	15.2	7.0
30–39	77.3	12.0	10.7
40–49	76.5	14.5	9.0
50–54	66.2	19.5	14.3
55–59	58.8	18.1	23.1
60–64	42.6	19.6	37.8
Job tenure (yr.)			
1–2	73.6	16.2	10.2
3–4	74.7	12.8	12.6
5–9	76.6	14.7	8.7
≥10	70.0	15.0	15.2

NOTE: The table shows the labor-force status in February 1996 of 20- to 64-year-old persons displaced from jobs lasting more than one year during the 1993–95 period.

SOURCE: Data are from the 1996 Displaced Worker Supplement and are weighted so as to be nationally representative.

Table 2.12 United States: Econometric Estimates of the Determinants of Postdisplacement Joblessness

Regressor	Probability of no joblessness[a]		Duration of joblessness			
			Conditional[b]		Unconditional[c]	
Job tenure (yr.)						
3–4	0.047	(0.089)	0.116	(0.073)	0.028	(0.055)
5–9	0.052	(0.090)	–0.017	(0.075)	0.006	(0.090)
≥10	0.095	(0.096)	–0.054*	(0.083)	–0.007	(0.073)
Age (yr.)						
30–39	–0.052	(0.094)	–0.118	(0.078)	–0.107	(0.069)
40–49	–0.134	(0.099)	–0.185**	(0.082)	–0.184**	(0.072)
50–54	–0.212	(0.133)	–0.479***	(0.113)	–0.442***	(0.100)
55–59	–0.138	(0.146)	–0.704***	(0.137)	–0.583***	(0.117)
60–64	–0.353*	(0.190)	–1.12***	(0.187)	–1.01***	(0.163)
Education						
High school grad.	0.321**	(0.134)	0.271***	(0.105)	0.303***	(0.096)
Some college	0.341**	(0.135)	0.319***	(0.105)	0.345***	(0.096)
College grad.	0.394***	(0.144)	0.387***	(0.115)	0.416***	(0.104)
Grad. school	0.480***	(0.170)	0.304**	(0.140)	0.381***	(0.125)
Married	0.135*	(0.069)	0.027	(0.058)	0.059***	(0.051)
Man	–0.007	(0.065)	0.231***	(0.055)	0.182***	(0.049)
Nonwhite	–0.285**	(0.113)	–0.188**	(0.087)	–0.228***	(0.080)
Native born	0.387***	(0.131)	–0.006	(0.090)	0.093	(0.084)
Source of job loss						
Plant closing	0.066	(0.084)	0.072	(0.058)	0.075	(0.060)
Slack work	0.034	(0.087)	0.010	(0.073)	0.021	(0.065)
Written notice (months)						
<1	–0.018	(0.112)	–0.036	(0.095)	–0.033	(0.084)

(continued)

Table 2.12 (continued)

Regressor	Probability of no joblessness[a]		Duration of joblessness			
			Conditional[b]		Unconditional[c]	
1–2	–0.139	(0.108)	–0.139	(0.086)	–0.154**	(0.078)
>2	0.209 **	(0.089)	–0.048	(0.082)	0.039	(0.070)

NOTE: Standard errors are in parentheses. The sample includes persons displaced from jobs lasting more than one year in 1993, 1994, or 1995 who were between the ages of 20 and 64 in February 1996. The reference groups for the sets of dummy variables are persons with 1–2 years of tenure on the predisplacement job, 20- to 29-year-olds, high school dropouts, those losing jobs due to a position or shift abolishment, and those with no written advance notice. *** = Statistically significant at the 1% level; ** = statistically significant at the 5% level; * = statistically significant at the 10% level.

[a] This column shows the results of a probit model where the dependent variable is equal to 1 if the respondent obtains a new job within one week of the displacement and zero otherwise.

[b] This column indicates coefficients for a Cox proportional hazard model where the dependent variable is weeks of joblessness and the sample is restricted to persons out of work for at least one week following displacement.

[c] This column shows results for a Cox proportional hazard model estimated over all displaced workers where the dependent variable is weeks of joblessness plus one-half week.

SOURCE: From the 1996 Displaced Worker Supplement.

Table 2.13 Netherlands: Displacement by Motivation and Transition

Worker category		Motivation[a] 1	2	3	4	5	All
Transition[b]	*E-E*	30	162	1	37	—	230
	E-U	6	47	0	15	—	68
	E-N	7	14	3	—	5	29
All		43	223	4	52	5	327
Workers with tenure ≥1 year							
Transition[b]	*E-E*	19	76	1	17	—	113
	E-U	1	21	0	10	—	32
	E-N	2	11	1	—	3	17
All		22	108	2	27	3	162

NOTE: Rows correspond to self-reported combinations of motivation for and voluntariness of transition.

[a] 1 = "would have lost job anyway"; 2 = "reorganization or plant closure"; 3 = "involuntary early retirement"; 4 = "DI"; and 5 = "voluntary disability" (E-N only).

[b] E-E = job-to-job transitions, E-U = employment-to-unemployment transitions, and E-N = employment-to-not-in-labor-force transition.

SOURCE: Based on the LFS.

Table 2.14 Netherlands: Reported Labor Market States of Separated Workers by Net Employment Change (%)

Group of firms	Layoff	New job	Early retirement	DI
Net employment changes < –30%				
All workers	24.9	19.4	2.9	1.9
Outflow	44.3	34.5	5.1	1.8
Other firms				
All workers	3.3	4.6	0.5	0.4
Outflow	31.0	43.4	4.9	3.5

NOTE: Workers older than 60 and workers with tenure less than one year have been excluded.

SOURCE: Based on weighted FE data.

Table 2.15 Netherlands: Labor Market State One Year after Displacement by Transition

Worker category		Labor market state[a]						
		E	*S*	*U*	*N*	*M*	*F*	All
Transition[b]	*E-E*	143	0	3	1	0	0	147
	E-U	17	2	27	1	0	1	48
	E-N	4	0	0	18	0	0	22
All		164	2	30	20	0	1	217
Workers with tenure ≥1 year								
Transition[b]	*E-E*	75	0	1	1	0	0	77
	E-U	6	1	17	0	0	1	25
	E-N	2	0	0	12	0	0	14
All		83	1	18	13	0	1	116

[a] *E* = "employed"; *S* = "self-employed"; *U* = "unemployed and searching"; *N* = "not-in-labor-force"; *M* = "military service"; and *F* = "full-time education."

[b] *E-E* = job-to-job transitions, *E-U* = employment-to-unemployment transitions, and *E-N* = employment-to-not-in-the-labor-force.

SOURCE: Based on the LFS.

Table 2.16 Netherlands: Median Residual Reemployment Durations (weeks)

Worker category	At 0 weeks	At 26 weeks
All workers	20.8	102.9
Sanction indicator		
Nondisplaced	23.9	86.2
Displaced	20.4	104.6
Displaced workers		
Age (yr.)		
<30	14.0	77.4
30≤ – <40	23.2	91.3
30≤ – <50	27.2	∞ [a]
≥50	∞	∞
Daily wage (guilders)		
<80	22.0	93.2
80≤ – <110	26.6	106.9
110≤ – <150	15.5	97.7
≥150	21.4	∞
Gender		
Female	25.8	93.3
Male	17.2	105.4
Urbanization		
Urban	25.5	100.0
Not urban	19.7	106.5
Hours		
Part-time	29.9	101.5
Full-time	18.0	107.9
Marital status		
Married	32.3	109.2
Not married	15.4	92.0

NOTE: Durations are observed in intervals and may be right-censored. Medians are computed using the actuarial method, i.e., assuming that censoring and reemployment durations are uniformly distributed within observational intervals.

[a] ∞ is used to denote medians larger than the longest completed spell observed, i.e., that are beyond the scope of the data set.

SOURCE: Based on the UI data.

Table 2.17 Netherlands: Mixed Proportional Hazard Estimates of Reemployment Durations

Variable[a]	Estimate (std. error)	
Nondisplaced (sanction)	–0.18***	(0.04)
Sanctions/cell member[b]	0.01	(0.07)
Predicted size cell ($\hat{c}$)	–1.42***	(0.15)
Residual size cell ($\hat{\mathcal{E}}$)	0.35***	(0.05)
log Age[c]	0.89***	(0.28)
$(\log \text{Age})^2$	–0.93***	(0.12)
log Wage[d]	0.18***	(0.03)
$(\log \text{Wage})^2$	0.09***	(0.02)
Right-censored wage[e]	–0.48***	(0.15)
Female	–0.09***	(0.02)
Urban	–0.01	(0.05)
Part-time	–0.00	(0.03)
Married	–0.15***	(0.03)
v_1	–2.80***	(0.19)
v_2	–3.74***	(0.15)
p_1	0.40**	(0.16)
p_2	0.60***	(0.16)
8–16 weeks	–0.13***	(0.04)
16–24 weeks	–0.26***	(0.05)
24–32 weeks	–0.43***	(0.06)
32–45 weeks	–0.80***	(0.07)
45–58 weeks	–1.05***	(0.10)
>58 weeks	–1.05***	(0.12)
log L	–40,739.8	
N	21,079	

Test	Statistic (d.f.)
IM mixing dist.[f]	6.95 (2)
Wald sectors	628.99 (16)

Test	Statistic (d.f.)
Wald months	108.54 (11)
Wald provinces	20.75 (11)

NOTE: Sector, month of inflow, and province dummy variables are included. *** = Statistically significant at the 1% level; ** = statistically significant at the 5% level.

[a] All variables are included in deviation from their sample means. Reference interval for the piecewise constant baseline hazard is 0–8 weeks.

[b] Cell refers to municipality × month of inflow UI × sector – groups. The sanction rate in each cell is included as a regressor. Also, the number of individuals in each cell is regressed on municipality, month of inflow UI, and sector dummies, which gives predicted cell counts $\hat{c}$ and residuals $\hat{\varepsilon}$.

[c] "Age" = age/10.

[d] Wage is daily wage in referral period in 100 Dutch guilders.

[e] Wages are right-censored at 430 guilders.

[f] IM = a test statistic for local parameter variation in (v_1, v_2), or, equivalently, (v_1, v_2, p_1, p_2); Wald-tests for the joint significance of the three groups of dummy variables. All tests are asymptotically χ^2 distributed with the degrees of freedom given in parentheses.

SOURCE: Based on the UI data.

Table 2.18 Netherlands: Simulated Reemployment Probabilities

Variable	Pr($t \leq 26$ weeks)	Pr($t \leq 52$ weeks)
Sample mean	0.54	0.72
Sanction indicator		
Nondisplaced	0.49	0.66
Displaced	0.55	0.73
Age (yr.)		
20	0.70	0.86
30	0.58	0.76
40	0.44	0.61
50	0.32	0.46
Daily wage (guilders)		
50	0.50	0.68
100	0.53	0.71
150	0.56	0.74
200	0.59	0.77
Gender		
Female	0.52	0.70
Male	0.56	0.74
Urbanization		
Urban	0.54	0.72
Not urban	0.54	0.72
Hours		
Part-time	0.54	0.72
Full-time	0.54	0.72
Marital status		
Married	0.51	0.69
Not married	0.56	0.74

NOTE: Probabilities are computed using the model estimates of Table 2.17. The sample mean is computed at the mean of the regressors in the sample used for estimation and the estimated mean of the unobserved heterogeneity component. All other rows correspond to single deviations from this mean.

Table 2.19 United States: Ratio of Average Survey Date and Predisplacement Weekly Earnings

Category	Conditional on survey date employment	Unconditional
All displaced workers	1.00	0.70
Initial jobless spell (weeks)		
0	1.19	1.14
>0	0.95	0.62
Gender		
Female	0.95	0.64
Male	1.03	0.75
Age (yr.)		
20–29	1.20	0.90
30–39	0.98	0.73
40–49	0.90	0.66
50–54	0.92	0.56
55–59	0.90	0.49
60–64	1.18	0.46
Job tenure (yr.)		
1–2	1.11	0.77
3–4	1.05	0.76
5–9	1.00	0.74
≥10	0.81	0.53
Year of displacement		
1993	0.96	0.75
1994	1.04	0.78
1995	0.99	0.62

NOTE: The table shows average values of the ratio of survey date (February 1996) to predisplacement weekly wages, both measured in February 1996 dollars, using the all-items Consumer Price Index to adjust for price changes. The sample includes persons aged 20–64 at the survey date who lost jobs lasting more than one year in 1993, 1994, or 1995 due to slack work, plant closing, or position or shift abolishment.

SOURCE: Data are from the 1996 Displaced Workers Supplement and are weighted so as to be nationally representative.

Table 2.20 Distribution of the Ratio of Survey Date to Predisplacement Wages

	All displaced workers		25- to 49-year-old men	
Wage ratio	Conditional[a]	Unconditional	Conditional	Unconditional
<0.75	0.323	0.523	0.276	0.449
0.75–0.89	0.136	0.096	0.134	0.102
0.9–1.09	0.262	0.184	0.286	0.218
1.1–1.25	0.096	0.068	0.105	0.080
>1.25	0.184	0.129	0.199	0.151

NOTE: The table shows the distribution of the ratio of survey date (February 1996) to predisplacement weekly wages. Predisplacement earnings are in February 1996 dollars, using the all-items Consumer Price Index to adjust for price changes. The sample includes persons aged 20–64 at the survey date who lost jobs lasting more than one year in 1993, 1994, or 1995 due to slack work, plant closing, or a position or shift abolishment.

[a] The conditional estimates are for reemployed workers only.

SOURCE: Data are from the 1996 Displaced Workers Supplement and are weighted so as to be nationally representative.

Table 2.21 United States: Econometric Estimates of the Determinants of Postdisplacement Earnings and Earnings Changes

Regressor[a]	Postdisplacement wages (1)[b]		(2)[c]		Change in wages (3)[d]	
Job tenure (yr.)						
3–4	0.062	(0.047)	0.039	(0.044)	–0.031	(0.047)
5–9	0.091**	(0.049)	0.018	(0.046)	–0.024	(0.049)
≥10	0.087	(0.054)	–0.081	(0.051)	–0.187***	(0.054)
Age (yr.)						
30–39	0.127**	(0.050)	–0.045	(0.048)	–0.153***	(0.050
40–49	0.142***	(0.053)	–0.041	(0.051)	–0.061***	(0.053)
50–54	0.067	(0.073)	–0.087	(0.069)	–0.181***	(0.073
55–59	0.018	(0.085)	–0.177**	(0.080)	–0.283***	(0.085)
60–64	–0.197*	(0.118)	–0.286***	(0.111	–0.345***	(0.119)
Education						
High school grad.	0.215***	(0.069)	0.081	(0.064)	–0.002	(0.068)
Some college	0.383***	(0.070)	0.144*	(0.065)	0.007	(0.069)
College grad.	0.546***	(0.075)	0.237***	(0.071)	0.027	(0.074)
Grad. school	0.766***	(0.091)	0.325***	(0.086)	0.029	(0.089)
Married	0.025	(0.037)	0.010	(0.035)	0.000	(0.037)
Male	–0.428***	(0.036)	0.201***	(0.036)	0.041	(0.036)
Nonwhite	–0.050	(0.057)	0.030	(0.055)	0.045	(0.058)
Native born	–0.010	(0.060)	–0.022	(0.057)	–0.048	(0.061)
Source of job loss						
Plant closing	–0.050	(0.043)	–0.010	(0.041)	0.039	(0.043)
Slack work	–0.026	(0.047)	0.061	(0.044)	0.120***	(0.047)
Written notice (mo.)						
<1	–0.045	(0.061)	–0.054	(0.057)	–0.056	(0.061)
1–2	0.025	(0.057)	0.002	(0.054)	–0.007	(0.058)
>2	0.023	(0.051)	–0.012	(0.048)	–0.050	(0.051)

(continued)

Table 2.21 (continued)

	Postdisplacement wages				Change in wages	
Regressor[a]	(1)[b]		(2)[c]		(3)[d]	
Year of displacement						
1994	–0.041	(0.043)	–0.013	(0.041)	0.016	(0.044)
1995	–0.075*	(0.042)	–0.039	(0.039)	–0.009	(0.042)
Union	0.032	(0.052)	–0.021	(0.049)	–0.061	(0.052)
Predisplacement wage	—		0.599***	(0.029)	—	

NOTE: Standard errors are in parentheses. The sample includes persons between the ages of 20 and 64 who were displaced from jobs lasting more than one year in 1993, 1994, or 1995 and were reemployed in February 1996. *** = Statistically significant at the 1% level; ** = statistically significant at the 5% level; * = statistically significant at the 10% level.

[a] The reference groups for the sets of dummy variables are persons with 1–2 years' tenure on the predisplacement job, 20- to 29-year-olds, high school dropouts, those losing jobs due to position or shift abolishments, and those with no written advance notice.

[b] The dependent variable is the natural log of weekly wages at the survey date. Predisplacement wage is not included as a regressor.

[c] The dependent variable is the natural log of weekly wages at the survey date. Predisplacement wage is included as a regressor.

[d] The dependent variable is the difference in (the natural logs of) weekly wages at the survey date and prior to displacement, both in February 1996 dollars.

SOURCE: Data are from the 1996 Displaced Worker Supplement.

Table 2.22 Netherlands: Estimates of Changes in Earnings after Displacement

Variable	All workers				Workers with tenure ≥1 yr.[b]	
	No tenure criterion		Tenure 1 yr. min.			
	estimate	(std. error)	estimate	(std. error)	estimate	(std. error)
Constant	0.160***	(0.036)	0.197***	(0.038)	0.199***	(0.046)
log Tenure[a]	0.016*	(0.009)	–0.011	(0.015)	–0.025	(0.018)
(log Tenure)2[b]	–0.004	(0.005)	0.001	(0.005)	0.009	(0.016)
log Age[c]	–0.101*	(0.053)	–0.087	(0.053)	0.002	(0.062)
(log Age)2[b]	0.272*	(0.153)	0.281*	(0.153)	0.190	(0.185)
Spell[d]	–0.008***	(0.003)	–0.008***	(0.003)	–0.008**	(0.004)
d^{I}_{displ} [e]	–0.003	(0.033)	—		—	
d^{II}_{displ} [f]	—		–0.049	(0.040)	–0.050	(0.038)
Female	–0.025	(0.024)	–0.024	(0.024)	–0.024	(0.030)
Education						
Intermediate	–0.002	(0.027)	–0.004	(0.027)	0.013	(0.032)
Higher	–0.022	(0.035)	–0.022	(0.035)	–0.043	(0.041)
University	–0.030	(0.056)	–0.029	(0.055)	–0.083	(0.068)
Married/cohabitating	–0.049	(0.029)	–0.051*	(0.029)	–0.067*	(0.035)
Non-Dutch	0.078	(0.074)	0.069	(0.074)	–0.012	(0.086)
Tenure <1 yr.	—		–0.104***	(0.040)	—	

(continued)

Table 2.22 (continued)

	All workers		
	No tenure criterion	Tenure 1 yr. min.	Workers with tenure ≥1 yr.[b]
Variable	estimate (std. error)	estimate (std. error)	estimate (std. error)
R^2	0.024	0.031	0.029
N	1,069	1,069	668
No. displaced	168	116	116

NOTE: Standard errors are in parentheses. Data on all transitions between jobs with or without intervening non-employment spells (*E-E*, *E-U-E*, and *E-N-E*) are included. Dependent variable is the change in log real after-tax monthly earnings between the pre- and postseparation employment spell. Reference states are "nondisplaced," "male," "primary/lower education," "unmarried and not cohabitating," "Dutch," and "tenure ≥ 1 year"; "log tenure," "log age," and "spell" are included in deviation from their sample means. *** = Statistically significant at the 1% level; ** = statistically significant at the 5% level; * = statistically significant at the 10% level.

[a] "Tenure" = tenure on the preseparation job (in months).

[b] In "(log tenure)^2" and "(log age)^2," both "log tenure" and "log age" are in deviation from their sample means, which correspond to geometric means of tenure and age equal respectively to 18.0 months and 28.9 years in the full sample and 39.8 months and 29.9 years in the tenure-restricted sample.

[c] "Age" = the age at the date of the first interview (in years).

[d] "Spell" = the duration of the non-employment spell between the pre- and postseparation jobs (in months); 0 for *E-E* cases.

[e] The variable d^{I}_{displ} = a dummy indicating whether the separation was caused by displacement, using the definition discussed in the text.

[f] The variable d^{II}_{displ} = a dummy indicating whether the separation was caused by displacement, using the definition discussed in the text.

SOURCE: Based on the LFS.

Table 2.23 United States: Survey Date Labor-Force Status of Displaced Workers (%)

	All displaced		Males		Females	
Age (yr.)	In labor force	Retired/disabled	In labor force	Retired/disabled	In labor force	Retired/disabled
30–39	81.3	1.5	95.6	2.0	81.6	1.0
40–49	91.0	1.2	93.4	1.9	87.6	0.3
50–54	85.7	6.5	92.5	3.8	76.1	10.3
55–59	76.9	13.5	81.5	13.9	69.9	12.8
60–64	62.1	30.5	68.8	28.4	54.9	32.8

NOTE: The table shows the labor-force status in February 1996 of persons displaced during the 1993–95 period, from jobs lasting more than one year.
SOURCE: Data are from the 1996 Displaced Worker supplement and are weighted so as to be nationally representative.

Table 2.24 United States: Survey Date Labor-Force Status of Displaced and Nondisplaced Males (%)

	Men, not displaced		Men, displaced	
Age (yr.)	In labor force	Retired/disabled	In labor force	Retired/disabled
44–46	90.4	5.9	93.8	1.6
47–49	90.0	7.1	91.5	3.0
50–52	86.4	11.1	95.0	2.2
53–55	81.5	14.1	90.8	4.7
56–58	75.3	21.5	81.9	16.5
59–61	68.0	29.3	79.7	16.7
62–64	46.0	52.1	61.8	34.9

NOTE: The table analyzes labor-force status in February 1996. "Displaced" individuals are those losing jobs during the 1993–95 period due to plant closing, slack work, or a position or shift abolishment.

SOURCE: Data are from the February 1996 Current Population Survey and Displaced Worker Supplement and are weighted so as to be nationally representative.

Appendix

Details of Dutch Data Sources

THE FE DATA

The Firm Employment (FE) data were collected by the Dutch "Labor inspection," which is part of the Ministry of Social Affairs and Employment, and contain administrative data on workers employed in both the private and the public sector. For our analyses we use only private sector workers below 60 years of age with at least one year of tenure (unless stated otherwise).

The data are collected yearly (in 1993–1996) as repeated cross-sections from administrative wage records of a sample of firms by means of a stratified two-step sampling procedure. In October of each year, in the first step a sample of firms is drawn. In the second step, workers are sampled from administrative records of these firms corresponding to two moments in time, one year before the sampling date and at the sampling date. As the two-step sampling procedure is repeated in 1993, 1994, 1995, and 1996, we have information on separation and displacement between October 1992 and October 1993, October 1993 and October 1994, October 1994 and October 1995, and October 1995 and October 1996. For notational convenience, we label these four data periods by 1993, 1994, 1995, and 1996, respectively. It should be noted that workers who enter and leave a firm between these two sampling moments are never sampled by this method.

Because both the first-step firm sample and the second-step worker sample are stratified, we have to reweigh the data before performing any (cross-) tabulation. Firm strata are distinguished by firm size (number of employees) and sector. The number of workers sampled per firm depends on firm size; whether the worker is a new entrant, a stayer, or one who left in the previous period; and whether the employee is covered by a collective agreement. Weights for the firm strata are computed from the "Business Statistics" of CBS. Employee weights are calculated from the CBS statistic "Jobs of Employees."

Table 2.A1 provides some sample characteristics. It is useful to mention that the data contain very few missing cases. Job-complexity levels, for example, are known for more than 99 percent of the workers. Below we provide information on the construction of some of the key variables.

Displacement

All workers with at least one year of tenure who are laid off, plus all separations because of disability (DI), early retirement, and transitions into other jobs directly at firms that face a (net) loss of more than 30 percent of their workforce.

Other Outflow

Workers who separate from a firm that is not shrinking by at least 30 percent because of (early) retirement, disability (DI), end of a test period, transition into another job, or expiration of a contract with a temporary work office.

Job-Complexity Level

We use the following classification of job-complexity levels:

Low

Simple, generally repetitive activities that take place under direct supervision. Little or no formal schooling or experience is required.

Intermediate

Less simple activities that partly take place without direct supervision. Administrative or technical knowledge is often required.

High

Activities that require a higher level of knowledge and experience and that take place without direct supervision. Also, management activities that require an academic degree or comparable level of learning.

Tenure

Measured in years (difference between starting and sampling dates).

Wage

Monthly wages (including extra-time payments, profit shares, and so forth) and hours worked are measured very accurately. We calculate gross hourly wages for each worker and deflate the wage by the all-item Consumer Price Index.

Wage Agreement

We distinguish three types of wage contracts. Most workers have a collective agreement (CAO) which is negotiated at the sectoral level or by leading firms within a sector. The Minister of Social Affairs and Employment has the right to force all other firms within a sector to follow an existing CAO, a practice which is labeled by AVV. The remaining workers have only bilateral employment contracts. These workers are, in general, employed at higher positions.

Part-Time–Full-Time

Part-time refers to working less than 100 percent of the regular number of hours in the worker's industry. Regular hours are determined by collective agreements; currently about half of Dutch industries set regular hours at 36 per week.

Education

Education refers to years of completed education. When it takes four years to complete higher vocational education, the reported years of schooling will be four years (plus the number of years it takes to finish high school and elementary school) even if the worker has spent more or fewer years to actually complete his higher vocational degree.

THE UI DATA

The UI data set is provided by Dutch Social Security Council (SVr) and contains administrative data from the sectoral organizations that implement the unemployment insurance system. Table 2.A2 reports results of our analysis of UI data. All cases of individuals applying for unemployment benefits in 1992 were included in the database, and, if necessary, followed up to September 1993. We create an initial data set by restricting the raw data to cases that can be linked to a local labor market—individuals who started collecting benefits in 1992 for whom sector, municipality, and month of inflow are known.[79] This data set contains 219,531 cases and is used for computing characteristics of local labor markets. Excluding all cases for which one or more regressor variables are missing leaves 209,478 cases. This data set is merged with local labor market characteristics computed from the initial data set and becomes the point of departure for the reemployment duration analysis. Below we give some details on measurement and construction of some of the variables.

Duration of Unemployment Insurance Benefits

Both the duration of the insurance benefits period and the destination state of individuals whose benefits expire are observed. Durations are observed in intervals. Thirteen biweekly intervals cover the first half year. Then we have one six-week interval, for durations between 26 and 32 weeks. On the interval 32 to 318 weeks we are able to distinguish 22 quarterly duration classes. The remaining durations are observed as being 318 weeks or longer. Since we are not considering benefit payments that started before 1992, and we are only following benefit recipients up to September 1993, there is no right-censoring because of observations in the residual class 318 weeks and higher. We observe unemployment spells that are continuing at the end of September 1993, however, and transitions out of unemployment insurance to destinations other than employment. In our analysis, both are considered to be right-censored.

Sanctions

The data set contains a variable indicating whether a sanction has been imposed at the start of the UI spell (because of a worker's responsibility for becoming unemployed). We do not use information on sanctions that are imposed during the UI spell, as these are related to behavior during the unemployment spell and not to any behavior that may have led to displacement.

Age

Age is computed as the age in years at the start of the individual's benefits spell.

Wage

Wage is the daily wage before taxes earned by the individual before becoming unemployed. It is the wage that is used by the administrative organization to compute the level of benefits. It is observed in 43 intervals—of width 10 f. up to 430 f.—and a residual interval for those earning over 430 f. The continuous wage variable is defined as the average wage in each wage class, or 435 f. for those in the highest wage class. An additional dummy variable is included for the highest wage class.

Provinces and Urbanization

Municipality codes are observed and recoded to provincial and urbanization dummies. The provinces are Groningen, Friesland, Drenthe, Overijssel, Flevoland, Gelderland, Noord-Brabant, Limburg, Utrecht, Noord-Holland, Zuid-Holland, and Zeeland. Urbanized areas are municipalities that are highly urbanized according to Statistics Netherlands (CBS): Amsterdam, Delft, The Hague, Groningen, Haarlem, Leiden, Rijswijk, Rotterdam, Schiedam, Utrecht, Vlaardingen, and Voorburg.

Part-Time–Full-Time

Like the wage information, this variable refers to the employment situation of the benefits recipient preceding the unemployment spell. Full-time refers to working 100 percent or more of the regular number of hours. Part-time refers to working less than 100 percent of the regular number of hours.

THE LFS DATA

The OSA Labor Force Survey follows a random sample of households in the Netherlands over time. On the basis of these data, sequences of labor market states occupied by the respondents are reconstructed. Table 2.A3 provides some characteristics of the sample that is used in this chapter. The following labor market states are distinguished: employed, self-employed, unemployed, not-in-labor-force, military service, and full-time education. For each transition between two of these labor market states, the respondent is asked to provide a motive or cause selected from an extensive list of possible motives and causes:

1. Due to *Tweeverdienerswet* (law on double-income households).
2. I wanted a more interesting job.
3. I wanted a more secure job.
4. I wanted a job with better career opportunities.
5. I wanted a better paying job.
6. I would have lost my job anyway.
7. Unemployment benefits are sufficient.
8. I wanted a job.
9. Reorganization or plant closure.
10. Bankruptcy.
11. Family business closed or reorganized.
12. Laid off for other reasons.
13. Early retirement.
14. Retired, living off my investments.
15. Disability.
16. Marriage.
17. Birth of a child.
18. Move of household or partner.
19. My family situation did not allow it anymore.
20. I wanted to earn my own wage or an extra wage again.
21. My family situation allowed it again.
22. I wanted to be more among people.
23. I wanted to attend classes again.
24. I just finished my education.
25. I had to fulfill military service.
26. I just fulfilled military service.

Most respondents, 78 percent, do not experience a labor market transition. Almost all respondents make fewer than four transitions (99 percent). The low number of transitions can be explained by the relatively short observation period (at most five years) and the fact that most respondents are breadwinners, who can be expected to have low job mobility. At the date of the first interview, 62 percent of the respondents are employed, whereas 27 percent are nonparticipants, and 7 percent are unemployed.

In the LFS, three types of transitions can be the result of displacement: job-to-job transitions (E-E), transitions from employment to unemployment (E-U), and transitions from employment to not-in-the-labor-force (E-N). As noted earlier, the LFS provides a self-reported motive or cause for each transition in the data set, and it provides information on whether the transition was made voluntarily. This information can be used to identify displacement. For instance, if "reorganization or plant closure" is reported as a cause for leaving a job, the worker is clearly displaced. There are several other motives which could indicate displacement. It could have occurred through DI, in which case disability may be reported as a cause for leaving employment. In deciding which motivation-voluntariness combinations identify displacement, we had to recognize that the reported motivations and voluntariness are heavily liable to subjective perceptions (like the distinction between a quit and a layoff). Having this in mind, we decided to consider transitions with the following motivation-voluntariness pairs as displacement.

The motivation "I would have lost my job anyway" will most likely be applicable to situations in which people anticipate displacement. In this case we take both voluntary and involuntary as involuntary transitions, because there seems to be no reason to believe that one or the other excludes displacement. The same holds for the cause "reorganization or plant closure." For the motivation "early retirement" involuntary transitions seem most likely to denote displacement. Voluntary early retirements, on the other hand, will probably cover individuals who prefer to stop working irrespective of economic conditions in the firm; these individuals would have reported "would have lost job anyway" in case of displacement. Finally, we have the transitions into DI. For this motivation we distinguish between E-E and E-U transitions, on the one hand, and E-N, on the other. We think that in case of an E-E or E-U transition, both voluntary and involuntary transitions denote displacement, because these people keep working or are searching for a job after the transition; they are not really incapacitated for work.[80] For E-N transitions, we assume that displacement is indicated by voluntary transitions, while involuntary transitions cover transitions for pure medical reasons.

More details on the LFS data can be found in van den Berg and Ridder (1998) and van den Berg (1992).

Table 2.A1 Netherlands: Weighted Means in FE Data for the 1993–96 Period

Variable	Mean
Year[a]	
1993	0.23
1994	0.24
1995	0.25
1996	0.28
Gender	
Female	0.37
Male	0.63
Coll. agreement	
CAO[b]	0.72
AVV[c]	0.05
None	0.23
Job-complexity level	
Low	0.19
Intermediate	0.70
High	0.11
Education (yr.)	11.3
Age (yr.)	34.1
Tenure (yr.)	4.1
Real gross hourly wage (guilders)	27.1
Total no. of workers	102,141

NOTE: Workers older than 60 and workers with less than one year's tenure are excluded.

[a] "Year" = the sampling year. Note that data on two consecutive years for each worker are collected at a single sampling date, October of the sample year, by reviewing the administrative records of both the sampling date and one year before the sampling date.

[b] "CAO" = coverage by a collective agreement.

[c] "AVV" = coverage by a mandatory extension of such a CAO.

SOURCE: FE data.

Table 2.A2 Netherlands: Some Characteristics of UI Data

Characteristic		
No. of spells	209,478	
Terminated by		
Reemployment	0.56	
Maximum entitlement	0.12	
Transition into DI	0.07	
End of observation period	0.17	
Other[a]	0.08	
	Mean	Std. dev.
Nondisplaced (sanction)	0.13	
Age (yr.)	32.0	10.9
Daily wage (guilders)	122.5	65.9
Female	0.43	
Urban	0.17	
Part-time	0.29	
Married	0.40	

NOTE: Wages are observed in 10-guilder intervals and are right-censored at 430 guilders. Sample mean and standard error of wages are computed by recoding wages to mean interval wages, or to 435 guilders if right-censored.

[a] "Other" includes reaching age 65, death, military service, and self-employment, among other things, all of which occur in less than 0.5 percent of the cases.

SOURCE: UI data.

Table 2.A3 Netherlands: Characteristics of LFS Earnings Sample

	All workers		Workers with tenure ≥1 yr	
Variable	Mean	Std. dev.	Mean	Std. dev.
Ratio post- to preseparation earnings[a]	1.22	0.62	1.24	0.55
Tenure (months)[b]	44.4	71.0	67.5	81.5
Age (yr.)[c]	30.0	8.1	31.0	8.3
Spell (months)[d]	0.7	3.5	0.6	3.3
Spell (nonzero spells only, in months)	8.8	9.5	10.4	10.1
Education				
Primary/lower sec.	0.36		0.34	
Intermediate	0.41		0.43	
Higher	0.18		0.19	
University	0.05		0.05	
d^{I}_{displ} [e]	0.16		—	
d^{II}_{displ} [f]	0.11		0.17	
Female	0.40		0.36	
Married/cohabitating	0.69		0.75	
Non-Dutch	0.03		0.03	
Total no. of individuals	1,069		668	
No. of nonzero intervening spells	81		37	

[a] "Ratio post- to preseparation earnings" = real after-tax monthly earnings in the preseparation and the first postseparation jobs.

[b] "Tenure" = tenure on the preseparation job; it is used to select the cases in the right panel.

[c] "Age" = age at the date of the first interview.

[d] "Spell" = the duration of non-employment spell between the pre- and postseparation jobs (0 for *E-E* cases).

[e] d^{I}_{displ} is a dummy variable indicating whether the separation was caused by displacement (1) or not (0), using the definition discussed in the main text.

[f] $d^{II}_{displ} = d^{I}_{displ}$ with the additional requirement that the tenure of the displaced individual equals at least one year.

References

Aarts, L.J.M., W.J. Dercksen, and Ph.R. de Jong. 1993. "Arbeidsongeschiktheid, een Internationale Vergelijking." (Disability, an International Comparison; in Dutch.) *Sociaal Maandblad Arbeid* 755–769.

Abbring, J.H., G.J. van den Berg, and J.C. van Ours. 1997. "The Effect of Unemployment Insurance Sanctions on the Transition Rate from Unemployment to Employment." Working paper, Tinbergen Institute, Amsterdam.

Addison, John T., and McKinley L. Blackburn. 1994. "Policy Watch: The Worker Adjustment Retraining and Notification Act." *Journal of Economic Perspectives* 8(1):181–190.

Addison, John T, and Pedro Portugal. 1987. "The Effect of Advance Notification of Plant Closings on Unemployment." *Industrial and Labor Relations Review* 41(1):3–16.

———. 1989. "On the Costs of Worker Displacement: The Case of Dissipated Firm-Specific Training Investments." *Southern Economic Journal* 56(1): 166–182.

Andersen, T.M. 1997. "French Unemployment: A Transatlantic Perspective (Discussion)." *Economic Policy, A European Forum* (25): 285–287.

CBS. 1991. *Maandschrift* (January; in Dutch). Statistics Netherlands (CBS), Voorburg.

———. 1996. *Tijdreeksen Arbeidsrekeningen* 1969–1993: *Ramingen van het Opleidingsniveau, een Tussenstand* (in Dutch). Statistics Netherlands (CBS), Voorburg.

CBS (Statistics Netherlands). 1998. "Statline (Labor Statistics)." Accessed July 22 at http://statline.cbs.nl/.

Chesher, A. 1984. "Testing for Neglected Heterogeneity." *Econometrica* 52: 865–872.

Cohen, D., A. Lefranc, and G. Saint-Paul. 1997. "French Unemployment: A Transatlantic Perspective." *Economic Policy* (25): 265–292.

Committee on Ways and Means, U.S. House of Representatives. 1996. *1996 Green Book: Background Material and Data on Programs within the Jurisdiction of the Committee on Ways and Means.* U.S. Government Printing Office, Washington, D.C.

CTSV. 1997. *Kroniek van de Sociale Verzekeringen 1996. Wetgeving en Volume-ontwikkeling in Historisch Perspectief* (in Dutch). College van Toezicht Sociale Verzekeringen, Zoetermeer.

Dertouzos, James N., and Lynn A. Karoly. 1993. "Employment Effects of Worker Protection: Evidence from the United States." In *Employment*

Security and Labor Market Behavior, Christoph F. Buechtemann, ed. Ithaca, New York: ILR Press, Cornell University, pp. 215–227.

Ehrenberg, Ronald G., and George H. Jakubson. 1988. *Advance Notice Provisions in Plant Closing Legislation.* Kalamazoo, Michigan: W.E. Upjohn Institute for Employment Research.

Emerson, M. 1988. "Regulation or Deregulation of the Labour Market: Policy Regimes for the Recruitment and Dismissal of Employees in the Industrialised Countries." *European Economic Review* 32(4): 775–817.

Evans, David S., and Linda S. Leighton. 1995. "Retrospective bias in the Displaced Worker Surveys." *Journal of Human Resources* 30(2):386–396.

Fallick, Bruce C. 1996. "A Review of the Recent Literature on Displaced Workers." *Industrial and Labor Relations Review* 50(1): 5–16.

Farber, Henry S. 1993. "The Incidence and Costs of Job Loss: 1982–91." *Brookings Papers: Microeconomics*, pp. 73–119.

———. 1997. "The Changing Face of Job Loss in the United States, 1981–1995." *Brookings Papers: Microeconomics*, pp. 55–128.

———. 1998. "Has the Rate of Job Loss Increased in the Nineties?" Photocopy, Princeton University, Princeton, New Jersey.

Gibbons, Robert and Lawrence F. Katz. 1991. "Layoffs and Lemons." *Journal of Labor Economics* 9(4): 351–380.

Hall, Robert E. 1995. "Lost Jobs." *Brookings Papers on Economic Activity* no. 1: 221–256.

Hamermesh, Daniel S. 1989. "What Do We Know about Worker Displacement in the United States?" *Industrial Relations* 28(1): 51–59.

———. 1991. "Wage Concessions, Plant Shutdowns, and the Demand for Labor." In *Job Displacement: Consequences and Implications for Policy,* John T. Addison, ed. Detroit: Wayne State University Press, pp. 83–106.

Hassink, W.H.J., J.C. van Ours, and G. Ridder. 1997. "Dismissal through Disability." *De Economist* 145(1): 29–46.

Heckman, J.J., and B. Singer. 1984. "A Method for Minimizing the Impact of Distributional Assumptions in Econometric Models for Duration Data." *Econometrica* 52(2): 271–320.

Herz, Diane E. 1990. "Worker Displacement in a Period of Rapid Job Expansion: 1983–1987." *Monthly Labor Review* 113(5): 21–33.

Jacobson, Louis S., Robert J. LaLonde, and Daniel G. Sullivan. 1993. "Earnings Losses of Displaced Workers." *American Economic Review* 83(4): 685–709.

Jovanovic, B. 1979. "Job Matching and the Theory of Turnover." *Journal of Political Economy* 87(5): 972–990.

Kletzer, Lori G. 1989. "Returns to Seniority after Permanent Job Loss." *American Economic Review* 79(3): 536–543.

———. 1991. "Earnings after Job Displacement: Job Tenure, Industry, and Occupation." In *Job Displacement: Consequences and Implications for Policy*, John T. Addison, ed. Detroit: Wayne State University Press, pp. 107–135.

———. 1998. "What Have We Learned about Job Displacement?" *Journal of Economic Perspectives* 12(1): 115–136.

Kodrzycki, Yolanda K. 1997. "Training Programs for Displaced Workers: What Do They Accomplish?" *New England Economic Review* (May-June): 39–59.

Krueger, Alan B. 1991. "The Evolution of Unjust-Dismissal Legislation in the United States." *Industrial and Labor Relations Review* 44(4): 644–660.

Lancaster, T. 1979. "Econometric Methods for the Duration of Unemployment." *Econometrica* 47(4): 939–956.

Layard, R., S. Nickell, and R. Jackman. 1991. *Unemployment; Macroeconomic Performance and the Labour Market*. Oxford: Oxford University Press.

Leigh, Duane E. 1995. *Assisting Workers Displaced by Structural Change*. Kalamazoo, Michigan: W.E. Upjohn Institute for Employment Research.

Nickell, Stephen. 1997. "Unemployment and Labor Market Rigidities: Europe versus North America." *Journal of Economic Perspectives* 11(3): 55–74.

OECD. 1995. *Economic Outlook*. Paris: OECD.

Office of Management and Budget. 1998. *Budget of the United States Government, Fiscal Year 1998*. Washington, D.C.: U.S. Government Printing Office.

Ruhm, Christopher J. 1987. "The Economic Consequences of Labor Mobility." *Industrial and Labor Relations Review* 41(1): 30–42.

———. 1990. "Do Earnings Increase with Job Seniority?" *Review of Economics and Statistics* 71(1): 143–147.

———. 1991a. "Are Workers Permanently Scarred by Job Displacements?" *American Economic Review* 81(1): 319–324.

———. 1991b. "The Time Profile of Displacement-Induced Changes in Earnings and Unemployment." In *Job Displacement: Consequences and Implications for Policy*, John T. Addison, ed. Detroit: Wayne State University Press, pp. 162–181.

———. 1992. "Advance Notice and Postdisplacement Joblessness." *Journal of Labor Economics* 10(1):1–32.

———. 1994. "Advance Notice, Job Search, and Postdisplacement Earnings." *Journal of Labor Economics* 12(1): 1–28.

Schoeni, Robert F. and Michael Dardia. 1996. "Earnings Losses of Displaced Workers in the 1990s." Photocopy, Rand Corporation, Santa Monica, California.

Siebert, Horst. 1997. "Labor Market Rigidities: At the Root of Unemployment in Europe." *Journal of Economic Perspectives* 11(3): 37–54.

Stevens, Ann Huff. 1997. "Persistent Effects of Job Displacement: The Importance of Multiple Job Losses." *Journal of Labor Economics* 15(1, part 1): 165–188.

Storer, Paul, and Marc Van Audenrode. 1997. "The Uncertainty of Displacement." Photocopy, Western Washington University, Bellingham, Washington.

Swaim, Paul L., and Michael J. Podgursky. 1991. "Displacement and Unemployment." In *Job Displacement: Consequences and Implications for Policy,* John T. Addison, ed. Detroit: Wayne State University Press, pp. 136–161.

Thio, V. 1997. "Why Do Workers Retire?" Photocopy, CERRA (Leiden University), Leiden.

Topel, Robert. 1990. "Specific Human Capital and Unemployment: Measuring the Costs and Consequences of Job Loss." *Carnegie-Rochester Conference Series on Public Policy* 33: 181–224.

U.S. Bureau of Labor Statistics. 1998. "Nonfarm Payroll Statistics from the Current Employment Statistics (National) Home Page." Accessed March 11 at http:146.142.4.24/cgi-bin/surveymost.

U.S. Bureau of the Census. 1997. *Statistical Abstract of the United States: 1997.* 117th ed. Washington, D.C.

van den Berg, G.J. 1992. "A Structural Dynamic Analysis of Job Turnover and the Costs Associated with Moving to Another Job." *Economic Journal* 102: 1116–1133.

van den Berg, G.J., M. Lindeboom, and G. Ridder. 1994. "Attrition in Logitudinal Panel Data, and the Empirical Analysis of Dynamic Labour Market Behaviour." *Journal of Applied Econometrics* 9: 421–435.

van den Berg, G.J., and G. Ridder. 1998. "An Empirical Equilibrium Search Model of the Labor Market." *Econometrica* 66: 1183–1221.

White, H. 1982. "Maximum Likelihood Estimation of Misspecified Models." *Econometrica* 50: 1–25.

3
Worker Displacement in Japan and Canada

Masahiro Abe
Dokkyo University

Yoshio Higuchi
Keio University

Peter Kuhn
University of California, Santa Barbara

Masao Nakamura
University of British Columbia

Arthur Sweetman
Queen's University

The profound institutional and structural differences between Japanese and North American labor markets are well known. Despite these differences, the two types of economies face a common problem: finding the best way to reallocate labor when technological, trade, and other shocks raise the demand for workers in some activities but reduce the demand in others. When these shocks occur, can permanent displacement, especially of vulnerable senior workers, be avoided? If not, what are the consequences of such displacements?

The purpose of this chapter is to provide a detailed description of the incidence and consequences of worker displacement in a North American economy—Canada—and in Japan. We begin with a brief description of the main modes of labor adjustment in the two countries, situating worker displacement in the broader context of how firms adjust to declines in product demand. Next we describe the legal and social institutions most likely to affect the displacement process and the general labor market conditions prevailing in each country at the time of our analysis. We then analyze, in turn, the frequency of displacement in each country and its consequences.

Our main findings are as follows. First, the primary mechanisms by which Japanese and Canadian firms shed workers differ. In Japan involuntary terminations can take three main forms: layoffs, mandatory retirement, and a kind of outplacement called *shukko*. In addition to simply laying workers off, Japanese firms often terminate workers as young as their mid 40s by forcing them to take a retirement package. *Shukko* involves placing workers at affiliated or related firms. Sometimes used as a means of transferring skills across company lines, it is also used, especially for older workers, simply as a means of reducing the workforce. While some younger *shukko* workers may be recalled to their original employer, this is seldom the case for older workers.

In Canada neither *shukko* nor mandatory retirement (at least for prime-age workers) is a common method of adjusting to demand shocks. Layoffs, which are common, take a different form there because their permanence is often unclear. Over half of all laid-off workers in Canada expect at the time of layoff to return to their original employer, and over 40 percent actually do so. Furthermore, neither workers nor firms are good predictors of actual recall probabilities. Thus the process of displacement in Canada, rather than being a sharp and permanent break, more typically begins with a layoff of no clear permanence and proceeds through an updating of probabilities of recall to the original workplace.

Second, perhaps surprisingly, institutional factors affecting displaced workers in Japan and Canada have as many similarities as differences. Both Japanese and Canadian firms, for example, are required to provide advance notice to workers being laid off, with statutory notice requirements actually somewhat higher in Canada. At the same time, however, Canadian firms can lay workers off for "economic" reasons without having to justify their actions legally; in Japan such layoffs must be justified, and certain procedural requirements satisfied, before they occur. Employment insurance benefits in both countries have similar replacement rates and are limited to less than a year in duration. Japan has a much more explicit and comprehensive program of adjustment subsidies for declining industries than Canada, but a number of such programs exist on an ad hoc basis in Canada as well.

Wage-setting institutions, such as unions and minimum wages, can be relevant to displaced workers by affecting the distribution of pre- and postdisplacement wages. In both countries only a minority of workers are unionized. In both countries, wage bargaining is at the enterprise level, although Japan has an element of coordination (*shunto*) not present in Canada. In both countries, statutory minimum wages are set at subnational (province or prefecture) levels and are only a small fraction of average wages, compared to many European countries. Unlike Canada, however, Japan has a system of industry-specific minimum wages which may provide a channel whereby collectively bargained wages can have some impact on the wages of unorganized workers.

Third, separations are much more frequent in the Canadian than the Japanese labor market, especially for men: in firms with at least five workers, and in jobs that have lasted at least a month, there are 0.36 separations per employed male in Canada per year; in Japan there are one-third as many, 0.12. A very large share of this difference, however, is due to the large number of temporary layoffs in Canada; when we look only at (*ex post*) permanent separations, overall separation rates are similar in the two countries. They are in fact higher among Japanese women than among Canadian women.

Fourth, a much larger share of separations is labeled as involuntary (in other words, firm-initiated) in Canada than in Japan. In Canada, about two-thirds of separating workers say they were "laid off"; this agrees roughly with the fraction of separations that firms label as due to "shortage of work." In Japan, under 10 percent of separations are labeled (by firms) as due to "management convenience" (which includes *shukko* workers). In fact, the total of all "involuntary" separations in Japan (which also includes mandatory retirements and the expiration of fixed-term contracts) is under one-third of all separations.

Fifth, the combination of similar permanent separation rates plus a larger involuntary share in Canada means that worker displacement—permanent, involuntary separation—is more common in Canada than Japan. The difference is very large if we focus only on men and on a narrow definition of displacement ("management convenience" only) in Japan: a displacement rate of 6.1 percent per year in Canada versus 1.3 percent in Japan. Smaller, but still substantial, differences exist for women and for broader definitions of displacement in Japan.

Sixth, we find a fascinating pattern (at least to a non-Japanese audience) in the age pattern of permanent layoffs in Japan and Canada. In Canada, as one might expect, layoff rates decline with age, as workers settle into jobs and accumulate seniority (which in North America tends to protect workers from a layoff). In Japan, young workers have very low layoff rates, but these layoff rates increase with age. This system of seniority-based (rather than inverse-seniority-based) layoffs in Japan appears to place a larger share of the employment adjustment burden on older, rather than younger, workers.

Seventh, despite frequent comments about the inability of Japanese labor markets to accommodate displaced mid-career workers, we find that unemployment durations of displaced Japanese workers are much shorter than those of displaced Canadian workers. Focusing on Japanese workers who separated due to a layoff, bankruptcy, declining business, expiration of a casual or fixed-term contract, or mandatory retirement, we find that median non-employment durations in the mid 1990s were under two months in Japan compared to just under six months for Canadian men and over eight months for Canadian women. The Japanese numbers would be even lower if we included the direct job-to-job transitions among *shukko* workers in our calculations. To some extent, these low relative durations reflect the lower overall Japanese unemployment rate even during the recessionary period of our data. However, they could also reflect low search intensities among Canadian workers hoping to be recalled to their former employer.

Eighth, for all workers under the age of about 50 in both countries, the mean wage consequence of displacement is essentially zero. Despite this, Canadian displaced workers are much more likely to experience large wage declines than Japanese displaced workers: all told, 14.5 percent of displaced Canadian men (16.4 percent of women) experience wage declines of more than 30 percent, compared with 8.7 and 4.3 percent respectively in Japan (the Japanese numbers are even smaller if we include *shukko* workers in the sample). These two facts are reconciled by the greater likelihood of large displacement-related wage increases in Canada: fully 17 percent of displaced Canadian men experience a wage gain of over 30 percent, compared with under 2 percent of displaced Japanese men; comparable numbers for women are 18 and 3 percent. These wage consequences of displacement may reflect a more compressed wage structure in Japan than Canada. Japanese displaced workers thus appear to face much less wage uncertainty than Canadian displaced workers.

Ninth, the mean wage loss associated with displacement increases with age in both countries, especially in Japan. In a sample of Japanese men over age 55 whose separation is due to management convenience, mandatory retirement, or contract expiration, mean wage losses are substantial (10 to 15 percent). It is unclear how much of this reflects mandatory "retirement" followed by lower-wage work, or simple layoffs (or, for that matter, whether this distinction is very meaningful). This age pattern in wage losses reinforces the notion that older workers bear a larger share of the adjustment burden in Japan than in Canada, which emerges from our examination of layoff rates.

Finally, we compute a simple summary measure of the combined employment *and* wage security experienced by Japanese and Canadian workers. Aside from combining the above information on the incidence and consequences of displacement, this measure has the advantage of not being affected by possible differences in the labeling of separations between countries. In particular, the measure we compute is the fraction of employed persons who, in a given year, are likely to experience a wage loss of 30 percent or more as a result of an employer change. This fraction is 1.9 percent for Canadian men versus 0.8 percent for Japanese men. This gap becomes much larger if we exclude older Japanese men: for example, for men aged 35–39, the rates are 1.7 percent in Canada versus only 0.2 percent in Japan. "Prime-age" Japanese men thus experience a level of wage and job security that may be unrivalled anywhere. This international gap in total earnings security is smaller for women and is dramatically reversed for older men: conditional on continuing to work, 6.8 percent of employed Japanese men over the age of 60 experience a separation resulting in a wage drop of more than 30 percent each year, compared to only 1.0 percent of Canadian men.

All told, despite a worsening Japanese recession and historically very high unemployment rates, our findings clearly show that—with one exception—Japanese workers are less likely to be displaced, experience less unemployment when displaced, and are less likely to suffer a large wage reduction as a consequence of displacement. That one exception is for men over the age of about 55 and reflects, at least in part, the common Japanese practice of mandatory retirement followed by work at lower wages in a more casual labor market. With that one potential exception, we do not find evidence that—at least compared to

Canada—Japanese labor markets are poorly adapted to the task of reemploying displaced mid-career workers.

EMPLOYMENT ADJUSTMENT MECHANISMS

Firms can adjust to declines in the demand for their products in a number of ways, many of which do not involve involuntary reductions in employment. These mechanisms include the development of new products, reductions in employee compensation, reductions in hours per worker, reductions in hiring, and voluntary workforce attrition. The mix of these mechanisms chosen by firms is known to vary substantially among countries. Nakamura and Nakamura (1991) showed, for example, that Japanese firms tend to adjust hours of work and wages, while U.S. firms tend to adjust employment. Despite this and other alternative forms of flexibility, involuntary employment reductions must sometimes occur in Japan, especially in the recent recession. The incidence and consequences of these reductions have, to date, been very little studied and are our main interests in this chapter. The remainder of this section describes the primary mechanisms by which involuntary workforce reductions occur in the two countries. As most readers will be less familiar with the Japanese case, our focus will be mainly on that country.

Japan

Mandatory retirement

As is well known, mandatory retirement at a prearranged age is a common feature of the Japanese labor market. Also, much more frequently than in Canada or the United States, it is followed by employment at a different firm, often on a part-time basis and usually at a lower wage.[1] The mandatory retirement age recommended by the government is 60 years; until very recently, however, many firms used 55 as the retirement age for many of their workers.[2] Mandatory retirement at age 55 is sufficiently common in Japan to be reflected in aggregate wage statistics. For example, Figure 3.1 shows cross-section age-wage

Figure 3.1 Wage Profiles by Age and Education, Japan

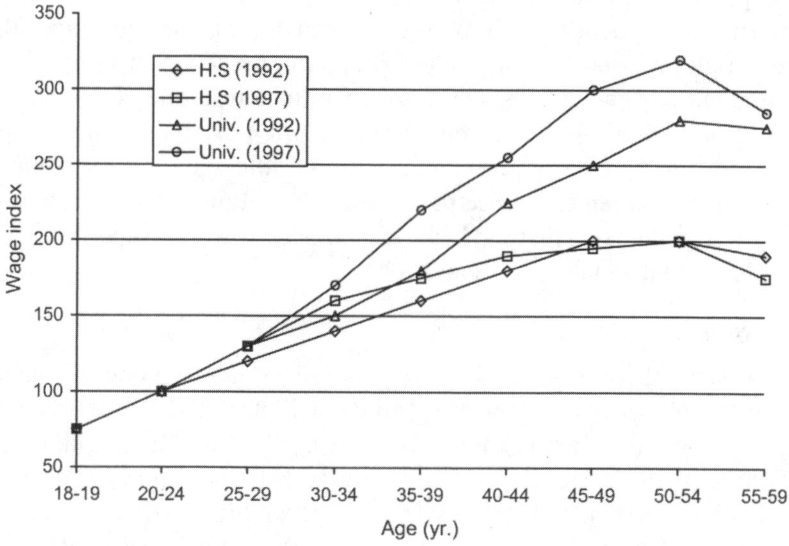

SOURCE: Japan Ministry of Labor.

profiles for regular Japanese workers in 1993. These profiles grow monotonically to age 54 but drop suddenly at age 55.

A less well-known feature of the Japanese labor market is the common use of mandatory retirement well in advance of the pre-arranged age as a means of labor adjustment. This can occur as early as a worker's early 40s. It is also known that so-called voluntary early-retirement programs are not always voluntary and that some targeted workers feel pressure to accept such packages. Early-retirement schemes are very common in large Japanese firms: almost half of firms with more than 5,000 employees had such programs in 1990, compared with under 2 percent of firms with 30–99 employees (Japan Ministry of Labor 1992).

Many Japanese firms provide workers with a lump-sum payment on retirement. The amount of such retirement pay depends on the number of years of service and the rank the worker has attained in the firm at the time of retirement; it can range from one year's to several years' salary. These retirement payments are separate from annual pensions and receive distinct, favorable tax treatment. Seike (1993) showed that the marginal gain workers get from their retirement lump-sum payments by staying with their present employer for another year is positive for younger age groups but negative for those above age 40. He concluded that for older age groups the presence of lump-sum retirement pay encourages workers' separations from their employers. A sweetened lump-sum retirement pay is often used as a bargaining tool for soliciting early retirements from middle-aged workers. One difference between severance pay in Canada and the lump-sum retirement pay in Japan is that the latter is paid even if workers quit prior to their normal mandatory retirement ages.

Shukko

A second form of involuntary separation in Japan occurs when firms simply assign their workers to an affiliate or otherwise-related firm; this arrangement is known as *shukko.* Most *shukko* assignments occur within vertically or horizontally related groups of firms (*keiretsu*) in Japan.[3] These new jobs are often with smaller firms and pay less than the workers' current jobs. There are two types of *shukko,* the first of which *(tenseki)* represents a one-way ticket to another firm with virtually no possibility of coming back to the original employer. The second type, *ichiji* (temporary) *shukko*, involves a substantial probability of returning to the original employer after a few years. It is more prevalent for younger workers. For example, younger workers may be assigned to some jobs at other firms as part of their job rotation for learning certain skills required by the original employer. More-experienced workers of a parent firm may also go on temporary *shukko* to its affiliated firms in order to teach some skill the parent firm wants the affiliated firms to possess. Many firms have agreements with their labor unions regarding the practice of calling back workers on temporary *shukko* within three or four years after their *shukko* assignments start.

For both temporary and permanent *shukko*, the original employer often pays most (or all) of the wages of the workers who are sent out, at least for the first year or two. After that, the new employer may start paying *shukko* workers' salaries, depending on the arrangement made between the two employers. At that point in time these workers may become regular employees of the new company and sever their ties to the old.

An example of the use of *shukko* in a Japanese firm is given in Figure 3.2, which shows the age distribution of employees at a large Japanese steel producer in 1997. About 4.5 percent of the firm's employees are 49 (34 + 15) years of age. Of those, fewer than two-thirds (under 3 percent) are actually working at the company, while the remainder are away on *shukko* assignments (on loan) to other employers. Those on *shukko* assignments may or may not be on the firm's payroll. The proportion of employees on *shukko* starts to increase rapidly beginning at about age 44 (15 + 29) and exceeds 50 percent of the total workforce by age 51. Most of the *shukko* employees older than their mid 40s will not come back to their original employer, while those in their 20s and 30s are quite likely to do so.

Because *shukko* workers, especially of the "permanent" type, experience involuntary employer changes, they can be thought of as a kind of displaced worker. In contrast to North American displaced workers, however, they do not experience any unemployment. As we shall see,

Figure 3.2 *Shukko* and Age Distribution of Workers at a Large Japanese Steel Company, 1977

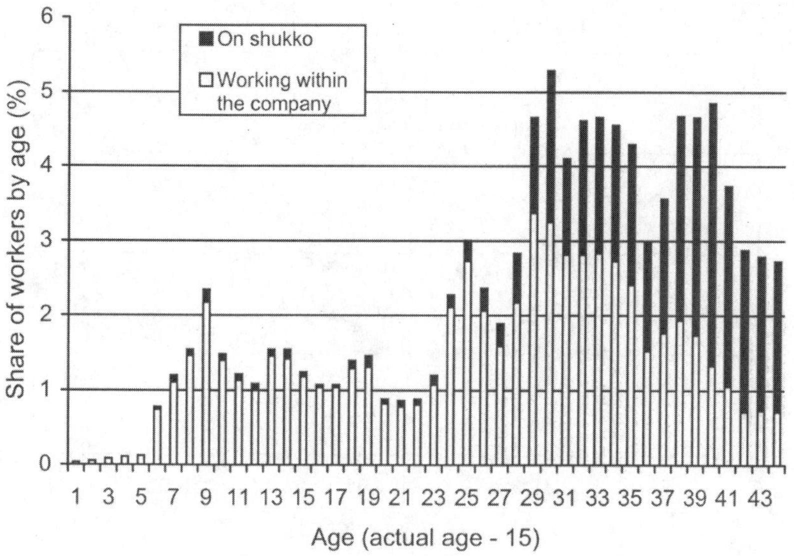

they also experience only very small wage changes, at least within one year of moving to the new firm.

Layoffs and the process of employment reduction

In Japan, there are also workers who lose jobs because employers cannot afford to keep them on, or because their employers have gone out of business. Generally, layoffs are used as a last resort after other mechanisms, like mandatory retirement and *shukko*, have been exhausted. As an illustration of this, Figure 3.3 shows how these processes were sequenced as Japanese manufacturers were forced to reduce employment from 1987 through early 1994. Clearly, the post-bubble recession had a major impact on employment adjustment, start-

Figure 3.3 Methods of Employment Adjustment at Manufacturing Establishments between 1987 (Q1) and 1994 (Q2)

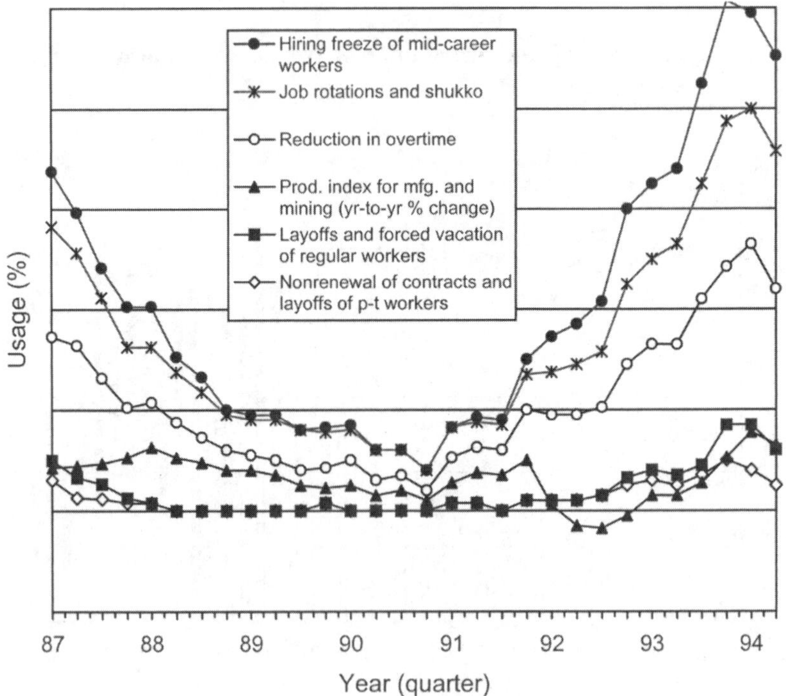

ing almost immediately after the bubble burst in 1990. As the change in the production index for manufacturing and mining registered a sharp decline in late 1991, reductions in overtime immediately followed.

These were joined by job rotations and *shukko* as well as reductions in, or complete termination of, new employment for mid-career workers. These methods, in turn, were followed by nonrenewal or cancellation of contracts with part-time employees. Next, temporary forced vacations of regular employees were implemented. Finally, after part-time workers were terminated, about 2 percent of Japanese manufacturers also implemented voluntary early-retirement programs and layoffs between 1992 and 1994 (see Higuchi 1996, for example). Thus, layoffs are clearly a last resort; but they do occur. They have been studied very little in Japan, and we hope to make an early attempt in this chapter at understanding their frequency and consequences.

Canada

Neither mandatory retirement for prime-age workers nor *shukko* is an important feature of firms' labor adjustment policies in Canada. The dominant form of involuntary downward employment adjustment used by Canadian firms is clearly layoff into unemployment. At the same time, however, it is important to realize that not all layoffs constitute what we normally think of as displacements. The main reason for this is that a large fraction of layoffs in North America are temporary, and the workers involved expect to return to the original employer after a short time. That a worker has been displaced, or permanently laid off, from her or his employer, may thus not be immediately obvious (to either the worker or the firm) at the time of separation. The sets of displaced and temporarily laid-off workers can be very fluid on the margin, and studies using *ex post* definitions will have quite different samples than those using *ex ante* ones.

The distinction between permanent and temporary layoffs figures prominently in the definition of displaced workers in Canada and has potentially important consequences for search intensities and unemployment durations. We explore this distinction in depth later in this chapter.

LEGISLATION AND INSTITUTIONS AFFECTING DISPLACED WORKERS

In this section we describe the main laws and institutions that are likely to affect the frequency and consequences of worker displacement in Japan and Canada. We begin with a discussion of employment-protection legislation, namely policies which limit firms' freedom to reduce employment, including mandatory advance-notice periods, mandated severance pay, unjust dismissal laws, and requirements to consult with local governments before engaging in mass layoffs.[4] We then discuss the "passive" income support (primarily employment insurance) available to unemployed workers in both countries. Next we focus on a set of policies that are particularly prevalent in Japan but probably less common, and certainly more ad hoc, in Canada: subsidies to employers and workers in "threatened" industries, designed both to maintain employment in the old firms and to encourage mobility into new product lines and industries. Finally, we briefly describe the main institutions, apart from firms, that shape the wage-setting process in both countries: collective bargaining and minimum wages. Because these institutions shape the distribution of wages among individuals, jobs, firms, and industries, they can have a significant effect on the wage changes experienced by displaced workers.

Our description of laws and other institutions in the two countries below is quite detailed and is meant to function both as background to the empirical work in this chapter and as reference material to researchers interested in displacement and related policy. Readers already familiar with Japanese and Canadian labor market institutions, or who are mostly interested in just what happens to displaced workers in the two countries, might happily skip ahead to our section on General Economic Conditions (p. 220).

Employment Protection Legislation

Japan

Japanese employment law, like that of many European countries, distinguishes between workers on "regular" employment contracts (usually long-term and full-time) and those working under other arrangements, including temporary and part-time workers. For workers on regular contracts, substantial legal precedent requires firms to demonstrate "just cause" to terminate their employment. Workers without regular contracts do not necessarily enjoy this just-cause protection, but they can qualify if they have worked for the same employer for a long time.[5] "Just cause" in Japan can include declines in business, but if firms want to invoke this reason to lay workers off, they must be able to demonstrate the following: 1) the necessity of the layoff, 2) that they have made efforts to avoid layoffs, 3) appropriate procedure, and 4) rational and fair choice of those to be laid off. Vol-untary early retirement programs are a typical part of the "efforts to avoid layoffs." To first lay off nonregular workers, such as temporary and part-time workers, is accepted as an "appropriate procedure." While negotiating with the labor union is considered to be an integral part of the procedure, employers can lay workers off even if no agreement with the labor union is reached after the employer has made a sincere effort.

The Japanese Labor Code requires that 30 days' advance notice be given to workers prior to a layoff; as in Canada firms have the option of paying the equivalent amount of severance in lieu of giving notice. Despite this low amount of statutory notice, it seems likely that, given the substantial procedural requirements that must be fulfilled to demonstrate the justification of layoffs in Japan, "effective" notice—the amount of time before the layoff when workers actually know it is coming—may in fact be substantially greater in duration.

Canada

In Canada, two main bodies of legislation restrict firms' abilities to terminate workers' employment.[6] The first and older of these is the common law, which governs the interpretation and enforcement of private employment contracts. According to Canadian common law, labor contracts without an explicit fixed duration can be terminated by the firm in two main ways: termination for cause or by giving notice. Permissible "causes" are defined by centuries of British and Canadian case law and include items such as repeated insolence, drunkenness, or morally improper behavior (Arthurs et al., 1993, pp. 153–155).

In contrast to dismissal for cause, termination of employment for "economic" reasons, such as a shortage of work, generally requires giving the employee a "reasonable" amount of notice under Canadian common law. In the event of a dispute, what is reasonable is determined by a judge, who is expected to consider the custom in the industry and geographical area, the periodicity of payment (hourly, weekly, or monthly, and so forth), and the difficulty the employee will have in finding a new job (Arthurs et al., 1993, pp. 146–149). As enforcing these common law provisions for reasonable notice generally requires workers to bring a civil suit against their employer, this option is typically exercised only by highly paid workers. It is worth noting, however, that in such situations the courts have determined advance-notice requirements of as much as 21 months to be "reasonable."[7]

The second main body of law regulating layoffs in Canada is contained in the Employment Standards Acts of its 13 labor jurisdictions.[8] These acts set minimum conditions that must be satisfied by all employment relationships, including minimum wages, paid vacations, and limits on overtime work. Of these, three main provisions would likely be considered "employment-protection laws": advance notice of layoff, severance pay, and consultation requirements.

Minimum mandatory notice statutes for permanent layoffs in each of the Canadian labor jurisdictions are summarized in Table 3.1, which shows the state of legislation as of September 1, 1997.[9] In most cases, mandated notice depends on the duration of employment, ranging from 1 week for relatively new workers to 8 weeks for workers with 10 or more years of experience. Generally, as in Japan, an employee can be given pay in lieu of notice.[10] Separate regulations exist for mass termination in 11 of the 13 jurisdictions. The number of workers necessary to constitute a mass termination is usually 50 or more in a period of four weeks. The amount of notice that must be given ranges from 4 weeks to 18 weeks, depending on the number of workers let go.

Employment-protection legislation in two Canadian jurisdictions also includes severance pay. In the federal jurisdiction, the amount of compensation is not large, consisting of two days' wages to be paid per year of service. In Ontario, severance packages apply only to employees with five or more years of service; the amount of compensation given is quite high, however, at one week of severance pay for each year of service, to a maximum of 26 weeks. Finally, most Canadian jurisdictions with mass-termination laws compel employers, in the event of a mass layoff, to establish and finance a "manpower adjustment committee" with worker representation to develop an adjustment program for workers and to help workers in finding new employment opportunities. Furthermore, the firms must advise and cooperate with local governments regarding the closure procedure.

Unlike the common law, employee remedies for employer noncompliance with minimum notice statutes are relatively fast and costless. In Ontario, for example, an employee has only to notify the local Employment Standards office and this can be done by telephone. The claim is then investigated and if the employer is found liable, he or she may be ordered by a judge to reimburse wages for the required notice period.

Given their universal application and ease of enforcement, one would expect the statutory notice provisions outlined above to be relevant to a much larger number of workers than those in the common law. While this is certainly true, Table 3.2 shows that even these minimum standards do not result in notice actually being received by the majority of workers experiencing a permanent layoff in Canada: only 35 percent of men and about 44 percent of women in such situations report receiving any formal notice at all. Of those who receive formal notice, about 30 percent obtain less than one week; only 6–10 percent (or 2–7 percent of all layoffs) receive more than one month (four weeks) of notice. The fraction *expecting* the permanent layoff is somewhat higher, at 63 and 60 percent for men and women, respectively, but even among these the vast majority learned of the impending job loss less than two weeks in advance. The principal reason for this lack of widespread notice is simply the preponderance of very short jobs in any sample of Canadian job losers. Thus, notice requirements are not binding on employers for the majority of job losers in Canada. It would be very useful to know how much "effective" notice of this kind is actually available to displaced workers in Japan, but we are not aware of any source of such information.

Finally, it is interesting to note that the current mix of employment-protection laws in Canada has resulted from a series of province-by-province increases in legislated notice starting in the 1960s. Indeed, despite the recent move to the political right in a number of jurisdictions, and despite significant retrenchment in a number of social programs and in labor relations legislation, as of January 1999 there has not been a single instance of a reduction in employment-protection law in Canada. In contrast to Europe, where employment-protection laws have been blamed for high unemployment rates and in many cases have been scaled back as a result, current levels of Canadian employment-protection legislation have not been perceived as a major obstacle to business. Instead, it appears that they are sufficiently valued by middle-class voters in a time of greater perceived job insecurity to make any attack on them politically unprofitable.

Comparing Canadian and Japanese employment-protection laws, it seems that, if anything, minimum statutory provisions for notice and severance are stronger in Canada. At the same time, however, it is not clear that these statutory provisions apply to most laid-off workers in Canada, and it may be the case that the stricter procedural requirements for layoffs in Japan give rise to greater "effective" notice than the statutory minimum in most cases. Ranking the two countries in terms of legal impediments to layoffs is therefore not clear; to this end, statistics on how far in advance Japanese workers actually knew of their layoff would be very useful in future research.

Passive Income Support

Japan

Japan's employment insurance (EI) system covers all employed workers except those aged 60 or older, government employees, and ship workers. Eligibility conditions include employment in EI-covered jobs for at least six months in the year prior to job separation and application to a government placement office for job-seeking status. Some restrictions apply for voluntary quits.

Statutory benefit levels under Japan's employment insurance system are presented in Table 3.3. EI payments range between 60 and 80 percent (50 and 80 percent for those 60 to 64) of the regular wage on the last job held, up to a maximum. The replacement rate declines with the rate of pay on the last job, while the maximum daily payment increases with age up to 59. Benefit duration varies from 90 to 300 days and is an increasing function of age, number of years insured, and full-time status. As the table indicates, somewhat longer benefits are available for disabled and other "hard to employ" workers.[11]

In addition to basic income support, Japanese EI provides numerous other allowances for items like learning a skill, lodging cost for job training, disability during unemployment, job search, preparation for a new job, and moving costs. There are also a number of programs for unemployed workers who are not eligible under the EI law, such as a training subsidy for changing jobs (*Shokugyo tenkan kyuuhukin*). Finally, in addition to EI, Japan also has a welfare system for its long-term unemployed. Households certified for welfare receive cash and in-kind payments in various forms.

Canada

In contrast to Japan's EI system, which in most cases requires at least half a year of work to qualify, Canada's EI system allows workers with quite short employment spells to qualify for benefits, especially in high-unemployment regions.

Canada's system of passive income support for the unemployed has two components: EI (called unemployment insurance [UI] before 1996), and Social Assistance, more commonly referred to as "welfare." EI, or UI, is federally operated, compulsory, and covers well over 90 percent of employed Canadians. During the 1990s, the program went through a series of substantial changes, primarily designed to reduce costs. In what follows we describe the main features of Canada's UI system in the period in which most of our data were collected—the mid 1990s. Information about subsequent reforms to the system, in particular in 1996, is available in Canada Employment Insurance Commission (1997).[12]

Despite the changes between 1990 and 1996, the main features of UI were reasonably constant over this period since most of the amendments were to parameters of the system rather than to the structure of the program itself. *Insurable employment* was deemed to be any paid employment over 15 hours per week, but earnings over a specified ceiling were not insurable. Premiums were (nominally) paid by both workers and employers, but collected and remitted by employers. In addition to sufficient earnings, qualifying for benefits required a minimum number of weeks of work during a 52-week qualifying period. The number of work weeks required varied across regions, from 20 in regions with a 6 percent or lower unemployment rate to 12 (10 in the early part of the period) where the unemployment rate was above 13 percent.[13]

All claimants received the same statutory replacement rate for earnings up to a weekly maximum. In 1995 this was 55 percent (60 percent for low-income individuals with a dependent) of the average weekly insurable earnings for the 20 weeks prior to the claim. The number of benefit weeks to which one was entitled varied from 14 to 50 as a function of the local unemployment rate and the number of qualifying weeks worked. In January 1995, after several cuts to the program's generosity, in a high unemployment-rate region 12 weeks of work entitled a worker to 32 weeks of benefits, while in a low unemployment-rate region 12 weeks was too few to obtain benefits, and the minimum number of weeks of work required for entitlement, 20, entitled a worker to 14 weeks of benefits. Workers with a full year of employment still qualified for a full year of benefits.

The broad magnitudes of Canadian UI entitlements are thus roughly comparable to those in Japan, summarized earlier. There seem to be two main differences, one of which is the greater generosity of the Canadian system to part-year, or seasonal, workers, who at the very most would be entitled to a lump sum of 50 days' worth of benefits in Japan. On the other hand, the Japanese system offers higher replacement rates, of up to 80 percent for low-wage workers, to displaced workers with steady work histories.[14]

In addition to employment insurance, all Canadians, including single men, are eligible for welfare (or in the case of those over age 65, other social benefits). Welfare is a provincial responsibility, and in some provinces it is administered at a municipal level; thus there is substantial inter- (and intra-) provincial heterogeneity. Welfare can be obtained after UI benefits are exhausted, and there is some evidence that the two programs substitute for one another. Like Japanese welfare, (but unlike the current U.S. welfare system), Canadian welfare has no benefit expiration.

Employment Maintenance and Adjustment Subsidies

Japan

Compared to the United States or Canada, Japan has a large number of programs specifically targeted at maintaining employment in designated declining industries. The Japanese programs are administered under two distinct bodies of legislation: EI laws and employment maintenance (EM) laws (*koyo taisakuho*). Programs under both systems consist largely of employment, outplacement, and training subsidies; in this section we describe the programs administered under the EI law only.[15]

Eligibility for most types of employment maintenance and adjustment subsidies requires the firm or worker to be in one of two lists of narrowly defined industries specified by the Ministry of Labor. Industries in both these lists are typically in need of significant downward employment adjustment. Industries in the first list, "special employment adjustment industries" (*tokutei koyo chosei gyoshu*), are considered to face little prospect for future recovery; this is not necessarily true of the second group, "employment adjustment subsidy industries" (*koyo chosei joseikin shitei gyoshu*). As of early 1998, there were 72 special employment adjustment industries comprising 86,954 establishments and 723,022 workers. As of mid 1998, there were 51 employment adjustment subsidy industries, comprising 511,921 establishments and 846,957 workers. Lists of both types of industries are provided in the appendix. Note that the average establishment covered by both laws is very small, with only 8.3 and 1.6 employees, respectively.

Employment maintenance and adjustment subsidies paid under Japan's EI program fall into four main categories, discussed in turn below. The first of these is available to workers and firms in both groups of industries described above. The other three are available only in special employment adjustment industries, those with little prospect for recovery.

Employment adjustment subsidy (*koyo chosei joseikin*). This law allows the Japanese government to subsidize the wages of workers who are laid off, are on educational or training assignments because of the lack of work, or are reassigned to another firm (*shukko*). Current subsidy rates are one-half of the wages of workers who are laid off or on *shukko*, with a higher rate of two-thirds in small and medium-size enterprises (SMEs).[16] The maximum subsidy duration is 200 days for laid-off workers and two years for *shukko* assignments. This program also pays half the cost of worker retraining or education (two-thirds in SMEs) for up to two years.

Labor movement employment-stability subsidy (*rodo ido koyo antei joseikin*). This subsidy is given to those firms in special employment-adjustment industries which invested in new lines of business in order to employ workers who have become redundant in the old operations. Interestingly, these subsidies are also payable to firms in *any* industry who *hire* workers displaced from special employment-adjustment industries. The subsidies are used for paying portions of workers' wages and/or relocation costs. Current subsidy rates are one-fourth of wages (one-third for SMEs) for up to one year. Other benefits are moving costs (actual cost up to a prespecified limit), housing costs (one-half of the cost paid by the employer for realtor fees and one year's rent), and special subsidies paid to firms for their new investment in plant and equipment and employment maintenance.

Labor movement ability-development subsidy (*rodo ido noryoku kaihatsu joseikin*). This subsidy is given to employers in special employment-adjustment industries who provide workers with education or training for the purpose of *shukko*, arranging for new jobs and reassignment of workers to new lines of business. The length of the subsidy is for one year prior to the relocation of workers. The subsidy takes the following forms: i) two-thirds of the wages (three-fourths for SMEs) with a maximum of 10,510 yen per day; ii) two-thirds of the training cost (three-fourths for SMEs) with a maximum of 100,000 yen; and iii) a subsidy to relocation costs for workers who receive retraining for new occupations. Components (i) and (ii) are also available to employers in any industry who employ and train workers who were laid off by firms belonging to special employment-adjustment industries.

Lifetime ability-development subsidy (*shogai noryoku kaihatsu kyuhukin*). Three distinct activities are subsidized under this program. "Ability-development subsidies" cover portions of employers' cost of training workers in their own company occupational skill-development programs. "Self-development subsidies" (*jiko keihatsu josei kyuuhukin*) reimburse a portion of employers' subsidy to their workers' cost of receiving outside education and training. Finally, a subsidy is also available for the development and testing of officially recognized tests of worker skill, the "skill evaluation promotion subsidy" (*gino hyoka sokushin kyuuhukin*).

Canada

Canada does not have a formal approach to government intervention in declining industries like Japan's. However, there is a mosaic of ad hoc initiatives and semi-permanent programs that perform a similar function, although not on as large a scale. The steel industry, for example, experienced a large downturn in the last few decades and the federal government funded a multiyear Canadian Steel Trades Employment Congress to aid workers in retraining and job search. Similar programs received funding to aid workers displaced as a result of international trade agreements, such as the North American Free Trade Agreement. In general, large failing firms and organized industries have frequently looked to the government for loan guarantees, tax concessions, or other forms of support. Although these "bailouts" are not as common as they once were, they occur regularly and, typically, each is a highly politicized event that is handled on an ad hoc basis by the government in power.

As in Japan, Canada's UI-EI system does play some role in retraining and in the explicit subsidization of labor mobility. UI-EI offers retraining assistance, for example, and in 1994, 6.2 percent of all UI weeks paid were in this category (combined with geographic mobility assistance). Furthermore, all formal tuition fees and moving costs can be deducted from taxable income; so the government implicitly subsidizes all such activity. Finally, there are smaller specialized UI-EI programs to promote temporary work sharing, job creation, and self-employment assistance, all of which have some parallels in the Japanese EI system. However, in 1994 these three specialized programs together accounted for only 1.5 percent of all UI benefit weeks paid.

Unions

A country's system of unionization is directly relevant to the experiences of its displaced workers in at least two ways. One of these is the effect of unions on the entire distribution of pre- and postdisplacement wages. For example, one might expect displaced workers in an economy with highly decentralized wage-setting institutions to face more wage uncertainty than workers in a more centralized economy. Second, unions sometimes intervene directly in the management of the displacement process. We provide a brief discussion of the possible effects of unions on displaced workers in Japan and Canada in this section.

Japan

In Japan, like Canada and the United States, only a minority of workers are unionized. The Japanese unionization rate (union members divided by the number of employed) peaked around 35.5 percent in the 1970s and gradually declined to the current level of 24 percent. As in Canada and the United States, unionization is highest in the government and public utilities sectors (about 67 percent), compared to 29 percent in manufacturing industries and 15 percent in the service sector. Also like Canada and the United States, Japanese unions are highly decentralized: the predominant form of private sector union in Japan is organized at the enterprise level. While legal provisions do exist for the extension of collective bargaining agreements to nonunion workers, these only set relatively low minimum wages within prefectures (see the following section on minimum wages).

Despite its low level of unionization and its enterprise-based structure, Japan's collective bargaining does contain one element of centralized coordination not present in the United States and Canada. This is the annual unified negotiation process, which takes place every spring between the Japanese Employers' Federation and various associations of labor unions (*shunto*). Wage settlements in *shunto* are determined at the firm level and vary across industries and firms, reflecting their industry- and firm-specific performance.[17] This process typically determines the formulas for general and individual annual increases in the level of regular pay. The formulas for bonuses, which are paid twice a year (usually in June and December), are also determined for unionized workers during the period between early spring and June. Bonuses generally constitute more than 25 percent of workers' annual pay and fluctuate more over time than regular (contract) pay.[18]

While nonunionized workers and government employees are not covered by *shunto*, it is widely argued that *shunto* wage settlements have a significant impact on the wages of these workers as well. Although the process by which this occurs is hard to document, Teulings and Hartog (1998), among others, have argued that this informal, economy-wide wage coordination has important effects on the national wage structure. If so, it is likely to have observable effects on the wage changes experienced by displaced workers as well—a question we address in detail later in this chapter.

Japanese unions also generally play at least some explicit role in the management of the displacement process at the firm level. According to the 1991 Survey of Labor-Management Agreements (Japan Ministry of Labor 1992), approximately 70 percent of unionized firms have some formal rules for employer-union consultation regarding job rotation, *shukko,* and rehiring of retired workers. Ninety percent of these firms have some formal rules for consultation regarding layoffs. On the other hand, a much smaller proportion of firms (30 percent) have formal rules for consultation regarding employment matters resulting from the introduction of new technology. It is unknown how common these arrangements are in nonunionized firms.

Canada

In 1997, Canada had a union membership rate of 31 percent of employed persons, with about 34 percent of workers covered by a collective bargaining agreement (Akyeampong 1997). While this is more than double the U.S. rate at that time, many aspects of Canada's industrial relations system are similar to that in the United States, from which Canada adapted much of its collective bargaining legislation.[19] Wage bargaining is done at the plant level, but not coordinated annually as in Japan. Most agreements are two or three years in duration, but this is an outcome of the bargaining process and single-year contracts are not unheard of. State-sanctioned extension of collectively bargained wages to nonunionized workers is essentially non-existent. As is well known, the average union/nonunion wage gap for observationally identical workers in North America is about 15 percent. Furthermore, relative to nonunion firms, North American unions compress wages across skill levels (see Lemieux 1993). Kuhn and Sweetman (1998) showed that the loss of union status plays a very significant role in the wage losses of Canadian displaced workers.

In sum, only a minority of workers are union members in both Canada and Japan. While there is some coordination of wage settlements in Japan, and some extension of union wage settlements to nonunion workers, both countries have quite decentralized wage-setting mechanisms in which conditions at the level of the individual firm play large roles in the setting of wages. Based on an examination of the collective bargaining system, one would therefore expect considerable dispersion in the wage outcomes of displaced workers in *both* countries, as compared, for example, with such highly centralized countries as Denmark or Austria.

Minimum Wages

Minimum wages, like unions, affect the entire distribution of pre- and postdisplacement wages. They could thus affect the distribution of wage changes experienced by displaced workers in each country.

Japan

Unlike U.S. or Canadian minimum wages, which are hourly rates, Japanese minimum wages are generally specified on a daily basis. Like Canada (and to a much lesser extent the United States) Japanese minimum wages vary among political subdivisions of the country, which in Japan are called prefectures. Unlike either the United States or Canada, Japanese minimum wages also vary across industries. Minimum wages are determined by Prefectural Minimum Wage Councils and are set in two main ways.[20]

District minimum wages. Each of the 47 prefectures has an overall minimum wage. These minimum wages are applicable to all workers including part-time workers, nonregular workers, and workers under other types of employment contracts. At the time of writing, most of the prefectural minimum wages were set on October 1, 1997; they range from 4,625 yen for Okinawa (lowest in the nation) to 5,368 yen for Tokyo and Kanagawa (highest).

Industry minimum wages. Within each prefecture, management and unions can agree on higher minimum wages for certain industries. There are currently 253 industry-level minimum wages of this type. Examples include the pulp and paper industry in Toyama Prefecture (5,637 yen, set on November 25, 1995); the pulp and paper industry in Shizuoka Prefecture (5,848 yen, set on December 31, 1997); the steel industry (5,487 yen in Oita; 5,970 in Tokyo; and 6,184 in Osaka); and the retail automobile industry (4,630 in Okinawa; and 6,049 in Saitama). These industry-specific minimum wages, which do not have a counterpart in Canada, may provide a channel whereby collectively bargained wages affect the wages of unorganized workers, and—because they exceed the overall district minimum—may work to compress wages in Japan more than minimum wages in Canada do.

Canada

As noted, minimum wages in Canada are a provincial responsibility, except for a small number of industries that are under federal jurisdiction, and are increased periodically on an ad hoc basis. With the exception of a small number of federally regulated industries, the minimum wage does not vary across industries. Benjamin, Gunderson, and Riddell (1998) described the trend of a population-weighted average of Canadian minimum wages. In the mid 1970s it was about 50 percent of the average manufacturing wage. It fell over the subsequent decade to about 35 percent and increased recently to about 38 percent.

In sum, both Canada and Japan have minimum wages that are set at subnational levels (provinces in Canada, prefectures and industry-prefecture cells in Japan). Clearly, these levels reflect local economic conditions, as they tend to be higher in higher-wage jurisdictions. Unlike Canada, Japan has a system of industry-specific minimum wages that exceed general local mimina and provide a channel whereby collectively bargained wages can affect nonunion wages. Finally, minimum wages are not very high relative to mean wages in either country. This is shown in Table 3.4: Japan, Canada, and the United States all have minimum wages between 36 and 38 percent of mean wages (though the definitions of mean wages vary somewhat), levels which are very low compared with France and Germany. We thus expect considerable heterogeneity in the wage outcomes experienced by displaced workers in both countries, with perhaps somewhat more legislation-induced wage compression in Japan than in Canada, given Japan's system of industry wage minima.

GENERAL ECONOMIC CONDITIONS

In this section, we briefly describe the overall macroeconomic and labor market conditions around the period (the mid 1990s) to which most of our analysis applies.

Japan

As is well known, the mid 1990s was a period of deepening recession for the Japanese economy. Unemployment rose from 2.1 percent in 1990 to 4.1 percent in 1998, and the number of vacancies per job seeker was cut by more than half, from 1.4 to 0.5. This recession has often been linked to the burst of the stock- and property-market bubble in 1990. The Nikkei stock price index climbed to its historical high of 38,916 yen on December 29, 1989. The bubble burst in 1990, and the Nikkei index fell to 20,222 yen on October 1, 1990 and then to 14,309 yen on August 18, 1992. Another factor contributing to the recession may have been Japan's recent deindustrialization, driven in part by the appreciation of the Japanese currency in the late 1980s. It is estimated that the fraction of overseas production in Japanese manufacturers' overall sales revenue, which had been about 3 percent in 1985, had risen to more than 8 percent by 1994 and was expected to approach 11 percent by 2000. At the same time the share of manufactured goods in total Japanese imports grew from 31 percent in 1985 to more than 55 percent in 1994. These trends were reflected in the much steeper declines in manufacturing employment than in overall employment during the 1980s and 1990s, and could be expected to put unprecedented pressure on Japanese firms, especially in manufacturing, to shed labor.

Canada

Canada's unemployment rate has been higher than Japan's throughout most of the postwar period and has exceeded that of the United States since the early 1980s. It peaked most recently in the 1992 recession at 11.3 percent, and declined only very slowly after that to 9.2 percent in 1997. The national number masks enormous regional differences, however, that have persisted for decades. Some areas have unemployment rates that are approximately 20 percentage points higher than others. The rate of employment growth also slowed markedly in the first half of the 1990s and the employment rate dropped from a peak in the low 60 percent range in the late 1980s to just under 60 percent.

Thus, during the mid 1990s, economic conditions were moving in opposite directions in Japan and Canada: deteriorating in Japan and improving in Canada. Despite this, it is important to note that there was a huge gap in unemployment rates in favor of Japan: in 1995, the Canadian unemployment rate of 9.5 percent was almost *triple* the Japanese rate of 3.2. This difference colors all discussion of comparative displacement and reemployment rates in the two countries. As we shall see, it shows up in large differences in both displacement rates and jobless durations among displaced workers in the two countries.

RATES OF SEPARATION AND DISPLACEMENT

Data

The goal of this section is to ascertain whether, and to what extent, job displacement is more or less common in Japan than in Canada. As displacements are a subset of all job separations, we present results on overall separation rates as well. In addition, we wish to see whether broad patterns of the incidence of separation and displacement among demographic groups (essentially age and gender groups) are similar in the two countries.

To accomplish this goal, we use one Japanese and two Canadian data sets. For Japan, we rely on the employment mobility survey (EMS), with its relatively large sample of persons leaving and entering firms. For Canada, we use a very large sample of separations drawn from administrative data collected by Human Resources Development Canada (HRDC). We supplement this with a much smaller, but richer, survey of separators called the Canadian Out-of-Employment Panel (COEP).

Japan's employment mobility survey ("Survey of Employment Trends") is an establishment survey that is conducted twice a year by the Ministry of Labor. The two surveys for each year (typically conducted during the periods July 1 to July 31 and January 16 to February 15) cover the employment changes which have taken place at surveyed establishments during the periods January 1 to June 30 and July 1 to December 31, respectively. This survey began in essentially the present form in 1964. Privately and publicly owned establishments with at least five employees in the following nine industries are covered: mining, construction, manufacturing, public utilities, transportation and communications, retail/wholesale and restaurants, finance/insurance, real estate, and service. In 1995, 14,000 establishments were surveyed. In addition to establishments' characteristics, the survey collects information on three subsets of their workers: 1) those who were hired during the six-month reference period, 2) those who left the firm during that period, and 3) those who experienced transfers from one establishment to another within the same firm (intrafirm transfers). For 1995, the workers surveyed comprise about 130,000 new hires, 120,000 departures, and 50,000 within-firm transfers. In this section we use the "departures" sample to compute separation and displacement rates; later we use the "hires" sample to examine the consequences of displacement.[21] We do not use the third, "transfers," sample.

The Canadian administrative data we use is collected as a by-product of administering the employment insurance system. Whenever a separation occurs, a Canadian employer is expected to submit to HRDC a form called a "Record of Employment" (ROE).[22] ROE forms contain information on the date and (firm-reported) reason for the separation, an indication of whether the separation is expected to be permanent or temporary, plus some limited demographic and firm information (including age, gender, job tenure, and firm size). Both the worker and firm are identified, so it is possible to see whether the person returned to the original firm after the separation.

Time series of separation rates based on the above data have recently been published in a series of Statistics Canada working papers (Picot and Lin 1996; Picot, Lin and Pyper 1997; Lin and Pyper 1997); these rates are not comparable to Japanese data derived from the employment mobility survey, however, for a number of reasons. In particular, the Japanese survey on which our results are based is restricted to establishments with five or more employees, to jobs lasting at least a month, and to a large but not exhaustive set of industries (for example, most of the public sector is excluded). To adjust for these differences (some of which make a considerable difference to the numbers), Garnett Picot and Leonard Landry of Statistics Canada have generously provided us with revised figures that impose the same restrictions as the Japanese numbers.

As mentioned, supplementary information on separating workers in Canada is available in a series of surveys called the COEPs. These use ROE forms as the sampling frame for a telephone survey which asks detailed questions about old and new jobs, unemployment durations, and search activities, among other items. In our work here, we use two merged COEP surveys: those which surveyed workers displaced between January and June of 1993 and of 1995. In 1995 this survey was conducted in two panels (or waves) approximately 8–9 and 13–14 months after the event; the 1993 survey had a third panel between these dates. Although much smaller in size than the Japanese employment mobility survey, the COEP gives us a comparable and representative sample of separations, combined with detailed information on their subsequent labor-force status and wages.

Separation and Displacement Rates

Total annual separation rates, calculated from the 1995 Japanese employment mobility survey and comparably defined Canadian administrative data, are presented in the first and third columns of Table 3.5. These rates give the annual number of separations from jobs which have lasted one month or more, from firms with five or more workers, expressed as a fraction of the employed population in June of 1995.[23]

Overall, the differences are striking: employed Canadian men are much more likely to experience a separation than Japanese men, with a separation rate of 35.9 percent, essentially triple the Japanese rate of 11.9 percent. The difference is considerably less dramatic for women, whose separation rates are essentially identical to men's in Canada, but much higher than men's in Japan. Thus Canadian women's separation rate (34.1 percent) is not even double that of Japanese women (18.3 percent). Ignoring teenagers, separation rates in both Canada and Japan seem to be U-shaped in age, especially in Japan, and especially for men.[24] Thus jobs are most stable for prime-age workers in both countries, as one might expect from a number of models, including job-shopping models and models where retirement is followed by one or more casual jobs.

To what extent are these apparently massive differences in turnover between Canada and Japan "real," in the sense that they actually result in a worker moving from one firm to another? With the exception of some *shukko* assignments, which are relatively infrequent, Japanese separations, especially as reported in Table 3.5, are essentially all permanent.[25] As in the United States, however, temporary layoffs constitute a large fraction of separations in Canada. To correct for this, the second column excludes from the count of separations all those workers who were observed working for their preseparation employer in the year following the separation. This dramatically reduces the Canadian separation rate, to the point where comparably defined permanent separation rates are very similar in Canada (16.8 percent) and Japan (14.3 percent). Previous analyses have often missed this because they included the huge volume of temporary separations in North American economies.

This overall similarity in permanent separation rates, however, obscures offsetting patterns by gender: in line with expectations, Japanese men do turn over substantially less than Canadian men (11.9 versus 16.8 percent per year), but this is offset by higher employment instability among Japanese women (18.3 versus 15.7 percent turnover). Overall rates also obscure a different age pattern in the two economies: while turnover is U-shaped with age in both, the ranking of the two countries is different at the top and bottom of the age distribution.[26] Consistent with a "job shopping" model, young Canadian workers, especially those in their 20s, turn over much more than workers in all other age categories. There is also some evidence of job shopping in Japan, but in stark contrast to Canada, the highest turnover rates in Japan are actually found among the oldest workers, aged 60 and over. These workers actually turn over much more rapidly in Japan than in Canada, suggesting the importance of both mandatory retirement and a casual labor market among "retirees."

Thus we find that overall permanent separation rates are not that different in Japan and Canada, but what about worker *displacements*, or the subset of separations that are involuntary from the worker's point of view? If a larger fraction of permanent turnover in Japan is voluntary, it may still be the case that displacement is less common there. We confront this issue in Table 3.6, which presents the distribution of firm-reported reasons for separation in Japan (from published EMS data), and Table 3.7, which examines both firm- and worker-reported reasons for separation in the Canadian COEP data.

In Table 3.6, the separation reason that corresponds most closely to what North Americans mean by layoffs is the "management convenience" category. In Japan in 1995, this category of separations constituted 8.7 percent of total separations, with a higher share for men (11.3 percent) than women (6.0 percent). Notably, this low "layoff" share includes *shukko* assignments, which do not result in unemployment; thus a count of layoffs that might conceivably cause unemployment would be even lower. At the same time, however, this rate does not include contract expirations or mandatory retirements, which might be considered a form of displacement. All told, *total* involuntary separations—which consist primarily of those based on the three reasons just mentioned—account for about one-third of all separations in Japan, with a higher involuntary share for men than women. The involuntary share increases strongly with age, echoing our earlier notion that job security falls with age in Japan. Importantly, this increase is *not* just due to mandatory retirement, which is important only for workers over 55 in these data. The great bulk of the increase in involuntary separations with age is in the "management convenience" category, which includes *shukko*. In stark contrast (as we shall see) to Canada, the vast majority of separations for all workers under 54 are voluntary; for both women and men, most of these voluntary separations are *not* related to marriage, childbirth, or nursing care.

For Canada, unlike Japan, the COEP survey allows a detailed examination of reported reasons for separation, including information on both the firm's and worker's perceptions. The employer's perceived separation reasons are those reported on the ROE form, which asks employers to choose one of 13 permitted answers: shortage of work (layoff), labor dispute, return to school, injury or illness, voluntary departure (quit), pregnancy, retirement, participation in a work-sharing program, apprenticeship, age 65, dismissal (for cause), leave of absence, and "other."[27] In addition to this information, however, the first panel of the COEP household survey asks each worker the primary reason for which the job ended. Only those whose self-reported reason for separation was either quit, dismissed or fired, laid off, injury or illness, or "other" were allowed to complete this survey (the survey was quickly terminated for separations due to retirement, maternity, labor dispute, and so forth, and these separations are not included in our data).[28]

Table 3.7 presents a cross-tabulation of firm- and self-reported reasons for separation for participants in the COEP survey. Interestingly, there is a divergence of opinion as to the nature of the separation in a substantial number of cases. For men (women) about 13 percent (7 percent) of those who label their separation as a quit have the separation labeled as a layoff by the firm. Almost 14 percent of women (11 percent of men) who said they quit were actually dismissed (i.e., terminated for cause) according to their employers. Further, only 60 percent of men (68 percent of women) whose separations are labeled as voluntary departures by firms label themselves as quits. While 89 percent of men (87 percent of women) reported by the firm as being laid off (a separation attributed to a shortage of work, that is, economic reasons) report themselves as having been laid off, only 76 percent of men (64 percent of women) who report that they were laid off are declared as such by the firm. A large part of this discrepancy results from the "other" category, which firms are much more likely to use than workers, but the number of separations labeled as quits by firms that are declared to be layoffs by workers is quite large, about 24 percent for men and 14 percent for women.

Overall, however, while Table 3.7 shows some discrepancy between worker and firm perceptions, it suggests that the large international differences we observe in the labeling of separations are common to workers and firms. In particular, no matter whether the worker's or the firm's label is used, a much higher share of separations in Canada (relative to Japan) are employer-initiated. Depending on whose label is used, layoffs constitute 62–72 percent of separations for men, and 48–65 percent for women. One reason for this might be Canada's UI-EI system, which disqualifies all workers labeled as quitters from benefits. This feature, combined with a lack of employer experience rating, might lead a much larger fraction of separations to be labeled as layoffs, even by the employer. Another reason might simply be cultural differences in labeling. It is sometimes claimed, for example, that a considerable number of forced resignations are reported under the category of voluntary separations in Japan, to preserve public appearances. If this is the case, our statistics in this section may underestimate the real rate of layoffs in Japan. We return to this issue in the section called "Combining Incidence and Consequences" (p. 243), which proposes and analyzes a definition of displacement that is not dependent on reported reasons for separation to make international comparisons. To anticipate, we find that the larger voluntary share in Japan is not illusory.

Given the rough similarity in overall permanent separation rates, plus the larger share of separations labeled as involuntary in Canada, one would expect the overall rate of displacement—of permanent, involuntary separation—to be higher in Canada than in Japan. This expectation is confirmed overall by Table 3.8, which presents our best estimates of displacement rates in the two countries. The Canadian numbers come from administrative data from Picot, Lin, and Pyper (1997) and simply restrict attention to separations labeled as due to "shortage of work" by the employer on the ROE form.[29] For Japan, the last three columns combine the published information in Tables 3.5 and 3.6 (multiplying separation rates by the fraction of separations in each category) to generate three alternative definitions of displacement rates.

According to Table 3.8, overall displacement rates are lower in Japan, no matter what definition of displacement is used. The overall annual displacement rate in Canada was 4.9 percent in 1995: conditional on being employed at least a month and on working for a firm with at least 5 employees, about 1 in 20 workers is permanently laid off each year in Canada. According to the narrowest definition of displacement in Japan (separations due to management convenience only), this fraction is only 1.2 percent, or 1 in 83 workers. This number would be even lower if we excluded *shukko* workers from the count of Japanese workers; these workers do not experience any unemployment and (as we shall see) face much more muted wage changes than those in other separations. The Japanese displacement rate *rises* substantially, to 2.7 percent, if we count workers whose temporary contracts end as being displaced.[30] Because they involve permanent, and (presumably) involuntary employment terminations, contract expirations may be considered a kind of displacement; as they typically involve short jobs and are not unanticipated, however, they may not be fully equivalent to layoffs. Finally, if mandatory retirements are included in the count of Japanese displacements, the overall displacement rate rises to 3.5 percent, still below the Canadian rate of 4.9 percent but much less dramatically so.[31]

Is the international difference in displacement rates shown in Table 3.8 an artifact of special features of work organization in one or two industries? One might imagine, for example, that the construction industry in Canada accounts for a very large share of annual separations nationwide. In that industry, many workers have a permanent affiliation to a craft rather than an employer and cycle through a large number of jobs with different employers in a given year. This is a fundamentally different form of labor market organization than almost all other industries. To check for this, we were able to generate separation and displacement rates for two roughly comparable industry groups—construction and manufacturing—for 1995 in both countries, according to the definitions used in Tables 3.5 and 3.8. The figures are for men and women combined. For construction, we find separation rates of 54 percent in Canada, but the permanent separation rate is only 22 percent. This compares to a permanent separation rate of 15 percent in Japan. The permanent layoff rate is 17.7 percent in Canada, compared to 1.1 percent in Japan, according to the "management convenience" definition in Table 3.8. Thus there is indeed a huge difference in displacement rates between the two countries in the construction industry. For manufacturing, the separation rate is 49 percent in Canada, but permanent separations are only 17.3 percent, compared to 12.1 percent in Japan. Manufacturing displacement rates, as defined above, are 6.1 percent in Canada and 1.1 percent in Japan. Thus, looking just at manufacturing, the international difference in displacement rates is smaller than in construction, but still very large. Indeed the rates for manufacturing are quite similar to those for the economy as a whole. We conclude that the differences seen in Table 3.8 are not an artifact of how the construction industry, or any other single industry, is organized.

Two other noteworthy features of Table 3.8 are the following. First, perhaps surprisingly, displacement rates are quite similar for Japanese men and women, but are considerably higher for Canadian men than Canadian women. In part due to differences in industry mix (men are overrepresented in construction, primary, and manufacturing industries) and to interindustry differences in adjustment patterns (the above industries have more volatile product demand and rely more on layoffs as an adjustment mechanism), displacement is thus disproportionately a "male" phenomenon in Canada. Second, and even more striking, are the opposite age patterns in Canada and Japan, which are particularly stark for men: *displacement rates fall with age in Canada but increase with age in Japan.* While mandatory retirement clearly plays some role here, Table 3.8 indicates that much more than this is going on: both layoffs due to "management convenience" and finishing a temporary contract also increase substantially with age in Japan. This trend highlights a key difference between the job markets of the two countries, which we explore further below: although Canadian workers operate in a less-secure job market overall, their job security tends to increase as they age, in part due to rising seniority levels and the widespread practice of ordering layoffs by inverse seniority. In Japan, the opposite occurs: while young workers experience very high job security, this security erodes with age, as more and more workers are forced out among the older age groups. Even excluding mandatory retirements, the displacement rate for Japanese workers over the age of 55 actually exceeds the Canadian displacement rate for workers of the same age.

In sum, our analysis of separation and displacement rates in Canada and Japan shows the following. There are large differences in total separation rates between Japan and Canada, with Canadian separations being much more frequent. Because a large fraction of Canadian separations are temporary (involving a return to the original employer), differences in *permanent* separations between the two countries are however much more modest. In fact this difference is reversed for women, who have a higher permanent separation rate in Japan than Canada. Finally, if we restrict attention to those separations that are labeled as firm-initiated (or as "layoffs"), the difference between Canadian and Japanese separation rates (which we can now consider as "displacement rates") again becomes much wider. The reason is that in Japan, a much larger share of separations tends to be labeled as "voluntary" from the worker's point of view. An implication, of course, is that the total rate of voluntary separation must actually be greater in Japan than in Canada; understanding this phenomenon would seem to be an important goal for further research.

The Permanence of Layoffs

A final, but key, element in our description of displacement rates in the two countries is a closer understanding of the North American phenomenon of temporary layoffs; as noted above, a very large fraction of separations in Canada involves a temporary sojourn on employment insurance, followed by recall to the preseparation employer. When workers are laid off in Canada, how certain are they about their recall prospects? Do their expectations coincide with the firm's, and how well do both parties' expectations predict what actually happens? These questions have important implications for workers' search strategies and provide a useful contrast to the Japanese case, where separations (except for certain types of *shukko*) almost always involve a permanent severing of ties with the employer. We use the COEP to answer these questions in Tables 3.9 and 3.10.

Table 3.9 contrasts worker and firm recall expectations among the subset of workers from Table 3.7 who are labeled as a layoff by either party. The firm data are from the ROE form which is filled out near the time of separation. The worker expectations are retrospective: workers were asked at the time of the first survey what their expectation was when the job ended. By this time, workers had had an opportunity to see the ROE form. On average, the fraction of laid-off women expecting recall (46.5 percent) is quite similar to the fraction of women employers expected to recall (49.2 percent). For men there is a somewhat larger gap, with 47.4 percent of workers expecting recall compared to 55.7 percent of firms. At the individual level, however, there are much larger differences in expectations; 34 percent of men (36 percent of women) who indicated that they expected to be recalled, for example, were not listed by the firm as workers they planned to recall.

Recall realizations are contrasted with expectations in Table 3.10 for the subset of workers from Table 3.9 who were reemployed by their last survey date (these are the only workers for whom we can identify the postseparation firm).[32] Clearly, neither firms nor workers are very reliable predictors of recall. For men, about 62 percent of workers who expected to be recalled and 51 percent of the workers firms expected to recall were actually back with their former employer. The corresponding numbers for women are about 70 percent and 63 percent. (This could reflect workers' exercising their option to search while unemployed, locating new jobs, and then declining the recall when it arrives.)[33] Perhaps more surprisingly, about 14 percent of the men and 15 percent of the women who expected not to be recalled were in fact reemployed by their former employer, and 33 percent of men and 35 percent of women with no indication of recall on their ROE were actually recalled. This suggests a reluctance by some firms to indicate an even weak commitment to recall workers in the face of uncertainty.

In sum, both the divergence in individual workers' and firms' expectations of recall and the inaccuracy of both firms' *and* workers' predictions of whether recall will occur mean that, in many cases, displacement in Canada does not constitute a sharp and well-defined event. Workers on EI may search at a low intensity for several months waiting to see whether they will be recalled or not. In contrast to Japan, where displacement constitutes a short, sharp, and permanent break with the firm, this more drawn-out process may contribute to the longer unemployment durations among displaced workers in Canada. We turn to this issue in the next section.

LABOR-FORCE TRANSITIONS AFTER DISPLACEMENT

In the previous section we established that, with the possible exception of older men, worker displacement is less common in Japan than in Canada. In this section we begin our analysis of the consequences of displacement in the two countries, focusing on the amount of time it takes displaced workers to find new jobs. In particular, we are interested in whether Japanese workers "pay" for their greater job security with worse unemployment consequences in the event of involuntary job loss. Because so few workers are displaced, are the few workers who are displaced seen by the labor market as "lemons," thus experiencing very long unemployment durations? Relatedly, does the widely cited "thinness" of Japanese labor markets for mid-career workers manifest itself in much longer unemployment durations of laid-off workers? Finally, we are also interested in the empirical correlates of long-term unemployment: are the same kinds of workers likely to experience long durations in both countries, or do patterns differ?

Table 3.11 contains our main results on the relative unemployment durations of displaced workers in Canada and Japan. The Japanese figures in that table are calculated from a special survey of workers entering unemployment, conducted in conjunction with the Japanese labor force survey in 1996 and 1997 (Japan Ministry of Labor 1996, 1997). This survey specifically interviewed workers who were employed one year before the survey date and experienced a separation within the prior 12 months. Individuals who had dropped out of the labor force (were neither working nor looking for work at the survey date) were not interviewed. With a sample size of about 5,200 persons, this special survey is small compared to the Employment Mobility Survey, but unlike that survey (and like the COEP) it contains relatively detailed information on jobless durations for an inflow-based sample. Our sample of displaced workers from this survey consists of all separations due to layoffs, bankruptcy, a decline in business, and other "management convenience" reasons.[34] This sample does not include workers on *shukko*, as such workers generally experience no unemployment. Both Japanese and Canadian samples, however, do include individuals who, despite being involuntarily and permanently terminated, moved directly into another job with no intervening joblessness.[35]

Canadian figures in Table 3.11 are based on the COEP survey. Canadian displaced workers are defined as those experiencing a separation due to a self-reported "layoff" who do not return to their preseparation employer within the (approximately) one-year panel of the COEP survey. For comparability with the Japanese statistics (which drop individuals who are not in the labor force on the single survey date on which they were interviewed), we impose two alternative restrictions on the Canadian sample: "Canada A" drops individuals who were out of the labor force at every date on which they were interviewed after the separation; Canada B drops individuals who were out of the labor force at *any* of the (postseparation) interview dates.[36] Together, results from these two samples should bracket what would be obtained from a sampling strategy identical to the Japanese one.

The numbers presented in Table 3.11 are cumulative reemployment rates derived from a Kaplan-Meier estimate of the survivor function. The Kaplan-Meier technique provides a simple way to adjust for the effect of censoring in the data, which is empirically fairly important: in Japan, 31 percent of men's and 30 percent of women's durations were censored; in Canada this fraction was higher, at 32 and 42 percent, respectively. Cumulative reemployment rates give the fraction of workers whose completed jobless durations are estimated to have ended by a specific amount of time after the layoff, and, by definition, cannot decrease with elapsed time.

Overall, the message of Table 3.11 is clear: even though displacement is much less common in Japan, Japanese displaced workers do not take longer to become reemployed than Canadian displaced workers. In contrast, their durations are much shorter, with a median of just under two months for both men and women, compared with between five and six months for Canadian men and between seven and nine months for Canadian women. Two months after displacement, over half of Japanese workers are reemployed, compared with under 30 percent of Canadian workers (according to either Canadian sample). Six months later, about three-quarters are reemployed in Japan compared with about 52 and 42 percent of Canadian men and women, respectively. It is worth reemphasizing that these results apply to involuntarily terminated workers only, and that they hold in spite of the fact that a much smaller fraction of separations are involuntary in Japan, and of the fact that we have excluded *shukko* workers (who experience involuntary mobility but no unemployment) from our calculations. Accounting for these factors would only widen the gap between Japan's low unemployment durations and Canada's higher ones.

Clearly, we do not find any evidence that "thinness" of mid-career labor markets or a "lemons" phenomenon hurts Japanese displaced workers, at least relative to Canadian ones. Instead, two other factors seem likely to be at work. One is simply the higher overall Canadian unemployment rate: as noted, despite the Japanese recession, unemployment rates in Japan were less than half of Canadian rates at the time of these surveys. The second may be the distinctly North American issue of recall expectations: the lack of a clean break with the old employer (even in the current sample of *ex post* permanent layoffs) may discourage search for a new job, thus contributing to the higher unemployment durations of Canadian displaced workers.

Results from modeling the impact of covariates on the reemployment hazard are presented in Tables 3.12 and 3.13 for Japan and Canada, respectively. In both cases we use a Cox partial likelihood specification, which assumes the covariates have a proportional effect on the hazard and allows for a fully general baseline hazard rate. The reported coefficients give the effect of each covariate on the log of the reemployment hazard. In Japan (Table 3.12), both the number of observed covariates and the sample size are small, and very few observed characteristics have a statistically significant effect on the hazard rate. A significant exception is that part-time workers, especially women, have higher reemployment hazards (and hence shorter jobless durations) than full-time workers. In addition, workers displaced from industry 14 ("other" industries, not elsewhere classified) have much lower hazards, and hence longer jobless durations, than the omitted industry, manufacturing.

In Canada we have both a larger sample and a more exhaustive set of covariates; as a result we are able to show quite a lot more about patterns in jobless durations in Table 3.13. All regressions in this table use the "Canada A" sample described earlier, though the results change very little when the smaller, "Canada B" sample is used. The specifications in columns 3 and 6 attempt to replicate the Japanese analysis in Table 3.12 as closely as possible. In contrast to Japan, these two regressions show that demographic and (predisplacement) firm characteristics matter a lot for the jobless durations of Canadian displaced workers. In particular, for men, lower reemployment rates are found among single workers, those displaced from firms with under 20 workers (the omitted category), visible minorities, and high-tenure workers. Age has a U-shaped effect on reemployment rates. All these patterns also hold for women, with two exceptions. Being single has the opposite, though not significant, effect—raising the reemployment hazard—and education has a strong, positive effect on reemployment rates (high school diploma is the omitted category). In contrast to Japan, being a part-time worker has no significant effect on reemployment rates, at least in the comparably specified regressions of columns 3 and 6.

The remaining columns in Table 3.13 add extra controls to check for the robustness of the correlations identified above. Columns 1 and 4 add a measure of predisplacement union coverage and province fixed effects; columns 2 and 5 add these plus the predisplacement wage—as a proxy for individual characteristics observable to the previous employer, but not to the econometrician. Interestingly, unionization is associated with a much *higher* reemployment hazard for men, but has no impact for women. In addition, and perhaps surprisingly, while the predisplacement wage (mean about 13.5) has a strong effect for men, it has no effect at all for women. Looking across the three specifications, most of the coefficient estimates are not strongly affected by the inclusion of additional controls.

In addition to reemployment rates, the COEP provides some related information concerning the search and employment behavior of displaced Canadians. For example, by the first survey date, 5.6 percent of Canadian displaced workers had started their own businesses after being laid off. Overall, 7.3 percent considered themselves to be self-employed at the first survey, 4.0 percent full-time and 3.3 percent part-time. But 28 percent of those who were full-time self-employed, and 51 percent of those who were part-time, were also searching for another job at that point. This compares favorably with the set of all workers reemployed at that point; 58 percent of all workers who were reemployed at the first survey date reported that they were still searching for another job. The fact that many Canadian displaced workers continue searching for other jobs even after becoming reemployed, combined (as we shall see) with the much higher fraction of Canadian displaced workers whose first postseparation job pays very much less than their previous one, suggests that postdisplacement "job shopping" may play a more important role in how Canadian workers "recover" from displacement than it does for Japanese workers.

WAGE CHANGES

In this section we conduct an econometric analysis of the wage changes experienced by displaced workers, using data from the 1993 and 1995 COEP for Canada and the 1995 Employment Mobility Survey for Japan. We first present comparable descriptive information on the distribution of wage changes, by age and sex, in both countries. We then examine the structure of displacement-induced wage changes in a regression framework. In both countries we compare the experiences of displaced workers to those of all workers experiencing a job separation. The Canadian sample of displaced workers consists of all permanent layoffs; in Japan we present results for two kinds of displaced workers: workers undergoing *shukko* and those experiencing other involuntary terminations (management convenience, contract expiration, and mandatory retirement).[37] The survey defines *shukko* workers as those who move to work under another employer's command by company order, or by agreement with another employer, regardless of their formal form of employment affiliation (Japan Ministry of Labor 1997a, p. 357).

The Distribution of Displacement-Induced Wage Changes

Detailed information on the distribution of wage changes experienced by Japanese job changers in the Employment Mobility Survey is provided in Table 3.14. As noted, Table 3.14 presents results for three groups of workers: all separations, workers undergoing *shukko,* and all other involuntary separations. The Japanese EMS does not ask workers directly about the level of preseparation wages; rather, it simply presents workers with the five percentage-change categories listed in the table and asks them to choose one. This makes it difficult to present results for mean wage changes, of course; we do provide a rough estimate of a mean, however, by assigning values to each category.[38] Finally, recall that, by definition, only workers who are reemployed after a separation can be included in these wage-change calculations and that the wage information refers to monthly wages excluding bonuses.

According to Table 3.14, the average Japanese male who changed jobs in 1995 experienced a 2.2 percent wage gain; if he changed jobs involuntarily without undergoing *shukko*, he lost 4.3 percent in wages. Closer examination of the data, however, reveals that the latter loss is entirely attributable to workers over 45 years of age: on average men under this age experience a mean wage gain after an involuntary separation. Men above 55, on the other hand, experience very large mean wage losses, many of which may be associated with mandatory retirement and with low-wage or part-time work after retirement. Indeed, the incidence of very large wage reductions among older men who separate involuntarily is remarkable, with almost 40 percent experiencing a wage reduction of over 30 percent. Also, again especially for men, a significant fraction of job changers (both overall and involuntary) experience wage gains, a fraction which declines strongly with age. Finally, the distribution of wage changes among workers undergoing *shukko* contrasts very strongly with the other distributions in Table 3.14: a much higher fraction of *shukko* workers experience wage stability across old and new jobs, with almost 90 percent experiencing a change of less than 10 percent in absolute value. The fact that, at least for a limited time, the old employer continues to pay the wage of such workers almost certainly contributes to this wage stability. These trends differ in two main ways for women. First, large wage reductions among older women undergoing permanent separations are much less common than among men. This reflects, at least in part, the less frequent use of mandatory retirement in women's labor contracts. Second, *shukko* is very rare among women in Japan.

Table 3.15 gives comparable numbers for Canada. As noted, these are derived from the merged 1993 and 1995 COEP surveys. Unlike the Japanese EMS, the COEP asked persons surveyed the actual level of wages in both the pre- and postseparation jobs; Table 3.15 uses these responses to compute percentage changes.[39] The table thus provides an actual mean wage change and an estimated mean using the same values as were assigned to the various categories in Japan, for comparability. In contrast to Japan, however, the Canadian wage data refer to hourly wages, a fact that is important to bear in mind when interpreting regression results on part-time work below.

The following trends are evident from an examination of Table 3.15. First, as in Japan, displaced workers under the age of about 45 do not experience economically significant mean wage losses. Also, as in Japan, mean wage changes among displaced workers, as well as among all separations, become more negative with age, but the decline is much less dramatic. Indeed, the fraction of displaced men experiencing large wage losses appears uncorrelated with age in Canada; the declining mean is largely due to a fall in the fraction of large, displacement-induced wage *gains* with age.

The clearest contrast in wage change patterns between Japan and Canada concerns their variance. Looking specifically at prime-age men (say, age 30–39, before mandatory retirement becomes an issue in Japan), and at the non-*shukko* involuntary separations in both countries, it is clear that the fraction of displaced workers experiencing wage changes of more than 30 percent in absolute value is much greater in Canada (17.20 + 14.66 = 31.86 percent) than in Japan (5.14 + 3.81 = 8.95 percent for 30- to 34-year-olds and 4.67 + 3.63 = 8.30 percent for 35- to 44-year-olds). This is particularly noteworthy when we recall that the Japanese figures are monthly wages, and thus they incorporate any monthly hours variation between jobs. This lower variance in wage changes in Japan is striking, given the relatively decentralized wage-setting regimes in both Japan and Canada. It may, however, reflect greater opportunities to extend collectively bargained wage settlements to nonunion workers, and industry minimum wages that reduce wage dispersion, in Japan. It clearly reflects something other than the institution of *shukko*, since it is very apparent even when *shukko* workers are excluded from the sample.

Finally, while (due to this greater dispersion) most age groups are much less likely to experience a large wage reduction when changing jobs in Japan than in Canada, the reverse is true for older workers, especially men separating involuntarily. Thus, our results again reaffirm the notion that adjustment burdens in Japan fall much more disproportionately on older workers than in Canada: not only does the involuntary separation rate rise with age (as we saw in the previous section), but so do the chances that such a separation will result in a large wage loss.

A reader might be surprised by the very small mean wage losses reported in Table 3.15 for older Canadian workers. Doesn't this contradict a large U.S. and Canadian literature which shows large wage losses among older displaced North American workers? The resolution to this puzzle can be found in Table 3.16, which breaks down Canadians' wage changes by tenure instead of age, and in Table 3.17, which provides supplementary information on the distribution of tenure by age in the two countries. Now, sizable mean losses (of 11.0 percent for men and 6.6 percent for women) are evident among workers with high tenure levels (more than 10 years), and losses increase rather steadily with tenure on the lost job. It therefore does *not* follow from Tables 3.14 and 3.15 that the Canadian labor market is kinder to high-tenure displaced workers than the Japanese market: the small wage losses of older Canadian displaced workers could be due largely to relatively low mean tenure levels among older workers in Canada relative to Japan.

Unfortunately, we do not have access to information about tenure levels of Japanese displaced workers in our microdata sample. However, the fact that older Japanese workers have higher tenure levels than older Canadian workers is documented in Table 3.17, which is based on calculations from general household surveys in both countries. This is especially the case for men; for example, a randomly selected, employed 50- to 54-year-old Japanese man has been on his current job for 22 years. The analogous figure for Canada is 14.7 years.[40] Women's age-specific tenure levels are remarkably similar in Japan and Canada. The other noteworthy feature of Table 3.17 is what happens after age 55: conditional on remaining employed, mean tenure continues to rise with age among Canadian workers, even past 65. This is not the case in Japan, at least for men, where the widespread practice of taking a low-wage "postretirement" job clearly shows up in the data.

The Structure of Displacement-Induced Wage Changes: Japan versus Canada

In this subsection we present regression analyses of displacement-induced wage changes in Japan and Canada. The goal is to see whether the same observable factors accentuate, or mitigate, wage losses experienced by displaced workers in both countries. As in the previous subsection, for Canada we present separate results for all permanent separations and for permanently laid-off workers. For Japan we consider three populations: all separations, workers undergoing *shukko*, and layoffs.

The Japanese results are presented for men and women separately in Tables 3.18 and 3.19. The dependent variable in all regressions is the percentage wage change reported by the (reemployed) worker; because both tails of this dependent variable are truncated, we use censored regression models for doubly truncated dependent variables.[41] For the "laid-off" and "*shukko*" samples, we report separate specifications with and without controls for industry wage premiums. The latter specification is for comparability with the Canadian data, when we cannot compute a similar variable.

Three main patterns are clear in Tables 3.18 and 3.19. First, as the "All Separations" column of both tables indicates (and as the simple wage-change distributions examined above suggested), separation reason matters. With the exception of workers experiencing outward *shukko*, who experience a small wage gain, workers experiencing involuntary separations experience larger wage losses than do voluntary separations. In particular, laid-off men (in other words, involuntary, non-*shukko* separations) are likely to lose 5 percent more in wages than men separating voluntarily. The somewhat surprising wage gains among outward-*shukko* workers might reflect pay incentives employers provide for encouraging workers to accept *shukko* assignments (to new jobs) willingly. Such incentives disappear as workers on *shukko* assignments are called back.

Second, among involuntary separations, the patterns of wage changes are very different for *shukko* versus all other involuntary separations. In virtually all cases, the absolute magnitudes of the coefficients are smaller for workers undergoing *shukko*. At the same time, as suggested by the wage-change distributions in the previous subsection, our estimate of unexplained wage-change variance, sigma, is also much smaller for *shukko* workers (less than half the value for laid-off workers among men). Thus, both measured and unmeasured personal and firm characteristics matter much less for wage changes among *shukko* workers. In part because the preseparation firm sometimes pays the worker his or her old wage during the initial period at the new firm, *shukko* workers thus seem to be relatively insulated from the heterogeneity in wage-change experiences of laid-off workers in Japan.

Third, focusing now on the "laid-off" workers columns, the wage consequences of displacement vary considerably with workers' characteristics in Japan. Compared with workers with less than high school (the omitted group), workers with more education experience larger wage losses in Japan, with the largest losses among those with junior college degrees. Firm size also matters: compared to workers remaining in a small firm before and after displacement, men moving into a large firm experience, on average, 3 percent larger wage gains, while those leaving a large firm lose 5 percent more. The large premium for full-time work, of about 10 percent, is unsurprising given that our monthly wage statistics will reflect hours variation between jobs. Men who change industry experience 4 percent larger wage losses (women, 2 percent), consistent with the existence of industry-specific capital (Neal 1995). Especially for men, industry-wage premiums are highly important in explaining wage changes. Moving into industries which pay above-average wages raises an individual's wages; leaving them reduces wages.[42] Finally, and again especially for men, older workers clearly lose more from displacement than younger workers. To some extent this surely reflects their higher tenure levels, which we are unable to control for in Japan. Especially for workers aged 55–64, it may also reflect the significant amount of work in "secondary" labor markets that occurs after mandatory retirement.

In sum, most of the patterns in displaced workers' wage changes in Japan will be familiar to analysts of displacement in other countries. The muted wage changes experienced by *shukko* workers are of distinct interest, however, as is the association of higher education with greater wage losses. The magnitudes of the effects of different variables may differ substantially from other countries, however—a question we address in our analysis of Canadian data next.

Results from wage-change regressions for Canada are shown in Table 3.20. Just as for Japan, we present one set of results for all job separations in columns 1 and 4 (though in Canada we require these separations to be permanent). The remaining columns restrict the sample to permanent layoffs only; of these, columns 2 and 5 provide the fullest possible description of the pattern of wage changes in Canada; columns 3 and 6 replicate the Japanese regressions essentially exactly by dropping those covariates not available in the Japanese data (union status and tenure).[43] The dependent variable in all regressions is the ratio of post- to preseparation hourly wages (based on wage levels reported by the worker); multiplying Table 3.20 coefficients by 100 thus makes them roughly comparable with those for Japan (Tables 3.18 and 3.19).

Table 3.20 shows the following. First, unlike Japan, education is essentially uncorrelated with wage changes among separating or displaced workers. Of course, higher education raises both pre- and post-separation wages in Canada (regressions not shown), but the effects are roughly equal. Thus it would appear that wage premiums associated with educational credentials are more likely to survive displacement in Canada than in Japan. Second, focusing on the comparable regressions in columns 3 and 6, it is clear that firm size "matters" in Canada, as it does in Japan. Perhaps more unexpectedly, *firm size appears to be much more important in Canada than in Japan*: displaced men who move from a large firm to a small firm in Canada lose 24 percent more in wages than those in small firms both before and after displacement. This compares to only a 5 percent larger loss in Japan, where the largest firm-size category (1,000 or more workers) actually refers to much larger firms than in Canada (500 or more).[44] Despite frequent comments about the importance of dual labor markets in Japan, we thus find larger firm-size premiums in a North American economy—Canada. This may reflect greater overall wage heterogeneity, as well as more idiosyncratic rent-sharing, as argued by Teulings and Hartog (1998).[45]

In contrast to firm size, part-time status matters much less in Canada than in Japan; in fact the only significant part-time coefficient implies an hourly wage *gain* for women moving into part-time jobs. As in Japan, older workers lose more from displacement, and the magnitude of the age effect is similar. As columns 2 and 5 indicate, controlling for tenure reduces, but does not eliminate, these age effects, suggesting that pure aging may play a role. Visible minorities lose significantly more from displacement than other Canadians. Because pure wage discrimination should affect both pre- and postdisplacement wages equally, this suggests that there might be a search component to discrimination—jobs in which visible minorities are welcome may be relatively scarce, prompting them to accept low-wage jobs while searching in this "thin" market.

Finally, the Canadian data provide evidence on the effects of a very important variable, aside from tenure, that is absent from the Japanese data: union status. Clearly, workers transiting from union to nonunion status ("UN") lose more from displacement, and workers transiting into union status ("NU") gain, by between 12 and 20 percent in all cases. While controlling for union status does not alter the other regression coefficients much (it reduces the firm size effects a little but to nowhere near the small Japanese levels), it would be interesting to see whether similar union effects are present in Japan, where union coverage rates are similar to Canada's but where more mechanisms exist by which union wage settlements might affect nonunion workers.

In sum, a regression-based examination of the patterns in wage losses experienced by displaced workers in Canada and Japan reveals both commonalities and differences. Commonalities include increasing wage losses with age, and wage losses that are accentuated when workers move out of large firms and into small ones. Differences revolve around the fact that some factors "matter" more for wage changes in one country than the other, or do not matter at all in one of the two countries. Firm size clearly matters more in Canada: in comparable wage-change regressions, estimated firm-size premiums are much larger there. In contrast, education and part-time status matter more in Japan. Further investigation into what might explain these wage-structure differences seems warranted. Finally, it is worth recalling the existence, in Japan but not in Canada, of a group of involuntarily displaced workers who experience no unemployment and whose wage changes are much more muted than those of laid-off workers: *shukko* workers. For some, at least, *shukko* might be a "kinder, gentler" alternative to displacement that permits industrial adjustment just the same.

COMBINING INCIDENCE AND CONSEQUENCES: THE PREVALENCE OF SEVERE SEPARATION-INDUCED WAGE LOSS

It would appear, based on the analysis so far, that—with the exception of older Japanese men exposed to early retirement risk—displacement, in the sense of involuntary, permanent job loss, is less common in Japan than Canada. Furthermore, it appears that, with the same exception, the likelihood of experiencing a large wage decline as a result of displacement is less in Japan as well. Overall, this would suggest that a randomly selected Japanese worker has more lifetime earnings security than a comparable Canadian worker.[46] In this section we quantify this difference between the two labor markets by computing a simple, comparable, summary measure of wage security for each. In particular, we ask: "In any given year, what is the probability that a randomly selected employed worker of a given age will experience a permanent job separation which results in an hourly wage loss of more than 30 percent?" For want of a better term, we call this the "risk of severe, turnover-induced, wage loss." In addition to combining information about both the incidence and consequences of displacement, this indicator might be thought of as a measure of displacement rates that is not dependent on potential differences in the labeling of separations across countries. Rather than restricting attention to particular separation reasons, we include all separations and, in a sense, weight their "severity" by the wage loss associated with them, thus circumventing these labeling and definitional issues.

Our estimates of per-worker frequencies of separation-induced wage gains and losses are presented in Table 3.21. The figures reported there combine the information on wage changes used in the previous section with the permanent separation rates calculated in Table 3.5. According to Table 3.21, men's overall risk of severe, turnover-induced wage loss is under one percent (0.8 percent) per year in Japan, and more than double that (1.9 percent) in Canada. As expected, this reflects both a higher male permanent separation rate *and* a greater likelihood of experiencing a large wage loss conditional on changing jobs in Canada. For women, the incidence of severe separation-induced wage loss is also greater in Canada than Japan, but the difference is much more moderate. This is because, as noted in Table 3.5, Japanese women actually have higher turnover rates than Canadian women.

Together, the age trends in Table 3.21 yield a perhaps-surprising finding that reinforces some trends noted much earlier, in Table 3.5: If *job security* is defined as freedom from the risk of a job change that results in a wage loss of over 30 percent (or 10 percent for that matter), *older Canadian workers (55+, both men and women) have greater earnings security than older Japanese workers.* Loosely, after a turbulent youth characterized by high turnover, both voluntary ("job shopping"), and involuntary (layoffs, which tend to be ordered by inverse seniority), Canadian workers tend to settle into permanent jobs where, by age 55, they are at relatively low risk of large, separation-induced wage losses. Japanese workers, especially men, enjoy unparalleled "wage security" when young, but face *increasing* wage-loss risk as they age. To some extent, then, older workers may bear a much larger share of the adjustment burden in Japan than in Canada.

A final question seems natural to ask: "Do younger Japanese workers 'pay' for their very high level of job and wage security in any way?" According to columns 3, 4, 7, and 8 of Table 3.21, which present parallel statistics on separation-induced wage gains, in at least one very important sense, the answer to this question is "yes": their prospects of increasing their wages by finding a new, better job are much lower. While in both countries the chances of "moving up" by switching jobs fall with age, the international differences are dramatic in all age categories. In any given year, a 20- to 24-year-old employed Canadian man has an 11.0 percent chance of raising his wage rate by 30 percent or more by switching employers. The equivalent probability in Japan is 1.3 percent. Even in a man's late 50s, the international difference is more than tenfold—1.1 percent in Canada versus 0.1 percent in Japan. Similar but less dramatic differences are present for women.

Thus, to some extent the greater protection from turnover-induced wage loss experienced in Japan, especially by young and prime-age men, is counterbalanced by the fact that fewer wage gains can be had from turning over. In general, this reflects the fact that the variance of separation-induced wage changes is much higher in Canada than Japan. Despite Japan's low level of unionization and enterprise-level wage bargaining, these wage-change results are suggestive of a more compressed overall wage distribution. To the extent that workers are risk averse, this lower variance can be thought of as raising the level of "effective" wage security in Japan, again especially among young and prime-age men.

EMERGING ISSUES: WHERE TO GO FROM HERE?

In this chapter we have described the main institutional elements of the Japanese and Canadian economies that affect displaced workers, and we have presented evidence on the incidence and consequences of displacement in both countries. Our main results have already been summarized in the introduction; in this concluding section we try to summarize the main outstanding puzzles our work leaves unanswered and provide suggestions for what needs to be done next to resolve them.

Concerning overall separation and displacement rates in Canada and Japan, a somewhat unexpected finding of this chapter is the rough similarity in permanent separation rates between the two countries. This phenomenon—reminiscent of Koike's (1984, for example) "revisionist" claim that Japanese employment systems do not necessarily provide more security than "Western" ones—is obscured in some published aggregate statistics by the inclusion of the large number of temporary separations in North American data, by a tendency to focus on male workers only, and by the tendency of Japanese statistics (because they are often based on surveys of firms) to restrict attention to workers in larger firms. When these factors are adjusted for, overall permanent separation rates in the two countries are similar, though they are higher for men in Canada and women in Japan. Clearly this finding needs to be explored in more detail, with as many data sources as possible, and with the closest attention to comparability of the data. If it is supported by further examination, it may have very important implications for understanding the process of industrial adjustment in Japan, compared to North American economies. The finding also needs to be reconciled with the very clear differences in age-specific mean job tenures we see between Canada and Japan. Tenure is much higher in Japan (at least among men); this could be consistent with the turnover data if turnover in Japan is more concentrated among low-tenure workers (for example, part-time and contract workers) than in North American economies.

A related puzzle concerns the very high fraction of Japanese separations that are voluntary, compared to Canada. Is this a genuine difference, or purely a labeling phenomenon?[47] The fact that many fewer Japanese separations result in large wage declines, plus the fact that in the aggregate, worker and firm labeling of separations seems to agree in Canada, certainly suggests that it is genuine. However, it is also true that many fewer separations result in substantial wage increases in Japan, so the phenomenon seems to warrant further investigation. Who are all these quitters in Japan? Are they concentrated in certain industries or demographic groups? Does the large fraction of voluntary turnover in Japan provide another mechanism for industrial adjustment that is less important in North America? Is the high fraction of involuntary turnover in Canada a "labeling" response to its particular employment insurance system?

Another aspect of the composition of separations that deserves further analysis is the much larger share of Japanese separations labeled as due to the expiration of a fixed-term contract. Despite recent concern over the growth of this form of work in Canada and the United States, it would appear to be much more prevalent in Japan. Does the much larger share of contract expirations in separations also substitute for displacement of "regular" workers as a form of industrial adjustment in Japan?

A final, and fascinating, issue concerning displacement rates that positively invites further exploration is the very different effect of age on the frequency of displacement in the two countries. In Canada, displacement becomes much less common as a worker ages, while in Japan the opposite occurs. Importantly, this phenomenon involves more than mandatory early retirement: it is clearly evident for simple layoffs as well. The Japanese and Canadian labor markets would thus appear to function very differently over a worker's lifetime: Canadian workers enter the market with low job and wage security, but over time accumulate greater security, in part due to a practice of layoffs by inverse seniority. In Japan, young workers, especially men, experience a level of job security that may be unparalleled worldwide. But this security erodes as they age. While each of these two systems may have its merits, one might imagine that the Japanese system (loosely one of layoffs by seniority rather than inverse seniority) might actually be better at allowing organizations to continue renewing their workforce during downturns in demand. The organizational, productivity, and other consequences of seniority-based, versus inverse-seniority-based, layoff rules seem to strongly invite further comparative research.

Turning now to the consequences of displacement, another very striking finding of this chapter is the much longer unemployment durations of Canadian versus Japanese displaced workers. To some extent this should not be surprising because, at the time of our data, Canada's national unemployment rate was more than double Japan's. Still, national unemployment rates are, to some extent at least, endogenous outcomes of institutional differences, and understanding these effects is particularly important from a policy perspective. Do long "effective" notice periods, resulting from the significant procedural requirements for layoffs in Japan, help explain the short unemployment durations there? (To answer this question it would be useful to have survey information on workers' advance knowledge of a displacement in Japan.) What is the effect of the significant share of involuntary Japanese separations that are due to the expiration of fixed-term contracts on mean unemployment durations there? Are the long unemployment spells in Canada related to its temporary layoff system, with its relative absence of a "short, sharp, and irrevocable" break from the previous employer?

Emerging issues in the analysis of the wage consequences of displacement are several. One concerns the experiences of *shukko* workers. On the surface, *shukko* appears to be an attractive alternative to "standard" layoffs when a firm needs to reduce its workforce, because no unemployment is experienced and much less wage uncertainty is involved: our data clearly show that wage changes are much more muted for *shukko* than other displaced workers. But are these changes truly more muted? The survey used here only captures workers within a year of the separation while most *shukko* workers are likely still on the original firm's payroll. In addition, some of these workers might still be benefiting from a long list of government wage subsidies available to workers leaving declining industries, described in detail in this chapter. Longer-term studies of *shukko* workers would seem to be very important, and might show much less benign wage effects of this practice.

Looking at wage changes among displaced workers not on *shukko*, our most striking finding concerns the much larger variance in wage changes experienced by Canadian displaced workers. Further study of this issue first needs to corroborate this very strong finding (which is based on reported percentage wage changes in Japan) with data based on reported levels of pre- and postdisplacement wages. Assuming it is genuine (which, given its magnitude, seems highly likely), further research needs to ask what explains it. Is it simply a result of a more compressed overall wage distribution in Japan than in Canada, and if so, which institutional features of the labor market explain this? Unionization and minimum wages are not that different in the two countries; perhaps greater Japanese uniformity in educational standards plays a role. Another contributing factor might be a greater role of postdisplacement "job shopping" in accounting for wage recovery from displacement in Canada: Canadian workers might be more willing, or able, to accept low-wage "stopgap" jobs after displacement than Japanese workers, so the short-term variation in wage changes overstates the long-term effects in Canada.

Relatedly, the current chapter suggests that a more-detailed study of the role of *voluntary* labor mobility in career wage growth may reveal some fascinating differences in how Japanese and North American labor markets work. Clearly, Canadian workers, especially when they are young, can achieve very substantial wage increases by switching firms. This is much harder to do in Japan, but most studies also indicate that the wage returns to staying with the same employer (i.e., the tenure-wage effect) are much higher in Japan than, say, the United States.[48] Thus, wages may grow at a similar rate with age in the two types of economies, but via very different processes. Relatedly, wage inequality within a cohort of workers may increase much more with age in Canada or the United States than in Japan, given the more varied consequences of turnover for wages in the two systems.

Two other issues emerge from a regression analysis of wage changes. For one, firm-size wage effects, as estimated from displaced-worker data, are (perhaps surprisingly) much larger in Canada than Japan.[49] This finding corroborates Teulings and Hartog's (1998) claim that "noncompetitive" wage differentials are actually larger in less-corporatist economies, suggesting that labor allocation may not be more efficient in those economies. Our findings here do not include annual bonuses, however, which are a large component of total compensation in Japan. It would be interesting to see whether the finding also holds when bonuses are included, and to extend our displacement-based estimates of firm-wage effects to other countries with different wage-setting institutions. The other aspect of wage changes that might warrant further exploration is the strong, positive effect of education on displacement-induced wage losses in Japan, but not in Canada. Is there any reason why educational credentials should be *less* portable across firms in Japan than elsewhere?

Finally, while many strides have been made with the coming-of-age of panel data sets outside the United States, an important remaining obstacle to further research on displaced workers outside North America remains gaps in data. As our investigation in this chapter clearly shows, our understanding of displacement in Japan would be much improved if the following information were available in microdata on separating workers: job tenure, union coverage, and a finer disaggregation of workers by separation reason. Job tenure and union coverage have been shown to have very large effects on wage changes experienced by displaced workers in Canada and elsewhere, and it would reveal much about the structure of the Japanese labor market to see if these same effects were present in Japan. Japanese microdata currently available do not allow us to distinguish separations due to "management convenience" (the closest analogue to a pure "layoff" in North

America) from mandatory retirements and expirations of fixed-term contracts. An analysis of just the first group might yield less benign consequences of displacement than we currently find for Japan.

In sum, this chapter shows that much can be learned, and that much remains to be learned, about the functioning of different national labor markets by comparing the experiences of displaced workers among countries. We can only hope that this chapter, and this volume, will stimulate more and more of this work.

Notes

NOTE: We thank Garnett Picot and Leonard Landry of Statistics Canada for generously providing customized counts of separation and displacement rates in Canada.

1. For example, according to Hashimoto (1990, p. 50), the labor-force participation rate among men over 65 was 35.8 percent in Japan, compared with only 16.7 percent in the United States in 1988.
2. Beginning in April 1998, firms were no longer permitted to impose mandatory retirement below age 60.
3. See Nakamura and Vertinsky (1994) for a more detailed description of *keiretsu* relationships.
4. Employment protection legislation has played a key role in the debate over the causes of high European unemployment over the last decade (see Bertola 1992, for example).
5. Another legal reason for the difficulty Japanese firms have in laying off workers is that the standard employment contract for regular workers simply states that a person is employed by a firm, meaning that workers will obey company orders to work. Because these contracts are not specific about the tasks workers are expected to perform, firms are expected to assign workers to whatever tasks are consistent with permanent employment.
6. A third set of restrictions concern discriminatory discharges, on such bases as race, sex, and union activity. Such restrictions are set out in provincial Labor Relations Acts, Human Rights Acts, and the Charter of Rights and Freedoms. See Arthurs, et al. (1993), pp. 88–95.
7. See, for example, Downey 1989.
8. Each of the ten provinces and two territories have their own employment standards acts and industrial relations acts, though there are many similarities and a good deal of borrowing and diffusion among jurisdictions. Unlike the United States, where federal statutes—such as minimum wage—supersede state laws, the Canadian federal labor jurisdiction is limited to a small subset of industries nationwide, including banks, transportation, communications, and the federal public service.

9. In most cases layoffs are classified as temporary, and hence not subject to notice requirements if their expected duration is fewer than 13 weeks or (in cases of mass layoffs) if the employer advises the Director of Employment Standards that he or she expects to recall the workers within a period of time approved by the Director. Some jurisdictions require notice of all large-scale layoffs, however, whether permanent or not.
10. Interestingly, a small number of Canadian jurisdictions require *workers* to notify their employers of their intent to quit, though it is unclear whether this provision has ever been enforced.
11. Other groups receiving special treatment in Japan's EI system are older workers, seasonal workers, and day laborers. Workers who become unemployed after 65 years of age receive a lump-sum payment ranging from 50 to 150 days' wages. Eligible seasonal workers receive a lump sum which is typically equal to 50 times the basic daily EI payment. Eligible day laborers receive daily EI payments, which are available for 13–17 days, depending on past earnings and the number of days of contribution to EI.
12. The major element of the 1996 reform was a move from weeks to hours of work to determine eligibility. For example, where previously 12 to 20 weeks of work were required to meet the entrance requirement, this was modified to 420 to 700 hours. (Many adjustments, such as these, are straightforward conversions based on a 35-hour week, which is very close to the average for Canadian workers.) In accord with the move to hours, coverage was extended to all hours of paid employment in the economy, including those in part-time jobs. In addition, a very mild degree of experience rating was added to the system which, unlike the system in the United States, had previously not been experience rated at all. However, again unlike the United States, the experience rating is based on the worker's history of EI use and not the employer's.
13. The actual rate used in administering the system is a seasonally adjusted 3-month moving average.
14. The rough comparability of Canada's EI system with Japan's does not extend to the United States. In 1993 the Canadian system paid Can$18.3 billion in benefits to a labor force of about 14.5 million people, whereas the American system paid about US$20.7 billion to a labor force of about 131 million. Given an exchange rate at that time of 1.30 (Can./U.S.), this implies that per-capita payments in Canada were about 6 times larger than those in the United States.
15. EM programs provide a kind of parallel system to the EI programs, but for workers who are ineligible for EI. Unlike the EI programs, which are financed by a payroll tax, EM programs are financed mostly by general revenue. One EM-law-based employment maintenance program of potentially considerable significance for displaced workers is the subsidy for promoting training of middle-aged and older workers (*Chuukonen rodosha to juko shoreikin*). Under this program, middle-aged and older workers (40 years or older) are eligible to get a 50 percent subsidy for taking training and education courses for the purpose of preparing themselves for new jobs after their retirement from their present jobs, up to a

maximum of 100,000 yen. For more information on EM-based employment maintenance programs, see Japan Ministry of Labor (1997c).

16. Small and medium-size enterprises satisfy one of the following conditions: 1) book-value capitalization does not exceed 10 million yen for firms in retail and service sectors; 30 million yen for firms in the wholesale sector; or 100 million yen in other sectors; or 2) the number of regularly employed workers does not exceed 50 for firms in retail and service sectors; 100 in the wholesale sector; or 300 in other sectors.
17. See Glenson and Odaka (1976), Higuchi (1991, 1996) and Okochi, Karsh, and Levine (1974) for a description of *shunto*, as well as other historical and institutional aspects of the Japanese labor market.
18. It should be noted that Japanese bonuses are paid to all regular workers regardless of their union status, including such nonmanagerial staff as security personnel, school teachers, and government employees. In this sense, unlike bonuses paid to executives in North America, Japanese bonuses are used primarily as a means to keep firms' wage bills flexible over time while maintaining employment.
19. One difference, which in part explains the Canada-U.S. gap in unionization rates, is that "certification votes" are not usually required to establish a union in Canada. Rather, signatures are collected over an extended period.
20. In addition to these two mechanisms, nationwide minimum wages exist for two industries: the metal mining industry (7,085 yen, effective March 30, 1997) and non-metal mining industries (5,772 yen, effective May 17, 1989). Minimum wages can also result from mandatory extension of collective bargaining agreements, although there are only two cases of this in all of Japan.
21. The "departures" sample does not contain information about the subsequent jobs or unemployment experienced by the workers involved.
22. It is generally thought that employer compliance with this reporting requirement is quite good, because, by submitting the form, the employer can cease remitting payroll taxes on behalf of the worker. One exception to this is for workers in jobs involving under 15 hours per week, who during our sample period were exempt from UI payroll taxes (and ineligible for UI benefits).
23. We also examined rates for 1988 in both countries and a number of intervening years in Canada. There are few differences and little evidence of a time trend, as Picot, Lin, and Pyper (1997) have already noted for Canada. It is perhaps worth noting, however, that imposing the firm-size and job-length restrictions in the Canadian data causes separation rates to drop quite precipitously: a large fraction of Canadian separations (and perhaps Japanese ones as well—we have no way of knowing for Japan) are from very short jobs in very small firms. Finally, note that in both the Japanese and Canadian data presented in Table 3.5 persons who separate more than once a year will be counted as adding to the separation rate more than once. Given the restriction to jobs lasting one month or more, a single individual could, potentially, contribute up to 11 separations per year to the counts in both countries.

24. In other work, Kuhn (1999) has argued that ROEs substantially undercount separations among teenage workers in Canada. This is especially important before 1997, because a much larger fraction of teens than any other age group work part time, and part-time workers were not subject to employment insurance premiums until 1997. Therefore, we shall largely ignore teens in our discussion of separation and displacement rates.
25. When work is very sparse, workers are sometimes told not to come in to work in Japan. Unlike in Canada, however, this would not be counted as a separation because the worker is still considered to be employed by the firm.
26. Recall that we are ignoring the numbers for teens in Canada, due to the likelihood of a large undercount of their separations in our data.
27. Presumably workers whose contract ended are included in the "other" category in Canada, though it is possible that some are coded in the "short work" category. In the Canadian UI (now EI) system, the category "dismissed" is read as "dismissed for cause" and implies that the worker would not, after 1993, normally be eligible for UI benefits.
28. For the purposes of this analysis, we further exclude multiple job holders who separated from a job which is not their "main" job.
29. Because there is no specific category on the ROE form for "end of contract," these may include some workers whose limited-term contracts ended. More likely, however, contract terminations will be coded as "other." According to Table 3.7, however, including these in our count of displacements would make only a minor difference to Canadian displacement rates, because firms use the "other" category for only 4.6 percent of male separations and 3.5 percent of female separations (compared with "shortage of work" frequencies of 61.8 and 47.5 percent, respectively).
30. As pointed out in the previous footnote, adding contract terminations to the count of Canadian displacements would increase the displacement rate only marginally.
31. Retirements (voluntary or otherwise) are not included in our Canadian data. Despite the fact that mandatory retirement remains legal in Canada (unlike in the United States), it is our impression that the vast majority of retirements in Canada are voluntary and thus should not properly be included in any count of displacements.
32. Although it is possible that some workers would have been recalled beyond the end of the survey, the final panel was approximately 57–63 weeks after the initial separation so any subsequent recall would have been beyond the maximum possible duration of unemployment insurance benefits. Also, although the survey experienced about 20 percent attrition between the first and last panels, when the same tabulations are performed on the subsample of those who responded to both, the column and row percentages are remarkably similar to those for the entire sample.
33. To investigate the possible influence of workers finding temporary jobs while awaiting recall, we calculated the fraction of workers who obtained a first job and were observed subsequently to return to their former employer. In our data win-

dow only about 0.8 percent of workers (from the set labeled as laid off by at least one party) did this; so we do not believe it would have a large influence.

34. In this survey, unlike the published statistics in Table 3.6, "management convenience" includes mandatory retirements and also job terminations of workers on nonregular contracts such as casual and term contracts. To the extent that these workers' unemployment durations are longer than layoffs of regular workers, our estimates for Japan will overestimate durations among the latter group.
35. As the advance-notice literature (Jones and Kuhn 1995, for example) shows, a substantial fraction of jobless durations will be exactly zero if workers receive, and make use of, substantial prenotification periods. This may be the case in Japan, though our data do not distinguish workers with exactly zero joblessness from others with under a month of joblessness.
36. Alternatively, we could have picked a single interview date and selected the sample based on labor-force attachment at that date. This raises the issues of which date to use, however, and how to treat individuals who exit from the survey between dates. Overall, we prefer the above "bracketing" approach because it is simpler.
37. It would, of course, be very interesting to dissaggregate these three forms of involuntary terminations, but this is not possible in the microdata file provided by the Ministry of Labor. Note also that the microdata file of Japan's Employment Mobility Survey does not distinguish temporary and permanent *shukko* assignments; thus our results should be interpreted as applying to a population-weighted average of the two.
38. Workers experiencing wage losses of over 30 percent were assigned a value of –30; those experiencing losses of 10 to 30 percent a value of –15. A similar pattern was followed for workers experiencing gains. Workers experiencing wage changes of –10 to +10 percent were assigned a value of zero.
39. The percentage change is calculated as 100 × (post – pre)/pre, where pre- and post- refer to wages before and after separation.
40. The Canadian figures in Table 3.17 are based on our own calculations from the 1994 Survey of Labor and Income Dynamics (Statistics Canada 1997). The nature of the establishment size question in this survey does not allow us to duplicate precisely the Japanese data's restriction to workers in establishments of at least 10 workers. Therefore, to "bracket" the Japanese definition, we provide results with no establishment-size restriction, and for workers in establishments of 20 or more persons. Usually the latter generate higher mean tenures, but for the specific case of men aged 50–54 the two measures happen to coincide exactly.
41. Just as for the calculation of means in Table 3.14, workers experiencing wage changes of –30 to –10 percent are assigned a value of –15, and workers experiencing gains of 10 to 30 percent are assigned a value of +15. Workers experiencing changes of –10 percent to +10 percent are assigned a value of zero.
42. Industry wage premiums were calculated from aggregate statistics as the average wage in the industry divided by the overall average wage. Statistics refer to

monthly regular wages (not including bonuses, overtime, and so forth) of workers on regular contracts (not fixed-term or part-time).

43. We keep visible minority status in the Canadian regressions, however, despite the absence of a Japanese counterpart. This does not affect the results materially.
44. In both Canadian and Japanese data sets, "firm" sizes actually refer to establishments, not (necessarily) entire companies.
45. Teulings and Hartog presented a wide array of evidence that corporatist countries (those with centralized wage setting) have fewer "noncompetitive" wage differentials, such as firm-size effects, than decentralized economies. In the case of Japan (p. 175) they found that its industry wages are less sensitive to output prices than those in Canada and the United States. They attribute this to informal bargaining coordination. Tachibanaki (1996) reported large firm-size wage premiums for Japan, probably larger than the United States (though he makes no direct comparison). Our much smaller estimates are most likely explained by the fact that our displacement-based measures implicitly control for individual fixed effects, unlike Tachibanaki's cross-section estimates. That said, our estimated firm-size wage premiums for Japan might be larger if bonuses were included in our wage measure, as they are in Tachibanaki's work. (Ito (1992, 234) presented simple tabulations suggesting that bonuses are a larger fraction of compensation in large than small Japanese firms.)
46. This greater level of security in Japan is also enhanced by the shorter unemployment durations there; because unemployment effects of displacement tend to be temporary we do not incorporate these differences in our summary measure of total earnings security here.
47. Hashimoto (1990, 77–81) argued that the quit-layoff distinction may be less meaningful in Japan than in the United States or Canada.
48. See, for example, Hashimoto and Raisian (1985, 1992), and Clark and Ogawa (1992). One limitation of these studies, however, is that they are all based on cross-section data. The limitations of using such data to estimate tenure-wage profiles are well known (see, for example, Topel 1991); thus it would be of great interest in future work to use Japanese panel data to estimate tenure effects, using techniques similar to Topel's.
49. Existing estimates of Japanese firm-size wage premiums (Tachibanaki 1996, for example) tend to be based on cross-section data only, and will therefore be contaminated by unobserved worker quality differences between firms.

Table 3.1 Notice Requirements for Termination of Employment in Various Jurisdictions of Canada, 1997

	Individual terminations		Mass terminations	
Jurisdiction	Length of service	Employer notice (wk.)	No. of employees	Employer notice (wk.)
Federal	3 months +	2	50+	16
Alberta	3 mo. – <2 yr.	1	No special provision	
	2 yr. – <4 yr.	2		
	4 yr. – <6 yr.	4		
	6 yr. – <8 yr.	5		
	8 yr. – 10 yr.	6		
	≥10 yr.	8		
British Columbia	3 mo. – <1 yr.	1	50–100	8
	1 – <3 yr.	2	101–300	12
	≥3 yr.	3	300+	16
	For each addit. year of employ., 1 wk. to max. 8 wk.	8		
Manitoba	1+ mo.	1 pay period	50–100	10
			101–300	14
			300+	18
New Brunswick	6 mo. – <5 yr.	2	10 or more, if they represent 25% of the employer's workforce	6
	≥5 yr.	4		
Newfoundland	1 mo. – <2 yr.	1	50–199	8
	≥2 yr.	2	200–499	12
			500+	16
Nova Scotia	3 mo. – <2 yr.	1	10–99	8
	2 – <5 yr.	2	100–299	12
	5 – <10 yr.	4	300+	16
	≥10 yr.	8		
Ontario	3 mo. – <1 yr.	1	50–199	8
	1 – <3 yr.	2	200–499	12
	3 – <4 yr.	3	500+	16
	4 – <5 yr.	4		
	5 – <6 yr.	5		
	6 – <7 yr.	6		
	7 – <8 yr.	7		
	≥8 yr.	8		

	Individual terminations		Mass terminations	
Jurisdiction	Length of service	Employer notice (wk.)	No. of employees	Employer notice (wk.)
Prince Edward Island	6 mo. – <5 yr.	2	No special provision	
	≥5 yr.	4		
Quebec	3 mo. – <1 yr.	1	10–99	2 mo.
	1 – <5 yr.	2	100–299	3 mo.
	5 – <10 yr.	4	300+	4 mo.
	≥10 yr.	8		
Saskatchewan	≥3 mo. – <1 yr.	1	10–49	4
	1 – <3 yr.	2	50–99	8
	3 – <5 yr.	4	100+	12
	5 – <10 yr.	6		
	≥10 yr.	8		
Northwest Territories	90 d. – 3 yr.	2	25–49	4
	For each addit. year of employment, add 1 wk. to max. 8 wk.	8	50–99	8
			100–299	12
			300+	16
Yukon	6 mo. – <1 yr.	1	25–49	4
	1 – <3 yr.	2	50–99	8
	3 – <4 yr.	3	100–299	12
	4 – <5 yr.	4	300+	16
	5 – <6 yr.	5		
	6 – <7 yr.	6		
	7 – <8 yr.	7		
	≥8 yr.	8		

SOURCE: Human Resources Development Canada, Employment Standards Legislation in Canada; latest figures are available at: http://labor-travail.hrdc-drhc.gc.ca/policy/leg/e/

Table 3.2 Worker-Reported Advance Knowledge or Formal Notice of Permanent Layoff among Workers Experiencing Permanent Layoffs in Canada (%)

Duration of notice (wk.)	Advance knowledge		Formal notice	
	Men	Women	Men	Women
<1	37.90	43.97	32.83	29.20
1	23.41	26.18	27.36	26.76
2	18.26	12.28	20.57	19.22
3	7.17	4.71	9.81	11.19
4	2.68	1.61	3.40	3.89
5–8	5.87	5.17	3.78	5.85
9–12	2.38	1.48	1.33	1.21
13–16	0.80	2.04	0.00	1.22
17+	1.50	2.49	0.95	1.46
Receiving notice	63.36	60.47	35.52	44.01

NOTE: The durations presented are conditional on having received notice, or having expected the layoff. The sample for this table is workers who were labeled as a layoff either by themselves or the firm and did not experience a recall in the survey window. Columns may not total to 100% due to rounding error.

SOURCE: Authors' calculations from the 1995 Canadian Out of Employment Panel Survey.

Table 3.3 Employment Insurance Entitlements in Japan

A. EI payments as replacement ratios

Daily wage on last job (¥)	Payment ratio (%)
Workers under age 60	
3,190–4,239	80
4,240–10,249	80–60
10,250–17,770	60
Workers age 60 to 65	
3,190–4,239	80
4,240–10,249	80–60
10,250–13,249	60–50
13,250–19,390	50

B. Duration of maximum EI entitlements (days)

	Full-time workers				Part-time workers			
Years insured	1–5	5–10	10–20	20+	1–5	5–10	10–20	20+
Regular EI program								
Age (yr.)								
Under 30	90	90	180	n.a.[a]	90	90	180	n.a.
30–44	90	180	210	210	90	180	180	210
45–59	180	210	240	300	90	180	180	210
60–65	240	300	300	300	210	210	210	210
Special provisions[b]								
Age (yr.)								
Under 45 (30 for part-time)	240	240	240	240	180	180	180	
45–65	300	300	300	300	210	210	210	

[a] n.a. = Not applicable.
[b] For disabled and other hard-to-employ workers.
SOURCE: Japan Ministry of Labor (1997c).

Table 3.4 Minimum Wages as a Percentage of Prevailing Wages in Selected Countries

Country	Minimum wage (as % of mean wage)	Definition, year
Japan	36	Weighted regional minimum wage (4,868 ¥ per day) over mean contract wage for establishments with at least 10 employees, 1995
Canada	38	Weighted jurisdictional averages over mean manufacturing wage, 1994
U.S.A.	38	Federal minimum over mean industrial wage (excl. agriculture and forestry), 1994
Germany	55	2,214 DM per day over mean manufacturing wage, 1993
France	84	36.98 F per hour over mean industrial wage (excl. agriculture and forestry), 1995

SOURCE: Japan Ministry of Labor (1997b).

Table 3.5 Annual Separation Rates for 1995

	Canada		
Gender/age (yr.)	All separations	Permanent separations	Japan, all separations
Men			
15–19	18.0	11.4	28.5
20–24	75.5	44.3	18.7
25–29	47.0	23.8	12.4
30–34	36.5	16.6	8.8
35–39	32.5	13.5	7.1
40–44	28.0	11.0	7.4
45–49	25.3	9.5	5.9
50–54	26.2	9.5	7.0
55–59	30.3	11.2	10.7
60+	29.0	12.4	31.7
All ages	35.9	16.8	11.9
Women			
15–19	16.6	11.1	20.7
20–24	66.9	42.3	24.9
25–29	45.0	21.9	26.4
30–34	35.6	14.5	19.4
35–39	30.7	12.0	15.2
40–44	25.3	9.0	12.6
45–49	24.8	8.5	10.9
50–54	24.1	8.1	11.9
55–59	27.6	9.6	13.7
60+	28.8	12.9	25.0
All ages	34.1	15.7	18.3

(continued)

Table 3.5 (continued)

	Canada		
Gender/age (yr.)	All separations	Permanent separations	Japan, all separations
Both			
15–19	17.3	11.3	24.7
20–24	71.4	43.3	21.7
25–29	46.1	23.0	17.7
30–34	36.1	15.6	12.0
35–39	31.7	12.8	9.8
40–44	26.7	10.1	9.4
45–49	25.1	9.0	7.9
50–54	25.3	8.9	8.8
55–59	29.2	10.5	11.8
60+	28.9	12.6	29.5
Total	35.1	16.3	14.3

NOTE: In both countries, the separation rate is defined by the number of job separations during the year divided by the number of regularly employed workers on June 30.

SOURCE: For Japan, calculated from Ministry of Labor (1989) for 1988 and (1996) for 1995. For Canada, the numerator comes from special tabulations from Statistics Canada, based on ROE files from Human Resources Development Canada. The denominator is from the June Labour Force Survey of the year in question.

Table 3.6 Reasons for Job Separations in Japan 1995 (%)

	Involuntary						Voluntary			
	Contract finished	Management convenience[a]	Mandatory retirement	Firing	Death or injury	Total	Marriage	Childbirth	Nursing care	Total[b]
Men	11.6	11.3	7.8	6.5	3.2	40.4	0.2	0	0.1	59.6
Women	8.6	6.0	3.0	3.5	1.6	22.7	8.7	5.5	1.0	77.4
Both	10.1	8.7	5.5	5.0	2.4	31.7	4.3	2.6	0.5	68.2
Age (yr.)										
<19	11.7	1.0	0.0	8.7	0.9	22.3	1.0	0.3	0.0	77.7
20–24	4.8	3.3	0.0	5.8	0.8	14.7	8.0	2.3	0.2	85.3
25–29	4.6	5.1	0.0	4.9	0.5	15.1	12.5	8.5	0.4	84.9
30–34	5.2	6.3	0.0	6.1	0.8	18.4	4.8	6.0	0.3	81.5
35–39	6.3	11.1	0.0	7.5	1.0	25.9	1.1	3.0	0.4	74.0
40–44	9.8	14.0	0.0	4.5	2.5	30.8	0.2	0.2	1.3	69.5
45–49	12.0	17.0	0.1	5.3	4.1	38.5	0.1	0.2	1.7	61.5
50–54	11.5	15.6	0.4	4.2	6.9	38.6	0.1	0.0	0.5	61.3
55–59	18.6	19.7	10.2	4.9	5.6	59.0	0.0	0.0	0.5	40.9
60+	23.6	8.8	34.2	1.4	4.8	72.8	0.0	n.a.[c]	0.8	27.1

[a] Management convenience in this table includes *shukko* assignments.
[b] Includes other voluntary reasons.
[c] n.a. = Not applicable.
SOURCE: Japan Ministry of Labor (1996).

Table 3.7 Firm- and Self-Reported Reasons for Separation in Canada

Firm-reported	Self-reported reason					
reason	Quit	Dismissed	Laid off	Illness	Other	Total
Men						
Voluntary	818	37	332	61	116	1,364
departure	59.97	2.71	24.34	4.47	8.50	100.00
	67.38	8.49	4.73	17.13	17.01	14.06
Dismissal	130	94	1,130	27	182	1,563
	8.32	6.01	72.30	1.73	11.64	100.00
	10.71	21.56	16.11	7.58	26.69	16.11
Shortage	155	136	5,331	38	342	6,002
of work	2.58	2.27	88.82	0.63	5.70	100.00
	12.77	31.19	75.98	10.67	50.15	61.85
Injury or	10	2	53	214	13	292
Illness	3.42	0.68	18.15	73.29	4.45	100.00
	0.82	0.46	0.76	60.11	1.91	3.01
Other	87	167	158	16	25	453
	19.21	36.87	34.88	3.53	5.52	100.00
	7.17	38.30	2.25	4.49	3.67	4.67
Return to	14	0	12	0	4	30
school	46.67	0.00	40.00	0.00	13.33	100.00
	1.15	0.00	0.17	0.00	0.59	0.31
Total	1,214	436	7,016	356	682	9,704
	12.51	4.49	72.30	3.67	7.03	100.00
	100.00	100.00	100.00	100.00	100.00	100.00

Women						
Voluntary departure	927	28	195	94	124	1,368
	67.76	2.05	14.25	6.87	9.06	100.00
	74.16	8.89	3.82	17.31	19.11	17.40
Dismissal	173	72	1,506	41	219	2,011
	8.60	3.58	74.89	2.04	10.89	100.00
	13.84	22.86	29.49	7.55	33.74	25.58
Shortage of work	88	106	3,247	23	277	3,741
	2.35	2.83	86.79	0.61	7.40	100.00
	7.04	33.65	63.59	4.24	42.68	47.58
Injury or illness	13	3	41	381	16	454
	2.86	0.66	9.03	83.92	2.47	3.52
	1.04	0.95	0.80	70.17	2.47	5.77
Other	45	106	111	4	12	278
	16.19	38.13	39.93	1.44	4.32	100.00
	3.60	33.65	2.17	0.74	1.85	3.54
Return to school	4	0	6	0	1	11
	36.36	0.00	54.55	0.00	9.09	100.00
	0.32	0.00	0.12	0.00	0.15	0.14
Total	1,250	315	5,106	543	649	7,863
	15.90	4.01	64.94	6.91	8.25	100.00
	100.00	100.00	100.00	100.00	100.00	100.00

NOTE: In vertical order, counts, row percentages, and column percentages are given respectively in each cell.

SOURCE: Authors' calculations from the Canadian Out-of-Employment Panel (COEP) survey. See Lacroix and Van Audenrode (2000) for a more detailed description of the COEP data and methods.

Table 3.8 Estimated Annual Displacement Rates in Canada and Japan, 1995 (various definitions)

	Canada[a]	Japan[b]		
Worker group/ age (yr.)	Permanent layoffs	MC[c]	MC + CF[d]	MC + CF + MR[e]
Men				
15–19	2.4	0.4	n.d.[f]	n.d.
20–24	12.3	0.8	n.d.	n.d.
25–29	7.9	0.9	n.d.	n.d.
30–34	6.3	0.8	n.d.	n.d.
35–39	5.7	0.1	n.d.	n.d.
40–44	5.0	1.6	n.d.	n.d.
45–49	4.5	1.3	n.d.	n.d.
50–54	4.5	1.5	n.d.	n.d.
55–59	5.1	2.3	n.d.	n.d.
60+	4.7	2.8	n.d.	n.d.
All ages	6.1	1.3	2.7	3.7
Women				
15–19	1.6	0.1	n.d.	n.d.
20–24	7.2	0.6	n.d.	n.d.
25–29	4.6	0.8	n.d.	n.d.
30–34	3.3	0.6	n.d.	n.d.
35–39	3.1	1.3	n.d.	n.d.
40–44	2.5	0.9	n.d.	n.d.
45–49	2.4	1.4	n.d.	n.d.
50–54	2.3	1.1	n.d.	n.d.
55–59	2.5	2.3	n.d.	n.d.
60+	2.8	2.1	n.d.	n.d.
All ages	3.4	1.1	2.7	3.2
Both				
15–19	2.0	0.2	3.1	3.1
20–24	9.8	0.7	1.8	1.8
25–29	6.4	0.9	1.7	1.7
30–34	4.9	0.7	1.4	1.4
35–39	4.5	1.1	1.7	1.7
40–44	3.8	1.3	2.2	2.2

Worker group/ age (yr.)	Canada[a] Permanent layoffs	Japan[b] MC[c]	MC + CF[d]	MC + CF + MR[e]
45–49	3.6	1.3	2.3	2.3
50–54	3.6	1.4	2.4	2.4
55–59	4.1	2.3	4.5	5.7
60+	4.0	2.6	9.6	19.6
Total	4.9	1.2	2.7	3.5

NOTE: In both countries, displacement is defined by the number of job separations during the year for specified reasons, divided by the number of regularly employed workers on June 30.

[a] In Canada we restrict attention to permanent separations only.

[b] In Japan, "management convenience" includes *shukko* assignments. We do not have access to separation shares for "contract finished" and "mandatory retirement" in Japan that are broken down by both age and gender.

[c] MC = management convenience.

[d] CF = contract finished.

[e] MR = mandatory retirement.

[f] n.d. = No data available.

SOURCE: For Japan, Ministry of Labor (1996) for 1995. For Canada, the numerator comes from special tabulations from Statistics Canada, based on ROE files from Human Resources Development Canada. The denominator is from the June Labour Force Survey of the year in question.

Table 3.9 Firm and Worker Recall Expectations in Canada

Firms' recall expectation	Men's recall expectation				Women's recall expectation			
	No	Yes	Unsure	Total	No	Yes	Unsure	Total
No	1,465	1,201	683	3,349	1,310	933	600	2,843
	43.74	35.86	20.39	100.00	46.08	32.82	21.10	100.00
	59.87	33.52	44.61	44.3	70.35	35.77	53.10	50.1
Yes	982	2,382	848	4,212	552	1,675	530	2,757
	23.31	56.55	20.13	100.00	20.02	60.75	19.22	100.00
	40.13	66.48	55.39	55.7	29.65	64.23	46.90	49.2
Total	2,447	3,583	1,531	7,561	1,862	2,608	1,130	5,600
	32.2	47.4	20.3	100.00	33.3	46.5	20.2	100.00

NOTE: In vertical order, counts, row percentages, and column percentages are given respectively in each cell.

SOURCE: Authors' calculations from the Canadian Out-of-Employment Panel (COEP) Survey.

Table 3.10 Recall Expectations versus Realizations in Canada

Observed returns	Workers' expectations No	Yes	Unsure	Total	Firms' expectations No	Yes	Total
Men							
No	1,281	919	403	2,603	1,292	1,311	2,603
	49.21	35.31	15.48	100.00	49.64	50.36	100.00
	85.51	38.31	59.26	56.87	67.50	49.23	56.87
Yes	217	1,480	277	1,974	622	1,352	1,974
	10.99	74.97	14.03	100.00	31.51	68.49	100.00
	14.49	61.69	40.74	43.13	32.50	50.77	43.13
Total	1,498	2,399	680	4,577	1,914	2,663	4,577
	32.73	52.41	14.86	100.00	41.82	58.18	100.00
	100.00	100.00	100.00	100.00	100.00	100.00	100.00
Women							
No	810	510	262	1,582	975	607	1,582
	51.20	32.24	16.56	100.00	61.63	38.37	100.00
	84.64	30.18	55.74	50.75	65.13	37.47	50.75
Yes	147	1,180	208	1,535	522	1,013	1,535
	9.58	76.87	13.55	100.00	34.01	65.99	100.00
	15.36	69.82	44.26	49.25	34.87	62.53	49.25
Total	957	1,690	470	3,117	1,497	1,620	3,117
	30.70	54.22	15.08	100.00	48.03	51.97	100.00
	100.00	100.00	100.00	100.00	100.00	100.00	100.00

NOTE: In vertical order, counts, row percentages, and column percentages are given respectively for each cell. The sample is those who are observed to be reemployed. The return to the predisplacement employer is not constrained to be the first job obtained by the worker following the separation.

SOURCE: Authors' calculations from the Canadian Out-of-Employment Panel (COEP) survey.

Table 3.11 Kaplan-Meier Cumulative Reemployment Rates for Displaced Workers in Japan and Canada

Duration	Japan		Canada A[a]		Canada B[b]	
(months)	Men	Women	Men	Women	Men	Women
0–1	0.314	0.313	0.164	0.115	0.171	0.124
1–2	0.576	0.526	0.269	0.196	0.283	0.215
2–3	0.633	0.619	0.364	0.264	0.386	0.290
3–4	0.701	0.696	0.425	0.308	0.449	0.339
4–5	0.732	0.721	0.469	0.351	0.495	0.388
5–6	0.767	0.747	0.515	0.402	0.543	0.443
6–7	0.795	0.776	0.546	0.440	0.577	0.482
7–8	0.805	0.802	0.577	0.473	0.613	0.518
8–9	0.828	0.844	0.621	0.519	0.660	0.568
9–10	0.834	0.867	0.654	0.550	0.697	0.601
10–11	0.859	0.892	0.682	0.572	0.728	0.624
12	n.d.[c]	n.d.	0.701	0.590	0.748	0.640
Median (interpolated)	1.7	1.9	5.7	8.6	5.1	7.5
Sample size	778	634	3,756	2,682	3,271	2,243
Total censored	243	192	1,208	1,138	932	858
Percent censored	31.2	30.3	32.1	42.4	28.4	38.2

NOTE: All columns present 1 minus the Kaplan-Meier survivor function for jobless durations. Medians are interpolated assuming a uniform distribution of durations within the cell containing the median.

[a] Canada A drops individuals who were out of the labor force at all dates they were interviewed after the separation.

[b] Canada B drops individuals who were out of the labor force at any date they were interviewed.

[c] n.d. = No data available.

SOURCE: Japanese numbers calculated from a Special Supplement (1996, 1997) to the Japanese Labor Force Survey (Japan Ministry of Labor 1996, 1997). Our sample includes separations due to the following reasons: layoffs, bankruptcy, declined business and other company convenience reasons, where the latter include mandatory retirements and expiration of fixed-term contracts. The vast majority of workers starting a *shukko* assignment would not be considered to be undergoing a termination of employment and would thus not be included in this sample. A small number of "one-way" *shukko* workers might be so classified, however, and would thus appear in our data. Canadian numbers are calculated from the 1993 and 1995 COEP surveys. The Canadian sample refers to "permanent layoffs": workers separating due to "shortage of work" who do not return to the preseparation employer.

Table 3.12 Cox Proportional Hazard Coefficients for Displaced Workers' Jobless Durations in Japan

Variable[a]	Men		Women	
Age	–0.0080	(0.0197)	–0.0389	(0.0269)
$(Age)^2$	–0.0001	(0.0002)	0.0003	(0.0003)
Junior high	0.0797	(0.0928)	–0.0190	(0.1093)
Junior college	0.0567	(0.1461)	–0.1209	(0.1128)
University	–0.0912	(0.1051)	0.0483	(0.2072)
Single	0.0006	(0.0010)	–0.0697	(0.1006)
Small firm	–0.0325	(0.0972)	0.0506	(0.1138)
Large firm	0.0905	(0.1454)	–0.2194	(0.1596)
Part time	0.1624*	(0.0986)	0.3083***	(0.0885)
IND4	–1.6202	(1.0117)	–0.1859	(1.0080)
IND5	0.2094*	(0.1213)	–0.1811	(0.2132)
IND7	–1.1779	(1.0098)	–0.1264	(1.0142)
IND8	0.3072	(0.1569)	0.2231	(0.2777)
IND9	–0.0296	(0.1133)	–0.0046	(0.1233)
IND10	0.1567	(0.3136)	0.5257*	(0.2979)
IND11	–0.0221	(0.3694)	0.1041	(0.4241)
IND12	–0.1211	(0.1230)	–0.0945	(0.1304)
IND13	0.6815	(0.5948)	–0.3231	(0.3162)
IND14	–0.4828***	(0.1194)	–0.4598***	(0.1337)
YUKO[b]	–0.1503	(0.1152)	0.0400	(0.1393)
No. of obs.	778		634	
N. of exiting	535		442	
N. of censored	243		192	
Log likelihood	–4514.792		–3541.226	
χ^2	69.72927***		64.35557***	

NOTE: Standard errors in parentheses. *** = Significant at the 1% level; * = significant at the 10% level.

[a] IND4 = mining; IND5 = construction; IND7 = electricity, gas, water service; IND8 = transportation; IND9 = wholesale and retail trade; IND10 = finance; IND11 = real estate; IND12 = service; IND13 = government service; IND14 = "other."

[b] YUKO is a published macroeconomic variable given the ratio of vacancies to job seekers by age-gender group.

SOURCE: Calculated from a Special Supplement to the Japanese Labor Force Survey (Japan Ministry of Labor). Our sample includes separations due to the following reasons: layoffs, bankruptcy, declined business, and other company convenience reasons.

Table 3.13 Cox Proportional Hazard Coefficients for Displaced Workers' Jobless Durations in Canada

	Men			Women		
Variables	1[a]	2[b]	3	4[a]	5[b]	6
Pre-union	0.202*** (0.051)	0.165*** (0.052)	—[c]	0.014 (0.083)	0.009 (0.084)	—
Age/10	0.068 (0.135)	0.016 (0.136)	0.080 (0.136)	0.180 (0.183)	0.174 (0.183)	0.161 (0.182)
Age^2/100	–0.036** (0.017)	–0.031* (0.017)	–0.042** (0.017)	–0.044* (0.024)	–0.043* (0.024)	–0.047** (0.024)
Single	–0.170*** (0.055)	–0.155*** (0.056)	–0.177*** (0.055)	0.109 (0.071)	0.110 (0.071)	0.111 (0.071)
Vismin[d]	–0.280*** (0.061)	–0.282*** (0.061)	–0.261*** (0.060)	–0.247*** (0.075)	–0.246*** (0.075)	–0.207*** (0.074)
Tenure	–0.025*** (0.005)	–0.026*** (0.005)	—	–0.033*** (0.009)	–0.033*** (0.009)	—
Part-time	0.029 (0.101)	–0.006 (0.103)	0.033 (0.102)	–0.111 (0.070)	–0.114 (0.071)	–0.095 (0.071)
Predispl. wage	—	0.009*** (0.003)	—	—	0.002 (0.004)	—
Firm size[e]						
20–99	0.271*** (0.063)	0.244*** (0.064)	0.290*** (0.063)	0.298*** (0.084)	0.297*** (0.084)	0.284*** (0.085)
100–499	0.136 (0.084)	0.093 (0.085)	0.174** (0.082)	0.216** (0.103)	0.212** (0.103)	0.216** (0.101)
500+	0.160 (0.120)	0.108 (0.122)	0.187 (0.118)	0.421*** (0.129)	0.416*** (0.129)	0.355*** (0.125)

Variables	Men 1[a]	Men 2[b]	Men 3	Women 4[a]	Women 5[b]	Women 6
Education						
Elem.	–0.097	–0.092	–0.090	–0.189	–0.186	–0.195
	(0.119)	(0.119)	(0.118)	(0.194)	(0.194)	(0.194)
Some high sch.	–0.080	–0.080	–0.080	–0.235**	–0.235**	–0.257***
	(0.062)	(0.062)	(0.061)	(0.094)	(0.094)	(0.094)
Some post-sec.	0.013	0.002	0.011	0.162*	0.161*	0.176*
	(0.072)	(0.072)	(0.072)	(0.091)	(0.091)	(0.090)
College	0.068	0.052	0.043	0.245***	0.243***	0.252***
	(0.077)	(0.077)	(0.077)	(0.083)	(0.084)	(0.084)
Univ.	–0.066	–0.090	–0.091	0.205**	0.201**	0.246***
	(0.086)	(0.086)	(0.085)	(0.089)	(0.089)	(0.088)
Trades	0.092	0.081	0.172*	–0.130	–0.131	–0.156
	(0.095)	(0.095)	(0.093)	(0.172)	(0.172)	(0.169)
Pseudo R^2	0.011	0.012	0.009	0.013	0.013	0.01
No. of obs.	2,988	2,988	2,988	2,191	2,191	2,191

NOTE: Standard errors are in parentheses. The dependent variable is the postdisplacement non-employment duration. Sample used is the "Canada A" sample described in Table 3.11. *** = significant at the 1% level; ** = significant at the 5% level; * = significant at the 10% level.

[a] Also included in the regression are 6 region dummy variables and 15 predisplacement industry variables.

[b] Also included are the variables from note a, and the predisplacement wage.

[c] A dash (—) indicates that the variable was not included.

[d] Vismin = visible minority.

[e] Firm sizes are only in the 1995 data, so these variables should be interpreted as firm size interacted with a dummy for the 1995 COEP. Size 1–19 is omitted.

SOURCE: Calculated by authors.

Table 3.14 Distributions of Wage Changes by Separation Reasons and Age in Japan (%)

Age (yr.)	Gain of over 30%	10% – 30% gain	10% loss – 10% gain	10% – 30% loss	Loss of over 30%	Mean[a] (estimated)	Sample
Men							
All separations							
All ages	5.44	28.48	47.74	12.25	6.09	2.2	53,175
<19	11.18	36.35	38.24	10.70	3.53	6.1	2,066
20–24	8.59	34.78	41.18	11.68	3.78	4.9	9,918
25–29	6.53	32.87	45.12	11.57	3.91	4.0	9,336
30–34	5.14	31.16	47.05	12.84	3.81	3.2	7,243
35–44	4.67	28.86	51.34	11.51	3.63	2.9	10,112
45–54	3.13	23.29	58.16	10.19	5.23	1.3	7,450
55–59	1.95	15.39	51.31	15.69	15.66	4.2	3,736
60–64	1.55	11.22	39.34	20.12	27.78	–9.2	2,585
65+	1.51	13.31	59.40	13.17	12.62	–3.3	729
Involuntary separations,[b] excluding *shukko*							
All ages	2.82	17.62	44.35	18.75	16.46	–4.3	4,683
<19	9.70	26.87	44.03	14.18	5.22	3.2	134
20–24	6.75	30.11	42.70	14.42	6.02	2.6	548
25–29	3.55	25.72	50.33	15.74	4.66	1.2	451
30–34	3.23	21.89	51.49	18.41	4.98	0.0	402
35–44	3.68	22.49	55.78	13.85	4.19	1.1	787

45–54	1.53	15.83	50.83	17.08	14.72	–4.1	720
55–59	0.91	8.85	36.33	25.39	28.52	–10.8	768
60–64	0.82	6.14	28.10	25.10	39.84	–14.6	733
65+	0	11.43	42.86	17.14	28.57	–9.4	140
Shukko							
All ages	0.71	5.58	87.79	4.25	1.67	–0.1	5,464
<19	1.92	9.62	82.69	5.77	0	1.2	52
20–24	0.60	6.55	87.50	4.17	1.19	0.2	336
25–29	2.27	7.85	83.42	2.79	3.66	0.3	573
30–34	1.22	7.15	85.69	4.72	1.22	0.4	657
35–44	0.27	6.65	89.17	3.02	0.89	0.4	1,459
45–54	0.45	3.85	90.90	4.19	0.61	–0.1	1,792
55–59	0.55	2.58	85.64	6.45	4.79	–1.9	543
60–64	0	12.5	47.92	25.00	14.58	–6.2	48
65+	—[c]	—	—	—	—	—	—

(continued)

Table 3.14 (continued)

Age (yr.)	Gain of over 30%	10% – 30% gain	10% loss – 10% gain	10% – 30% loss	Loss of over 30%	Mean[a] (estimated)	Sample
Women							
All separations							
All ages	5.32	27.87	47.91	13.58	5.32	2.2	34,886
<19	5.48	35.62	45.37	10.89	2.64	4.6	1,589
20–24	4.52	27.55	46.73	16.21	4.98	1.6	9,702
25–29	4.78	25.23	43.65	17.36	8.98	–0.1	5,478
30–34	6.89	29.15	44.46	13.31	6.19	2.6	3,005
35–44	7.52	30.63	47.20	10.77	3.88	4.1	7,782
45–54	4.23	26.61	53.47	11.80	3.89	2.3	5,035
55–59	2.87	24.05	58.72	9.19	5.17	1.5	1393
60–64	2.79	19.35	59.24	9.24	9.38	–0.5	682
65+	2.27	16.36	65.45	7.27	8.64	–0.6	220
Involuntary separations,[b] excluding *shukko*							
All ages	3.00	21.34	55.73	14.79	5.14	0.3	3,131
<19	5.59	24.48	54.55	12.59	2.80	2.6	143
20–24	3.21	24.78	52.62	16.18	3.21	1.3	686
25–29	3.27	17.44	51.50	20.16	7.63	–1.7	367
30–34	3.27	22.86	55.10	10.20	8.57	0.3	2,760
35–44	4.27	23.61	54.62	14.08	3.41	1.7	703
45–54	1.34	15.63	64.71	14.45	3.87	–0.6	595

55–59	1.70	24.68	54.89	13.19	5.53	0.6	235
60–64	0.79	17.46	51.59	11.90	18.25	–4.4	126
65+	3.23	12.90	61.29	12.90	9.68	–1.9	31
Shukko							
All ages	2.61	9.26	81.00	5.46	1.66	0.9	421
<19	0.00	0.00	90.91	9.09	0.00	–1.4	11
20–24	0.00	6.36	90.00	3.64	0.00	0.4	110
25–29	5.00	6.25	81.25	6.25	1.25	1.1	80
30–34	9.30	9.30	74.42	6.98	0.00	3.1	43
35–44	0.00	12.50	77.5o	7.50	2.50	0.0	80
45–54	1.56	12.50	81.25	3.13	1.56	1.4	64
55–59	7.41	14.81	66.67	3.70	7.41	1.7	27
60–64	—[c]	—	—	—	—	—	—
65+	—	—	—	—	—	—	—

NOTE: Wage changes refer to monthly wages which do not include bonuses. Involuntary separations consist of mandatory retirement, company convenience, contract termination, and *shukko*.

[a] Estimated mean assigns valules 30%, 15%, 0, –15%, and –30% to each of the five-wage categories.

[b] Involuntary separations consist of mandatory retirement, company, convenience, contract termination, and *shukko*.

[c] Cell sizes too small to report.

SOURCE: Japan Ministry of Labor (1997).

Table 3.15 Distributions of Wage Changes by Separation Reasons and Age in Canada (%)

Age (yr.)	Gain of over 30%	10% – 30% gain	10% loss – 10% gain	10% – 30% loss	Loss of over 30%	Mean[a] (estimated)	Mean[b] (actual)	Sample
Men								
All permanent separations								
All ages	19.46	15.86	34.50	16.47	13.70	1.6	5.9	3,278
15–19	27.88	22.42	21.82	17.58	10.30	6.0	17.9	165
20–29	24.85	17.51	28.95	16.65	12.04	4.0	9.0	1,171
30–39	17.20	16.13	35.97	16.03	14.66	0.8	2.1	1,023
40–49	15.21	12.94	38.51	17.64	15.70	–0.9	1.9	618
50–59	9.41	10.98	51.37	13.33	14.90	–2.0	–9.2	255
60 +	15.22	10.87	41.30	19.57	13.04	–0.7	6.0	46
Permanent layoffs								
All ages	17.03	14.66	36.99	16.82	14.50	0.4	–0.4	2,455
15–19	18.07	25.30	21.69	22.89	12.05	2.2	3.3	83
20–29	22.52	16.09	31.02	16.60	13.77	2.5	3.6	777
30–39	16.00	14.41	38.34	16.73	14.53	0.1	–0.6	819
40–49	13.98	13.01	39.81	17.28	15.92	–1.2	–3.1	515
50–59	9.05	10.86	51.13	14.48	14.48	–2.2	–3.3	221
60 +	12.50	12.50	42.50	17.50	15.00	–1.5	–3.0	40

Women								
All separations								
All ages	19.13	16.32	30.00	18.97	15.58	0.7	2.8	2,420
15–19	27.45	19.61	27.45	16.67	8.82	6.0	14.2	102
20–29	21.86	16.99	28.20	18.57	14.38	2.0	6.0	883
30–39	17.45	16.01	30.97	18.90	16.67	–0.2	–0.8	762
40–49	16.25	15.83	28.96	22.08	16.88	–1.1	–2.5	480
50–59	16.76	13.29	37.57	14.45	17.92	–0.5	0.5	173
60 +	10.00	20.00	45.00	15.00	10.00	0.8	–3.3	20
Permanent layoffs								
All ages	18.38	14.26	31.50	19.39	16.48	–0.2	–2.4	1,578
15–19	26.83	12.20	34.15	14.63	12.20	4.0	4.7	41
20–29	20.91	15.38	29.59	18.54	15.58	1.1	–1.0	507
30–39	17.86	13.79	32.04	20.00	16.31	–0.5	–1.9	515
40–49	15.60	14.76	29.81	22.01	17.83	–1.8	–3.9	359
50–59	16.67	10.14	38.41	15.94	18.84	–1.5	–5.4	138
60 +	11.11	22.22	44.44	11.11	11.11	1.7	1.4	18

[a] "Actual" mean is the percentage difference between mean pre- and postseparation wages in each age-gender category.

[b] Estimated mean assigns values 30%, 15%, 0, –15%, and –30% to each of the five wage change categories. "Actual" mean is the percentage difference between mean pre- and postseparation wages in each age-gender category.

SOURCE: Derived from the merged 1993 and 1995 COEP surveys.

Table 3.16 Mean Wage Changes by Tenure for Permanently Laid-Off Workers in Canada

Group	All	<1	1–3	3–5	6–10	>10
Men						
Change (%)	–1.34	2.61	–0.31	–5.48	–5.13	–11.05
N	2,497	1,382	382	223	187	323
Women						
Change (%)	–2.42	0.81	0.79	–7.84	–4.35	–6.59
N	1,610	853	336	177	129	115

SOURCE: Authors' calculations from 1994 Survey of Labour and Income Dynamics.

Table 3.17 Mean Tenure by Age and Gender for All Employed Workers in Japan and Canada

	Japan		Canada A[a]		Canada B[b]	
Age (yr.)	Men	Women	Men	Women	Men	Women
All	12.9	7.9	9.0	6.7	9.6	7.9
<17	1.1	1.2	0.5	0.5	0.5	0.5
18–19	1.1	1.0	1.0	0.8	1.0	0.9
20–24	2.7	2.7	1.8	1.6	2.1	1.6
25–29	5.1	5.2	3.1	3.4	3.1	3.6
30–34	8.5	7.7	5.5	5.2	6.3	6.1
35–39	11.9	9.3	7.8	6.3	8.4	7.4
40–44	15.8	10.5	10.8	8.6	12.4	10.0
45–49	19.3	11.2	13.0	8.8	14.4	9.7
50–54	22.1	13.0	14.7	11.7	14.7	13.1
55–59	21.8	14.4	17.8	12.7	18.3	15.4
60–64	13.4	13.3	18.2	15.6	16.1	15.1
65+	12.8	16.1	21.0	14.5	24.1	15.0

NOTE: The sample consists of employees at establishments with 10 or more workers in June 1995. Figures are for the individual's "main" job, defined as the one with the highest annual hours in 1994.

[a] Specification A imposes no establishment-size restriction.

[b] Specification B restricts to establishments with at least 20 employees.

SOURCE: For Japanese data, Japan Ministry of Labor, Survey of the Wage Structure (1996). For Canadian data, authors' calculations from the Survey of Labour and Income Dynamics for 1994.

Table 3.18 Determinants of Wage Changes for Male Workers Who Found Jobs within One Year in Japan

Variable	(1) All separations	(2A)[a] "Laid-off" workers	(2B)[a] "Laid-off" workers	(3A) *Shukko* workers	(3B) *Shukko* workers
Constant	15.985***	10.036***	1.559*	3.248***	–0.028
	(0.905)	(3.141)	(0.823)	(0.988)	(0.450)
High school	–1.003***	–2.037***	–2.472***	0.119	–0.083
	(0.179)	(0.599)	(0.597)	(0.333)	(0.330)
Junior college	–3.256***	–5.299***	–5.940***	–0.272	–0.499
	(0.340)	(1.369)	(1.370)	(0.587)	(0.585)
University	–1.770***	–1.327	–2.153***	0.167	–0.124
	(0.225)	(0.843)	(0.830)	(0.352)	(0.345)
Firm >1,000	5.032***	3.3970***	3.302***	0.930***	1.077***
(postsep.)	(0.180)	(0.720)	(0.722)	(0.281)	(0.277)
Firm 100–999	0.781***	–0.562	–0.476	0.981***	1.100***
(postsep.)	(0.164)	(0.583)	(0.583)	(0.287)	(0.285)
Firm >1,000	–7.415***	–5.911***	–5.337***	–0.566**	–0.474**
(presep.)	(0.190)	(0.725)	(0.722)	(0.243)	(0.241)
Firm 100–999	–2.606***	–0.685	–0.262	–0.907***	–0.848***
(presep.)	(0.152)	(0.604)	(0.603)	(0.246)	(0.246)
Part time	–9.154***	–13.869***	–13.76***	2.521	2.4
(postsep.)	(0.398)	(1.287)	(1.290)	(1.869)	(1.872)
Part time	7.929***	11.025***	11.187***	8.401***	8.392***
(presep.)	(0.352)	(1.553)	(1.557)	(2.103)	(2.106)

(continued)

Table 3.18 (continued)

Variable	(1) All separations	(2A)[a] "Laid-off" workers	(2B)[a] "Laid-off" workers	(3A) *Shukko* workers	(3B) *Shukko* workers
*Shukko*1 (out)	2.257*** (0.299)	—	—	—	—
*Shukko*2 (back)	–4.665*** (0.309)	—	—	—	—
Laid off	–5.399*** (0.232)	—	—	—	—
Change IND	–0.781*** (0.137)	–3.250*** (0.5348	–4.422*** (0.506)	0.223 (0.200)	–0.0790 (0.185)
Industry wage premium (postsep.)	–0.887 (0.857)	7.607** (3.153)	—	–1.317 (0.888)	—
Industry wage premium (presep.)	–8.4258*** (0.734)	–16.575*** (2.455)	—	–2.121*** (0.761)	—
Year	–1.677*** (0.137)	4.687*** (0.616)	5.303*** (0.577)	–0.230 (0.191)	–0.017 (0.182)
Age 35–44	–1.037*** (0.172)	0.799 (0.727)	0.757 (0.721)	0.058 (0.243)	0.088 (0.242)
Age 45–54	–2.387*** (0.200)	–3.946*** (0.773)	–4.243*** (0.774)	–0.332 (0.237)	–0.361 (0.237)
Age 55–64	–9.415*** (0.222)	–11.251*** (0.706)	–12.166*** (0.696)	–2.401*** (0.342)	–2.542*** (0.340)

Σ	14.402***	16.311***	16.377***	6.664***	6.674***
	(0.049)	(0.200)	(0.201)	(0.065)	(0.065)
Log likelihood	–197583	–16607.1	–16630	–17874.5	–17882.4
No. of obs.	52,414	4,603	4,603	5,443	5,443

NOTE: Double-truncated censored regression results by job-loss status. Numbers in parentheses are asymptotic standard errors. *** = Significant at the 1% level; ** = significant at the 5% level; * = significant at the 10% level, all based on asymptotic *t*-ratios.

[a] Laid-off workers category includes all involuntary separations excluding *shukko*: management convenience, contract termination, and mandatory retirement.

SOURCE: Authors' calculations.

Table 3.19 Determinants of Wage Changes for Female Workers Who Found Jobs within One Year in Japan

	(1) All separations	(2A) "Laid-off" workers[a]	(2B) "Laid-off" workers[a]	(3A) *Shukko* workers	(3B) *Shukko* workers
Constant	6.030***	7.799**	4.485***	2.697	3.402
	(1.163)	(3.288)	(0.814)	(5.977)	(1.667)
High school	–1.642***	–1.573*	–1.634***	–1.821	–1.784
	(0.224)	(0.593)	(0.591)	(1.285)	(1.279)
Junior college	–3.566***	–4.486**	–4.560***	–2.676	–2.648
	(0.290)	(0.894)	(0.892)	(1.638)	(1.627)
University	–3.151***	–3.456**	–3.507**	–3.632**	–3.605**
	(0.424)	(1.464)	(1.464)	(1.690)	(1.671)
Firm > 1,000 (postsep.)	3.007***	3.848***	3.873***	–0.629	–0.621
	(0.211)	(0.685)	(0.684)	(1.177)	(1.153)
Firm 100–999 (postsep.)	1.153**	1.029**	1.064**	–0.370	–0.367
	(0.179)	(0.517)	(0.515)	(1.121)	(1.116)
Firm > 1,000 (presep.)	–6.523***	–6.170***	–6.167***	–0.002	–0.048
	(0.247)	(0.788)	(0.788)	(1.121)	(1.117)
Firm 100–999 (presep.)	–2.743***	–3.100***	–3.085***	–0.378	–0.393
	(0.174)	(0.526)	(0.526)	(1.004)	(1.003)
Part time (postsep.)	–11.700***	–9.117***	–9.176***	–2.501	–2.481
	(0.206)	(0.654)	(0.653)	(1.978)	(1.974)
Part time (presep.)	10.643***	10.006***	10.049***	4.469***	4.464***
	(0.200)	(0.651)	(0.650)	(1.697)	(1.697)

*SHUKKO*1 (out)	0.687 (0.900)	—	—	—	—
*SHUKKO*2 (back)	–3.286*** (1.070)	—	—	—	—
Laid off	–1.736** (0.265)	—	—	—	—
Change IND	–0.861*** (0.165)	–2.028*** (0.507)	–2.263*** (0.476)	1.854* (0.981)	2.057** (0.880)
Industry wage premium (postsep.)	1.825* (1.075)	–0.269 (3.124)	—	–2.372 (6.755)	—
Industry wage premium (presep.)	–2.572*** (0.949)	–3.141 (2.520)	—	3.121 (5.588)	—
Year	–0.947*** (0.162)	–0.722 (0.529)	–0.492 (0.484)	–1.000 (0.970)	–1.118 (0.854)
Age 35–44	0.952*** (0.203)	–0.623 (0.625)	–0.677 (0.617)	–1.984* (1.162)	–1.945** (1.158)
Age 45–54	–0.796*** (0.246)	–2.996*** (0.698)	–3.125*** (0.686)	–0.691 (1.295)	–0.587 (1.276)
Age 55–64	–2.153*** (0.361)	–3.303*** (0.858)	–3.515*** (0.844)	–3.540* (1.849)	–3.330* (1.810)

(continued)

Table 3.19 (continued)

	(1) All separations	(2A) "Laid-off" workers[a]	(2B) "Laid-off" workers[a]	(3A) *Shukko* workers	(3B) *Shukko* workers
Σ	13.939***	12.580***	12.584***	8.393***	8.397***
	(0.058)	(0.171)	(0.171)	(0.301)	(0.302)
			3,109		417
Log likelihood	–130038	–11,639.7	–11,640.6	–1,448.45	–1,448.6
No. of obs.	34,551	3,109	3,109	417	417

NOTE: Double-truncated censored regression results by job-loss status. Numbers in parentheses are asymptotic standard errors. *** = Significant at the 1% level; ** = significant at the 5% level; * = significant at the 10% level, all based on asymptotic *t*-ratios.

[a] Laid-off workers category includes all involuntary separations excluding *shukko*: management convenience, contract termination, and mandatory retirement.

SOURCE: Authors' calculations.

Table 3.20 Determinants of Wage Changes for Permanent Separations and Laid-Off Workers Who Found Jobs within One Year in Canada

	Men			Women		
	All separations	Displaced workers		All separations	Displaced workers	
Variable	(1)	(2)[a]	(3)[b]	(4)	(5)[a]	(6)[b]
UU[c]	0.045**	0.030	—	0.102***	0.110***	—
	(0.020)	(0.021)		(0.034)	(0.042)	
UN[d]	–0.136***	–0.164***	—	–0.124***	–0.151***	—
	(0.024)	(0.028)		(0.034)	0.041	
NU[e]	0.196***	0.184***	—	0.180***	0.128***	—
	(0.031)	(0.038)		(0.036)	(0.043)	
Elem.	0.030	0.031	0.023	0.052	0.106**	0.120**
	(0.041)	(0.043)	(0.042)	(0.045)	(0.052)	(0.055)
Some high	–0.032*	–0.014	–0.026	0.005	0.012	0.007
	(0.020)	(0.022)	(0.022)	(0.028)	(0.033)	(0.034)
Some post	–0.024	–0.025	–0.010	0.009	0.003	0.005
	(0.024)	(0.028)	(0.029)	(0.025)	(0.031)	(0.030)
College	–0.017	–0.022	–0.026	0.037	–0.002	–0.004
	(0.026)	(0.032)	(0.033)	(0.027)	(0.033)	(0.034)
Univ.	0.011	–0.025	–0.036		0.070**	0.042
	(0.028)	(0.034)	(0.034)	(0.028)	(0.034)	(0.034)
Trades	–0.041	–0.027	–0.029	0.023	0.004	0.025
	(0.026)	(0.029)	(0.029)	(0.039)	(0.050)	(0.053)

(continued)

Table 3.20 (continued)

	Men			Women		
	All separations	Displaced workers		All separations	Displaced workers	
Variable	(1)	(2)[a]	(3)[b]	(4)	(5)[a]	(6)[b]
Firm 20–99 (pre)[f]	–0.013	–0.022	–0.031	–0.029	–0.056	–0.065
	(0.025)	(0.030)	(0.031)	(0.030)	(0.044)	(0.044)
Firm 100–499 (pre)	–0.059	–0.057	–0.075	–0.180***	–0.204***	–0.254***
	(0.036)	(0.049)	(0.051)	(0.049)	(0.062)	(0.060)
Firm 500+ (pre)	–0.207***	–0.176**	–0.244***	–0.158**	–0.121	–0.193***
	(0.061)	(0.071)	(0.073)	(0.073)	(0.078)	(0.073)
Firm 20–99 (post)	0.029	0.009	0.026	0.044	–0.005	–0.002
	(0.023)	(0.028)	(0.029)	(0.030)	(0.043)	(0.042)
Firm 100–499 (post)	0.083***	0.077*	0.103***	0.138***	0.141**	0.163***
	(0.032)	(0.039)	(0.039)	(0.049)	(0.066)	(0.062)
Firm 500+ (post)	0.167***	0.149**	0.221***	0.197***	0.041	0.094
	(0.055)	(0.064)	(0.070)	(0.060)	(0.098)	(0.101)
Part-time (pre)	–0.029	–0.044	–0.034	–0.008	–0.023	–0.014
	(0.037)	(0.050)	(0.052)	(0.024)	(0.029)	(0.029)
Part-time (post)	–0.080***	–0.020	–0.028	0.042**	0.059**	0.071***
	(0.030)	(0.033)	(0.035)	(0.020)	(0.024)	(0.024)
Change industry	–0.019	–0.026*	–0.019	–0.012	–0.018	–0.033
	(0.014)	(0.016)	(0.016)	(0.018)	(0.022)	(0.021)

Tenure (pre)[g]	–0.007***	–0.007***	–0.007***	–0.006**	—	—
	(0.002)	(0.002)	(0.002)	(0.003)		
Age 35–44	–0.027	–0.024	–0.043**	–0.022	–0.012	–0.015
	(0.018)	(0.020)	(0.019)	(0.020)	(0.025)	(0.024)
Age 45–54	–0.070***	–0.062**	–0.094***	–0.035	–0.063*	–0.058*
	(0.024)	(0.027)	(0.027)	(0.028)	(0.032)	(0.031)
Age 55–64	–0.053*	–0.053	–0.092***	–0.007	–0.029	–0.039
	(0.031)	(0.033)	(0.032)	(0.057)	(0.066)	(0.067)
Vismin	–0.058***	–0.043*	–0.040*	0.052*	0.040	0.037
	(0.020)	(0.023)	(0.023)	(0.027)	(0.030)	(0.030)
Intercept	0.173***	0.188***	0.059***	0.005	–0.026	–0.024
	(0.029)	(0.037)	(0.019)	(0.031)	(0.038)	(0.027)
Industry	Yes	Yes	No	Yes	Yes	No
Province	Yes	Yes	No	Yes	Yes	No
R^2	0.096	0.094	0.013	0.073	0.08	0.015
N[h]	2,697	1,995	1,995	2,027	1,289	1,289

NOTE: Ordinary least squares regression results (heteroskedasticity consistent standard errors in parentheses). The dependent variable is the ratio of pre- to postdisplacement wages. *** = Significant at the 1% level; ** = significant at the 5% level; * = significant at the 10% level.

[a] Restricted to permanent layoffs. Equations 1, 2, 4, and 5 include 15 predisplacement industry dummy variables.

[b] Restricted to permanent layoffs. Equations include 15 predisplacement industry variables but drop union status and tenure.

[c] UU = union to union.

[d] UN = union to nonunion.

[e] NU = nonunion to union.

[f] Firm sizes are only in the 1995 data, so the variables should be interpreted as firm size interacted with a dummy for the 1995 COEP.

[g] Tenure is measured in years.

[h] The number of observations in each regression reflects the number of respondents who answered all of the relevant questions.

Table 3.21 The Incidence of Severe and Moderate Separation-Induced Wage Losses and Wage Gains in Canada and Japan (% of employed workers)

	Canada				Japan			
Group	Wage loss >30%	Wage loss >10%	Wage gain >10%	Wage gain >30%	Wage loss >30%	Wage loss >10%	Wage gain >10%	Wage gain >30%
	(1)	(2)	(3)	(4)	(5)	(6)	(7)	(8)
Men								
15–19	1.1	3.1	5.1	3.0	0.4	1.7	8.7	1.3
20–24	4.7	11.0	18.8	11.0	0.8	2.5	8.0	1.3
25–29	2.6	6.0	8.3	4.7	0.5	2.2	4.9	1.2
30–34	1.9	4.1	4.6	2.5	0.4	1.5	3.3	0.5
35–39	1.7	3.4	3.8	1.9	0.2	1.0	2.0	0.2
40-44	1.2	2.9	2.6	1.4	0.4	1.3	1.9	0.1
45–49	1.3	2.5	2.3	1.3	0.4	0.8	1.6	0.2
50–54	1.2	2.3	1.7	0.7	0.6	1.2	2.0	0.3
55–59	1.1	2.3	2.1	1.1	1.5	2.9	1.5	0.1
60+	1.0	2.4	3.1	1.9	6.8	10.5	4.1	0.2
All ages	1.9	4.2	5.1	2.8	0.8	2.1	3.8	0.6
Women								
15–19	0.9	2.7	4.7	2.7	0.8	2.6	8.0	1.8
20–24	4.9	12.0	15.9	8.7	2.0	6.5	8.4	2.6
25–29	2.5	5.7	7.0	3.8	2.3	7.9	6.6	2.2
30–34	1.7	4.0	4.3	2.1	2.0	5.2	6.5	2.3

35–39	1.5	3.3	3.4	1.7	0.6	3.1	4.0	1.0
40–44	1.1	2.4	2.5	1.3	0.5	2.3	4.9	0.8
45–49	1.1	2.5	1.9	0.8	0.5	1.8	3.4	0.7
50–54	1.0	2.0	2.2	0.8	1.4	3.8	3.3	0.3
55–59	1.1	1.8	1.8	1.0	1.0	2.4	3.9	0.7
60+	1.2	2.6	3.2	1.3	2.8	4.8	3.0	0.0
All ages	1.9	4.2	4.8	2.4	1.4	4.4	5.6	1.4
Both								
15–19	1.1	2.9	4.9	2.9	0.6	2.1	8.3	1.5
20–24	4.6	11.4	17.5	10.0	1.3	4.2	8.3	1.9
25–29	2.5	5.8	7.8	4.3	1.1	4.1	5.8	1.6
30–34	1.8	4.0	4.5	2.3	0.8	2.5	4.3	0.9
35–39	1.6	3.4	3.6	1.8	0.3	1.7	2.6	0.4
40–44	1.1	2.7	2.6	1.4	0.4	1.7	3.0	0.4
45–49	1.3	2.5	2.1	1.0	0.5	1.2	2.3	0.4
50–54	1.1	2.2	2.0	0.8	0.9	2.0	2.5	0.4
55–59	1.1	2.1	2.0	1.0	1.4	2.9	2.1	0.3
60+	1.0	2.4	3.2	1.7	5.7	8.9	3.8	0.2
All ages	1.8	4.2	5.0	2.6	1.0	2.9	4.5	0.9

NOTE: All data refer to 1995, except the Canadian wage-loss distributions which are from the merged 1993 and 1995 COEP surveys.

Appendix

Japanese Industries Eligible for Employment Maintenance and Adjustment Subsidies

SPECIAL EMPLOYMENT ADJUSTMENT INDUSTRIES

As of January 29, 1998, there were 72 special employment adjustment industries in Japan. Together these industries included 86,954 establishments employing 723,022 workers. They are listed below.

As an example of how such industries become designated, consider the most recent. On January 29, 1998, the Ministry of Labor designated part of industry 2969, in particular the manufacturing of stone cutting machines, as a special employment adjustment industry. The stated reason for this designation was a decline in output due to increased imports of cheap tombstones and other stone products from China and South Korea; the period of designation (which can be extended) was February 1, 1998 to January 31, 2000. This industry has 12 establishments and 187 workers.

Table 3.A1 Special Employment Adjustment Industries

Industry	Description	Effective period
2969 (part)	Stone cutting machines	1998.2.1~2000.1.31
1465 (part)	Coloring process of Yuzen silk cloth	1998.2.1~2000.1.31*
1226 (part)	Manufacturing frozen seafood (herring, salmon, cod, . . .)	1996.7.1~1999.6.30*
1229 (part)	Preprocessing of herrings	1996.7.1~1999.6.30*
1362, 1363	Manufacturing fish powder	1998.7.1~1999.6.30*
1423	Wool textile manufacturing	1996.7.1~1999.6.30*
1425 (part)	Flax textiles (excl. jute)	1995.8.1~1999.7.31*
143	Throwing (silk) manufacturing	1996.4.1~1999.3.31
1441	Cotton, synthetic textiles	1996.9.1~1999.8.31*
1442 (part)	Silk textiles	1996.9.1~1999.8.31*
146 (part)	Textile coloring process (excl. manual coloring, lace coloring and textile, piecemeal coloring processes)	1996.8.1~1999.7.31*
1465 (part)	Manual textile coloring (excl. coloring of Yuzen, scarfs, and handkerchiefs)	1996.7.1~1999.6.30*
1472, 1479	Fish net and other net production (incl. repair)	1996.9.1~1999.8.31
1481	Embroidery lace manufacturing	1997.11.1~1998.10.31
1484	Cloth string manufacturing	1996.4.1~1998.3.31
1485	Thin width textile products	1996.4.1~1998.3.31
1491	Hair processing	1996.4.1~1998.3.31
151	Production of overcoats and shirts (excl. traditional Japanese types)	1996.4.1~1998.3.31
152	Knit jackets and shirts	1997.7.1~1999.6.30
1541, 4921 (part), 4922 (part), 4929 (part),	Leather clothing and products manufacturing and wholesale	1995.7.1~1999.6.30*
1564	Socks manufacturing	1995.7.1~1999.6.30*
1595	Towel manufacturing	1997.1.1~1998.12.31

Industry	Description	Effective period
1622 (part)	Wood sheets manufacturing (excl. bamboo plated and decorative sheets)	1995.9.1~1999.8.31
1633	Wooden box manufacturing (excl. lunch boxes)	1995.7.1~1999.6.30
1811	Chemical pulp production	1997.10.1~1999.9.30
1852	Paper bags with square bottoms	1996.12.1~1998.11.30
1899 (part)	Cloth paper pipes	1995.7.1~1999.6.30*
2297 (part)	Flat yarn	1995.7.1~1999.6.30*
2312	bicycle tires and tire tubes	1995.7.1~1999.6.30*
232	rubber and plastic sandals	1995.7.1~1999.6.30*
2391	Cloth with rubber back and related products	1995.11.1~1999.10.31*
2393	Rubber material	1996.9.1~1998.8.31
2395	Recycled rubber manufacturing	1995.8.1~1999.7.31 extended
241	Tanned leather production	1995.7.1~1999.6.30*
244	Leather shoes and sandals	1995.7.1~1999.6.30*
2461, 2472 (part)	Bags and briefcases	1995.7.1~1999.6.30*
248	Fur manufacturing	1995.7.1~1999.6.30*
2514	Glass ware	1997.1.1~1998.12.31
2523 (part)	Steel framed concrete pipes	1996.4.1~1998.3.31
2529 (part)	Cement sheets	1995.7.1~1999.6.30*
2542, 2547 (part)	Kitchen pottery products	1995.12.1~1999.11.30*
2543, 2547(part)	Pottery decorative products	1995.12.1~1999.11.30*
2551	Fire resistant bricks	1995.10.1~1999.9.30*
2583 (part)	Stone products for buildings	1996.4.1~1998.3.31
2584 (part)	Insulation plats (excl. wall material)	1995.8.1~1999.7.31*
2595	Asbestos products	1995.8.1~1999.7.31*
2645	Iron processing	1995.10.1~1999.9.30*

(continued)

Table 3.A1 (continued)

Industry	Description	Effective period
2662	Die production	1995.7.1~1999.6.30*
2811 (part)	Production of cans	1995.7.1~1999.6.30*
2821	Western kitchen silverware	1995.7.1~1999.6.30*
2824	Tools (excl. grinding metals)	1996.6.1~1998.5.31
2831 (part)	Steel connecting pipes (excl. die pipes)	1995.7.1~1999.6.30*
2842 (part)	Metal window frames and doors	1996.5.1~1998.4.30
2851 (part)	Aluminum, aluminum kitchenware	1996.6.1~1998.5.31
2892	Metal spring	1996.5.1~1998.4.30
295 (part)	Textile mills production (excl. sewing machines)	1996.9.1~1998.8.31
2981 (part)	Typewriter production	1996.4.1~1998.3.31
3012	Transformer production (excl. those for electronic equipment)	1995.11.1~1999.10.31
313	Bicycles, parts	1995.11.1~1999.10.31*
3251 (part), 3254 (part)	Binoculars, parts	1995.12.1~1999.11.30*
3253, 3254 (part)	Motion picture machinery, parts	1996.4.1~1998.3.31
332	Gun production	1996.10.1~1998.9.30
3432 (part)	Cloth dolls production	1995.8.1~1999.7.31*
3434 (part)	Baseball gloves, mitts	1995.7.1~1999.6.30*
3434 (part)	Ski equipment	1995.12.1~1999.11.30*
3434 (part)	Air guns, hunting rifles	1996.6.1~1998.5.31
3453	Button production	1996.10.1~1998.9.30
3454 (part)	Needle production	1995.12.1~1999.11.30*
3475 (part)	Umbrellas, parts	1995.7.1~1999.6.30*
3476	Matches	1997.7.1~1999.6.30
3911 (part)	Railway (freight only)	1997.3.1~1999.2.28
459 (part)	Volume measurement industry	1996.6.1~1998.5.31

*The effective periods for these industries have been extended.

The following is the list of employment adjustment subsidy industries as of January 29, 1998.[a]

Table 3.A2 Employment Adjustment Subsidy Industries

Industry	Description (effective region)	Effective period
1299(part)	Kaiware daikon salad leaf sprouts (all)	1996.10.18~1998.9.30*
1465(part)	Scarf and handkerchief coloring (all)	1996.11.1~1998.10.31*
1532,1534	Knit underwear and pajamas (all)	1997.12.1~1998.11.30
1611	General lumber mills (all)	1997.10.1~1998.9.30
1622 (part)	Wood sheets (all)	1997.11.1~1998.10.31
1711	Wood furniture, excl. lacquer painted (all)	1998.2.1~1999.1.31
2242 (part)	Synthetic foam (Komatsu, etc.)	1997.4.1~1998.3.31
2513 (part)	Glass light bulbs (all)	1997.4.1~1998.3.31
2523 (part)	Concrete pile	1998.2.1~1999.1.31
2544	Electrical pottery insulation material (all)	1996.10.1~1998.9.30*
2546	Pottery tiles (all)	1997.7.1~1998.6.30
2549 (part)	Pottery plant pots (all)	1998.2.1~1999.1.31
2644	Steel pipes (all)	1997.7.1~1998.6.30
2663	Die production	1997.11.1~1998.10.31
2864	Electric gilding (all)	1996.6.1~1998.5.31*
4232 (part)	River cruising operator	1996.10.1~1998.9.30*
452 (part) 459 (part)	Port transportation	1997.7.1~1998.6.30

*The effective periods for these industries were extended.

[a] As of June 1, 1998 this list grew: a total of 51 industries with 511,921 establishments were certified to be employment adjustment subsidy industries. They employed 846,957 employees.

References

Akyeampong, E. 1997. "A Statistical Portrait of the Union Movement." Statistics Canada, *Perspectives on Labour and Income* 9(1): 45–54.

Arthurs, H. W., D.D. Carter, J. Fudge, H.J. Glasbeek, and G. Trudeau. 1993. *Labor Law and Industrial Relations in Canada.* Fourth ed. Markham, Ontario: Butterworths Kluwer.

Benjamin, D., M. Gunderson, and W.C. Riddell. 1998. *Labour Market Economics.* Fourth ed. Toronto: McGraw-Hill Ryerson.

Bertola, Giuseppe. 1992. "Labor Turnover Costs and Average Labor Demand." *Journal of Labor Economics* 10(4): 389–411.

Canada Employment Insurance Commission. 1997. *Employment Insurance Monitoring and Assessment Report 1998.* Human Resource Development Canada, Catalogue no. WSP-102-01-98. Ottawa: Minister of Public Works and Government Services Canada.

Clark, Robert L., and N. Ogawa. 1992. "Employment Tenure and Earnings Profiles in Japan and the United States: Comment." *American Economic Review* 82(March): 336–345.

Downey, Don. 1989. "Man Awarded $1 Million in Wrongful Dismissal Suit." *Globe and Mail* (October 31): B1, B4.

Glenson, W., and K. Odaka. 1976. "The Japanese Labor Market." In *Asia's New Giant,* H. Patrick and H. Rosovsky, eds. Washington, D.C.: The Brookings Institution, pp. 587–671.

Hashimoto, M. 1990. *The Japanese Labor Market in a Comparative Perspective with the United States.* Kalamazoo, Michigan: W.E. Upjohn Institute for Employment Research.

Hashimoto, M., and J. Raisian. 1985. "Employment Tenure and Earnings Profiles in Japan and the United States." *American Economic Review* 75(September): 721–735.

———. 1992. "Employment Tenure and Earnings Profiles in Japan and the United States: Reply." *American Economic Review* 82(March): 346–354.

Higuchi, Y. 1991. *Japanese Economy and Employment Behaviour.* Tokyo: Toyo Keizai.

———. 1996. *Labour Economics* (in Japanese). Tokyo: Toyo Keizai.

Human Resources Development Canada. 1993. *Labour Program: Employment Standards Legislation in Canada.* Available at http://www.hrdc-drhc.gc.ca/menu/pub.shtml.

———. 1998. *Employment Standards Legislation in Canada.* Ottawa: HRDC.

Ito, Takatoshi. 1992. *The Japanese Economy.* Cambridge, Massachusetts: MIT Press.

Japan Ministry of Labor. 1989. *Employment Mobility Survey Report: 1988* (in Japanese). Tokyo.

———. 1992. "1991 Survey of Labor-Management Agreements." In *Yearbook of Labor Statistics.* Tokyo.

———. 1996. *Special Survey of the Labor Force.* Tokyo.

———. 1997. *Special Survey of the Labor Force.* Tokyo.

———. 1997a. *Employment Mobility Survey Report: 1995* (in Japanese). Tokyo.

———. 1997b. *Employment Report'97* (in Japanese). Tokyo.

———. 1997c. *Employment Related Payments* (in Japanese). Tokyo.

Jones, Stephen G.R., and Peter Kuhn. 1995. "Mandatory Notice and Unemployment." *Journal of Labor Economics* 13(4): 599–622.

Koike, K. 1984. "Skill Formation Systems in the U.S. and Japan." In *The Economic Analysis of the Japanese Firm*, M. Aoki, ed. Amsterdam: North-Holland.

Kuhn, Peter. 1999. *Cross-Subsidization between Full- and Part-Time Workers under the Employment Insurance Act.* Report prepared for Human Resources Development Canada, March.

Kuhn, Peter, and Arthur Sweetman. 1998. "Wage Losses of Displaced Workers: The Role of Union Coverage." *Industrial and Labor Relations Review* 51(3): 384–400.

Lacroix, Guy, and Marc Van Audenrode. 2000. *An Assessment of Various Components of Bill C-12 on the Duration of Unemployment Spells: Final Report.* Ottawa: Strategic Evaluation and Monitoring and Data Development Branch, Human Resources Development Canada, Catalogue no. SP-AH130-10-00, October.

Lemieux, Thomas. 1993. "Unions and Wage Inequality in Canada and the United States." In *Small Differences that Matter: Labor Markets and Income Maintenance in Canada and the United States,* D. Card and R. Freeman, eds. Chicago: University of Chicago Press.

Lin, Zhengxi, and Wendy Pyper. 1997. "Job Turnover and Labor Market Adjustment in Ontario from 1978 to 1993." Analytical Studies Branch Research Paper no. 106, Statistics Canada.

Nakamura, M., and A. Nakamura. 1991. "Risk Behavior and the Determinants of Bonus versus Regular Pay in Japan." *Journal of the Japanese and International Economies* 5(2): 140–159.

Nakamura, M., and I. Vertinsky. 1994. *Japanese Economic Policies and Growth: Implications for Businesses in Canada and North America.* University of Alberta Press; distributed by the University of British Columbia Press, Vancouver, Canada.

Neal, Derek. 1995. "Industry-Specific Human Capital: Evidence from Displaced Workers." *Journal of Labor Economics* 13(4): 653–677.

Okochi, K., B. Karsh, and S.B. Levine, eds. 1974. *Workers and Employers in Japan: The Japanese Employment Relations System.* Princeton: Princeton University Press.

Picot, Garnett, and Lin, Zhengxi. 1996. "Are Canadians More Likely to Lose Their Jobs in the 1990s?" Analytical Studies Branch Research Paper no. 96, Statistics Canada.

Picot, Garnett, Zhengxi Lin, and Wendy Pyper. 1997. "Permanent Layoffs in Canada: Overview and Longitudinal Analysis." Analytical Studies Branch Research Paper no. 103, Statistics Canada.

Seike, A. 1993. *Labor Markets in the Aged Society* (in Japanese). Tokyo: Toyo Keizai.

Statistics Canada. 1997. *Survey of Labour and Income Dynamics (SLID) Microdata User's guide.* Statistics Canada Catalogue no. 75M0001GPE. Ottawa: Minister of Industry.

Tachibanaki, T. 1996. *Wage Determination and Distribution in Japan.* Oxford: Clarendon.

Teulings, C., and J. Hartog. 1998. *Corporatism or Competition: Labour Contracts, Institutions and Wage Structures in International Comparison.* Cambridge: Cambridge University Press.

Topel, R. 1991. "Specific Capital, Mobility, and Wages: Wages Rise with Job Seniority." *Journal of Political Economy* 99(February): 145–176.

4
They Get Knocked Down. Do They Get Up Again?

Displaced Workers in Britain and Australia

Jeff Borland
University of Melbourne

Paul Gregg
University of Bristol

Genevieve Knight
Policy Studies Institute

Jonathan Wadsworth
Royal Holloway, University of London

"I get knocked down, but I get up again."
Chumbawumba, 1997

Industrial restructuring, changes in technology, and recession are all associated with worker displacement, the involuntary separation of an employee from a job. Workers also leave jobs for personal reasons, but because these are considered voluntary actions and presumably not as closely linked with economic hardship, there is less concern over the consequences of this type of movement. The media in Britain and Australia, and perhaps because of this the general public, are also preoccupied with the idea of declining job security (see, for example, Kelley, Evans, and Dawkins 1998). Whilst job security is difficult to quantify, public concern could arise not only from a belief that a long-term employment relationship is now less likely, but also from a belief that, if unlucky enough to lose a job, a replacement job is likely to be of lower quality, to pay lower wages, and to be less stable.

In this chapter we examine the consequences of job loss for displaced workers in Britain and Australia. Fallick (1996) and Kletzer (1998) provide useful summaries of over ten years of research into the issue in North America. As yet, however, the evidence from Britain and Australia is sparse.

For Britain, Gregory and Jukes (1997) provided the first evidence of the effects of unemployment on the subsequent earnings of a sample of unemployed male benefit claimants. They find, on average, an earnings penalty of around 10 percent compared with men who remain in jobs. The research in this chapter draws on data from the British Household Panel Survey (BHPS) over the period 1991 to 1996 to broaden the scope of inquiry on job displacement in Britain by including all unemployment spells (claimant or otherwise) and spells of economic inactivity (allowing for discouraged job seekers), together with information for women and/or part-time working. The analysis highlights which groups are most likely to experience displacement, which groups are most likely to get back into work, and the earnings changes associated with reentry into work.

For Australia, a range of case-study–type evidence is available which suggests that displaced workers face considerable difficulties in obtaining new jobs, but does not provide clear conclusions on the effects of displacement on future wages (Borland 1998). In this chapter, data from two sources are used to extend existing research. First, aggregate-level data from the Australian Bureau of Statistics (ABS) and Labor Force Survey (LFS) are used to describe patterns and trends in the incidence of displacement and labor market outcomes for displaced workers. Second, individual-level data from the Youth in Transition Survey (YTS) are used to examine the consequences of displacement for young workers in Australia in the mid 1980s and early 1990s. The analysis provides a more detailed treatment of post-displacement employment and wage outcomes for displaced workers in Australia than in previous studies—for example, by presenting information on average employment outcomes over the two-year period following displacement.

The next section provides background information on the labor markets in Britain and Australia in the 1980s and 1990s. The third section describes the institutional and legal framework surrounding job displacement in Britain and Australia. The fourth section outlines the data sources used for each country and presents findings from analysis of the incidence of displacement and the consequences of job loss. The last section presents a summary of the main results for each country and attempts to offer a comparative perspective on how institutional differences between Britain and Australia might have affected wage and employment outcomes for displaced workers in those countries. Differences between the data sources—in particular, the Australian data source is restricted to younger workers whereas the British data source covers all age groups—mean that the scope for such comparisons is somewhat limited. However, some conclusions regarding the role of institutional factors are preferred.

LABOR MARKET BACKGROUND

Britain

At the beginning of the nineties, Britain entered a recession that was to last until the end of 1992. Unemployment reached a peak of around 3 million, some 10.5 percent of the workforce, in the spring of the following year. The recession primarily affected men. Male employment fell by 1.3 million in the three years between 1990 and 1993, while female employment fell by only 150,000 over the same period. The economic downturn helped increase the movement of many men—mostly, but not entirely, over age 50—into economic inactivity. The number of men outside the labor force grew by around 700,000 over the recession period and continued to rise over the rest of the nineties, albeit more slowly. Manufacturing and the distribution and retail sectors bore the brunt of the fall in employment: 600,000 jobs were lost in manufacturing between 1990 and 1993 and 400,000 jobs in distribution and trade. Younger workers were hit worst by the recession. The employment rate for those aged 20–24 years fell from 75.5 percent to 66.0 percent, some 500,000 workers, from 1990 to 1993, compared with the national fall from 75.2 percent to 70.6 percent over the same period.

The labor market in the early years of recovery was dominated by a rise in the share of part-time and temporary jobs. By the end of 1996, when the British sample stops, the employment rate had recovered to 72 percent, up by some 600,000 from its 1993 low. Of the net new-job creation 200,000 were for full-time work and 400,000 for part-time work. Half of the net growth in employment was accounted for by temporary jobs. Youth (20–24) employment fell, however, by a further 300,000. This may, in part, be explained by an increased enrollment in tertiary education. Three-quarters of all net employment growth between 1993 and 1996 was accounted for by the public sector and finance industries. Over the same period the increase in earnings inequality that had begun at the start of the eighties continued apace, until 1996 when inequality stopped rising. By 1996, the gross hourly earnings of the lowest decile had fallen to 53 percent of the median, while hourly earnings of the top decile had risen to 220 percent of median earnings. The typical entrant back into work after a spell of non-employment could expect to receive earnings around the bottom quartile of the aggregate earnings distribution, some 69 percent of median earnings in 1996.

Australia

Individual-level data on displaced workers in Australia used in this study are from the early to mid 1980s and early 1990s, and primarily for workers aged 18 to 22 years. Hence in this subsection a range of descriptive information on the Australian labor market in the 1980s and 1990s—in aggregate and for persons aged 15–24 years—is presented.

In 1978, the average unemployment rate in Australia was 7.8 percent, with that for 15- to 24-year-olds at 14.4 percent. Both these rates attained a local maximum in 1983 at 9.9 and 17.9 percent, respectively; declined to a trough of 5.7 and 10.4 percent in 1989; and rose to a higher peak in the recession of the early 1990s of 10.7 percent for the population as a whole in 1993, and 19.5 percent for youth in 1992. This 1990s recession was also distinguished by a substantially larger share of the unemployed population in long-term unemployment; for example in 1993, 36.9 percent of the unemployed had been in that state for over a year, compared with 31.2 percent in 1984. Some reversal of the above increases has now taken place. In May 1998 the rate of unemployment for the working-age population was at 8 percent.

Along with being higher for younger than older labor-force participants, the incidence of unemployment has been particularly high for those with low levels of educational attainment or whose last job was in an unskilled blue-collar occupation, and for some immigrant groups (Borland and Kennedy 1998).

Changes in employment/population and labor-force participation rates also took place in the 1980s and 1990s. The aggregate employment/population rate varied procyclically but displayed little overall trend. As in most industrialized countries, however, the stability of the aggregate employment/population rate disguises opposing trends for males and females. For females both employment and labor-force participation have increased since the mid 1970s, while for males there has been a decrease in participation over this period (see for example, Gregory 1991 and EPAC 1996).[1] Focusing on persons aged 15–24 years, employment and labor-force participation also remained remarkably constant throughout this period (employment at about 60 percent, participation at about 68 percent). However, significant changes occurred in the composition of employment: the full-time employment/population rate declined substantially—from 52 percent in 1980 to 38 percent in 1995—while the part-time employment/population rate increased to compensate. Underlying the change in the composition of employment has been an increase in schooling and university participation, from 34 percent in 1987 to 44 percent in 1995.

The 1980s and 1990s in Australia were characterized by relatively little real wage growth. Between 1978 and 1984, average real weekly earnings of full-time employees grew by a total of 7.6 percent, but fell after that. Only by 1995 had average real weekly earnings recovered to their 1984 level. These trends were similar for youths, although declines in the 1980s were larger for them. (This latter finding could be due to changes in the composition of the full-time youth labor force.) Earnings dispersion was relatively stable from the early to late 1980s, but then increased during the first half of the 1990s (Gregory 1993 and Borland and Wilkins 1996).

INSTITUTIONS

Institutional factors are generally supposed to have an important role in determining both the incidence of worker displacement and subsequent outcomes for displaced workers. In this section we identify the key institutional features which are likely to be relevant for understanding what happens to displaced workers—employment-protection legislation; the unemployment benefit system; and wage-setting institutions. Employment-protection legislation may affect whether and how firms are able to lay off workers. Differential costs of layoffs may also influence the incidence of worker displacement. Unemployment benefits may affect the jobless duration and search activities of displaced workers. Wage-setting institutions help determine both the wages displaced workers surrender and their wages at reemployment.

Britain

Employment protection

How easy is it for firms to make their employees redundant in Britain and what are the costs to firms? Employment-protection legislation, as covered by the Statutory Redundancies Payments Scheme (1965), has operated largely unchanged since its inception. This covers mandatory severance pay, advance notice, legal requirements, and procedures for dismissal. There are relatively few legislative constraints on the ability of firms to make redundancies. The qualifying period—before general rights exist to claim redundancy payments and unfair dismissal—was extended, first, from six months to one year in 1979 and, then, to two years in 1985 for full-time jobs and five years for part-time jobs. In 1995, an EU antidiscrimination ruling was brought in which equalized the qualification period at two years tenure for all. If a worker qualifies for redundancy rights then the entitlements are as follows:

- there is a minimum notice period of one week for each year of service, up to a maximum of 12 weeks.
- an employer must make a lump-sum payment to any employee dismissed because of redundancy, calculated using a formula based on length of service and age. This is then multiplied by the

worker's weekly earnings (with a ceiling imposed currently at £210), as follows:

- 0.5 week's pay for each complete year of service between ages 18 and 21,
- 1 week's pay for each complete year of service between ages 22 and 40,
- 1.5 weeks' pay for each complete year of service between ages 41 and 60.

There is maximum, national, service period of 20 years. Service before age 18 and after age 60 does not count toward redundancy-compensation entitlement. Since qualification for these general rights requires two years' tenure, then the minimum notification period is two weeks, irrespective of hours worked, and the minimum compensation lies between one and three weeks' pay. The maximum amount an employer might be required to pay as a statutory redundancy payment is £6,300 (20 x 1.5 x 210), around one-third average annual earnings. Unions tend to negotiate supplements that raise the compensation and notification period substantially. Employers sometimes make larger payments as an incentive for the workforce to take "voluntary" redundancy. A statutory redundancy payment is not liable to tax and any nonstatutory "golden handshake" is also tax free if it is under £30,000. If the employer fails to make the statutory payment, the employee must present a complaint in writing to an Industrial Tribunal within six months. A right to time off during the period of dismissal notice to look for work or make arrangements for training exists after two years of employment. There is a penalty of two-fifths of weekly pay for each week if the employer does not allow this. The employee also has the right to have recognized trade unions consulted by employers before redundancy proposals are put into effect. This requires no minimum length of employment. Employers wishing to make 100 or more workers redundant at the same time are obliged to give 90-days' notice to the Secretary of State for Employment and to consult with the employees' representatives. Firms wishing to make between 20 and 100 workers redundant are obliged to give 30-days' notice to the same parties (Selwyn 1996). Workers on fixed-term contracts are excluded from redundancy rights if they agree in writing to exclude their rights to make any claim, even if their jobs last for more than two years. Such a clause is now common in many fixed-term contract agreements. General rights apply against "unfair dismissal" after two years, including an award of compensation by an Industrial Tribunal if a claim is made within three months of the dismissal. Any employer who dismisses a woman for some reason connected to her pregnancy, for example, may well be dismissing her unfairly.

Unemployment benefits

Once displaced, what can workers expect to receive from the state? To receive any benefit workers must first register with the state employment service and sign a weekly declaration that they are available for, and actively seeking, work. The British unemployment benefit system encompasses both contribution-based insurance (UI) and means-tested assistance (UA). Both benefits are paid out of general taxation revenue. National Insurance Contributions (NIC) are compulsory for all employees earning above a minimum level, currently £63 a week, as a given percentage of gross pay. Employees who do not pay NICs are not eligible for UI payments and must therefore apply for means-tested assistance. No contributions are required on jobs paying below £63 a week, but NICs are levied on all earnings once the wages rise above this threshold. This profile creates what is called an "entry fee," crossing above which incurs a sharp rise in the tax burden. As a result, more part-time jobs may be created than would otherwise be, and this may affect the new-job wage-offer distribution and hence the cost of job loss.[2]

To be entitled to contributory unemployment benefit a displaced worker must have been employed continuously for two years immediately prior to displacement and must have earned a wage higher than the contribution lower limit (£63 per week). Before 1988 a worker could have been credited with NICs during a spell of unemployment and still qualified for benefit. Since 1983, unemployment benefit in Britain has been paid at a flat rate (£48.25 in 1996), irrespective of previous earnings for a set period. In 1996, the duration period for receipt of UI was reduced from 12 to 6 months. After exhaustion of UI, claimants are transferred to means-tested assistance payments. This benefit is levied at the level of the household rather than the individual and pays a claimant the difference between the household's weekly net income and their needs level or "applicable amount." UI claimants can also claim UA simultaneously since the flat rate UI payment is normally below the amount a family would get on UA. In addition, those living in rented accommodations can claim means-tested help with their housing costs (Housing Benefit). Successful claimants will normally have all of their rent paid, except a nominal amount. Those who own their residences can claim help with their mortgage payments after a 6-month spell of unemployment. Council Tax Benefit, help with local authority taxes, is also paid to those on means-tested benefit, such that 100 percent of their Council Tax is paid.

Individuals can receive means-tested assistance indefinitely, provided they satisfy eligibility requirements. For an unemployed worker this requires a weekly declaration of availability for work at the local Jobcentre, administered by the government employment service. Recent attention has been given to the growing numbers of economically inactive men of working age. Over most of the period covered by this chapter, many of these individuals were claiming long-term sickness benefit (SI). This is a means-tested benefit paying around £30 above the rate for UA, with eligibility determined by a general practitioner. Claimants could move off unemployment benefit into SI after a period of six months claiming means-tested income support. Claims were also allowed after a 6-month period out of work receiving employer-contributed statutory sick pay. It is possible therefore that some displaced workers who could not find a job immediately may have ended up receiving a sickness benefit. In 1995, concerned with the growth in claims, the government replaced SI with Incapacity Benefit, restricting the role of the general practitioner to an "objective" test of a medical basis for the ability to perform work-related activities.

These myriad variations in benefits and the uncertainty surrounding likely wage offers make the calculation of potential replacement rates facing displaced workers very difficult. OECD estimates of "typical replacement ratios" for the United Kingdom are shown in Table 4.A1 in the appendix. Replacement rates are relatively low until housing benefits are taken into account. Thereafter they approach parity with the income brought home by a worker earning two-thirds of the average production worker's salary.

The employment service offers a range of training, advice, and support schemes aimed at helping the unemployed back into work.

Claimants are required to produce evidence that they are actively seeking work and/or had "good cause" for turning down a job they were offered. They are also encouraged, but not obliged, to complete a Back to Work Plan containing goals that they have to achieve during the unemployment spell. This is reviewed after an unemployment spell of 13 weeks and from then on the claimant is referred to the plethora of support schemes and advisory networks available at that time. These initiatives target various categories of unemployment duration—currently *JobClubs* (6 months unemployed), *JobPlan Workshops* (12 months), *Restart* courses (24 months)—and try to match jobseekers to posted vacancies, placement in relevant employment-subsidy programs, remotivation counselling, and improvement in the extent and quality of their job search. Recruitment subsidies and work programs were not in place during the sample period, though the government has recently introduced a wage subsidy scheme, *The New Deal*, for those unemployed in excess of six months. Schmitt and Wadsworth (1998) provide more details on changes to the benefit system over time and the consequences for unemployment outflows.

Wage-setting institutions

What are the principal forces shaping wages in Britain and what might be the consequences for displaced workers looking to reenter work? Wages are relatively free of regulations governing pay determination. Over the sample period, the Conservative administration encouraged, but did not mandate, decentralized determination of wages. There was no national minimum-wage regulation applicable in the United Kingdom over the sample period. Wages Councils, which had previously set minimum rates of pay for around 2 million low-paid workers in selected industries, were abolished in 1993, except in agriculture. Union density in Britain, which continues to fall, is currently estimated to be around 30 percent, and only around 20 percent in the private sector. Collective bargaining coverage has no legal status. Employers must agree as to whether unions are recognized for negotiation purposes. Recent estimates show that collective representation has also been considerably undermined, with just 37 percent of employees covered by collective agreements in 1996, but with 70 percent coverage in large public sector workplaces (Cully and Woodland 1997). If pay is not determined through collective bargaining, then management or a "review body" in the public sector decides (Beatson 1995). Gregg and Wadsworth (1997) provided an analysis of the changing nature of wages being offered to the non-employed.

Australia

The Constitution of the Commonwealth of Australia assigns powers to make legislation between state and federal governments. The power to regulate industrial relations matters is divided between these two: Federal powers are those explicitly stated in the Constitution, and residual powers are assigned to the states. For example, section 51(xxxv) of the Constitution allows the federal government to make laws with respect to "conciliation and arbitration for the prevention and settlement of industrial disputes extending beyond the limits of any one state."

Regulation of the terms and conditions of employment in Australia occurs through: a) Provisions of state and federal government workplace relations legislation; and b) The "award system" whereby a system of industrial tribunals specify and enforce a set of minimum terms and conditions for workers in specific occupation or industry groups.

In what follows we discuss these two sources of employment regulation in turn.

Employment protection

In Australia any employment contract of indefinite duration between an employer and employee will generally be terminable by notice (Creighton, Ford, and Mitchell 1993, p. 225). Currently, regulation of the appropriate notice period for worker retrenchment in Australia occurs through workplace relations legislation and through the wage-setting system. First, some states in Australia have enacted legislation which requires (or can be used to require) employers to provide advance notification of dismissal (Social Justice Consultative Council, 1992). Second, awards setting out minimum terms and conditions of employment may contain provisions relating to minimum-notice periods.

Prior to 1984 most awards (federal and state) contained provisions to the effect that "Employment . . . shall be terminated by a week's notice on either side given at any time during the week or by the payment or forfeiture of a week's wages at the case may be" (Creighton, Ford, and Mitchell 1993, p. 225). The *Termination, Change and Redundancy (TCR) Test Case* decision handed down by the Federal Conciliation and Arbitration Commission in 1984, however, provided a stronger set of conditions governing worker retrenchment which could henceforth be included in awards. These conditions specify minimum requirements for advance notification of retrenchment, severance payments, and such other employer obligations as providing time off for job interviews.

Provisions from the TCR Test Case relating to advance notice and severance payments for retrenched workers are as follows (Creighton, Ford, and Mitchell 1993, pp. 225–226):

- Advance Notice:

  "(i) Where an employer has made a definite decision that the employer no longer wishes the job the employee has been doing done by anyone and this is not due to the ordinary and customary turnover of labor and that decision may lead to termination of employment, the employer shall hold discussions with the employees directly affected and their union.

  (ii) The discussions shall take place as soon as practicable after the employer has made a definite decision . . .

  (iii) For the purposes of the discussion the employer shall, as soon as practicable, provide in writing to the employees concerned and their union, all relevant information about the proposed terminations including the reasons for the proposed termination, the number and categories of employees likely to be affected, and the number of workers normally employed and the period over which the terminations are likely to be carried out."

- Severance Pay:

"... an employee whose employment is terminated [made redundant] . . . shall be entitled to the following amount of severance pay in respect of a continuous period of service:

Period of continuous service	Severance pay
1 year or less	nil
1 year and less than 2 years	4 weeks' pay
2 years and less than 3 years	6 weeks' pay
3 years and less than 4 years	7 weeks' pay
4 years and over	8 weeks' pay

*Week's pay means the ordinary time rate of pay for the employee concerned."

Incorporation of these TCR Test Case conditions into awards seems to have been far from complete. Pearce, Bartone, and Stephens (1995, p. 20) reported that in 1990 only 25 percent of federal awards included provisions from the TCR Test Case. Moreover, it is important to note that the redundancy conditions from the TCR Test Case do not apply to employees with less than one year's continuous service, where an employer can demonstrate incapacity to pay, and in some circumstances, to employers who employ fewer than 15 workers. On the other hand, there are other groups of employees—such as public sector employees for whom redundancy conditions are specified in special legislation regulating public sector employment—who would have much stronger notice provisions than those specified in the TCR Test Case.

Unemployment benefits

The Australian social security system is primarily a social assistance scheme. Payments are funded from general taxation revenue and are based on a person's current need, rather than on previous levels of earnings or duration of employment. Payments are generally available to all residents of Australia, subject to eligibility and duration of residency.

Unemployment benefit payments are available to persons who have lost or left employment and to persons who are unable to obtain work on leaving school. Receipt of benefits is subject to an income test that allows some nonbenefit earnings before benefits are withdrawn at a dollar-for-dollar rate. A waiting period of 13 weeks applies for persons who should be able to support themselves during the initial period of an unemployment spell (for example, persons who have received recreation leave or termination payments from an employer, or who have considerable financial assets).

There is no limit on the duration of receipt of unemployment benefits provided that an unemployed person is willing and able to undertake paid employment and is actively seeking work (for example, for some unemployed persons the "activity test" involves keeping a job-search diary).

Unemployment benefit replacement rates vary, depending on whether an unemployed person is single or married, has any children, and owns or rents housing. For example, in 1983 the unemployment benefit for a married person with dependent spouse was $137.30, for unmarried persons aged 16–17 years without dependents was $40.00, for unmarried persons aged 18 years and above without dependents was $68.65, for unmarried persons aged 18 years and above with dependents was $82.35, and for each child of an unemployed person with dependents was $10 (Commonwealth Department of Social Security 1983). At the same time, average weekly earnings for a full-time employee were $172 for a 15- to 19-year-old, $270 for a 20- to 24-year-old, and $318 for employees as a whole (Australian Bureau of Statistics 1983).

Table 4.A2 in the appendix presents some more-recent summary information on replacement rates in Australia compared to average rates for the OECD. Three main features are evident. First, for none of the cases where an unemployed person would shift to full-time employment at the average earnings level do unemployment benefits exceed average earnings. Second, both in absolute terms and relative to OECD averages, replacement rates in Australia are higher for couples with children than couples with no children, and higher for couples than for single persons. Third, the longer duration of unemployment benefits in Australia than in most other countries means that, whereas replacement rates in Australia are below the OECD average in the first month of unemployment, this ordering is reversed in the sixtieth month of unemployment. It is also important to note that in Australia persons receiving unemployment benefits are eligible for other non-cash benefits—in particular, the Health Care card provides access to reduced-cost medicines and public transport travel.

Displaced workers who shift out of the labor force will also be eligible for social security benefits. Age pensions are available to males over age 65 and females over 61. Persons who have a medical condition which prevents full-time work are eligible for disability support pensions. And service pensions are available to male war veterans over age 60 and female war veterans over age 55. Each of these pensions is subject to income and assets tests (see Commonwealth Department of Social Security 1997).

Wage-setting institutions

There are three main dimensions to the regulatory structure for wage setting in Australia:

a) Regulation of the wage bargaining process and of the form of agreement over terms and conditions of employment which can be made between a worker and employer;

b) Regulation providing for intervention by a third party (industrial tribunal) in the process of wage bargaining, and in the determination of terms and conditions of employment; and

c) Regulation promoting collective organization of workers and providing a right for collective organizations to represent workers in negotiations over terms and conditions of employment.

Most workers in Australia have minimum terms and conditions specified in "awards." These are written documents which are ratified and enforced by industrial tribunals at either the state or federal level. Individual awards generally cover workers within specific occupation or industry groups. Each award specifies a range of minimum wage rates for workers with different skill levels in that occupation or industry group. Hence a multitude of different minimum wage rates exist in the economy. The conditions in an award may be agreed by consent between a union and employers and then ratified by the relevant industrial tribunal or may be arbitrated by the industrial tribunal.

The principle of "common rule" means that any decision of an industrial tribunal about conditions in an award will be extended to all workers in the workforce group covered by that award, regardless of union status. Award coverage remained high and relatively constant in the period from the 1950s to 1990s. In 1954 the proportion of workers covered by awards was 90 percent (Dabscheck and Niland 1981, p. 274), and in May 1990, this proportion was 80 percent—33.5 percent covered under federal awards, and 46.5 percent under state awards (Australian Bureau of Statistics 1990). It is important to note, however, that for a large proportion of these workers minimum wage conditions specified in awards are not binding. Estimates for 1995 suggest that about 25 percent of workers had rates of pay at award levels (Australian Industrial Relations Commission 1997, p. 124).

Industrial tribunals have an important function in wage determination in Australia. These tribunals exist at both the federal and state level, and may have general coverage (for example, the Federal Industrial Relations Commission) or coverage restricted to specific occupation groups (such as the Federal Coal Industry Tribunal). At the federal level the wage-determination process involves a three-tier system: a) national wage cases where the federal industrial tribunal adjusts wages for all workers covered by federal awards (often with flow-ons to workers covered by state awards); b) industry cases where the federal industrial tribunal is concerned with setting conditions in a specific award; and c) over-award negotiations or enterprise-level negotiations which occur directly between employers and employees and do not involve an industrial tribunal. Although a greater proportion of workers are covered by state tribunals than federal tribunals, federal tribunals are generally considered to be more important in the regulation of wage setting in Australia (see, for example, Dabscheck and Niland 1981, p. 273). In particular, wage increases granted to workers covered by federal awards in national wages cases would usually flow on to workers covered by state awards.

The importance of industrial tribunals in wage setting—and hence the degree of centralization in wage bargaining—has varied over time. In some periods, uniform national wage increases have constituted the only source of wage increase for workers covered by awards (wage indexation phases of 1975–1981 and 1983–1985, for example). At other times, the most important source of wage increases is from over-award or enterprise-level negotiations (for example, between 1974 and 1975).

Trade unions have a key role in representing workers in bargaining over terms and conditions of employment in Australia. The important function of unions, and incentives for union organization, have been effected through legislation which assures access to industrial tribunals for registered trade unions and which provides exclusive jurisdiction over members through the process of registration (Creighton, Ford, and Mitchell 1993, pp. 923–925). The main types of unions in Australia are occupational unions which cover workers performing tasks in a single generic category (for example, Federated Clerks Union); partial industrial unions which draw members from a single industry but do not have exclusive jurisdiction of that industry (for example, Australian Railways Union); and general unions which organize workers irrespective of occupation or industry classification (for example, Australian Workers' Union).

As in a number of other industrial countries, union density has declined in Australia over the past two decades. In 1976, 51 percent of workers were union members; but by 1996 this had declined to 31 percent (Australian Bureau of Statistics 1996). Between 1990 and 1996 a dramatic decrease in the number of trade unions (from 299 to 132) also occurred, largely reflecting a process of union amalgamations.

The description of the regulation of wage setting in Australia applies to most of the period after the 1940s. Since 1993, however, there have been a number of important developments in the regulation of wage bargaining in Australia. Since these developments have not had a significant effect on wage outcomes until very recently, they are not directly relevant for the analysis of the experiences of displaced workers in Australia that will be undertaken in this chapter. Nevertheless it seems worthwhile to present a brief overview of the main changes. The primary recent developments in federal regulation of wage bargaining in Australia (Commonwealth Department of Industrial Relations 1996) have been to

- Change legislative provisions for wage bargaining so that enterprise-level bargaining is the main method for workers to obtain changes in terms and conditions of employment.
- Reduce the role of the federal industrial tribunal in wage setting, its main function now being to guard the interests of employees not able to gain wage increases through enterprise bargaining via arbitration on general "safety net" wage increases.
- Provide scope for employers to enter formal agreements with workers without a legal requirement for union involvement in the wage-bargaining process.

Summary

A fair degree of similarity appears to exist between institutional factors in Britain and Australia. In both countries, levels of employment protection are relatively low. The OECD ranks Britain and Australia as having respectively the fourth and seventh lowest levels of employment protection out of 20 OECD countries (see Nickell and Layard 1999). The unemployment benefit system in the two countries are also quite similar. Benefits are provided for an unlimited period, but subject to a job-search activity test (which has been progressively tightened in each country from the 1980s onwards). Benefit replacement rates in both countries are below the OECD average in the first month of unemployment for single adults and couples with no children. They are about the same as the OECD average for couples with children. In the sixtieth month benefit replacement rates in Britain and Australia are above the OECD average for couples both with and without children. The main difference between the two countries appears to be in wage-setting institutions. Wage setting in Australia—over the relevant periods for this study—appears to have been more highly regulated than in Britain. There has been a more comprehensive system of minimum wages in Australia, and wage setting has involved a much greater role for centralized regulatory bodies. Trends in union density in the two countries, however, have been quite similar.

What do institutional factors suggest about the experiences of displaced workers in Britain and Australia? First, the similarity in levels of employment protection indicates that this should not be a source of significant differences in rates of worker displacement between Britain and Australia (although employment protection might be important for explaining differences between these countries and European countries with much stricter regulation of worker dismissals). Second, differences in wage-setting institutions might be expected to cause differences in the way in which displaced workers respond to job loss. In particular, the system of minimum wages and centralized wage setting in Australia—compared to Britain—may reduce the chances that displaced workers find new jobs with earnings below those in their predisplacement jobs. Hence, differences in wage-setting institutions may cause adjustment to job loss to occur through non-employment to a greater degree in Australia than Britain. By contrast, the unemployment benefit system in each country does not seem likely to be a source of differences in job-search behavior or non-employment durations of displaced workers in the two.

RESULTS

This section presents findings on the experiences of displaced workers in Britain and Australia. The data sources used for the empirical analysis for each country are described, and some descriptive information on the incidence of worker displacement is presented. The main parts of the empirical analysis involve an examination of the earnings and employment consequences of job loss for displaced workers.

Several authors have provided evidence from the United States to the effect that job displacement involves reductions in wages (Hamermesh 1987; Topel 1991; Jacobson, LaLonde, and Sullivan 1993; Stevens 1997; Farber 1993, 1997). The reasons advanced for this are loss of firm-specific human capital, loss of good job-match capital, or loss of wage premiums. United States evidence also suggests that the costs of job displacement rise with age, tenure in previous job, and loss of a union job. Moreover, earnings appear to fall within the job prior to displacement. Earnings do recover after a new job is secured, but not all these losses are recouped after reentry. Stevens (1997) suggested that this occurs largely because of subsequent, repeated job loss.

For Britain, Gregg and Wadsworth (1997) have shown that the wages of jobs taken by those who were out of work have fallen relative to others in work. In part this decline is due to higher job-specific returns, rewards to seniority, and experience at the firm, which cannot be transferred. As the wage returns to experience rise within any occupation or skill group, then the job currently held is likely to pay more than any new job gained after a displacement. The longer a worker has been in the job, the greater this penalty will be if some or all of the returns to accumulated on-the-job experience are lost in the next job. So the costs of job loss may be higher among older and more experienced workers or wherever job loss is a relatively rare event.

Evidence from the United States also suggests that displaced workers experience increases in non-employment and a reduction in hours of employment following displacement (Swaim and Podgursky 1991; Ruhm 1991; Farber 1993). Important determinants of the duration of non-employment for displaced workers appear to be macroeconomic conditions prevailing at the time of displacement and factors, such as a worker's job tenure and union membership status, which affect the extent of earnings losses from cross-industry mobility (and hence determine the scope of a displaced worker's job search).

Kletzer and Fairlie (1998) found that earnings losses for young displaced workers in the United States are substantial and persistent (around 10 percent five years following job loss). Gustafson (1998) obtained similar results on earnings losses and also found that young displaced workers have significantly lower employment probabilities and (for those obtaining jobs) lower hours of work than young labor-force participants who have not experienced displacement. This research suggests that young workers potentially have as much to lose from displacement as their older counterparts.

Britain

Data

There is no equivalent to the Displaced Workers Survey in Britain with which to try and investigate the costs of displacement. Our estimation of the cost of job loss utilizes the information contained within the labor market histories embedded in the British Household Panel Survey, a panel survey of around 5,500 households. The BHPS has been carried out annually since 1991 and currently runs for six waves. Information on labor market status for around 8,000 working age individuals—together with gross monthly pay, hours, and other job characteristics, if in work—is recorded between September and December of each year. Details of any changes in labor market status from the September of the previous year until the interview date are recorded in a series of job history spell data.[3] Data on monthly earnings in each spell are also recorded, and respondents are asked why they left their previous employment.

Our basic strategy is to compare earnings data in the current job with earnings in the previous job, with or without an intervening spell out of employment. The principal earnings information in the BHPS is the individual's usual gross monthly pay in the job. Because hours of work are only asked at the date of interview and not in the job history data, we are unable to calculate hourly earnings. There is information on whether each job is full- or part-time and we use this wherever possible. We exclude those who report very low earnings, below £5 a week. At these earnings, if true, most recipients will be transitory labor market participants. Earnings are deflated by the Retail Price Index into September 1995 prices. Students in full-time education and individuals on maternity leave are removed from the sample, as are those under the age of 18 and those over pensionable age. Missing data on several variables, notably previous job tenure, reduce the final sample to 25,442 person years, of which 791 are displaced workers with weekly wage information before and after displacement.

We focus on the earnings changes of four groups: 1) workers reporting no change in employer over the year (stayers);[4] 2) workers who lost a job either through redundancy or dismissal (displaced); 3) workers who came to the end of a temporary contract (temporary); and 4) workers who left their last job for other reasons, such as for family or health or retirement (leavers). The sum of the displacement, temporary, and leaver rates gives the total separation rate. We also distinguish between those who found a job without an intervening spell of joblessness and those who did not.

The British institutional system often blurs the distinctions among the four categories. If employed for less than two years prior to displacement, a worker is not eligible for redundancy pay. Yet the term "redundancy" is a commonly accepted phrase used to cover any involuntary separation. Also, unlike in the United States, "getting the sack" is a common phrase that does *not* necessarily imply that the dismissal was justified by the behavior of the individual (for example, poor time keeping). Hence for many workers the terms are essentially interchangeable. We do distinguish, however, between workers displaced from industries where employment is falling and those displaced from industries where employment is rising, in an attempt to enforce some exogeneity over the cause of job loss. Temporary contract holders are exempt from redundancy rules and so are best looked at separately. Unlike in continental Europe a temporary contract is not normally a probationary period prior to starting a permanent job.

Incidence of displacement

Our first step is to identify the principal characteristics associated with displacement in Britain. Table 4.1 outlines average annual separation and displacement rates derived from pooling the six years of the BHPS. We calculate for each wave how many were in work at September 1 of the previous year, and then count how many were observed separating from that job within a year. On average, one in five employees, some 5 million workers, separated from their jobs over a year. Some 4.7 percent of employees lost their jobs each year as the result of displacement. Of these, one-third did not experience any joblessness (data not shown). The ending of a temporary contract was around one-third as common as displacement in the stock of jobs as a whole, but since only 7 percent of employees were on such contracts, the separation rate is very high. Displacement rates are around 1 percentage point higher in industries in which net employment falls over the year. One in 8 displacements are classified as sackings by the respondents but when focusing on those with more than two years of job tenure this ratio falls to 1 in 12. The final two rows contrast separation rates between industries with growing and falling workforces. Separation rates in the former are higher, because a larger quit rate dominates the lower displacement rate.

Men are more than twice as likely to be displaced as women, 6.4 percent compared to 2.9 percent (Table 4.2). The displacement rate for younger workers, under the age of 25, at 7.3 percent, is nearly twice that of other age groups. There is less evidence that education affects displacement. The difference between the highest and lowest education groups, at around 0.7 percentage points, is not large. There is some variation in displacement rates across industries. Construction has the highest rate at 13.2 percent and public services the lowest, at around 1.4. Displacements in the service sector are less common than in manufacturing. The incidence of displacement falls with job tenure. There is a 7.9 percent chance that a worker in a job for less than 12 months will lose his or her job and a less than 4 percent chance of displacement for a worker in a job for five years or more. These numbers are consistent with the findings of Gregg and Wadsworth (1998) for Britain who used a different data source. Longer job tenure is not associated with a lower likelihood of displacement followed by a spell out of employment. This is a little surprising, since longer tenured workers should have longer official notification periods with which to try and find alternative work.

In order to determine the principal characteristics associated with displacement, holding other observed factors constant, we next consider multinomial logit estimates of the probability that, within a year, the worker will 1) be displaced, 2) quit his or her job, or 3) come to the end of a temporary contract. The default category is the set of job stayers. Table 4.3 gives the results. The coefficients are marginal effects relative to the sample mean probabilities of belonging to each category.[5] Consistent with Table 4.2, young, single males with less education working in a full-time job in a small firm in manufacturing or construction with job tenure under two years are all more likely to be displaced from work, though the gender and age differences are statistically significant only for temporary contract terminations. The last column of Table 4.3 gives marginal effects from a binary logit estimation of the probability that a displaced worker will find a new job only after a spell of joblessness. Here we remove those in temporary contracts from the sample so that the base category is the set of displaced workers who undertake a job-to-job move. The estimates are less precise, but part-time and low-tenured workers appear much more likely to experience a spell out of work between jobs.

Time out of work

We next examine the duration pattern of joblessness following displacement in more detail. Table 4.4 takes the sample of workers in a job in September of the year prior to the survey and compares the likelihood of being in work one year later by type of job separation. The numbers are annual averages over the six waves. Around one-half of all displaced workers are in employment one year after the initial September observation, compared with around two-thirds of all those who separate from their jobs. Those displaced workers with no nonemployment spell between jobs are nearly twice as likely to be in work in the two observation points than displaced workers who are out of work for some finite length of time.

Kaplan-Meier estimates of monthly survival and hazard rates for the time taken to return to work, allowing for censoring based on the Cox likelihood model, are outlined in Table 4.5. We follow Gu and

Kuhn (1998) by including any displaced workers with no jobless spell in the likelihood function with duration set to one month and all other durations increased by one month.[6] Any displaced workers not back in employment are treated as right censored at the number of months of the ongoing jobless spell. The first observation on the hazard is therefore the proportion of displaced workers who find a new job without a spell of joblessness (21.6 percent). Thereafter the hazard falls with the duration of joblessness to around 10 percent at month 10.

The determinants of the probability of displacement and the time taken to return to work are given in Table 4.6. The first columns present Cox proportional hazard estimates of jobless duration including job-to-job movers; the second columns exclude job-to-job movers. Men are both more likely to lose their jobs and are some 10 percent less likely to return to work. Long job tenure is associated with a quicker return to work. However, as column 2 shows, once job-to-job moves are excluded, long job tenure is no longer associated with a longer period of joblessness.

Earnings consequences of job loss

How much do displaced workers lose? Table 4.7 summarizes the mean of the difference in weekly log real earnings before and after displacement. As a comparison we show the annual earnings change recorded for workers who remain in the same job over the year. Weekly wages of the average displaced worker are around 10 percent lower in the new job than in the job lost (row 3). If the displaced worker moves from one full-time job to another, the penalty is only around 4 percent.[7] Weekly earnings of those who remain with their employer rise by around 5 percent over a year. So displaced workers not only experience wage losses relative to their previous job but they also forego general increases in wage levels. The total pay penalty is then 14 percent and 10 percent for those working full-time both before and after displacement. For those moving directly from one job to another the wage falls by just 2 percent. Hence wage falls are mainly limited to those displaced workers experiencing some time out of work, and some of the observed fall is due to shorter hours after displacement. The wage gaps for all exits into non-employment (including quits and those leaving temporary jobs) are smaller, which suggests that displacement does have distinct labor market effects. Those leaving temporary jobs or quitting a job and moving directly into a new job achieve wage gains above those staying with the same employer.

There is considerable variation around these averages. Comparison of earnings changes by individual characteristics are given in Table 4.8. Part (a) of the table looks at all reemployed workers; part (b) restricts attention to workers in full-time jobs both before and after separation. Women experience weekly wage losses around twice those of men, but the gap is lower for full-time job changes. Older workers and those out of work longer also face higher pay cuts than the average. The weekly wage loss for those over 50 is around 18 percent. Education is not correlated with the size of earnings loss. There is little evidence that the pay gap widens with job tenure, beyond one year in the previous job. Coming from a declining industry also makes little difference. The biggest variations, however, remain where displacement results in a spell out of work.

We now explore the size of these wage changes, controlling for observed differences in worker and firm characteristics in Table 4.9. We present weekly, full-time to full-time moves only and regressions that control for part-time status, to be as clear as possible about what is going on. Displacement that results in time out of work remains strongly significant, but this increases with longer durations out of work. The biggest falls in earnings are associated with those coming back into smaller firms than the ones they left. The results do not confirm the effect of job tenure on displacement found elsewhere (Kletzer 1998). Age is a weakly significant determinant of earnings changes but the point estimates for over 50s are large. Gender only matters for weekly wages, reflecting a greater propensity for women to return part-time after displacement. Displacement from a declining industry makes little difference. This is important as displacement here is perhaps a little more exogenous to the abilities of the worker.

Table 4.9 also examines whether there are any distinguishing characteristics between displaced and temporary-contract workers that are associated with lower earnings on return to work. We present results for the entire set of displaced and temporary workers with or without a spell out of work and the subsets who move full-time to full-time. The results are not always well determined, but the length of time out is negatively associated with the change in earnings for displaced workers. Those out for more than 12 months experience a cost of job loss

17 percent greater than displaced workers who move immediately to another job. For the full-time sample, older workers experience wage losses around 15 percent above the base group.

Table 4.10 estimates the cost of job loss for displaced workers relative to stayers, conditional on the characteristics outlined in Table 4.8. We present simple OLS estimates of the difference in log wage growth between job stayers and displaced workers. Other types of separation are included as intercept terms. The raw weekly cost is 16.9 percent if a spell out of work is observed. Controlling for worker and firm characteristics makes little difference to these estimates. Termination of a temporary contract that results in a spell out of work reduces earnings growth by only around 2 percent. Moving to a new job directly after displacement leads to a loss of earnings in the order of 5 percent. However, compared to those quitting and moving to a new job the gap is large.

Australia

Data

The empirical analysis in this section draws on two main types of data. First, we use aggregate-level evidence on the rate of worker displacement and reemployment probabilities for displaced workers, which are available for various years between 1975 and 1997. Second, we use individual-level data on earnings and employment outcomes of young workers in Australia that allow displaced workers to be identified.

The sources for the aggregate-level data are the Australian Bureau of Statistics (ABS) Labor Mobility Survey, a periodic supplement to the ABS Labor Force Survey; and two special surveys of displaced workers, also undertaken as supplements to the ABS Labor Force Survey. The first of these (Australian Bureau of Statistics 1993) focused on the state of Victoria only; the second (Australian Bureau of Statistics 1997) was Australia-wide. The displaced worker surveys collected information on whether a respondent had been displaced from a job in the previous three-year period; the characteristics of the job from which the respondent had been displaced; reason for displacement; respondent's labor-force status at the survey date; and the respondent's personal characteristics.

The data source for detailed analysis of displaced workers in Australia is the Youth in Transition Survey (YTS). This is a series of longitudinal surveys conducted by the Australian Council for Educational Research. Surveys of cohorts born in 1961, 1965, 1970, and 1975 have been undertaken.[8] Individuals in each cohort were initially sampled in their mid teens (for example, the 1961 cohort were initially sampled as 14-year-olds), and then in each subsequent year through to 1995.[9] In the initial survey for each cohort a range of background information was collected relating, for example, to country of birth, parents' educational attainment, and mathematics aptitude. In each subsequent annual survey two main types of information relevant to this study were collected. First, respondents completed a diary showing educational and labor-force status in each month throughout the preceding year. Second, respondents provided information on details of labor-force status, earnings, hours and weeks worked, and occupation in the survey month (October).

A sample of displaced workers was extracted from the YTS by defining displacement to occur where being "laid off" was a "very important" or "fairly important" reason for losing their last job. Information on reason for job loss in the preceding year is available for persons in the 1961 cohort for 1981, 1982, 1983, and 1993, and in the 1965 cohort for 1983, 1984, 1985, and 1993. Information on the construction of other variables is presented in the appendix.

Data from the YTS has a number of shortcomings for analyzing experiences of displaced workers. The primary one is that the sample is likely to display length sampling bias. That is, since the sample of displaced workers is drawn from a subset of respondents who were unemployed at the survey date (only those persons were asked questions about reasons for job loss), displaced workers who have relatively long spells of unemployment will tend to be overrepresented, and those with short spells of unemployment will tend to be underrepresented. To attempt to overcome this problem, each observation is weighted by the inverse of the duration of the completed non-employment spell. The rationale for making this correction is that, in a steady state, the probability of sampling a spell at any instant of time is proportional to its completed length. Hence, by weighting each observation by the inverse of its length, the entire density function for completed new spell durations is obtained.[10] For an incomplete spell, a completed spell duration is estimated as the weighted average of all completed spells lasting longer than that incomplete spell. The weights are used in all subsequent analyses of the sample of displaced workers.[11]

One aspect of the length bias problem which cannot be addressed is that—since a displaced worker must be unemployed to be observed as displaced—there is no information on displaced workers who had an immediate transition to employment following displacement. For this reason the results should be interpreted as conditional on experiencing some joblessness. Two other shortcomings should also be noted. First, since a question on reason for job loss was asked only in four years for each cohort, the sample of displaced workers which can be obtained is quite small. Second, the sample of displaced workers from the YTS is unrepresentative of the general population of displaced workers in that it is restricted to a group of relatively young workers who were displaced at trough points in the Australian labor market.[12] For example, Farber (1993) found that the difference in employment outcomes between displaced and nondisplaced workers is greater during recessions than expansions.

Incidence of displacement

Time-series information on annual rates of job separation from the ABS *Labor Mobility Survey*—together with the rate of unemployment—are displayed in Table 4.11. "Rate of job separation—displacements" can be interpreted as the rate of worker displacement. This is equal to the number of workers who ceased a job during the year whose reason for ceasing that job was being laid off or a business closure divided by the total number of persons who held a job during the year. Other rate-of-separation measures are similarly defined.[13] It is evident that the annual rate of aggregate job separation is about 25 percent. The annual rate of job separation due to displacement is about 5 percent; and the rate due to job loss is about 9 percent. The aggregate rate of job separation is inversely correlated with the rate of unemployment. Job separation rates due to displacement and job loss display a positive correlation with the rate of unemployment. Over the period between 1975 and 1997, the aggregate rate of job separation displays a slight downward trend. The rate of job separation due to displacements does not show any particular trend.

Average displacement rates for workers in disaggregated gender and tenure categories can also be calculated using information from the ABS *Labor Mobility Survey*.[14] Table 4.12 shows the average rate of displacement in Australia from 1983 to 1997. A number of findings emerge. First, displacement declines with years of tenure of an employee (in particular for employees with up to five years of tenure); second, the rate of displacement is generally higher for male than female workers; and third, the amount of cyclical variation in the rate of displacement is largest (in absolute terms) for workers with low tenure.

Other evidence on the incidence of worker displacement is available from the population surveys of displaced workers undertaken in Victoria in 1993, and for Australia in 1997. The main findings from the surveys—summarized in Table 4.13—are that

- Between October 1990 and 1993 about 10 percent of workers in Victoria were displaced from a job. Between July 1994 and 1997 about 7 percent of workers in Australia were displaced.
- Rates of displacement are higher for male than female workers, but they do not display a strong correlation with age.

Farber (1997, p. 121) reported that the proportion of persons in the United States displaced from employment between 1991 and 1993 was 12.8 percent, and between 1993 and 1995 was 15.1 percent. Over the period from 1981 to 1995 in the United States the three-year displacement rates for various subperiods were found to range from 9.0 to 15.1 percent. Hence it appears that the three-year job displacement rate found from the Australian displacement survey is quite similar to rates found for the United States.

Time out of work

Aggregate-level information on labor market outcomes for displaced workers is available from the ABS surveys of retrenched workers. This information—on the labor-force status at the survey date of workers displaced in the previous three years—is also presented in Table 4.13. It shows that

- In October 1993 the rate of employment of persons in Victoria who had been displaced in the previous three-year period was

50.8 percent; and in July 1997 the rate of employment of persons displaced in Australia in the previous three years was 54.7 percent.

- The probability of reemployment among displaced workers was lowest for persons in older age groups (50+ years), whose last job was in a blue-collar occupation, and who were from a NESB country. It is higher for men than women, and lower for persons without postschool qualifications than for those with postschool qualifications.

Information on the employment status of displaced workers from the ABS retrenched worker surveys appears comparable to information presented by Ruhm (1998, Table 4) on the labor-force status at February 1996 of workers displaced in the United States between 1993 and 1995. Ruhm found that 71.6 percent of displaced workers were in employment at the survey date. This is considerably higher than the employment ratios for displaced workers of around 50 to 55 percent found from the Australian surveys. It suggests the possibility that employment costs of displacement are higher in Australia than the United States. However, it is also necessary to take into account that the labor market in the United States was much stronger than in Australia during this period of the mid 1990s, so that at least part of the difference in employment outcomes for displaced workers may be explained by cyclical factors.

Tables 4.14 to 4.17 present information on labor-force outcomes for young displaced workers using individual-level data from the YTS. These tables are based on a sample of persons unemployed at the survey dates who are classified as displaced workers. In the calculations for each table the weighting method (using the inverse of completed duration of the spell of non-employment) described above has been applied.

Table 4.14 presents information on the labor-force status of the sample of displaced workers at 6 and 12 months after the date of displacement. First, it is clear that a substantial proportion of displaced workers remain unemployed and out of the labor force in the year after displacement. Second, there is no significant change in the non-employment probability of displaced workers between 6 and 12 months. What does happen, however, is that the composition of employment for displaced workers in employment shifts to some degree from part-time to full-time jobs. Third, some effect of educational attainment is apparent—in particular, having completed high school or having a postschool qualification is associated with a higher probability of full-time employment for female displaced workers.

An alternative aspect of labor-force transitions for displaced workers is to examine the duration of spells of non-employment which follow displacement. The Kaplan-Meier hazard results for exit from non-employment and survival function in non-employment for displaced workers are presented in Table 4.15. Over the 12 months following displacement the hazard rate displays a downward trend; however, there is a relatively large degree of month-to-month volatility.

To further explore the process of transition to reemployment, regression analysis of the determinants of the time to exit from non-employment for displaced workers has been undertaken. The analysis involves estimation of a weighted probit regression where the dependent variable is a monthly observation of whether a displaced worker exited from non-employment in that month, conditional on not having exited previously. Explanatory variables included are age at time of displacement, reading and mathematical aptitude test scores (with interactions with a dummy variable for the 1961 cohort to allow for differences in the tests between cohorts), rate of unemployment in last occupation, and dummy variables for gender, year, country of birth, and whether a respondent completed high school or had a postschool qualification.

The main results from the regression analysis of determinants of exit from non-employment are shown in Table 4.16. A first main finding is that—consistent with the Kaplan-Meier hazard function—the probability of reemployment declines with spell duration. For each extra month of non-employment the probability of exit from non-employment declines by about 1 percent (evaluated at the mean value of other explanatory variables). Alternative specifications of the spell-duration variable (quadratic and cubic specifications) were also tested; however, F-tests could not reject the hypothesis that the extra explanatory terms were insignificant. The second finding is that a range of other explanatory variables—age, whether completed high school or have a postschool qualification, gender, and rate of unemployment in last occupation—are found to affect the probability of exit from non-employment. Age is inversely related to the probability of reemployment, suggesting that older displaced workers (more than 30 years old) find it relatively more difficult to find a new job. One explanation for this finding may be that rates of job turnover are higher for workers aged 15–24 years than for those 25–34 years, so that the flow of job vacancies may also be higher for the younger group of workers (Borland and Kennedy 1998). However, it is important to note that—due to collinearity between the age and year variables—age is only significant in specifications without year dummy variables. Hence the age variable may be proxying for year effects. Males who are displaced have a higher probability of reemployment than do female displaced workers, and displaced workers in occupations with relatively high rates of unemployment have a relatively lower probability of reemployment. Finally, it appears that high-skill workers—who have completed high school or have a postschool qualification and have higher levels of aptitude in reading—have higher exit probabilities from non-employment than low-skill workers. Other explanatory variables, such as reading and math aptitude, are not found to affect the probability of exit from non-employment.

An alternative perspective on the labor-force experience of displaced workers is to examine average hours and weeks of work in the period following displacement. Table 4.17 shows the weighted average ratio of weeks and hours of work in the quarter preceding displacement to weeks and hours of work in each of the first eight quarters after displacement. Displaced workers are found on average to have worse employment outcomes in every quarter in the two years following displacement than in the quarter preceding displacement. This difference is generally statistically significant for the first six to seven quarters following displacement.

Findings from the YTS therefore suggest that the costs to displaced workers from time out of employment may be quite substantial. However, in interpreting results on employment outcomes for displaced workers from the YTS, a number of factors must be taken into account. First, since the sample of displaced workers excludes those who moved immediately to a new job, the adverse employment consequences of displacement may be overestimated. Second, labor-force mobility (transitions into and out of employment, for example) is higher for younger than older labor-force participants so that the apparent employment consequences of displacement may be in some part due to the age of the sample of workers.

Earnings consequences of job loss

The other main cost of job loss occurs through changes in earnings following displacement. To address this issue in the YTS, data on weekly earnings for both displaced and nondisplaced workers can be taken from the years prior to and following each sample year in which information on reason for job loss is available. For displaced workers, weekly earnings in the predisplacement job are observed for the sample of workers who were in their predisplacement job 12 months prior to the time of the survey question on displacement (that is, in the preceding October). Hence this information on earnings ranges from 1 to 11 months prior to displacement. Weekly earnings in postdisplacement jobs are observed for the samples of workers in employment 12, 24, and 36 months following the time of the survey question on displacement (that is, in October in subsequent years). For nondisplaced workers, weekly earnings data that will match with data for displaced workers is obtained by using the same set of years around those sample years in which information on reason for job loss is available. All displaced and nondisplaced workers with observations on weekly earnings are included in the respective samples.

As an example, for the 1961 cohort, information on reason for job loss is available in 1981. Hence, information on weekly earnings is obtained (if available) for 1980, 1982, 1983, and 1984 for all workers who were displaced and nondisplaced in October 1981. This means that the sample of nondisplaced workers may include some workers who experienced job loss during this period but did not have the status of a displaced worker in October 1981; and it will also include voluntary job switchers. Unfortunately the data set does not allow these separate types of workers to be identified.

Weekly earnings in different years are adjusted to constant dollars, using the Consumer Price Index. Note that since the information is on weekly earnings it may reflect changes in weekly hours of work as well as hourly wage rates. Information on hours of work is not available for a sufficient number of observations to allow the analysis to be undertaken using hourly wage rates.

A factor to take into account in interpreting findings on the effect of job loss on earnings is the potential role of selection effects. One aspect of selection effects is that to the extent that displaced workers who obtain reemployment are not representative of all displaced workers—and, as seems likely, are of higher ability than average—the change in weekly earnings may be an overestimate of the change for all displaced workers.

Table 4.18 shows the weighted average difference between log real weekly earnings in displaced workers' jobs 1–2, 2–3, and 3–4 years after displacement and log real weekly earnings in the predisplacement job, and data on average changes in log real weekly earnings for nondisplaced workers taken from the same time periods as for displaced workers. It is evident that both displaced and nondisplaced workers experience growth in weekly earnings over time. Some differences, however, do emerge in comparing earnings changes over time. Focusing on the sample of full-time workers (in order to minimize composition effects) it appears that the difference in earnings outcomes between displaced and nondisplaced workers tends to increase over time. In the period 1–2 years after displacement there is no significant difference in the change in log weekly earnings for displaced and nondisplaced workers. In the period 2–3 years after displacement, earnings of nondisplaced workers are about 7 percent higher than for displaced workers, and by 3–4 years this difference has become 16 percent. (These latter findings, however, are based on a very small number of observations for displaced workers.)

To conclude the analysis of earnings outcomes for displaced workers, a regression analysis of the determinants of earnings and changes in earnings was undertaken using data on real weekly earnings predisplacement and 1–2 years postdisplacement. The effect of displacement is examined by including as an explanatory variable a dummy variable for whether a worker was classified as displaced at the relevant survey date.

The findings are presented in Table 4.19. Log weekly earnings in pre- and postdisplacement years are significantly lower for females than males, are decreasing with the rates of unemployment in a worker's occupation category, higher for full-time than part-time workers, and follow a quadratic pattern with age. Displaced workers have lower weekly earnings than nondisplaced workers although the effect is only statistically significant for postdisplacement earnings where year dummies are included as explanatory variables. The change in log weekly earnings is significantly negatively related to age (reflecting a decreasing rate of increase in earnings), and is significantly affected by switching between part-time and full-time employment. The effect of displacement on the change in log real weekly earnings is not statistically significant. Hence these findings provide some limited evidence that displaced workers have a lower level of earnings than nondisplaced workers, but little evidence of short-term earnings losses due to job loss.

Summary

Analysis of the experiences of Australian displaced workers suggests two main findings. First, these workers experience substantial periods of non-employment following displacement. Second, for younger displaced workers there do not appear to be significant short-term earnings consequences from displacement.[15] One possible explanation for these findings is the nature of labor market institutions in Australia. The absence of a wage adjustment for displaced workers — or more generally in response to adverse demand conditions—would suggest that adjustment should then take place through employment. This appears to be consistent with our findings on employment outcomes for displaced workers. It is also worth noting that other case-study evidence on displaced workers has generally found little effect on earnings of displaced workers who are reemployed but significant effects on employment outcomes for displaced workers (see Borland 1998).

As has been noted earlier, it is also necessary, however, to recognize how selection effects might have affected the findings. First, the sample of displaced workers excludes those workers who shifted to a new job without an intervening period of non-employment. Second, the sample of displaced workers in new jobs—from whom earnings information is obtained—may be of greater average ability than the entire group of displaced workers. Hence, estimates of the employment and wage costs of job loss for Australia derived in this chapter are likely, respectively, to over- and underestimate the true consequences.

CONCLUSIONS

Every year around 5 to 6 percent of workers in Britain and Australia will lose their jobs as a result of layoff, plant closure, or the end of a contract. Job loss is most likely to occur within the first year of any job. Most displaced workers will return to work within a year, though a significant proportion do not.

In Britain, the median length of joblessness is around three months. Displaced workers will enter jobs that pay weekly wages, on average, around 10 percentage points less than those they left behind. Compared with those who remain continuously in the same post, the wage gap is around 15 percent. However, much larger penalties are experienced by displaced workers with longer seniority, and those out of work for 12 months or more.

In Australia, for the sample of young displaced workers examined, job loss has significant consequences for future employment. A large proportion of displaced workers remain out of work for some period following displacement, and average hours of work per quarter postdisplacement remain below average hours of work in the quarter preceding displacement for the two years after job loss. By contrast, for the sample of young workers examined, there do not appear to be significant short-term consequences for labor market earnings due to job loss.

What do these findings suggest about the role of institutional factors in determining experiences of displaced workers? Differences between the data sources make it very difficult to provide any definitive answers to this question. One point to emerge is that rates of separation and worker displacement do appear quite similar in Britain and Australia for the 1990s. In both countries the average rate of separation is about 20 percent; and the average rate of worker displacement around 5 percent. Hence displacements constitute about 25 to 30 percent of total separations.

It is more difficult to make comparisons of the process of adjustment to job loss for displaced workers in Britain and Australia. The case of Australia—with its highly regulated system of wage setting where there have been relatively large costs to displaced workers in the form of time out of employment but little apparent effect on earnings from job loss—does seem consistent with the hypothesis that where institutional factors prevent wage adjustment to an adverse demand shock there will be greater employment adjustment. However, it is also necessary to note that for Britain there is no evidence of large earnings losses for young displaced workers. This suggests that it would be necessary to exercise caution before attributing the absence of earnings losses in Australia to the effects of wage-setting institutions rather than to age-specific determinants of the adjustment process.

Notes

We are grateful for many helpful comments from Jaap Abbring and Peter Kuhn. LFS and BHPS data for Britain are supplied by the ESRC Data Archive at Essex University with permission of OPCS. YTS data for Australia are supplied by the Australian Council of Education Research.

1. Specifically, men's employment rate fell from 74.4 percent in 1978 to 67.4 percent in 1995; women's increased from 40.5 to 49.7 percent over the same period. Trends in labor-force participation rates were very similar.
2. The government explicitly recognized this problem in its 1998 budget, raising the zero contribution threshold by one-third and imposing a flat NIC rate of 12.5 percent on all earnings above this threshold. This change came too late for the period covered by our data.
3. Attempts to match the current spell in the last wave to a particular spell in the job history data in the following wave proved fraught with errors. The September data across the waves matches better. This is because the September first information is requested in every wave. The spell histories then count forward from this point until the date of interview and backward to September first of the previous year. Matching the current job from the previous wave is hampered both because the interview date floats between September and April of the following year and because of resulting recall error in dating events between last September and the previous interview data. See Halpin (1997) or Paull (1997) on problems in spell data and recall error across waves in the BHPS.
4. "Stayers" includes individuals promoted within a firm to a new job title.
5. The marginal effect of variable x_i on the probability of being in category j, P_j is given by $dP_j/dx_i = P_j[bj - \Sigma_k P_k b_k]$ where b_j is the coefficient on variable i in category j. The sample means of the stayer, quit, temporary, and displaced categories are 0.78, 0.14, 0.03, and 0.03.
6. Gu and Kuhn (1998) pointed out that the Cox likelihood function depends only on the ranking of the durations and therefore is invariant to the addition of a scalar. This allows the inclusion of the zero duration job-to-job displaced in the likelihood, unlike other parametric models.

7. These numbers are similar to the findings of Gregory and Jukes (1997) for unemployed men. There is only a very small hourly wage penalty, on average, to being displaced but this is mainly a selection effect, as the monthly wage gap is much smaller for those where hourly wages are defined. *t*-Tests on the equality of the means of the stayer and displaced groups confirm that the weekly and hourly mean pay changes are significantly different in the two groups.
8. Further details on the Youth in Transition survey are available from Marks (various years) and from http://www.acer.edu.au/lsay/longitud.htm.
9. The only exception is that a survey for the 1961 cohort was not undertaken in 1985 or 1988 due to resource constraints.
10. Let $f(d)$ be the density of completed new spell durations, and $g(d)$ be the density of completed durations of spells observed at any point in time. In a steady state: $f(d) = k(g(d)/d)$ where k is a constant. Because $f(d)$ must integrate to one, therefore k is equal to the integral over d of $g(d)/d$. Hence, weighting each observation by the inverse of its length gives the density for all new completed spell durations.
11 An alternative approach would be to use maximum likelihood techniques to jointly address the length-sampling bias and censoring issues.
12. Cyclical peaks in the rate of unemployment occurred in quarter 2 of 1983 and quarter 3 of 1993.
13. "Rate of job separation - aggregate" is equal to the number of workers who ceased a job during the year divided by the total number of persons who had a job during the year; and "Rate of job separations - job losers" is equal to the number of workers who ceased a job during the calendar year whose reason for ceasing that last job was retrenchment or ill health, seasonal or temporary job divided by the total number of persons who had a job during the year.
14. Average rates of job separation - displacement for employees in disaggregated tenure (or gender) categories are calculated as

$$\text{Prob}(D_{it} = 1 | T_{it} = j) = [\text{Prob}(T_{it} = j | D_{it} = 1) \times \text{Prob}(D_{it} = 1)] \,/\, [\text{Prob}(T_{it} = j)]$$

where $\text{Prob}(D_{it} = 1 | T_{it} = j)$ is the probability that an employee is displaced in time period t given that the employee is in tenure (or gender) category j; $\text{Prob}(T_{it} = j | D_{it} = 1)$ is the probability than an employee is in tenure (or gender) category j given that the employee has been displaced in time period t; and $\text{Prob}(D_{it} = 1)$ and $\text{Prob}(T_{it} = j)$ are, respectively, the probabilities than an employee is displaced and that an employee is in tenure (or gender) category j in time period t (Farber 1993, p. 89).
15. These findings seem consistent with Gray (1999), who finds—using a different longitudinal data set covering young workers in Australia in the early 1990s—that in general unemployment experience does not have a strong effect on future hourly wages, but does have a significant influence on future hours of work.

Table 4.1 Average Annual Separation and Displacement Rates in Britain, 1990–96 (%)

		Job to job						Exit						
					Displacements						Displacements			
Categories	Total separations	Total	Temp. job	Quit	Total	Redundant	Sack	Total	Temp. job	Quit	Total	Redundant	Sack	All displacements
All industries	20.9	11.9	0.7	9.8	1.6	1.4	0.2	9.0	0.9	5.0	3.1	2.7	0.4	4.7
Declining industry	19.4	10.9	0.7	9.8	1.6	1.4	0.2	8.2	0.7	4.0	3.5	3.2	0.3	5.1
Growing industry	22.8	12.9	0.7	9.8	1.5	1.3	0.2	9.9	1.0	6.1	2.8	2.3	0.5	4.3
Tenure in previous jobs ≥2														
All industries	15.9	8.7	0.4	7.1	1.2	1.1	0.1	7.1	0.3	4.3	2.5	2.3	0.2	4.0
Declining industry	14.8	8.2	0.4	6.5	1.3	1.2	0.1	6.5	0.2	3.4	2.9	2.7	0.2	4.5
Growing industry	17.0	9.2	0.3	7.8	1.1	1.0	0.1	7.7	0.4	5.2	2.1	1.9	0.2	3.5

SOURCE: BHPS.

Table 4.2 Separation and Displacement Rates by Worker and Firm Characteristics in Britain

Category	Separation rate	Displacement rate	Job-to-job displacement	Exit and displacement	% job to job in displacements
Gender					
Female	18.6	2.9	1.0	1.9	35.0
Male	23.1	6.4	2.1	4.3	32.7
Age (yr.)					
Youths <25	35.9	7.3	2.1	5.1	29.8
Prime 25–49	18.9	4.3	1.6	2.7	37.6
Mature 50+	16.9	4.4	1.1	3.3	23.9
Marital status					
Single	26.1	5.8	1.8	4.0	30.6
Married	18.8	4.4	1.5	2.8	34.7
Qualifications					
None	19.0	5.5	1.4	4.1	26.0
Lower Intermed.	21.8	4.8	1.7	3.1	35.6
Upper Intermed.	19.2	2.6	1.1	1.5	41.2
Degree	20.6	6.2	2.0	4.2	31.9

Job tenure (yr.)					
<1	35.9	7.9	2.8	5.1	36.0
≥1 – <2	23.8	5.3	1.7	3.6	31.5
≥2 – <5	16.7	3.7	1.1	2.6	30.9
≥5 – <10	13.1	3.3	1.2	2.1	37.2
10+	13.6	3.5	1.0	2.5	28.5
Industry					
Agriculture/energy	18.3	5.4	2.0	3.3	38.0
Manufacturing	21.9	7.8	2.1	5.6	27.6
Construction	36.9	13.2	5.0	8.2	37.7
Distribution	24.4	5.0	1.9	3.1	37.4
Transport	18.7	4.7	1.7	3.0	36.5
Banking	22.8	4.8	2.0	2.8	42.1
Private services	23.9	2.5	1.2	1.2	50.0
Public services	14.6	1.4	0.4	1.0	27.7

Table 4.3 Who Is Displaced? Multinomial Logit and Binary Logit Estimates for Britain

	Multinomial logit			Binary logit
Independent variables	Quit	Temporary	Displaced	Prob. (jobless spell), given displaced
Characteristic				
Male	–0.042**	–0.003	0.002	0.075
	(0.004)	(0.001)	(0.002)	(0.045)
Single	–0.001	0.003	0.004	0.004
	(0.005)	(0.001)	(0.003)	(0.050)
Children	–0.044**	0.004**	0.001	0.049
	(0.005)	(0.001)	(0.003)	(0.047)
Age 25–49 yr.	0.032**	0.010**	0.003	0.052
	(0.008)	(0.002)	(0.004)	(0.082)
Age ≥ 50 yr.	–0.009	0.002	–0.001	–0.056
	(0.007)	(0.002)	(0.003)	(0.065)
Qualifications				
Upper intermed.	–0.030**	–0.006**	0.009**	–0.013
	(0.008)	(0.002)	(0.004)	(0.085)
Lower level	–0.018**	–0.010**	0.006	–0.003
	(0.006)	(0.002)	(0.004)	(0.073)
None	–0.034**	–0.011**	0.012**	0.058
	(0.009)	(0.002)	(0.004)	(0.091)
Occupation				
Professional	0.010	0.005	0.005	0.017
	(0.008)	(0.003)	(0.003)	(0.067)
Other nonmanual	0.044**	0.012**	0.005	–0.023
	(0.008)	(0.002)	(0.004)	(0.067)
Unskilled manual	0.035**	0.007**	0.005	–0.077
	(0.006)	(0.002)	(0.003)	(0.055)
Job tenure (yr.)				
<1	0.049**	0.016**	0.028**	0.220**
	(0.005)	(0.002)	(0.003)	(0.048)
1–2	0.013**	–0.001	0.006**	0.073
	(0.006)	(0.001)	(0.003)	(0.058)
5–10	–0.056**	–0.017**	–0.009**	–0.106
	(0.007)	(0.003)	(0.003)	(0.068)
10+	–0.068**	–0.023**	–0.008**	–0.193**
	(0.008)	(0.004)	(0.003)	(0.077)

Independent variables	Multinomial logit Quit	Temporary	Displaced	Binary logit Prob. (jobless spell), given displaced
Industry				
Agriculture/energy	0.004	0.007**	0.030**	–0.022
	(0.007)	(0.003)	(0.007)	(0.128)
Manufacturing	0.005	–0.001	0.040**	–0.023
	(0.007)	(0.002)	(0.003)	(0.092)
Construction	0.028**	0.005	0.049**	–0.217**
	(0.013)	(0.003)	(0.005)	(0.108)
Retail	0.050**	–0.002	0.034**	–0.061
	0(.006)	(0.002)	(0.004)	(0.090)
Transport	0.010	–0.001	0.028**	–0.167
	(0.010)	(0.003)	(0.005)	(0.114)
Financial sector	0.018**	–0.002	0.028**	–0.149
	(0.007)	(0.002)	(0.004)	(0.097)
Private services	0.061**	0.001	0.029**	–0.082
	(0.009)	(0.002)	(0.007)	(0.119)
Industry declining	–0.015**	–0.005	0.002	0.025
	(0.004)	(0.003)	(0.002)	(0.046)
Firm size				
<10	0.035**	0.001	0.011**	–0.005
	(0.005)	(0.001)	(0.002)	(0.053)
10–25	0.014**	0.003**	0.008**	–0.006
	(0.005)	(0.001)	(0.002)	(0.054)
Part-time	–0.121**	–0.004**	–0.014**	0.310**
	(0.007)	(0.002)	(0.003)	(0.083)
N	23,346			781
Psuedo *R*	0.095			0.135

NOTE: Standard errors are in parentheses. Coefficients in logits are marginal effects and their standard errors relative to sample mean of each category. Equations also include controls for region and year. ** = Statistically significant at the 5% level.
SOURCE: Authors' calculations from BHPS data.

Table 4.4 Labor-Force Status One Year Later in Britain (annual averages)

Group	Self-employed	Employed	Unemployed	Inactive
All separations	6.3	65.3	15.9	12.5
All displaced	7.0	53.6	34.9	4.5
Job to job	13.4	79.5	5.2	1.9
Exit	3.8	40.5	49.9	5.8
All not displaced				
Job to job	7.8	88.6	2.8	0.8
Temporary job	8.6	84.3	6.6	0.5
Not temporary job	7.8	88.9	2.5	0.8
Exit	2.9	33.6	23.6	39.8
Temporary job	4.7	47.0	35.6	12.7
Not temporary job	2.6	31.3	21.5	44.6

SOURCE: Authors' calculations from BHPS data.

Table 4.5 Kaplan-Meier Estimates of Hazard and Survival Rate of Return to Work in Britain

Time out after displacement (months)	Hazard rate	Survival rate
0	0.366	0.633
1	0.204	0.504
2	0.178	0.414
3	0.201	0.331
4	0.154	0.279
5	0.128	0.243
6	0.172	0.202
7	0.120	0.178
8	0.110	0.158
9	0.132	0.137
10	0.106	0.123

NOTE: Job-to-job moves all measured as ending spell at month 0. Initial sample = 853, of which 313 are job-to-job, 475 displaced, and 75 right-censored.
SOURCE: Authors' calculations.

Table 4.6 Cox Estimates of Time to Return to Work for Displaced Workers in Britain

	Including job-to-job movers		Excluding job-to-job movers	
Independent variables	Coeff. (std. err.)	Fraction of baseline	Coeff. std. err.)	Fraction of baseline
Male	0.049 (0.089)	1.05	0.093 (0.119)	1.09
Single	–0.010 (0.093)	0.99	–0.014 (0.122)	0.98
Children	–0.241** (0.091)	0.79	–0.304** (0.121)	0.74
Age 25–49 yr.	0.252 (0.157)	1.28	0.321 (0.194)	1.38
Age ≥ 50 yr.	0.367** (0.128)	1.44	0.338** (0.170)	1.40
Qualifications				
Upper intermed.	–0.065 (0.167)	0.94	0.001 (0.230)	1.00
Lower level	–0.061 (0.143)	0.94	0.019 (0.200)	1.01
None	–0.036 (0.174)	0.96	0.134 (0.234)	1.14
Occupation				
Professional	–0.010 (0.131)	0.99	0.016 (0.172)	1.01
Other nonmanual	–0.200 (0.131)	0.82	–0.362** (0.171)	0.70
Unskilled manual	–0.059 (0.110)	0.94	–0.233 (0.150)	0.79
Job tenure (yr.)				
<1	–0.496** (0.095)	0.61	–0.481** (0.124)	0.62
1–2	–0.187 (0.116)	0.83	–0.198 (0.155)	0.82
5–10	0.167 (0.134)	1.18	0.072 (0.206)	1.07

(continued)

Table 4.6 (continued)

Independent variables	Including job-to-job movers Coeff. (std. err.)	Fraction of baseline	Excluding job-to-job movers Coeff. (std. err.)	Fraction of baseline
10+	0.076 (0.151)	1.07	–0.264 (0.247)	0.77
Industry				
Agriculture/energy	0.376 (0.249)	1.45	0.489 (0.329)	1.63
Manufacturing	0.330 (0.173)	1.39	0.369 (0.224)	1.44
Construction	0.525** (0.207)	1.69	0.425 (0.281)	1.52
Retail	0.315 (0.171)	1.37	0.326 (0.221)	1.39
Transport	0.444** (0.214)	1.55	0.404 (0.291)	1.50
Financial sector	0.369** (0.184)	0.45	0.196 (0.246)	1.22
Private services	0.706** (0.228)	2.02	0.852** (0.313)	2.35
Industry declining	–0.046 (0.090)	0.95	–0.002 (0.114)	1.00
Firm size				
<10	–0.076 (0.103)	0.93	–0.129 (0.138)	0.88
10–25	–0.053 (0.102)	0.94	–0.116 (0.134)	0.89
Part-time	–0.544** (0.141)	0.58	–0.299 (0.166)	0.75
N	853		540	

NOTE: Standard errors are in parentheses. Additional coefficients in Cox are measured relative to baseline hazard. Equations also include controls for region and year. ** = Statistically significant at the 5% level.

SOURCE: Authors' calculations.

Table 4.7 Mean Log Weekly Wage Growth by Labor Market Status in Britain

Labor market status	Mean change[a]	Full time – full time[b]
Stayers (22,113)	0.045	0.055
	(0.302)	(0.283)
All exits (1,770)	–0.073	–0.004
	(0.582)	(0.503)
All displacements (791)	–0.097	–0.044
	(0.581)	(0.509)
Job to job (297)	–0.015	0.009
	(0.486)	(0.469)
Exit (494)	–0.146	–0.081
	(0.626)	(0.534)
All temporary (485)	0.013	0.086
	(0.552)	(0.495)
Job to job (199)	0.066	0.098
	(0.553)	(0.502)
Exit (286)	–0.023	0.076
	(0.548)	(0.491)
Exit and quit (990)	–0.052	0.013
	(0.566)	(0.487)
Job to job and quit (1,754)	0.210	0.237
	(0.572)	(0.554)

[a] Sample size in parentheses.
[b] Standard errors in parentheses.
SOURCE: Authors' calculations.

Table 4.8a Mean Weekly Wage Growth by Labor Market Status in Britain (%)

	Stayers	All displaced	Job to job and displaced	Exit and displaced	Temporary	Other exits
Independent variables						
Women	4.9	−15.9	−4.3	−24.7	−0.1	−6.4
Men	4.2	−6.2	0.4	−9.7	3.8	−4.0
Age (yr.)						
Youths (< 25)	10.7	−5.2	1.8	−7.9	4.3	−3.4
Prime (25–49)	4.4	−9.6	0.0	−16.1	0.9	−2.9
Mature (50+)	1.3	−18.0	−15.1	−19.8	−6.4	−20.9
Time out						
<6 months	n.a.[a]	−11.8	n.a.	−11.8	−1.9	−12.4
6+ months	n.a.	−15.6	n.a.	−15.6	−5.2	−24.0
Education						
None	2.6	−10.2	−0.5	−16.4	−8.8	−7.5
0 level and equiv.	5.0	−10.0	−2.3	−14.5	1.2	−4.0
A level/degree	4.5	−8.6	−0.2	−13.8	7.4	−8.1
Job tenure (yr.)						
<1	6.1	−13.3	−3.9	−16.4	0.8	−3.7
≥1 – <2	6.4	−7.7	−4.0	−9.8	3.6	0.4
≥2 – <5	5.1	−6.5	3.5	−14.1	6.4	−5.8
≥5 – <10	2.7	−7.9	−1.9	−15.9	−13.2	−8.6
Industry						
Expanding ind.	5.1	−8.2	0.9	−14.3	2.7	−4.0
Declining ind.	3.9	−10.7	−3.4	−14.7	−0.2	−6.3

[a] n.a. = not applicable.
SOURCE: Authors' calculations.

Table 4.8b Mean Log Weekly Wage Changes: Full-Time to Full-Time in Britain (%)

	Stayers	All displaced	Job to job and displaced	Exit and displaced	Temporary	Other exits
Independent variables						
Women	7.0	–5.6	0.4	–12.3	10.1	2.5
Men	4.6	–3.9	1.2	–6.8	7.4	0.3
Age						
Youths (<25)	11.7	3.2	7.0	1.7	14.8	4.4
Prime (25–49)	5.2	–5.6	0.8	–10.7	6.5	2.3
Mature (50+)	2.7	–11.5	–7.1	–14.6	–0.7	–11.0
Time out						
<6 months	n.a.[a]	–7.3	n.a.	–7.3	7.8	–0.4
6+ months	n.a.	–8.4	n.a.	–8.4	5.8	–15.3
Education						
None	3.3	–2.3	7.5	–10.4	–5.8	–2.1
0 level and equiv.	6.1	–6.7	–2.0	–9.9	10.0	1.1
A level/degree	5.4	0.5	3.4	–1.6	13.2	2.3
Job tenure (yr.)						
<1	7.6	–5.7	–3.1	–6.8	9.1	3.7
≥1 – <2	6.9	0.5	–0.3	1.0	14.2	4.2
≥2 – <5	6.1	–5.2	5.2	–14.3	4.9	–1.4
5+	3.5	–6.5	0.5	–17.5	3.6	0.6
Industry						
Expanding ind.	6.5	–2.6	3.0	–7.2	10.1	3.0
Declining ind.	4.7	–5.6	–0.8	–8.6	6.9	–0.2

[a] n.a. = not applicable.

SOURCE: Authors' calculations.

Table 4.9 OLS Log Wage-Growth Regressions for Separating Groups in Britain

	Displaced		Temporary contract	
Independent variables	All	FT-FT[a]	All	FT-FT
Constant	0.089	0.101	0.105	0.197**
	(0.066)	(0.069)	(0.072)	(0.070)
Male	0.018	0.050	–0.002	–0.003
	(0.042)	(0.042)	(0.052)	(0.054)
Age 25–49 yr.	–0.063	–0.098	–0.012	–0.094
	(0.052)	(0.056)	(0.056)	(0.056)
Age 50+ yr.	–0.112	–0.152 **	–0.049	–0.133
	(0.070)	(0.071)	(0.089)	(0.094)
Higher intermediate	0.050	0.072	0.065	0.061
	(0.044)	(0.044)	(0.056)	(0.059)
Degree	0.081	–0.016	–0.155	–0.191
	(0.053)	(0.053)	(0.236)	(0.293)
Tenure 2–5 yr.	0.004	–0.030	0.025	–0.063
	(0.054)	(0.054)	(0.077)	(0.079)
Tenure 5+ yr.	0.019	–0.075	–0.082	–0.049
	(0.093)	(0.040)	(0.106)	(0.122)
Firm size down	–0.102**	–0.021	–0.086	–0.089
	(0.039)	(.039)	(0.052)	(0.050)
Industry declining	–0.012	–0.106	–0.002	–0.012
	(0.039)	(0.046)	(0.048)	(0.050)
Out <6 mo.	–0.096**	–0.105**	–0.040	–0.035
	(0.045)	(0.046)	(0.065)	(0.067)
Out 6–12 mo.	–0.113 **	–0.110**	–0.040	–0.047
	(0.054)	(0.055)	(0.063)	(0.064)
Out 12+ mo.	–0.179	–0.170**	0.314	0.141
	(0.110)	(0.111)	(0.191)	(0.223)
Part-time then	0.519**	—	0.139	—
	(0.147)		(0.131)	
Part-time now	–0.611**	—	–0.496**	—
	(0.147)		(0.085)	
R^2	0.150	0.027	0.131	0.025
N	791	688	485	398

NOTE: White adjusted standard errors in parentheses. ** = Statistically significant at the 5% level.

[a] FT = Full-time.

SOURCE: Authors' calculations.

Table 4.10 OLS Log Wage-Change Estimates for Britain

Independent variables	All		FT–FT	
Constant	0.046**	0.095**	0.044**	0.088**
	(0.002)	(0.006)	(0.003)	(0.006)
Job to job and displaced	–0.061**	–0.054**	–0.061**	–0.055*
	(0.028)	(0.027)	(0.026)	(0.028)
Exit and displaced	–0.169**	–0.169**	–0.131**	–0.152**
	(0.028)	(0.026)	(0.023)	(0.027)
Job to job and temp.	0.020	0.022	0.009	0.015
	(0.039)	(0.038)	(0.032)	(0.036)
Exit and temp.	–0.069**	–0.040	0.042	–0.013
	(0.034)	(0.031)	(0.033)	(0.034)
Exit and quit	–0.098**	–0.0077**	–0.047**	–0.057**
	(0.018)	(0.017)	(0.016)	(0.016)
Job to job and quit	0.164**	0.161**	0.166**	0.159**
	(0.014)	(0.015)	(0.013)	(0.014)
Men	—	–0.025**	—	–0.020**
		(0.005)		(0.005)
Youth (<25 yr.)	—	0.058*	—	0 .068**
		(0.007)		(0.007)
Age (50+ yr.)	—	–0.024**	—	–0.023**
		(0.006)		(0.006)
Degree	—	–0.001	—	–0.014**
		(0.005)		(0.006)
Previous tenure (yr.)				
≤2 – <5	—	–0.012**	—	–0.014**
		(0.006)		(0.006)
≤5 – <10	—	–0.025**	—	–0.025**
		(0.005)		(0.006)
Industry declining	—	–0.020**	—	–0.016**
		(0.004)		(0.005)
Sample size	25,276	25,276	22,424	22,424
R^2	0.023	0.101	0.026	0.036

NOTE: White adjusted standard errors in parentheses. A dash (–) means the variable was not included. ** = Statistically significant at the 5% level; * = statistically significant at the 10% level.

SOURCE: Authors' calculations.

Table 4.11 Annual Rates of Job Separation

Year	Unemployment rate	Rate of separation: Displaced	Job losers	Aggregate
1975	4.6	5.9	9.8	24.9
1976	4.7	n.d.[a]	n.d.	n.d.
1977	5.7	n.d.	n.d.	n.d.
1978	6.2	5.7	9.5	24.8
1979	5.9	5.1	8.5	23.0
1980	5.9	n.d.	n.d.	n.d.
1981	5.6	4.4	6.2	25.0
1982	6.7	7.2	10.2	24.8
1983	9.9	5.6	8.4	22.4
1984	8.5	4.7	8.0	23.3
1985	7.9	4.1	7.6	24.6
1986	8.0	4.6	8.8	24.5
1987	7.8	4.4	9.0	25.4
1988	6.8	4.1	7.6	26.2
1989	5.7	4.4	9.3	25.5
1990	7.0	6.5	10.1	23.2
1991	9.5	6.4	10.1	21.4
1992	10.5	n.d.	n.d.	n.d.
1993	10.7	5.4	9.3	22.2
1994	9.2	n.d.	n.d.	n.d.
1995	8.1	4.6	8.7	23.0
1996	n.d.	n.d.	n.d.	n.d.
1997	8.4	4.4	7.6	21.4

[a] n.d. = No data available.

SOURCE: Australian Bureau of Statistics, *Labor Mobility Survey,* various years.

Table 4.12 Average Rate of Job Displacement in Australia from 1983 to 1997

	1983	1985	1987	1989	1991	1993	1995	1997
Gender								
Male	0.059	0.043	0.046	0.045	0.073	0.060	0.052	0.048
Female	0.050	0.038	0.041	0.043	0.052	0.043	0.039	0.038
Tenure (yr.)								
<1	0.136	0.096	0.097	0.095	0.131	0.104	0.098	0.096
≥1 – <3	0.051	0.036	0.042	0.044	0.084	0.062	0.045	0.046
≥3 – <5	0.040	0.022	0.030	0.023	0.045	0.044	0.028	0.031
≥5 – <10	0.023	0.016	0.019	0.017	0.028	0.027	0.024	0.026
10+	0.020	0.015	0.012	0.014	0.029	0.024	0.020	0.020

SOURCE: Australian Bureau of Statistics, various years, Catalogue no. 6209.0.

Table 4.13 Incidence of Displacement and Reemployment of Displaced Workers in Australia

Population	Probability of displacement	Probability of reemployment at survey date
Victoria: 1990–93		
Total	0.108	0.508
Gender		
Male	0.129	0.525
Female	0.082	0.472
Age (yr.)		
18–24	0.103	0.501
25–34	0.117	0.597
35–44	0.105	0.571
45–54	0.100	0.471
55–64	0.122	0.197
Education		
Univ. degree +	—	0.584
Trade qualification	—	0.648
Completed H.S.	—	0.490
Not completed H.S.	—	0.358
Country of birth		
Australia		0.528
Immigrant – ESB[a]	—	0.581
Immigrant – NESB[b]	—	0.418
Tenure (yr.)		
<1	—	0.430
≥1 – <3	—	0.595
≥3 – <5	—	0.581
≥5 – <10	—	0.587
10+	—	0.386
Occupation		
Manager/professional	—	0.591
Tradesperson	—	0.604
Clerical/sales	—	0.517

Population	Probability of displacement	Probability of reemployment at survey date
Plant and machine operators, laborers etc.	—	0.383
Australia: 1994–97		
Total	0.073	0.547
Gender		
Male	0.091	0.552
Female	0.052	0.536
Victoria: 1994–97		
Total	0.078	0.536
Male	0.098	0.560
Female	0.055	0.466
Age (yr.)		
18–24	—	0.486
25–34	—	0.593
35–44	—	0.620
45–54	—	0.575
55–64	—	0.326
Tenure (yr.)		
<1	—	0.451
≥1 – <3	—	0.606
≥3 – <5	—	0.634
≥5 – <10	—	0.626
10+	—	0.579
Occupation		
Manager/professional	—	0.648
Tradesperson	—	0.591
Clerical/sales	—	0.550
Plant and machine operators, laborers, etc.	—	0.452

[a] ESB = English-speaking background.
[b] NESB = Non-English-speaking background.
SOURCE: Australian Bureau of Statistics 1993, 1997.

Table 4.14 Labor Force Status of Displaced Workers in Australia

Population	Employed, full-time	Employed, part-time	Unemployed	Out of labor force	No. of observations
Six months after displacement					
Aggregate					
Male	0.44	0.18	0.26	0.12	198
Female	0.36	0.21	0.31	0.12	178
Educational attainment					
Male					
NCHS	0.43	0.15	0.30	0.12	104
CHS/postschool qualif.	0.46	0.21	0.22	0.11	94
Female					
NCHS	0.27	0.25	0.35	0.13	73
CHS/postschool qualif.	0.42	0.19	0.29	0.10	105
Twelve months after displacement					
Aggregate					
Male	0.51	0.10	0.22	0.17	179
Female	0.43	0.09	0.26	0.22	162

Educational attainment					
Male					
NCHS	0.48	0.13	0.21	0.18	88
CHS/postschool qualif.	0.54	0.07	0.22	0.17	91
Female					
NCHS	0.28	0.08	0.38	0.24	60
CHS/postschool qualif.	0.52	0.10	0.19	0.19	92

Table 4.15 Estimated Kaplan-Meier Hazard and Survival Rate of Return to Work in Australia

Time out after displacement (months)	Hazard rate	Survival rate
1	0.284	0.716
2	0.168	0.596
3	0.241	0.454
4	0.184	0.365
5	0.145	0.314
6	0.134	0.274
7	0.114	0.246
8	0.108	0.224
9	0.183	0.190
10	0.083	0.178
11	0.065	0.170
12	0.159	0.151

NOTE: Sample size is 390, of whom 305 are observed returning to work. Maximum observed duration in sample is 40 months.
SOURCE: Authors' calculations.

Table 4.16 Determinants of Probability of Exit from Non-employment—Marginal Effects for Australia

Covariates	Col. 1	2
Year dummies	No	Yes
Observations	4,403	4,403
Spell duration	–0.0082**	–0.0077**
	(0.0010)	(0.0010)
Age	–0.0063**	0.0078
	(0.0019)	(0.0222)
Immigrant	–0.0458	–0.0382
	(0.0246)	(0.0243)
Completed high school/postschool qualification	0.0307**	0.0342**
	(0.012)	(0.0123)
Reading aptitude	0.0028	0.0040
	(0.0026)	(0.0027)
Reading aptitude × cohort 1	0.0001	–0.0019
	(0.0031)	(0.0038)
Math aptitude	0.0024	0.0016
	(0.0020)	(0.0021)
Math aptitude × cohort 1	–0.0005	–0.0007
	(0.0021)	(0.0030)
Female	–0.0238**	–0.0271**
	0.0115)	(0.0115)
Rate of unemployment in last occupation	–0.0074**	–0.0074**
	(0.0023)	(0.0025)

NOTE: Standard errors are in parentheses. Marginal effects are calculated at average values of other explanatory variables. Marginal effects for dummy variables are for effect of a change from 0 to 1 in that variable. ** = Statistically significant at the 5% level.

Table 4.17 Predisplacement and Postdisplacement Work Time in Australia (ratio of worktime in quarter postdisplacement to worktime in quarter prior to displacement)

Quarter postdisplacement	Total hours			Total weeks			Observations		
	All	Males	Females	All	Males	Females	All	Males	Females
1	0.213**	0.214**	0.220**	0.221**	0.203**	0.223**	389	205	184
2	0.518**	0.533**	0.519**	0.556**	0.585**	0.520**	377	198	179
3	0.576**	0.591**	0.578**	0.598**	0.599**	0.597**	354	189	165
4	0.631**	0.649**	0.631**	0.619**	0.651**	0.578**	345	183	162
5	0.701**	0.740**	0.676**	0.677**	0.727**	0.616**	332	176	156
6	0.717**	0.802**	0.630	0.703**	0.776**	0.610**	309	165	144
7	0.743**	0.780	0.718	0.723**	0.767	0.664	276	152	124
8	0.791	0.831	0.764	0.748	0.796	0.684	268	148	120
Average predisplacement	425.13	433.97	398.34	12.06	12.06	12.06	n.a.[a]	n.a.	n.a.

NOTE: ** = Statistically significant at the 5% level.
[a] n.a. = not applicable.
SOURCE: Authors' calculations

Table 4.18 Predisplacement and Postdisplacement Average Log Weekly Earnings in Australia (postdisplacement job minus predisplacement job)

Years after displacement	Full-time + part-time			Full-time		
	All	Males	Females	All	Males	Females
1 – <2 yr.						
Displaced						
Difference	0.456 (0.058)	0.456 (0.070)	0.455 (0.112)	0.342 (0.048)	0.355 (0.064)	0.312 (0.060)
No. of obs.	94	61	33	74	47	16
Nondisplaced						
Difference	0.428 (0.017)	0.407 (0.022)	0.449 (0.026)	0.324 (0.014)	0.336 (0.019)	0.310 (0.019)
No. of obs.	1,085	539	546	921	492	429
≥2 – <3 yr.						
Displaced						
Difference	0.593 (0.063)	0.637 (0.086)	0.518 (0.101)	0.460 (0.061)	0.511 (0.073)	0.366 (0.113)
No. of obs.	56	35	21	43	28	15
Nondisplaced						
Difference	0.700 (0.024)	0.700 (0.034)	0.700 (0.035)	0.537 (0.019)	0.561 (0.027)	0.511 (0.028)
No. of obs.	670	329	341	549	282	267

(continued)

Table 4.18 (continued)

Years after displacement	Full-time + part-time			Full-time		
	All	Males	Females	All	Males	Females
≥3 – <4 yr.						
Displaced						
Difference	0.764	0.723	0.819	0.581	0.592	0.561
	(0.123)	(0.159)	(0.193)	(0.100)	(0.145)	(0.191)
Obs.	33	19	14	27	17	10
Nondisplaced						
Difference	0.903	0.877	0.929	0.746	0.775	0.713
	(0.032)	(0.042)	(0.050)	(0.026)	(0.035)	(0.036)
Obs.	412	207	205	345	181	164

NOTE: Standard errors are in parentheses.

Table 4.19 Determinants of Ratio of Predisplacement and Postdisplacement Weekly Earnings in Australia

Explanatory variables[a] / Dependent variable	Log (weekly earnings 1–2 yr. postdisplacement)		Log (weekly earnings predisplacement)		Log (weekly earnings 1–2 yr. postdisplacement/weekly earnings predisplacement)	
Year dummies	No	Yes	No	Yes	No	Yes
Observations	1,177	1,177	1,177	1,177	1,177	1,177
Constant	–2.806**	–3.136**	1.013	2.082**	1.222**	1.310**
	(0.759)	(0.937)	(0.596)	(0.771)	(0.106)	(0.324)
Displaced	–0.137	–0.199**	–0.084	–0.055	0.007	0.070
	(0.084)	(0.084)	(0.066)	(0.070)	(0.089)	(0.091)
Female	–0.086**	–0.068**	–0.092**	–0.093	–0.003	–0.022
	(0.025)	(0.024)	(0.019)	(0.020)	(0.027)	(0.026)
Age	0.517**	0.547**	0.257**	0.154**	–0.036**	–0.044**
	(0.066)	(0.082)	(0.052)	(0.068)	(0.003)	(0.017)
Age^2	–0.008	–0.008**	–0.003**	–0.001	—	—
	(0.001)	(0.001)	(0.001)	(0.001)		
Complete H.S./post-school qualifications	–0.012	–0.010	–0.011	–0.010	–0.006	–0.008
	(0.026)	(0.025)	(0.021)	(0.021)	(0.028)	(0.027)
Rate of unemployment in last occupation	–0.014**	–0.002	–0.011**	–0.011**	0.003	–0.009
	(0.004)	(0.004)	(0.003)	(0.004)	(0.005)	(0.005)

(continued)

Table 4.19 (continued)

Explanatory variables[a] \ Dependent variable	Log (weekly earnings 1–2 yr. postdisplacement)		Log (weekly earnings predisplacement)		Log (weekly earnings 1–2 yr. postdisplacement/weekly earnings predisplacement)	
Immigrant	0.023	0.024	0.012	0.015	–0.007	–0.007
	(0.044)	(0.042)	(0.034)	(0.034)	(0.047)	(0.046)
FT	1.007**	1.067**	0.056**	0.086*	—	—
	(0.034)	(0.033)	(0.031)	(0.031)		
FT to FT	—	—	—	—	–0.090	–0.139**
					(0.054)	(0.053)
FT to PT	—	—	—	—	–0.859**	–0.914**
					(0.082)	(0.079)
PT to FT	—	—	—	—	0.926**	0.934**
					(0.067)	(0.065)
Adj. R^2	0.720	0.750	0.652	0.654	0.427	0.421
F-statistic	380.39**	268.79**	277.49**	172.45*	98.44**	75.01**

NOTE: Standard errors are in parentheses. A dash (—) means the variable was not included. ** = Statistically significant at the 5% level.

[a] FT = full-time; PT = part-time.

SOURCE: Authors' calculations.

Appendix

Data Construction

BRITAIN

Each wave of the BHPS has an individual file and a job-history file. The individual file contains three reference points about jobs, the *current* job, the *Sept. 1 this year* job and the *Sept. 1 last year* job. Each of these has a job identifier, in the form of the spell number in the spell history that relates to this reference point. For some individuals whose current state is the same as that in the previous year, the *current spell identifier* in later waves links these jobs. Otherwise, linking job spells between waves is tenuous, based upon matching information about the jobs. The simplest way to join the waves is to assume that the Sept. 1 reference points can be reasonably linked. Thus the *Sept. 1 this year* of the previous wave should correspond to the *Sept. 1 last year* of the current wave.

Problems can arise, resulting from the nature of the *current* job, which corresponds to the interview date in that wave. This job spell has the only recorded information about certain important job-description variables, specifically the variables for the number of hours worked, full-time or part-time status, temporary or permanent status, and union membership. Only six observation points are available for these variables. It can be difficult to match this *current* job spell to a subsequent wave, except by matching such basic information about the jobs as the start date, occupation, and industry. Inconsistencies in recorded information can make this very difficult, since even the labor-force state for the spell does not always match for the best link points of *Sept. 1 this year* and *Sept. 1 last year*. The design of the survey provides some overlap information when the waves are linked, and also when the job history is linked to the individual response, such that corresponding dates or periods of any state might be matched.

DEFINING DISPLACEMENT

To define a displaced worker, responses are coded on the basis of a self-defined "reason for leaving last job" question.[1] The range of classifications allows us to separate *layoffs* from *redundancy* and *end-of-temporary-job-contract.* In Britain the two categories *layoffs* and *redundancy* are usually synonymous. "Short-term layoffs," after which workers can be recalled to the same job, do not usually occur in Britain. Britain also differs from many mainland European countries, in which (sometimes enshrined in law) short-term contracts must be followed by a permanent job if the contract is renewed. Short-term contracts are used in Britain but they are not linked explicitly to any future permanent status.

The tenure of the job is an important part of statutory redundancy provisions, however, with two years' tenure being the significant threshold within this law beyond which entitlement to redundancy and sickness pay begins.

Inconsistencies in recorded information can mean that the spell lengths are not always clear. One obvious example is that some exit job spell lengths are greater than the age of the respondent. Both start and end dates suffer problems and spells can overlap, or there can be undefined gaps, even when only months and years are used.

Reconciling the data from the individual (*indresp*) and job-history (*jbhist*) record files, sourced from different question specifications and sequences within the survey, there is a reasonable level of agreement, but some differences exist which are not generally systematic. Reconciling information within a wave (matching the *indresp* and *jbhist*) results in generally better agreement than reconciling consecutive waves, but data conflicts between them result in multiple possible records rather than a single panel record for some individuals. The analysis relies on spell lengths, so for missing start dates substantial effort was spent in processing the data, but only if the start year was not missing (since it was deemed too difficult to make any reasonable assumptions about the year). Thus an effort was made to reduce *untrue* left and right censoring. Following Paull (1997), only months and years are used for dates. Seasons are recoded to months. We assume that years suffer less recall error than months and that any time gap is an error, since spells in the job history are recorded consecutively. Where consecutive spells exist within a wave, the previous spell end month is substituted for a missing start month *if* the year is the same, and for the current spell the interview month is substituted if the start year is the same as the interview year. For end dates (which only exist for job history spells, not the current job), where consecutive spells exist within a wave, the missing previous spell end month is replaced with the following spell start month.

Spell lengths for the current spell are created by taking the recorded tenure variable measured in days and dividing by 30, since no end date exists. For all other spells, (the end year × 12 plus the end month) – (start year × 12 plus the start month) is constructed.

Race, age, and gender are only asked when the respondent first enters the panel, and must be copied across. Spell identifiers and job identifiers are used to match job information in the spells and the only file data where a job descriptor data item is missing.

The annual *employment by industry* is also added to the data set in the form of a change variable. This data is sourced from the published statistics 1990–1995 in the Employment Gazette. It is matched to the industry the displaced worker left from.

In order to minimize selection bias due to attrition, we use all individuals observed at any wave and do *not* restrict the panel to only those present in all waves.

AUSTRALIA

Variable Definitions

Displaced worker: Persons who did not have a job at the time of the survey and who responded that being "laid off" was a "very important" or "fairly important" reason for ending their last job. Questions on reasons for job loss were asked in October 1981, 1982, 1983, and 1993 for the 1961 cohort, and in October 1983, 1984, 1985, and 1993 for the 1965 cohort.

Months since displacement: Date of displacement is identified as first month prior to survey date in which the respondent did not work full-time or part-time.

Educational attainment: Variable constructed from information on years of schooling and on whether a postschool qualification was obtained. Individuals reporting having completed high school or reporting having any postschool qualification are classified as being in the category "Complete HS/ Postschool qualifications."

Age: Equal to year of displacement minus year of birth.

Year: Equal to year of displacement.

Reading aptitude/Math aptitude: Scores from tests administered to respondents as 14-year-olds by Australian Council of Education Research.

Rate of unemployment in last occupation: Rate of unemployment by 1-digit CCLO occupation (From ABS, *Labor Force Survey*, Catalogue No. 6203.0, selected issues).

Weekly earnings in predisplacement job/Weekly earnings X to $(X + 1)$ years after displacement: Information obtained from question on "weekly earnings last week."

Total weeks of work in quarter, x months after displacement: Information from labor market diary. Respondents answering that they were employed part-time or full-time in a month were assumed to have 4 and one-third weeks of work in that month.

Total hours of work in quarter x months after displacement: Information from labor market diary. Respondents answering that they were employed part-time in a month were assumed to have worked for 85 hours in that month.

Respondents answering that they were employed full-time in a month were assumed to have worked 170 hours in that month.

Total weeks/hours of work in quarter prior to displacement: Information from labor market diary. Date of displacement is identified as first month prior to survey date in which the respondent did not work full-time or part-time. Total weeks/hours of work in the preceding quarter are then calculated using the same assumptions as for weeks/hours of work per quarter after displacement.

Appendix Note

1. The following choices are offered: promoted/left for a better job, left for a different job, was made redundant/company went bankrupt, was dismissed or sacked, a temporary job ended, took retirement, stopped for health reasons, left to have a baby, children/home care, care of other person, other reason.

Table 4A.1 Unemployment Benefit Replacement Rates for Single-Earner Households in Britain, 1995

Group	% of APW[a]	% of 2/3 APW
First month, no social assistance		
Gross – single	16	24
Net of tax/other		
Couple – no children	26	39
Couple – 2 children	35	52
Couple – 2 children – housing benefit	77	90
60th month, with social assistance		
Gross – couple no children	25	38
Net of tax/other		
Couple – 2 children – housing benefit	77	90

NOTE: Gross replacement rates are before tax. Net replacement rates are after tax and other benefits.

[a] APW = average production worker earnings.

SOURCE: OECD (1997, Table 2.1).

Table 4A.2 Unemployment Benefit Replacement Rates for Single-Earner Households in Australia, 1995

	Australia	OECD
Replacement rate in 1st month of unemployment		
Gross replacement rate		
Single	22	52
Couple (no children)	40	52
Net replacement rate		
Couple (no children)	49	60
Couple (2 children)	64	68
Couple (2 children, housing benefits)	71	73
Replacement rate in 60th month of unemployment		
Gross replacement rate		
Couple (no children)	40	19
Couple (2 children, housing benefits)	71	67

NOTE: Gross replacement rates are before tax. Net replacement rates are after tax and other benefits.

SOURCE: OECD (1997, Table 2.1).

References

Australian Bureau of Statistics. Various years. *Labor Force Survey—Supplementary Labor Mobility Survey.* Catalogue no. 6209.0.

———. 1983. *Weekly Earnings of Employees (Distribution), Australia.* Catalogue no. 6310.0, August.

———. 1990. *Award Coverage, Australia.* Catalogue no. 6315.0, May.

———. 1993. *Retrenched Workers and Workers Who Accepted Redundancy Packages, Victoria.* Catalogue no. 6266.2, October.

———. 1996. *Trade Union Members, Australia.* Catalogue no. 63250.

———. 1997. *Retrenchment and Redundancy, Australia.* Catalogue no. 6266.0, July.

Australian Industrial Relations Commission. 1997. *Safety Net Review—Wages.* Melbourne, April.

Beatson, M. 1995. "Progress towards a Flexible Labor Market." *Employment Gazette.* Employment Department (UK), pp. 55–66, February.

Borland, J. 1998. "Microeconomic Reform and Displaced Workers—An Introduction." In *Microeconomic Reform and Productivity Growth,* Productivity Commission, pp. 365–399. Canberra: AusInfo.

Borland, J., and S. Kennedy. 1998. "Dimensions, Structure and History of Australian Unemployment." In *Unemployment and the Australian Labor Market*, G. Debelle and J. Borland, eds. Sydney: Reserve Bank of Australia, pp. 68–99.

Borland, J., and R. Wilkins. 1996. "Earnings Inequality in Australia." *Economic Record* 72: 7–23.

Creighton, W., W. Ford, and R. Mitchell. 1993. *Labor Law—Text and Materials.* Sydney: The Law Book Company.

Commonwealth Department of Industrial Relations. 1996. "The Reform of Workplace Relations—Legislation Guide." Photocopy, Canberra.

Commonwealth Department of Social Security. 1983. *Annual Report 1982–83.* Canberra: Australian Government Publishing Service.

———. 1997. *Annual Report 1996–97.* Canberra: Australian Government Publishing Service.

Cully, M., and S. Woodland. 1997. "Trade Union Membership and Recognition." *Labor Market Trends Employment Gazette.* Employment Department (UK), pp. 231–240, June.

Dabscheck, B., and J. Niland. 1981. *Industrial Relations in Australia.* Sydney: George Allen and Unwin.

EPAC. 1996. *Future Labor Market Issues for Australia.* Canberra: Australian Government Publishing Service.

ESRC Data Archive. Various years. *British Household Panel Survey and Labor Force Survey.* Essex University.

Fallick, B. 1996. "A Review of the Recent Empirical Literature on Displaced Workers." *Industrial and Labor Relations Review* 50: 5–16.

Farber, H. 1993. "The Incidence and Cost of Job Loss: 1982–91." *Brookings Papers on Economic Activity: Microeconomics,* pp. 73–132.

Farber, H. 1997. "The Changing Face of Job Loss in the United States, 1981–1995." *Brookings Papers on Economic Activity: Microeconomics,* pp. 55–128.

Gray, M. 1999. *The Effects of Unemployment on the Earnings of Young Australians.* Unpublished Ph.D thesis, Australian National University.

Gregg, P., and J. Wadsworth. 1997. "Mind the Gap: The Changing Distribution of Entry Wages in Great Britain." Discussion Paper no. 303, Centre for Economic Performance, London School of Economics.

———. 1998. "Job Tenure in Britain." Working Paper no. 823, Centre for Economic Performance, London School of Economics.

Gregory, M., and R. Jukes. 1997. "The Effects of Unemployment on Subsequent Earnings: A Study of British Men, 1984–94." Department of Education and Employment Working Paper, London.

Gregory, R. 1991. "Jobs and Gender: A Lego Approach to the Australian Labor Market." *Economic Record* 67(Supplement): 20–40.

———. 1993. "Aspects of Australian and U.S. Living Standards: The Disappointing Decades." *Economic Record* 69: 61–76.

Gu, W., and P. Kuhn. 1998. "A Theory of Holdouts in Wage Bargaining." *American Economic Review* 88: 428–449.

Gustafson, C. 1998. "Job Displacement and Mobility of Younger Workers." Working paper no. 8, Center for Labor Economics, University of California, Berkeley.

Halpin, B. 1997. "Unified BHPS Work-Life Histories: Combining Multiple Sources into a User-Friendly Format." Technical paper no. 13, ESRC Research Centre on Micro-Social Change, University of Essex.

Hamermesh, D. 1987. "The Costs of Worker Displacement." *Quarterly Journal of Economics* 52(1): 51–76.

Jacobson, L., R. LaLonde, and D. Sullivan. 1993. "Earnings Losses of Displaced Workers." *American Economic Review* 83: 685–709.

Kelley, J., M. Evans, and P. Dawkins. 1998. "Job Security in the 1990s: How Much Is Security Worth to Employees?" Photocopy, ISSP, RSSS, Australian National University.

Kletzer, L. 1998. "Job Displacement." *Journal of Economic Perspectives.* 12(Winter): 115–136.

Kletzer, L. and R. Fairlie. 1998. "The Long-Term Costs of Job Displacement among Young Workers." Photocopy, Department of Economics, University of California, Santa Cruz.

Marks, G. Various years. "The Youth in Transition Project." Photocopy, Australian Council for Educational Research.

Nickell, S., and R. Layard. 1999. "Labor Market Institutions and Economic Performance." In *Handbook of Labor Economics,* O. Ashenfelter and D. Card, eds. Amsterdam: North Holland.

Organisation for Economic Co-operation and Development (OECD). 1997. "Making Work Pay." In *Employment Outlook 1997.* Paris: OECD, pp. 25–58.

Paull, G. 1997. "Dynamic Labor Market Behaviour in the BHPS: The Effects of Recall Bias and Panel Attrition." Discussion paper no. 10, Centre for Economic Performance and Institute of Economics and Statistics Programme into Labor Market Consequences of Technical and Structural Change, London School of Economics.

Pearce, A., S. Bertone, and J. Stephens. 1995. *Surviving Retrenchment—Experiences of NESB Immigrants in the Western Region of Melbourne.* Canberra: Australian Government Publishing Service.

Ruhm, C. 1991. "Are Workers Permanently Scarred by Job Displacements?" *American Economic Review* 81(1): 319–324.

———. 1998. "Labor Displacement in the United States." Photocopy, University of North Carolina, Greensboro.

Schmitt, J., and J. Wadsworth. 1998. "You Won't Feel the Benefit: Changing Unemployment Benefit Entitlement and Unemployment Outflows." *Oxford Economic Papers.*

Selwyn, N. 1996. *Selwyn's Law of Employment.* London: Butterworths.

———. 1998. *Tolley's Social Security and State Benefits Handbook.* London: Tolley Publishing Company Great Britain, United News and Media Publications.

Social Justice Consultative Council. 1992. *Social Justice: Economic Restructuring and Job Loss.* Melbourne: Department of Premier and Cabinet.

Stevens, A. Huff. 1997. "Persistent Effects of Job Displacement: The Importance of Multiple Job Losses." *Journal of Labor Economics* 15(1, part 1): 165–188.

Swaim, P., and M. Podgursky. 1991. "Displacement and Unemployment." In *Job Displacement: Consequences and Implications for Policy,* J. Addison, ed. Detroit: Wayne State University, pp. 147–148.

Topel, R. 1991. "Specific Capital, Mobility, and Wages: Wages Rise with Job Seniority." *Journal of Political Economy* 99(1): 145–175.

5
Worker Displacement in France and Germany

Stefan Bender
Institute fur Arbeitsmarkt- und Berufsforschung, Nurnberg

Christian Dustmann
University College London, and *Institute for Fiscal Studies*

David Margolis
Centre National de Recherches Scientifiques, Université de Paris 1
and
Centre de Recherches en Economie et Statistique

and

Costas Meghir
University College London, and *Institute for Fiscal Studies*

INTRODUCTION

In this chapter, we describe the evolution of earnings and employment, postdisplacement and post-other-separation, for workers in France and Germany. Although the literature on displaced workers (those who experienced involuntary separations from stable jobs for reasons beyond their control) in North America is already extensive, the European literature is limited. We consider two labor markets in which layoffs are heavily regulated (as opposed to the relatively flexible Canadian and United States labor markets). We exploit administrative data from both countries that match workers to their employers and have the advantages (relative to survey-based analyses) of providing large, representative samples of a wide range of workers from all sectors, thereby allowing for the straightforward construction of control groups. Administrative data have the additional advantage that reported earnings and employment durations are precisely measured and not subject to recall bias.

One particularity of our approach is that we focus our attention on workers whose separation is a result of the closure of the employing firm (in the case of France) or plant (in the case of Germany). This is for two main reasons. First, our administrative data do not allow us to distinguish the reason for separation when the separation is not related to the employer's shutting down. Second, our measure avoids the frequently cited problem of relying on workers to accurately report the reason for separation. This is particularly important in heavily regulated labor markets like those of France and Germany, since the administrative procedures that must be followed in the case of layoffs are typically much longer and more complicated than the procedures surrounding quits. For this reason, declared quits in these countries may frequently be layoffs disguised so as to avoid the administrative complications. Furthermore, workers often misreport firing for cause as a layoff—and these two events can have very different implications for the non-employment durations and earnings losses involved.

A second issue is that we consider non-employment, as opposed to unemployment, durations following displacement. We do so partly because our data for France do not allow us to discern whether the worker is actively looking for employment when not employed (as the ILO definition of unemployment requires). In Germany we observe only unemployment benefit and unemployment assistance durations, although individuals may experience spells of unemployment while being ineligible for benefits. We also limit ourselves to non-employment because the complexity of the unemployment insurance schemes (see the section on institutions below) brings the explicit modeling of their role beyond the scope of this chapter.[1]

In addition to describing the institutional context in France and Germany, our analysis focuses on non-employment durations and earnings changes experienced by workers who have stayed with a single firm for at least four years as the principal measures of interest. More precisely, we look at prime-age males in the age range of 26–55 (for France) and 25–56 (for Germany). We distinguish between workers who separate from their firm (in the case of France) or plant (in the case of Germany) as a result of a closure (referred to as displaced workers) and those who separate for unknown reasons. This last category includes workers who are fired for cause, workers who leave the firm or plant because they receive a better offer, and workers who drop out of the labor force.[2] The literature has concentrated primarily on these measures,[3] finding that displaced workers tend to experience earnings losses both pre- and postdisplacement and that workers displaced as a result of a firm or plant closure tend to have shorter non-employment durations than workers who separate from from their employers involuntarily for other reasons (Gibbons and Katz 1991).

The structure of our chapter is as follows. We begin by describing the institutional setting surrounding layoffs and unemployment benefits in France and Germany. This discussion provides the context in which the subsequent results need to be considered. Then, after describing the data sources we use, we describe the incidence of displacement in the two countries. We then proceed with a more detailed analysis of the non-employment durations following displacement, followed by a description of the earnings changes associated with displacement. The next section provides results of a regression analysis of earning changes before, around, and after displacement, and the final section summarizes our results and concludes.

INSTITUTIONS

Both France and Germany have detailed regulations concerning layoffs and unemployment compensation. For each country, we describe the institutions surrounding layoffs, followed by a brief description of the unemployment benefit system and the main prevailing-wage-setting mechanisms.

France

Following is a brief summary of the labor law and jurisprudence surrounding worker displacement, or layoffs for economic reasons.[4] An excellent reference for this (in French) is Lefebvre (1996).

Laws concerning layoffs for economic reasons (displacements)

The legislation and jurisprudence surrounding displacements distinguishes four classes of layoffs: individual, fewer than 10 employees over 30 days, more than 10 employees over 30 days, and bankruptcy or reorganization.[5] One common characteristic of all displacements is that the employer is required to offer the option of participating in a partially employer-funded retraining scheme to all employees who will be laid off. This retraining program is run by the fund that finances unemployment benefits (ASSEDIC) and made available.

- Individual displacements have to meet the obligations surrounding both individual layoffs for personal reasons and layoffs of fewer than 10 employees over 30 days (with the exception of the obligation to inform the works council; see below). The obligations attached to the layoffs for personal reasons include an invitation to a "reconciliation" meeting at which the layoff will be discussed, an actual holding of the reconciliation meeting (to which the worker can bring an outside representative), and a notification-of-layoff letter, all with required delays and notice periods. The displaced employee must also be guaranteed priority in future hiring for all jobs for which he or she is qualified, and this obligation runs for one year following the layoff.
- The case of displacements involving fewer than 10 employees in a 30-day period is more complicated than that of individual displacements. First, the works council (or personnel representatives in firms too small to have a works council, that is, with fewer than 50 employees) must be consulted. The employer must provide all useful information to the works council concerning the economic circumstances that motivate the layoffs, the number of employees to be laid off by occupational category, the criteria used to determine the order of layoffs (in other words, which employees will go), and a preliminary calendar for the layoffs. Each employee must still be invited to a "reconciliation" meeting, and the layoff letters can be sent out only after the appropriate waiting period following this meeting.
- In the case of displacements involving more than 10 people in a 30-day period, things become even more complicated. The enter-

prise must devise a "social plan" which, in addition to proposing ASSEDIC retraining programs, must describe the possibilities for an internal reclassification within the enterprise (when the enterprise is larger than 50 employees) and the steps the enterprise is prepared to take in terms of helping laid-off employees become self-employed, providing training in new fields, or reducing the workweek. Along with all of the information described in the previous case, this plan has to be given to the works council, when one exists, or to the personnel delegates for consultation. The works council can request the help of an "expert accountant" to evaluate the different aspects of the employer's social plan and explanations for the layoffs. The local labor ministry office also receives a copy of the social plan, and both the works council and the labor ministry can make suggestions to which the employer must respond. There must be two meetings held with the works council, or three if the works council brings in an accountant. There are specified delays between the meetings which vary with the size of the proposed layoff, but there is no obligation to meet individually with each employee in this case. The selection of the individuals to be laid off will typically be determined by a governing collective agreement, but in the absence of such an agreement it is the employer who fixes the criteria after consultation with the works council. The layoff letters can be sent out only after a fixed delay following the final meeting with the works council.

- The conditions surrounding layoffs in the case of bankruptcy or court-ordered reorganization are similar to those for the previous case, except that it is the court-appointed administrator who makes the proposals, and the judge responsible for overseeing the liquidation or reorganization must approve all layoffs.

Advance notice and severance pay

The forewarning that workers receive before being laid off varies according to the size of the layoff, whether or not an expert accountant is called in, the size of the firm, and whether the employer and employee agree upon a buyout of the notice period. The time taken by just following the legal procedure (prior to the official advance notice that starts running from the moment the layoff letter is received) can vary from 1) 35 days between the mailing of the invitation to the "reconciliation" meeting to 2) the sending out of the layoff letter (in the case of an individual displacement), to 3) 74 days or more from the date at which the first works council meeting is held (in the case of a layoff of 10 or more people in 30 days, with expert accountant called in, not counting the time it takes to devise the social plan or respond to suggestions made by the works council and the labor ministry). After the layoff letters are sent out, the official advance-notice period begins. This period is a function of seniority: a minimum of one month for employees with six months to two years of seniority, and two months for employees with at least two years of seniority. If a collective agreement exists that provides for longer notice periods, the longer periods prevail.

Severance pay is a function of seniority, whether or not the employee had accrued unused paid vacation time, and whether the employer buys off the official notice period. In general, the base rate of severance pay is 1/10th monthly earnings per year of seniority (if seniority is greater than two years), with an additional 1/15th monthly earnings per year of seniority if seniority is greater than 10 years. The worker also recovers the value of unused paid vacation time, plus one to two months of earnings in the case where the notice time is bought off, corresponding to the level of seniority.

Unemployment benefit eligibility and levels

To be eligible for unemployment benefits, workers must meet the following conditions.[6] First, they must have been employed for a sufficiently long period preceding the start of the episode of unemployment. There are five criteria defining the minimum number of days or hours worked over a reference period.[7]

Second, they must be enrolled on the National Job Search Agency (ANPE) lists. Third, they cannot have voluntarily quit their previous job although layoffs, even for cause, are acceptable.[8] Fourth, they must be actively looking for a job or, if over 57-1/2 years old, must reside in France. Fifth, they must be younger than 60 or between 60 and 65 and ineligible for retirement with full benefits. Sixth, they must be physically able to hold down a job. Finally, they cannot be "seasonally unemployed"; that is, they can not have come from a job that is classified as seasonal, nor can they have had a job that, for two of the prior three years, had regular periods of inactivity at more or less the same calendar dates each year.

Unemployment benefits are taxable as revenue and are made up of a base rate that applies for a first period, then a "digressivity coefficient" which lowers the benefits for a second period. The daily base rate is comprised of a fixed component (56.95 francs in June 1996) and a variable component corresponding to 40.4 percent of reference earnings. The total can neither exceed 75 percent of the reference level of earnings nor be less than a statutory minimum level (138.84 francs in June 1996). There are also provisions relating to high-earnings workers that guarantee them at least 57.4 percent of their reference earnings.

The digressivity coefficient and the durations of the benefit periods are functions both of the age of the worker and his or her "length of affiliation" (cumulative seniority in any covered employers during a reference period). Durations range from 1) 122 days (four months) for workers with only 122 days or 676 hours of eligibility over the previous eight months (all at the second-period rate with a digressivity coefficient of 0.75) to 2) an 821-day (27-month) first period and a 1,004-day (33-month) second period, with digressivity coefficient of 0.92, for workers over 55 years old with 821 days or 4,563 hours of eligibility over the preceding 36 months. Thus, if a 56-year-old person worked 27 out of the 36 months preceding a spell of unemployment, he or she would have a right to five years of benefits, with the lowest rate still being 92 percent of his or her previous benefit level.[9]

Wage-setting institutions

During the period of time covered by our French data (1984–1989), the French industrial relations environment was undergoing significant changes. Although union membership was steadily declining, union coverage remained relatively stable. This phenomenon was due largely to the policy of contract extension. This policy allows the Ministry of Labor to take a collective agreement negotiated by an employers' association and several union confederations and extend its coverage to all other enterprises in the same region or sector, or all individuals in the same occupation, as those covered by the contract, regardless of their participation or membership in the employers' association or union confederation that actually negotiated the contract.[10]

Despite the high level of contract coverage, important modifications of the structure of collective bargaining were brought about by the Auroux laws of 1982. Two of the most important features were 1) the establishment of works councils and the definition of their consultative role in mass layoffs (see above) and 2) the requirement to engage in bargaining at the enterprise level for all firms over a minimum size. Although there was no obligation to come to an agreement, the fact that employers were required to negotiate locally encouraged a gradual shift of collective bargaining over wages from a centralized to a more decentralized level. This shift reduced the frequency with which the national, often extended, agreements had their salary grids renegotiated. Given the constant increase in the real minimum wage over the period (see below), the share of contracts for which the lowest earners on the salary grid earned more than the minimum wage fell from 15.3 percent in January of 1983 to 3.6 percent in January of 1985.[11]

The first minimum-wage law in France was enacted in 1950, creating a guaranteed hourly wage rate that was partially indexed to the rate of increase in consumer prices. Beginning in 1970, the original minimum-wage law was replaced by the current system (called the SMIC, for *salaire minimum interprofessionnel de croissance*), linking the changes in the minimum wage to both consumer price inflation and growth in the hourly blue-collar wage rate. In addition to annual formula-based increases in the SMIC, the government legislated increases many times over the next two decades. The statutory minimum wage in France regulates the hourly regular cash compensation received by an employee, including the employee's part of any payroll taxes.

Although the original minimum wage program (called the SMIG, for *salaire minimum interprofessionnel garanti*) was only partially indexed—in particular, the inflation rate had to exceed 5 percent per year (2 percent from 1957 to 1970) to trigger the indexation—the real minimum wage did not decline measurably over the entire post-war period and increased substantially during most decades.[12] The French minimum wage lies near most of the mass of the wage-rate distribution for the employed workforce. In 1990, the first mode of the wage distribution was within 5 francs of the minimum wage and the second mode was within 10 francs of the minimum. In the overall distribution, 13.6 percent of the wage earners were at or below the minimum wage and an additional 14.4 percent were within an additional 5F per hour of the SMIC.[13]

Germany

Employment security and dismissal protection

German dismissal protection is based on an extensive system of legal rules and collective contracts. Historically, dismissal protection is rooted in a framework of directives developed during the Weimar Republic. It was developed in the 1950s to 1970s, and went through a process of amendments during the 1970s and 1980s (see Büchtemann 1990).

One can distinguish between general dismissal protection and specific dismissal protection, with the latter applying to individuals in specific situations. The general dismissal protection was first regulated in the *Burgerliches Gesetzbuch* (BGB) and in the *Kündigungsschutzgesetz* (KSchG). Since those were enacted, however, it has undergone a number of slight revisions.[14] The most notable is the Employment Promotion Act (*Beschaftigungsforderungsgesetz*), or EPA of 1985, which is discussed below in more detail.

The KSchG applies to all blue- and white-collar workers with more than six months of uninterrupted tenure in firms with more than six regularly employed workers. According to Büchtemann (1990), it covers about 80 percent of all blue- and white-collar workers.

The general dismissal protection regulations as laid out in the KSchG are supplemented by regulations which apply to individuals in specific circumstances. For instance, specific regulations apply to handicapped people, people on maternity leave, and people who are serving in compulsory military or civil service. In 1987–1988, 16 percent of all dismissals fell under these complementary rules (see Büchtemann 1990).

According to the KSchG, all dismissals of employees who are employed for more than six months without interruption, which are initiated by the employer, are invalid if they are socially unacceptable. Accordingly, dismissals of all individuals to whom the KSchG applies have to be justified by the employer. Acceptable reasons for dismissal may be due to the firm's concerns or macroeconomic shocks (or the employee's absenteeism or illness, for example). In the case of dismissals caused by economic difficulties on the side of the firm, the KSchG stipulates that social criteria (such as seniority) should be used to determine which employees are to be dismissed. Employees who feel that they have been unjustly dismissed have the right to sue the employer in the labor courts. In 1987, about 10 percent of dismissals were brought to court by dismissed employees, although in very few cases did this lead to a continuation of the employment relation (see Büchtemann 1990). In addition, German dismissal protection has a strong collective component. For every dismissal, the works council has to be consulted.

Concerns about the negative effects of the rather rigid dismissal-protection regulations on firms' employment policies led to the Employment Promotion Act of 1985. The EPA introduced some deregulating measures which do not replace, but rather complement, existing employment-protection regulations. They mainly promote fixed-term contracts as an instrument for enhancing flexibility. More specifically, the EPA allows fixed term contracts to be established without a particular reason (which was not the case before). Contracts are limited to a duration of 18 months, and they are not renewable. The EPA originally limited them to five years, but this was extended twice. At present its applicability lasts until the year 2000 (see Rogowski and Schömann 1996).

Advance notice and severance pay

The advance-notice period in Germany varies according to the size of the layoff, the seniority of the worker, and whether he or she is a blue- or white-collar worker.[15] Furthermore, there are a number of collectively bargained regulations as well as firm-worker specific agreements that include notice provisions. The legal advance-notice regulations stipulate four weeks of notice for blue-collar workers who have been employed for at least five years, and 12 weeks for white-collar workers. After 20 years of employment with the same firm, these periods rise to 12 weeks and 24 weeks for blue- and white-collar workers, respectively (see Buttler, Brandes, Dorndorf, Gaum, and Walwei 1992).

If a firm dismisses a considerable fraction of its workforce, the layoffs have to be reported to the local employment office and to the works council. For instance, a firm which employs between 21 and 59 workers has to report if the number of dismissals exceeds six workers within a period of 30 working days; a firm which employs between 60 and 499 employees has to report layoffs of more than 25 workers, or when layoffs exceed 10 percent of the firm's workforce; a firm which employs more than 499 workers has to report if layoffs exceed 30 workers.

If the reduction in the firm's workforce exceeds certain numbers, the works council can demand a social plan. For instance, when dismissals exceed 20 percent of the workforce (or at least six workers for a firm of size 21–59 or more than 36 workers for a firm of size 60 to 249), a social plan can be demanded. Social plans describe the conditions surrounding severance pay and other payments.

Unemployment benefit eligibility and levels

The German unemployment compensation scheme distinguishes between unemployment insurance benefit (*Arbeitslosengeld* (AG)) and unemployment assistance (*Arbeitslosenhilfe* (AH)). To be eligible for AG, the employee must have contributed to the system for at least 12 months over the preceding three years. The system is financed by employer and employee contributions in equal parts (each part amounting to 3.25 percent of the employee's salary). There is a waiting period of 12 weeks if the separation was induced by the employee, but receipt of AG starts immediately if the separation was caused by the employer. The compensation is based on previous *net* earnings, and it amounts to 67 percent of the previous net wage (60 percent for employees without children). There is an upper threshold (5,200 DM in 1984 and 6,000 DM in 1990, for instance). AG can be received for up to 32 months, with the duration of the entitlement period depending on age and the length of contributions to the scheme.[16]

If AG is exhausted, or if the employee is not eligible for AG, he can claim AH. A condition for receiving AH in case of non-eligibility for AG is having been in insured employment for at least 150 days during the prior year. Like AG, AH is based on previous earnings; it amounts to 57 percent of previous net earnings (50 percent for employees without children). AH is means tested, and its duration is unlimited.

Both AG and AH are granted conditional on the recipient's agreement to accept reasonable employment (*zumutbare Beschaftigung*) and are not subject to income tax.

Wage-setting institutions

In Germany, wages are determined by (annual) negotiations between unions and employer federations (tariff parties, or *Tarifparteien*). Workers are represented in collective bargaining by unions that are organized nationwide according to industries (see Schmidt 1994 for more details). Union membership is not tied to a particular job or firm; union workers usually remain with the union irrespective of their mobility decisions, as well as through spells of non-employment.

Collective bargaining takes place on industry and regional levels. During negotiations, parties have legally guaranteed autonomy. The results of the negotiations are laid down in tariff contracts (or *Tarifvertraege*), which determine working conditions and wages. These contracts are registered at the Ministry of Labor. Since the union is the legal representative of all workers covered by collective bargaining (irrespective of the workers' union status), collective agreements apply to all workers within the respective segment.

There are no legal minimum wages in Germany; however, tariff contracts which specify wage levels for specific groups in specific sectors can be considered as an elaborate system of minimum wages.

To enforce their bargaining position, unions have the right to call strikes and employers have the right to lock out employees (*Aussperrung*), although this latter instrument is regulated by a number of legal rules. If the two parties have difficulties reaching a compromise, they may call for a mediator. The legal rules concerning the bargaining procedures, as well as the commitment that binds the two parties to the agreed contract, are laid down in the tariff contract law (*Tarifvertragsgesetz*).

DATA

We use administrative data from Social Security records for Germany, and payroll taxes for France, in some cases supplemented with data from other sources. We briefly describe these data sources below.

France

Base data set

The base data set for France is the Annual Social Data Reports (Déclarations Annuelles des Données Sociales, or DADS), which is a random 1/25 sample of the French population.[17] All people born in October of an even-numbered year, with the exception of civil servants (but including those employed by publicly held companies), are in the data set whenever they are employed.[18] These data cover the period 1976–1996, with the exception of 1981, 1983, and 1990, since the French National Statistics Institute (INSEE) did not collect the 1/25 sample in those years. These data include earnings information from all employers of all of these individuals, with both individual and employer identifiers attached to each year-individual-enterprise-establishment observation.[19] We also have the number of days worked during the course of the year and the job start and end dates (if the job began or ended during the year). We impute information using auxiliary regressions run on other data sets to determine the job start dates for the left-censored spells.[20] Temporary layoffs (of a length shorter than one calendar year) are not considered as interruptions of an employment spell. With this information, we can calculate seniority at each job for each year. We observe seniority, gender, age, occupation, region, full- or part-time employment status (but not hours), and sector on all jobs held by the individual, and we can measure the length of non-employment spells between jobs.

There are two problems with using this data set to study displaced workers. First, we do not know education, marital status, or number of children, for example. The Permanent Dynamic Sample (*Echantillon Dynamique Permanent*, or EDP), provides some additional information though. INSEE collected data on individuals born on the first four days of October that could be located in the 1968, 1975, 1982, or 1990 censuses, or for whom one of the following was available: the individual's birth, marriage, or death certificate or the birth, death, or marriage of a parent or child of the individual concerned. Most of the demographic information of interest comes from matches with the censuses. Since the EDP sampling frame overlaps that of the DADS in even-numbered years, it was possible to obtain a data set with all of the relevant variables from the combination of the DADS and the EDP.[21]

The remaining problem is to know the reason behind a separation.[22] We use a two-step approach to identifying displacements, or more precisely, firm deaths.[23] First, we use the Unified System of Enterprise Statistics (*Systeme Unifie de Statistiques d'Entreprise*, or SUSE), to determine the last year in which the employing firm filed accounts with any of France's administrative authorities.[24] We then look at all of the observations in the DADS that correspond to a given enterprise (not establishment). If the last year in which we observe data corresponding to the enterprise is 1996, we consider all separations from that employer as being for reasons other than firm death.[25] If, on the other hand, we observe a firm for which the last year with DADS data is, say, 1985, we compare this date to the date found in the SUSE (where available). We consider the latter of the two dates for a given enterprise as its estimated death date, and we consider enterprises that filed accounts or were paying employees in 1996 as ongoing.

For the "dying" enterprises, we attempt to control for false firm deaths (change of firm identifier without cessation of activity) with the following procedure. Given that we only observe a random sample of 1/25 of any firm's employment, we apply the procedure only to firms with at least three observed employees.[26] For these firms, we test the hypothesis that 50 percent or more of the firm's actual employees leaving the enterprise at its estimated death date were employed by the same subsequent employer, conditional on the total number of observed employees and the share of those who move together to the same subsequent firm identifier. This procedure is described in detail in Appendix A.[27]

Based on this dating procedure and correction, we construct two definitions of displacement. In the first, the worker separates from the firm within the calendar year preceding the calendar year of the firm's death.[28] In the second, we widen the window to two years preceding the year of the firm's death. We report below results based on the two-year window definition, since our procedure for dating firm deaths is not very precise (particularly when SUSE data are involved) and because advance-notice provisions may mean that some workers separate from their firm prior to its actual shutdown (see Appendix B).[29] All other separations are classed as "other separations."

It should be noted that, given the sampling scheme of the DADS, this approach over-attributes separations to the "displaced" category. This is even more likely to be the case for separations from small firms, especially when the separation occurs near the end of the sample period. Our selection criterion reduces the risk of this source of overclassification somewhat (see below). Nevertheless, all of our results for France should be interpreted with this in mind.[30]

The sample retained for analysis

From the overall data base, we focus in particular on men between 26 and 50 years of age with four or more years of seniority in 1984.[31] These restrictions were imposed so that we could restrict our attention to adult,[32] high-attachment workers without a risk that they would take early retirement in the later years in the sample.[33] We exclude all individuals with more than three different employers in any given year, as well as all individuals who held multiple jobs simultaneously at any point during our analysis window.[34] As a further control against early retirement, our duration analyses exclude all workers who, following separation from their employer, experienced a censored non-employment spell that pushed them above 56 years old (the minimum age for men to receive early retirement). Appendix C shows the differential effect of imposing this latter restriction by age at separation.[35]

We focus on individuals observed during the window of 1984–1989 for three reasons. First, given our definition of firm death for workers not matched to SUSE firms, we wanted to allow a time period after the end of the analysis period during which we might observe people in a "dead" firm, in order to minimize incorrect classifications. Second, given the data missing from 1983 and 1990, this is the longest period without interruption in our data. Finally, this sample window makes the French data comparable with the German data (see below).

In general, we concentrate on the first separation observed for the individual in the sample window (1984–1989), and, in so doing, ignore the issue of multiple displacements (Stevens 1997).[36] As mentioned above, our data include information on the year, age, education, seniority, log real annual gross earnings, sector of activity, skill level (unskilled blue-collar, skilled blue-collar or white-collar), region and, of course, the reason for separation (displacement or other, calculated according to the procedures described above), if it occurred. Appendix D provides descriptive statistics for the full sample in 1984.

For the analyses of displacement incidence and earnings changes surrounding separations, we aggregated our data to one observation per individual per year.[37] In years preceding the separation, if the individual was employed by the employer from whom he or she will eventually separate, we keep the descriptive information (sector, occupation, seniority) corresponding to that job. For all other individual-year combinations, the descriptive information corresponds to the job the person held for the longest duration during the year, and in the case of ties, the job that provided the highest gross earnings.

The earnings measure used for the French data is the log of Total Average Real Daily Earnings,[38] corresponding to the log of the average of daily labor earnings from all sources, weighted by the number of days worked in the particular job (measured in thousands of 1980 francs).[39] The precise formula is

$$\text{(1)} \quad LARDE_{i,t} = \log\left(\frac{\sum_{j \in J(i,t)} \left(\frac{RAE_{i,t,j}}{dw_{i,t,j}} \right) dw_{i,t,j}}{\sum_{j \in J(i,t)} dw_{i,t,j}} \right)$$

where RAE is the real gross annual earnings received by individual i in year t from firm j, $dw_{i,j,t}$ is the number of days worked by individual i in firm j during year t, and $J(i,t)$ is the set of firms j in which individual i worked during year t.

Germany

Base data set

The data used for Germany, which will be referred to as the IAB data, are comprised of three components. The core data are drawn from the *Beschaftigungsstichprobe* (BS) of the *Institut fur Arbeitsmarkt- und Berufsforschung* (IAB) in Nürnberg. The BS is a 1 percent sample from the overall employees' statistics, the so-called historic file *Historikdatei* (HD), of the Federal Department of Employment in Nürnberg, which is constructed as an insurance account, and contains a continuous employment history for each employee covered by the social security system. The BS is drawn in two stages (see Bender, Hilzendegen, Rohwer, and Rudolph 1996 for details) and covers a period of 16 years (1975–1990). It comprises 426,363 individuals in the longitudinal dimension and, on average, around 200,000 individuals in the yearly cross-sectional dimension.

On January 1, 1973, an integrated reporting procedure for health, retirement, and unemployment insurance was introduced in Germany. The data collected using this process form the basis for the HD. The procedure requires employers to report any commencement and termination of an employment relation which is subject to social security contributions. Additionally, to guarantee continuity in the registration of employment histories, employers have to provide information on every ongoing employment relation which is subject to social security payments on December 31 of every year. The information reported by the employer each time includes individual characteristics, such as gender, nationality, and educational attainment, as well as gross earnings over the past employment spell which served as the basis for social security contributions.[40] Furthermore, the HD also contains information on spells of interrupted employment relations, like maternity leave or obligatory military and civil service.

The HD does not include individuals who are below the earnings threshold which makes social security contributions compulsory unless they have been in an employment relation which was subject to social security contributions at an earlier stage of their career. It further excludes the self-employed, state civil servants, and individuals who are in compulsory military service or alternative compulsory activities. For 1980, Herberger and Becker (1983) estimate that the HD comprises 79 percent of the total labor force.

In addition to information available in the BS, the IAB data contain information from a second important data source, the *Leistungsempfangerdatei* (LD) of the employment office. The LD contains data covering spells for individuals who received certain benefit payments from the Federal Department of Employment. These payments include unemployment benefits, unemployment assistance, and payments while participating in training and retraining programs. This additional data source allows us to follow individuals during periods of registered non-employment, too. It is important to note, however, that not all spells of registered non-employment are included in the LD. For instance, active labor market programs (*Arbeitsbeschaffungsmassnahmen*) are not covered. Furthermore, individuals have to fulfill certain requirements to be eligible for unemployment benefits or unemployment assistance (see above). Those who do not fulfill these requirements are likewise not included in the LD.

The IAB data set combines information on individual employees (from the BS and the LD) with plant information. Every individual in the HD is associated to a plant with a plant identifier. In a separate step and using the entire database, information about individuals is regrouped at the plant level. This allows us to add plant information to individual records contained in the IAB data. In particular, information about plant size and the educational structure of the workforce, as well as industry information, is added. The plant-level statistics, however, concern only those individuals who are covered by the social security system.

The sample retained for analysis

From the overall database, we extract a sample of high-attachment workers. We select male workers who were between 25 and 50 years old in 1984. We use this age group to avoid including separations for early retirement and to exclude individuals who might not yet have finished their schooling.

Although our observation window covers the period between 1975 and 1990, we concentrate our analysis on the last decade. The reason is that the earnings information before 1984 is only of limited use. Until 1983, whether wages reported to the authorities contained additional payments, like holiday or Christmas money, was up to discretion of the employer. It was compulsory to include these payments after 1983. Additional payments constitute a substantial part of the wage bill of German employees—around 7 percent (see Dustmann and Van-Soest 1997). Furthermore, these payments are likely to be correlated with variables like seniority, industry, and firm size. For these reasons we decided to use earnings information only for the period between 1984 and 1990.

We select all workers who had been continuously employed with the same establishment for at least four consecutive years in 1984. Between 1984 and 1990 (the last year of our observation window) these workers either stayed with their establishment or they separated. Temporary spells of unemployment or non-employment with subsequent continued employment at the previous plant are not considered as separations.

We distinguish two types of separations: separations due to plant closure and separations for other reasons. We define a worker as a displaced worker if his separation is related to the establishment closing down or to a significant reduction in the number of employees. We adopt three alternative definitions: a worker is displaced if his plant closes down within one year of his departure (definition 1), within two years of his departure (definition 2), or if he separates from a plant at which employment falls by at least 40 percent within two years of his departure (definition 3). A plant closure occurs if the number of employees within a plant drops to zero.[41]

The strictest definition is the first one. By using this definition, we may exclude workers who left earlier because they foresaw a closure, or who were dismissed while the firm cut down on size prior to closure. The last definition avoids this problem, but it may include workers who separate for other reasons. In most of the analysis, we adopt the second definition. We use the first and last definition to check the robustness of our results. Appendix Table 5.B1 describes how these measures differ.

Another problem with the type of data we use is censoring. If individuals lose their jobs, they may or may not return to the sample within the observation window. Those who do not return may change into states not recorded by our data, like nonparticipation, retirement, self-employment, or civil service; they may also leave the country. This type of censoring is a particular problem with administrative data. The question is how to treat censored observations. Analyses of non-employment duration, or reemployment probabilities, are sensitive to the definition of the underlying sample and have to be understood in that light. We decided not to impose any restrictions; results should therefore be understood as referring to the whole population of workers conditional on separation or displacement.

For illustrative purposes we use information about whether individuals claim unemployment insurance or unemployment assistance after separations as a device to sort out individuals with a high likelihood of leaving the sample. After at least four years of continuous employment (which is one of our criteria to enter the sample), every individual is, in principle, eligible for both types of benefits. Workers who intend to return to the labor market are most likely to claim benefits. We single out workers who do not return to the sample after separation and who do not claim benefits. Appendix E splits up the total sample of workers who separate from a firm into those who return into employment within the observation window (74 percent) and those who do not (26 percent). Of those who do not return, 30.6 percent claim benefits.

Appendix F displays sample statistics of worker characteristics for the year 1984: we distinguish among workers continuously employed between 1980 and 1990; workers whose first separation between 1984 and 1990 was a displacement (where displacement refers to separation from a plant within two years of the plant closing down); and workers whose first separation between 1984 and 1990 was for unknown reasons.

The numbers in the table indicate that average gross daily earnings of workers who are in continuous employment over the entire period are higher than those of workers who separate for unknown reasons or who are displaced. Continuously employed workers also have higher seniority in 1984, with more than 44 percent being with their firm for more than 10 years (as compared to 27 percent for displaced workers, and 24 for workers who separate for unknown reasons). Interesting are the numbers on plant size, which we measure in 1982, two years before any closure can take place in our sample. The average plant size for continuously employed workers is 3,086, as compared to 1,653 for other separations, and 160 for displacements. Accordingly, workers who are displaced according to our definition separate predominantly from small firms. The distributions are not symmetric, as indicated by a comparison between the median and the mean.

The Incidence of Displacement in France and Germany

We address the question of the incidence of permanent job loss, or displacement, in our data by two approaches. First, we look at the share of observations that correspond to displacements and separations for other reasons in our data, and then we estimate probit models of the incidence of displacements and other separations. We follow different approaches for the two countries.

For France, we consider the share of individuals in a given year who experience each sort of separation. Whereas Table 5.1 breaks annual incidence for our sample down by year, we restrain our attention to the 1984 sample year for the decomposition of the incidence of separation and the estimation of its determinants in Tables 5.2 and 5.3. This is because all individuals in the 1984 sample year have at least four years of seniority on their first job that year, whereas individuals observed in later years may be on postseparation jobs with low seniority, and thus the distribution of job types in later years will not necessarily be comparable with that of the year on which the sample selection criterion was applied.

For Germany, we split our sample into three groups: Those who are continuously employed with the same firm over the entire period between 1980 and 1990 (32,594 individuals), those whose first separation (after 1984) is a displacement (3,273 individuals), and those whose first separation (after 1984) is a separation for unknown reasons (12,933 individuals). In Table 5.4, we display characteristics of these three samples, where the decomposition is by variables measured in 1984. In Table 5.5, we estimate simple probability models, which relate the probabilities of being in any of the three groups to individual characteristics, again measured in 1984.

France

Table 5.1 describes the incidence of permanent separation, defined as the share of individuals in a given year experiencing a given type of permanent separation, in our data for all unique individual-year combinations.[42] Note that, as we are aggregating jobs to the individual-year level, a person can experience both displacement and other separation in the same year. Thus, the sum of the number of individual-years with displacements and other separations may exceed the number of individual-years with any separation. This table covers all separations that occur in our sample window, not just first separations, since (as noted above) considering only first separations would bias our sample increasingly toward stable individuals in the later years, thereby seriously underestimating the incidence of separation toward the end of our sample window. The spike in 1989 is due to the fact that we are missing data from 1990 (see below), and our coding algorithm would attribute all changes in employer identifier between 1989 and 1991 to the 1989 observation year, whereas at least some changes in employer certainly occurred during the (missing) 1990 observation year.[43] We include women as a reference, although in what follows we restrict our attention to men.

We find that the incidence of separation increased in France to a peak at 1987 for both men and women, and then declined in the remainder of the sample window. Whereas the share of individuals experiencing displacements seems to have peaked in 1988 for men, the figures for women suggest a peak around 1986. The increase for men toward the end of the sample is likely related to the onset of the recession that began in the early 1990s, while the peak for women in 1986 corresponds to the slump that began in mid 1986 and ran through spring 1987.[44] Furthermore, there seem to be no major, consistent differences between men and women over the entire sample period in terms of either the share of separations in the total or the share of displacements. Since maternity leave, albeit generous by North American standards, typically does not last longer than a full calendar year, and since women are guaranteed a job with their previous employer upon returning from maternity leave, such a lack of differences in separation and displacement rates is less surprising.[45]

A similar breakdown of our data, aggregated to the individual-year level, by seniority on the lost job and by age, all measured in the 1984 data year is presented in Table 5.2. Although 96 individuals experienced both a displacement and another separation, we count only the first separation in the top half of the table, since the elimination of multiple-job holders implies that the second separations are from low-seniority jobs that follow the first separation.

Table 5.2 shows that, although there is a clear decline in the share of separations in total observations and the share of displacements in total observations with previous job seniority in France (with the exception of the relatively underpopulated 8–10 years of seniority category), the share of separations represented by displacements (defined as separations in the two calendar years preceding the calendar year of firm closure) is relatively invariant to seniority, and may even be slightly increasing.[46]

Although the share of displacements and separations in the total seems reasonable by North American standards, the share of separations attributed to the displaced category is quite high. This is likely due to two main reasons. First, given the sampling frames in our data, most departures from small firms will be classed as displacements, since the chances of observing another sampled individual in the firm or observing firm financial data after the separation are very low. Second, we are classifying separations occurring in a relatively long window preceding the calendar year of firm death as displacements. This approach will mislabel all separations that occur within the window but are independent of the firm's impending demise as displacements. Unfortunately, given our data constraints, there is little we can do about these problems.

A final point worth noting regarding Table 5.2 is that the share of individuals experiencing a displacement, or any sort of separation, is highest for the youngest and oldest age categories. Given that younger workers are less stable than older workers, the results for young people are not surprising. Despite our restraining our attention to workers who are at most 50 years old in 1984, the possibility that some of these workers' employers may offer exceptional early retirement plans could explain the results for older workers.[47] For this reason (as mentioned above), we impose an additional control for early retirement in our analyses for postseparation non-employment durations.

In order to get a more precise view of the determinants of displacement, we estimate probit models of the incidence of 1) displacement, 2) other types of separation, and 3) all separations combined on our data from 1984. The reference category is all alternative states (other separations and no separations for model 1, displacements and no separations for model 2, and no separations for model 3). Constraining ourselves to 1984 data provides us with estimates of the determinants of annual probabilities of each sort of separation, and has the advantage of substantially reducing the risk of separations into early retirement, as the oldest workers at this date are 50 years old. Table 5.3 presents the results of these models.[48]

The table suggests that the highest educational categories are the most likely to separate for reasons other than firm closure, while the only diploma that affects displacement is an advanced vocational education (which reduces the risk of displacement relative to those without any educational certification). The probability of both displacement and other sorts of separations is not significantly related to age in 1984, a result which has also been found for the United States (Seitchik 1991). However, the most senior workers are clearly less likely to experience a separation, *ceteris paribus*, among the workers in our sample. Although the differences among 4–6, 6–8, and 8–10 years of seniority are not significant, all have a significantly higher probability of experiencing a displacement than workers with 10 or more years of seniority. These results are consistent with Table 5.2 and further reinforce the idea that the incidence of worker displacement declines with the seniority of the worker. Similar results are found for workers with 4–8 years of seniority (relative to 10 and above) when considering separations for other reasons. Many theoretical models predict a decline in mobility with job seniority, so this result is not surprising.

Germany

In Table 5.4 we report numbers on continuously employed workers over the period 1980–1990 (our reference group), and the number of displaced workers and workers who separate for unknown reasons during our sample window.[49] Recall that our selection criterion is that all workers joined the plant in 1980 or earlier. Seniority and age refer to 1984.

On average, 6.71 percent of all workers who have been in continuous employment with one firm between 1980 and 1984 experience a separation between 1984 and 1990 because the plant closes down. This percentage is slightly higher at the lower seniority levels, and lower at the higher seniority levels, indicating that plants which close down tend to have workers with lower levels of seniority. One reason may be that these plants are younger. There is no clear age pattern; displaced workers account for 20.19 percent of the by-age sample of separated workers.

Among the continuously employed workers, 44 percent have been with the same plant for at least 10 years in 1984; for displaced workers and workers who separate for unknown reasons, this number is lower: 26 percent and 24 percent respectively. Accordingly, although we used the same selection criterion to construct our samples (to have been with the same firm for at least four years in 1984), the distribution of seniority differs according to their future separation status. The age distribution is more similar among the three groups, with more than 70 percent of workers concentrated in the age range between 30 and 50.

To investigate the effect of observables on the separation and displacement probability in finer detail, we estimate simple probit models (Table 5.5), where the dependent variable is equal to 1 if the individual is displaced or separated for unknown reasons ("other separations") over the period 1984–1990.[50] The values of regressors refer to 1983, the last year before a separation could take place. The benchmark group are workers who are continuously employed with the same firm between 1980 and 1990.

We first discuss displacement. The estimates compare characteristics of workers in plants which close down between 1984 and 1990 with characteristics of workers in plants which do not; this is conditional on the two groups being employed for at least four years in 1984, and the latter group being employed between 1980 and 1990 with the same plant.

Age has a nonsignificant effect on the displacement probability (Table 5.5). This may be interpreted as an indication that the age structure of workers in firms which close down is not different from that of the reference group. The displacement probability decreases slightly with seniority—workers affected by a closure over the 1984–1990 window are characterized by less tenure than workers who are not. The benchmark for the education categories are workers without apprenticeship and without a high school degree. The negative signs of higher education dummies indicate that the skill mix of workers affected by displacement is weighted toward lower education groups, compared to our reference group.

The results for "other separations" are quite different. Remember that workers separated for unknown reasons include workers who are fired for cause, as well as workers who quit. Here, age has a strong negative effect. This is to be expected, given that age should affect the separation probabilities for both groups of workers in this category negatively. First, firing of workers becomes more expensive the older they are because of institutional regulations; and second, age is positively related to the match quality, and the mobility of workers decreases with age. Unlike displaced workers, higher education now has a positive effect on the separation probability. This may indicate a higher degree of mobility for the well educated.

Durations out of Work

In North America, displaced workers often experience periods out of work following their displacement prior to finding another job. In the more heavily regulated labor markets of France and Germany, advance-notice requirements are meant to reduce or eliminate periods out of work. The analysis of non-employment durations following displacement in France and Germany may provide additional insight into the functioning of the labor markets in these countries, and into the role that differences in the institutional environment might play in determining the speed of reemployment. In both countries, we focus on the first separation that occurs within our sample windows.

France

Table 5.6 breaks down all first separations in our data by seniority and describes the share of separations which are followed by a period out of work. This is further broken down into displacements and other sorts of separations.

The numbers in Table 5.6 demonstrate that the percentage of those who experience a non-employment spell after separating from the firm declines with seniority in France. Furthermore, the share of positive-duration non-employment spells is lower in general for displaced workers than for workers who separate for unknown reasons, with the difference being the most flagrant for the least senior workers.

Overall, Table 5.6 shows that approximately 22 percent of workers who lose stable jobs because of firm closure never experience an interruption in their employment histories as a result of their displacement. This may be due to the employment-protection legislation described above. In fact, given the rigidity of the employment-protection legislation and the long advance-notice periods it implies, one might wonder why the share of direct transitions is not higher. This is probably due to the length of the window we use for defining displacement, which includes separations that are not necessarily related to the firm closure and thus do not necessarily benefit from such generous employment-protection legislation.

To offer a sense of the duration of non-employment spells when they do occur, we show the Kaplan-Meier estimates of the nonparametric survival functions of postseparation non-employment spells for all spells of positive duration (in Figure 5.1). Note that these results are conditional on experiencing a non-employment spell of positive length, and that (as is always the case in duration modeling) our estimates are sensitive to the treatment of censored observations.[51]

Displaced workers clearly leave non-employment at a faster rate than workers who separate for other reasons. These differences are highlighted by the differences in long-term non-employment between displaced workers and those who separate for other reasons. In France, less than 18 percent of displaced workers who experience a non-employment spell are still without employment five years after displacement, while roughly 30 percent of workers who separate for other

Figure 5.1 Kaplan-Meier Survivor Functions, France

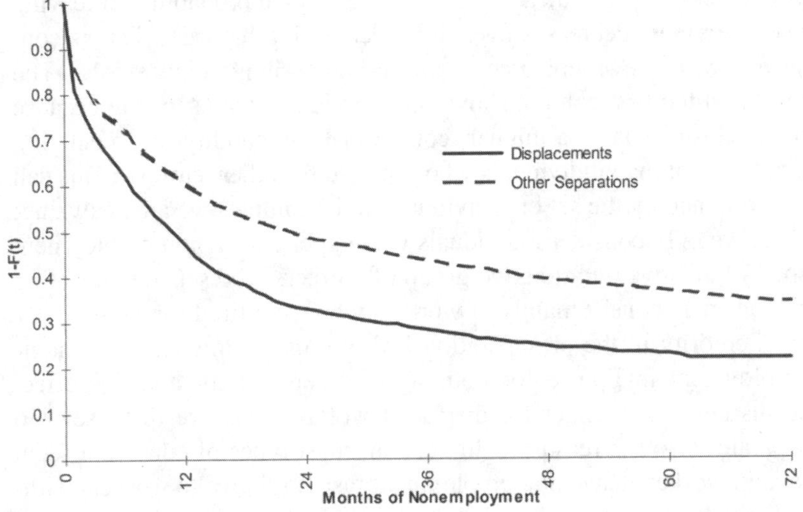

reasons and enter non-employment are without a job five years after separation.[52]

Of course, the differences between displaced workers and other separators in France may only be superficial: the Kaplan-Meier survivor functions we have drawn in Figure 5.1 do not consider the differences in the characteristics of the two populations. It may simply be the case that other separators have characteristics that make finding a new job harder and, thus, these workers would take longer to find new jobs irrespective of the reason for the separation. To control for observable heterogeneity in the populations, we estimate durations of non-employment by using proportional hazard models with Weibull-distributed baseline hazards for France.[53] The effects of different covariates on non-employment durations following separations are given in Table 5.7 for workers with at least four years of seniority on the job of their first separation.[54]

We estimate models with 1) both types of workers and an indicator variable for firm closure, as well as separately for 2) displaced workers and 3) workers who separate for other reasons. The first specification is equivalent to imposing an identical baseline hazard and identical coefficients on all covariates except the constant across the second and third specifications.

Table 5.7 shows that the shape parameter of the Weibull model is always less than 1, indicating that the conditional probability of leaving unemployment decreases over time (decreasing hazard). This is consistent with the nonparametric hazard underlying Figure 5.1. The results in the first column show that individuals who separate because of a closure have a higher conditional probability of reentering employment than individuals who separate for other reasons. This can be explained by the set of individuals in the samples we are analyzing; since we only consider individuals who experience a non-employment spell of positive duration, the group of workers who separate for other reasons may consist mainly of workers who were fired for cause.

Seniority in the preseparation firm seems to slow exit from non-employment in France for both sorts of separations, and this effect seems slightly stronger for displaced workers (relative to those who separate for other reasons). In general, most types of education seem to help workers leave non-employment faster, relative to workers without any degree, although which degrees help the most varies by reason for separation. For displaced workers, those with an advanced vocational school or a graduate school or grande école degree find new jobs the fastest, while among workers who separate for reasons other than firm closure, the degrees that count are a high school baccalauréat, an undergraduate, or a grande école or graduate school degree (the vocational degrees are marginally less important). The results for displaced workers suggest the importance of being able to signal a particular competency after one's firm closes via an advanced vocational certification or a relatively specialized graduate degree. One explanation could be that since firm closure is such a dramatic event, when a firm closes it may be a sign of ill health in the industry in general. As such, workers who are able to point to advanced skills may find it easier to get new jobs than those whose abilities are more closely linked to their previous employer's industry. The results for other separators may reflect the value that a more general education might have in counterbalancing the negative signal sent by a firing for cause, as well as the extensive networks that some grandes écoles have available to help place their alumni who might otherwise have difficulty.

Germany

The number and the percentage of workers who experience a non-employment spell in Germany are reported in Table 5.8. On average, about 50 percent of workers who separate from their firms immediately find another job. The number is slightly lower for displaced workers (39.5 percent), and slightly higher for workers who separate for unknown reasons (51.6 percent). The likelihood of a non-employment spell decreases slightly with job tenure, particularly for displaced workers.

Figures on non-employment include all individuals who do not experience a job-to-job transition, including individuals who leave the labor force into other states (see discussion above). The numbers are therefore not directly interpretable as the percentage of individuals who experience non-employment after a separation and would like to remain in the labor market. Figures for this type of worker will generally be lower.

Next, we investigate the duration of spells of non-employment for those individuals who experienced a non-employment spell after separation. Figure 5.2 shows the Kaplan-Meier estimates of the survival

Figure 5.2 Kaplan-Meier Survivor Functions, Germany

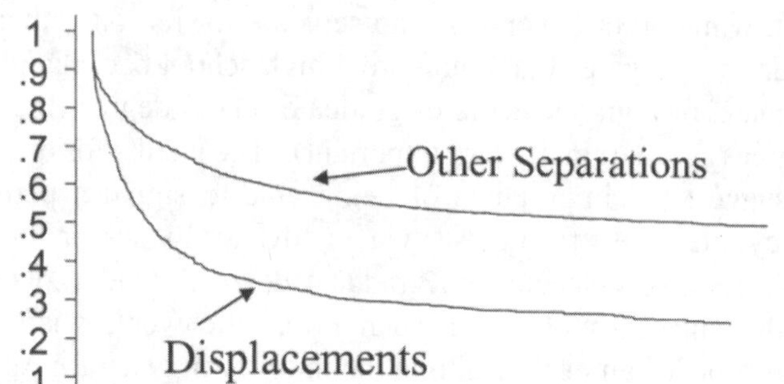

functions of postseparation non-employment spells for all spells of positive duration. Observations are treated as censored if they have not reentered the workforce at the end of the observation window (December 1990). The graphs indicate that displaced workers leave non-employment at a faster rate than workers who separate for other reasons.

In order to learn about the relation between individual characteristics and the conditional probability of reentering employment after a separation, conditional on having had a non-employment spell, we estimate durations of non-employment using Cox models, which avoid parametric assumptions about the baseline hazard. The effect of different covariates on non-employment durations following separation are given in Table 5.9. We estimate the models separately for displaced workers and workers who separate for other reasons.

In the first model, we do not distinguish between the two types of separation. We include an indicator variable which is equal to 1 if separation is due to closure. As already indicated by the Kaplan-Meier estimates, workers who are displaced and experience a subsequent non-employment spell are more rapidly reabsorbed by the labor market than workers who separate for other reasons. This latter group is likely to include primarily workers who were dismissed for cause, since workers who quit because they received better outside offers are unlikely to experience non-employment spells after separation.

The seniority variables refer to seniority prior to separation. Seniority plays no role in changing the rate of exit from non-employment for workers who are displaced for unknown reasons, but it increases the conditional probability of a return to work for displaced workers. Recall that seniority also reduces the probability of experiencing a non-employment spell for these workers. Age has a negative effect for both groups, indicating that older workers find it more difficult to get a job offer than younger ones, regardless of the reason for separation. The educational indicators are marginally significant. They indicate a negative relationship between education and the conditional probability of exit from non-employment for displaced workers. This may reflect the higher level of benefits for educated workers.[55]

Earnings before and after Separation

The literature notes that wage losses occur, in particular, for workers who lose jobs in which they had a high level of seniority. It has also been noted that these wage losses begin prior to displacement, and that measuring wage losses by comparing only the final wage on the job from which the worker was displaced with the new wage is likely to underestimate the size of these losses. In this section, we describe the time paths of daily earnings and changes in earnings growth in the years surrounding separations.

France

Figure 5.3 plots average daily earnings for French workers who were continuously employed over the at-risk period (1984–1989), workers whose first separation was a displacement during that period, and workers whose first separation was for another reason during that period. We include only individuals with strictly positive average daily earnings for our calculations.[56] For expository purposes, we look in particular at individuals whose first separation took place in 1987, if

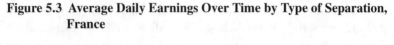

Figure 5.3 Average Daily Earnings Over Time by Type of Separation, France

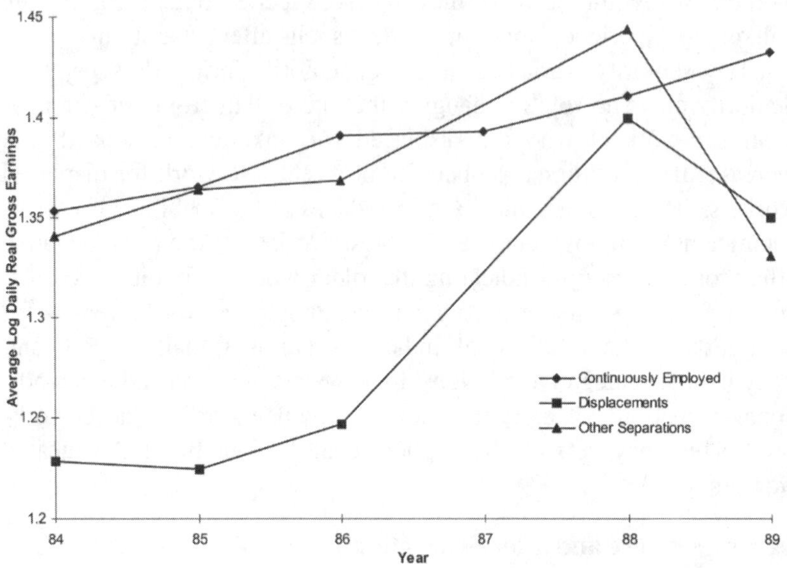

at all. We consider separations from all years combined starting with the next table.

In France, average daily earnings increased faster between 1986 and 1988 for workers displaced in 1987 than for workers who were continuously employed over the entire 1984–1989 period with the same employer and for those whose first separation was in 1987 and for reasons other than firm closure. Figure 5.3 illustrates that average real daily earnings grew by 2.01 percent for continuously employed workers between 1986 and 1988 and by 7.80 percent for other separators over the same interval, while average daily earnings jumped by 16.43 percent for displaced workers across the 1986–1988 interval.[57] Part of this might be due to what is called "partial unemployment" in the period leading up to firm closure. In France, a firm can negotiate a contract with the unemployment insurance fund to put its workers on partial unemployment, in which case the worker receives a fixed fraction of his or her prior salary with the costs split between the employer and the unemployment insurance fund. The worker does not report to work, but maintains the employment relationship. If employers report only their (lower) share of the (lower) workers' earnings paid during this period while not reducing the reported number of days for which compensation was paid, this would artificially lower the predisplacement earnings level. However, Figure 5.3 does not show such a preseparation drop in relative earnings, and even if such a phenomenon were present, it seems unlikely that average daily earnings in France would decline around separation.[58]

Another interesting point to draw from Figure 5.3 is the order of earnings levels among the three categories. It appears that in the time before separation, displaced workers have earnings that are, on average, lower than other sorts of workers, be they continuously employed or separated for reasons other than displacement. Workers who separate from their employers in France for the first time (in the 1984–1989 window) by displacement in 1987 earn 11.8 percent less in 1984 than those whose first separation is for other reasons, who in turn earn 1.3 percent less than workers who are continuously employed over the whole period. During the period preceding separation, there seems to be very little difference between continuously employed workers and those who separate for reasons other than displacement, while throughout this period displaced workers earn less. Still, in the period immediately after the separation, average daily earnings for displaced workers who have found new jobs have almost completely caught up with continously employed workers, being only 1.2 percent below, while workers who separate for other reasons and are employed in the year after separation pull ahead of continuously employed workers, earning 3.2 percent more.

A final point worth noting is the dip in average real daily earnings between the year following separation and two years after separation, for both displaced workers and those who separate for other reasons. Since we are calculating the averages used to draw Figure 5.3 from employed individuals only, this dip (or rather, lack of recovery) could be due to a composition effect. It may be that workers who take longer to find a job after separation earn less on their new job than those who find their new job sooner (and already have a year of seniority). We explore this idea further below.

Table 5.10 considers the raw averages in more detail, looking at long differences (of at least two periods) in average daily earnings around the displacement or separation date by seniority (prior to separation), distinguishing among continuously employed workers, displaced workers, and workers who separate for other reasons. For the continuously employed, the table simply provides two-year differences in average real earnings. For displaced and other separated workers, the numbers refer to the earnings difference between the new job in the year after the separation year (if a new job has been found) and the old job in the year prior to the separation year. Otherwise the numbers refer to the difference between the earnings in the first year in which a new job has been found and the old job. We have also differentiated workers who are observed in employment, at the earliest, two calendar years after separation; we refer to these workers as "slow displaced" and "slow other separations."

Table 5.10 confirms the intuition derived from Figure 5.3. Considering all displacement dates simultaneously, we find that displaced workers as a whole make faster earnings gains than continuously employed workers or workers who separate for other reasons. Earnings losses occur on average for both displaced and other separating workers who take more than a year to find a new job. Despite the fact that slow job finders make up a relatively small share of workers who eventually find jobs following separation within our sample window, it will become clear in our earnings regressions below that it is important to distinguish them from workers who find new jobs within the first calendar year after separation.

Germany

Average daily earnings for German workers who were continuously employed over the at-risk period (1984–1990), workers whose first separation was a displacement and took place in 1988, and workers whose first separation was for another reason and took place in 1988 are plotted in Figure 5.4. The separation year 1988 is omitted. Only employed individuals contribute to the averages on which the figures are based. We do not include workers who are not employed in a given year after separation.

The figure indicates that displaced and other separated workers experience earnings growth at a rate similar to continuously employed

Figure 5.4 Average Daily Earnings Over Time by Type of Separation, Germany

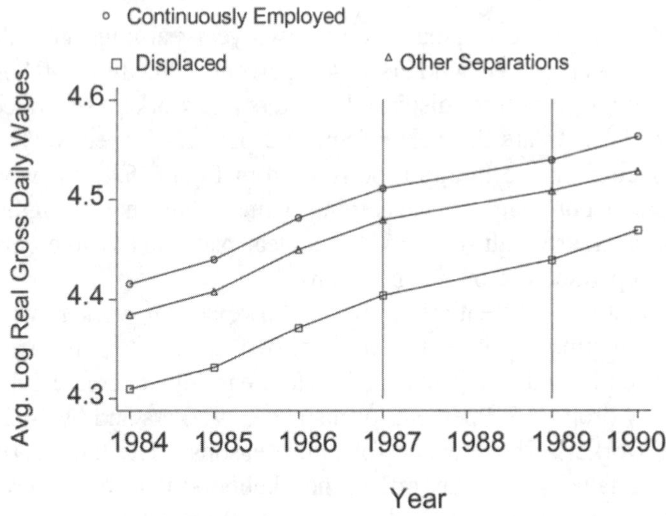

workers between the pre- and postseparation year. Another interesting point is that it appears that displaced workers have daily earnings that are, on average, lower than other sorts of workers, be they continuously employed or separated for reasons other than displacement.

Table 5.11 considers the raw averages in more detail, looking at long differences (of at least two years) in average earnings around the displacement or separation date. We distinguish among different levels of seniority (prior to separation), and among continuously employed workers, displaced workers, and workers who separate for other reasons. For the continuously employed, the table simply provides two-year differences in average earnings. For displaced and separated workers, the numbers refer to the earnings difference between the new job in the year after the separation occurs and the old job in the year prior to the separation. Obviously, this includes only workers who have found a job in the year after separation. The columns "Displaced I" and "Separated I" report earnings growth of workers who are observed in employment, at the earliest, two calendar years after separation. Although the earnings data are top coded—overall, 12.7 percent of the sample is affected in 1983 (see data section for details)—we do not account for this in Table 5.11. This point is considered explicitly below.

Table 5.11 indicates that average two-year earnings growth for continuously employed workers is 4.6 percent. Pre- to postdisplacement earnings growth for displaced workers and workers separated for unknown reasons are 2.8 percent and 3.2 percent, respectively. The numbers confirm the intuition derived from Figure 5.4 that workers who separate continue to make earnings gains. Gains have a slight tendency to decrease with seniority, but a clear pattern is visible only for workers separated for unknown reasons.

The picture looks entirely different, however, for workers who are only able to find a job, at the earliest, two years after displacement ("Displaced I" and "Separated I"). Here earnings decrease substantially: they drop by 7.3 percent for displaced workers and by 14.2 percent for workers who separate for other reasons. The large earnings loss of the latter group may reflect the likelihood that this group consists mainly of workers who have been laid off for cause.

A problem in our data is that we observe closures only at the plant level. Therefore, some plants may disappear due to reorganization, and workers may continue to work in the same firm, but in a plant with a different identifier. Although this event is not likely to be frequent, it may distort our results. On the basis of the data we have available, it is not possible to sort out these "false" plant closures.

Workers whose plants disappear because of a reorganization should appear as direct transitions. We have therefore computed earnings losses for displaced workers who have experienced a non-employment spell after separation lasting at least one week. This will most likely eliminate workers who change plant numbers for reorganizational reasons. However, it also restricts the sample to lower quality workers—workers who are not able to find a new job immediately. Accordingly, the corresponding numbers may be seen as lower bounds for earnings losses incurred by displacement. We report these results in the column, "Displaced II." A total of 644 displaced workers experience a non-employment spell of at least six days after displacement and are reemployed in the year after displacement. Their average earnings loss is –1.46 percent. Earnings losses are clearly higher for workers with higher levels of seniority before displacement. This may be an age effect, or it may indicate the loss of firm-specific human capital incurred by these workers.

We conclude from these numbers that average losses incurred by displacement are, in the worst case, around 1.5 percent. At the same time, those workers who are continuously employed experience an earnings increase of about 4.6 percent. Assuming that this number reflects the earnings growth that workers who are displaced would have experienced had their plants not closed down, the worst case scenario is that the decline in earnings growth associated with a plant-closure-related displacement is about 6 percent. More serious earnings losses are experienced by workers who are not able to rejoin the labor market in the year after displacement, however.

Regression Analysis of Pre- and Postseparation Earnings

In this section, we compare the pre- and postseparation earnings paths of displaced and continuously employed workers more generally. As a descriptive tool, we estimate simple earnings regressions on various subpopulations. The general estimation strategy is as follows.[59]

We regress the logarithm earnings on time-invariant and time-varying individual specific characteristics (x_i and z_{it}), time effects δ, and a vector of indicator variables k_{is}, which switch from 0 to 1 s years after separation, or $-s$ years before separation. Depending on the specification, the coefficients on the k_{is} variables measure the difference in the level of earnings of workers s years before or after separation and the earnings of either continuously employed workers, or the difference in earnings with respect to other workers who separate for the same reason measured in a reference year,[60] conditional on time effects and observable individual characteristics. We also add the variables $ks_{\iota\varpi}$ which take on the value 1 in the after-separation period for those individuals who are not observed in employment in the year after separation. The parameter on these variables, ξ, picks up a negative permanent effect for those individuals who remain out of work for more than one year after separation. Finally, u_{it} is a disturbance term. Thus, our estimation equation is as follows:

$$\text{(2)} \quad \ln \omega_{it} = X_i \beta_1 + z_{it} \beta_2 + \delta_t + \sum_{r \in \omega} ks_{ir} + u_{it},$$

where (w) is the set of postseparation dates and (A) is the set of pre- and postseparation dates (with or without an indicator for the year immediately preceding separation, depending on the specification).

France

The results of estimating this model on average daily earnings in France are shown in Table 5.12.[61] To ease interpretation of the results, we replace the indicator variable for five years before separation with an indicator variable that takes on the value 1 for all individuals who separate (the variable Separated). This allows us to sweep out the average difference between separators and the continuously employed, and we can interpret the coefficients on the other relative year indicators (Sep_i) in terms of an earnings path for workers who separate.

The first column compares workers who are displaced because of plant closure between 1984 and 1989 with workers who are continuously employed over that period. The second column compares continuously employed workers with workers who separate for unknown reasons. As mentioned above, these latter separations consist of voluntary quits and firings for cause. The variable *Perm* takes on the value 1 in all years following the first separation if it took the individual more than 12 months to find a job after displacement. As mentioned above, the variable Separate takes on the value 1 for all workers who separate, and the Sep_i variables assume the value 1 in the ith year prior to or following the worker's first separation. Thus the coefficient on *Separate* can be interpreted as the difference in earnings five years prior to separation for workers who will eventually separate from their employers relative to the continuously employed, and the coefficients on the Sep_i variables are interpreted as variations in earnings for workers who will eventually separate relative to their earnings five years before separation. Note that we are considering only the first separation as the reference in these regressions, and that we have excluded earnings in the separation year for workers who separate. The reason is that the earnings in the separation year may come from both pre- and postseparation employers, and the interpretation of this coefficient would be unclear.

Table 5.12 shows that, even after controlling for observable individual characteristics, workers who separate because of firm closure earn 8.8 percent less than continuously employed workers five years prior to the actual separation.[62] This could be due in part to unobserved heterogeneity across individuals, in other words, to individuals employed by firms that will close who would be earning less anyway.[63] Alternatively, it could be that low-wage firms have a higher risk of going out of business than better paying firms.[64]

This gap increases slightly as the displacement date approaches, with the dip being significant only in the year immediately preceding displacement, in which earnings of displaced workers are approximately 2.8 percent lower than they were five years before displacement. Workers who separate for reasons other than firm closure start with earnings closer to the continuously employed (5.4 percent below), but the preseparation dip starts sooner (three years prior to separation) and is much larger, with earnings in the year preceding separation being approximately 5.1 percent lower than they were five years before separation.

Table 5.12 also shows that both displaced workers and other separators make earnings gains between the year before separation and the year after separation. However, as suggested by Figure 5.3 and Table 5.10, there is a significant additional penalty to taking a long time to find a job after separation. For displaced workers, slow job finders earn an extra 4.7 percent less than other displaced workers postseparation, while the penalty for slow job finding is more than twice as large (10.1 percent) for workers who separate for other reasons. The result for displaced workers could be interpreted in the context of a declining reservation wage, in which case workers who take longer to find jobs would have, on average, lower reemployment wages. On top of this "penalty" comes an additional negative signal for workers who separate for other reasons: For workers who take longer than a year to find a new job, the separations are more likely to have been firings for cause than voluntary quits, and thus these workers would receive, on average, lower wage offers as the market infers that they have a lower value of marginal product.

Finally, the earnings path in the postseparation period shows that, on average, the gains made by workers around the separation date are eliminated and become losses as time passes, so that displaced workers five years after displacement are earning essentially the same as they were earning in the year immediately preceding displacement. The postseparation decline is not as dramatic for workers who separate for other reasons. Given the concave form of seniority returns in France, such a pattern is surprising, since returns are steepest in the first few years with an employer.[65] This declining pattern may suggest that our specification of a fixed-intercept shift in the postseparation period for all slow job finders may not be a flexible enough functional form to capture the heterogeneity in earnings that is correlated with the speed of reentry into the labor market.[66]

Germany

Parameter estimates of Equation 2 for Germany, where we use the sample of displaced workers and the year preceding displacement as the reference earning level are displayed in Table 5.13. All regressions are tobit specifications, which take care of the top coding occurring in our data. The first column includes all workers who separate from a plant that closes down within two years of the worker's departure. Relative to the workers' average earnings in the year before a closure, displacement leads to a 1–2 percent wage decrease in the years after closure; four years after closure, their wage disadvantage relative to their position before a closure becomes insignificant. Workers who are not observed in employment in the year after displacement face a permanent additional wage loss of about 19 percent. Wages more than one year before displacement do not vary much from wages in the predisplacement year.

We have run the same regression, using our alternative definitions for displacement. When considering a worker as displaced if he separates from a firm within one year of the firm's closing down (which reduces the number of observations to 13,539), the permanent loss for workers who have not rejoined the labor market in the year after displacement is again 19 percent; the average wage loss in the three years after displacement is 3 percent. Using the third definition (contraction by at least 40 percent), the respective numbers are 20 percent and 4.3 percent (this corresponds to 35,031 observations). All these numbers are fairly close, indicating that our results are quite robust to the definition of a displacement.

The second column in Table 5.13 reports results for displaced workers who experienced a non-employment spell of at least six days after separation. The permanent effect of not having found a job in the year after displacement reduces now to 12 percent (which is probably due to a change in average wages of the reference group). Displacement is associated with a wage loss in the first job in the year after displacement of 4.1 percent, and of 2.0 percent two years after displacement, both relative to wages in the year before displacement. The difference becomes insignificant thereafter.

These results, which are quite robust to different definitions of displacement and different samples indicate that wage losses of displaced workers relative to their predisplacement wages are fairly moderate. Furthermore, there is a slight decline of wages in the three years before separation. As already indicated in Table 5.11, losses are substantial if the worker does not find a job in the year after separation.

In Table 5.13 we compare the wage position of a displaced worker after displacement to his predisplacement wage. Next, we estimate a specification similar to the one underlying the results in Table 5.13, where this time we pool displaced workers (or workers separated for unknown reasons) and continuously employed workers. We add an additional indicator variable for the year immediately preceding displacement. This gives us the wage profile of displaced (separated) workers, relative to continuously employed workers, in the years before and after displacement. Results are displayed in Table 5.14.

As already indicated in Figure 5.4, wages of displaced workers are, on average, 10 percentage points lower than wages of continuously employed workers. This difference may be due to firm effects, or may be a result of workers of lower quality selecting into firms which close down. The immediate pre- to post-wage difference is again small—about 0.9 percent. Compared with continuously employed workers, displaced workers continue to have lower wages. Again, those who are not in work in the year after displacement suffer substantial permanent losses.

The second column displays results for workers who separate from their firm for unknown reasons. Here, wages begin to decline about two years before separation, but do not differ from those of continuously employed workers before that. After separation, wages are on average 4 percentage points lower, as compared to those of continuously employed workers. Again, workers who have not found a job in the years after displacement suffer substantial losses.

DISCUSSION AND CONCLUSIONS

In this section, we bring together the results from the two countries and briefly relate them to the existing literature from North American studies of worker displacement. It bears repeating that we focus on prime-age men in stable jobs (at least four years of job seniority). Furthermore, our definition of displacement, used throughout this chapter, is a separation within two years of firm closure in France and within two years of plant closure in Germany.

Incidence

Worker displacement seems to be slightly more frequent in France than in Germany.[67] Among our sample of high-seniority workers, 2.78 percent experienced a displacement in France in 1984, whereas 6.71 percent of eligible German men had a displacement as their first separation during the 1984–1990 window (a seven-year interval). This suggests that a lower bound on annual incidence of worker displacement due to plant closures might be below 1 percent in Germany. Both of these numbers, and the German figures in particular, are lower than what has been found for the United States; Farber (1997) found a probability of experiencing a displacement of 6.9 percent for the 1984–1985 two-year period using the Displaced Worker Supplements of the Current Population Survey. However, this may be due largely to the fact that Farber (1993) considered all self-reported displacements, whereas (for data reasons) we restrict our attention to firm and plant closures.[68]

As a share of total separations, worker displacements are more important in France than in Germany. Part of this difference may be due to our different definitions of displacement (firm closure in France, plant closure in Germany).

In both France and Germany, age is not significantly related to the probability of displacement. The highest levels of education are negatively related to the probability of being displaced in both countries as is seniority in 1984. All of these results are generally consistent with what has been found for the United States (Fallick 1996).

Duration

In both France and Germany, a large share of displaced workers transit to their subsequent employers without spending any time in non-employment. The share of direct transitions is always higher for displaced workers than for workers who separate for other reasons, and the share of displaced workers making direct transitions increases slightly with seniority. There is a larger share of direct transitions in the German data than in the French data, which may be due to the differences in the definitions of displacement (firm closure in France versus plant closure in Germany).

The durations of spells out of the workforce, when they occur, are shorter in both countries for displaced workers than for those who separate for other reasons. The long-term non-employment rate for displaced workers in France seems slightly lower (around 20 percent after five years) than that of Germany (around 27 percent), and the gap in the survivor functions between displaced and other separating workers is larger in Germany. Recall that our administrative data suffer from the problem of censoring—some individuals do not return into the labor force after separating from their job within the observation window. They may have changed into other states, like self-employment (in Germany), or retirement, or they may have left the country. Therefore, one has to be cautious when interpreting these results as durations in non-employment.

Estimations of duration models confirm the faster exit of displaced workers in both countries. However, displaced workers with high seniority tend to leave non-employment more slowly than those with low seniority in France, whereas the reverse is true in Germany.[69]

Earnings Changes

In both countries, we find a result that is contrary to the majority of North American results on worker displacement. Displacement does not seem to be associated with large earnings losses. In the French case, average daily earnings of displaced workers actually increase, relative to continuously employed workers, between the year preceding and the year following displacement. In Germany there is still a small drop in average daily earnings relative to continuously employed workers, but the drop is less than 1 percent in relative earnings terms. One explanation for our different results may be the way the earnings variable is constructed: While we use data on daily earnings, which are calculated using employment periods only, many North American studies use data on quarterly or yearly earnings, without taking account of the number of days worked. Furthermore, some studies (Jacobson, LaLonde, and Sullivan 1993) substitute zero earnings for workers who are not in work, while we construct our comparisons conditional on employment.

We do find an important earnings differential associated with taking longer than a year to find a new job following displacement for both countries. In France, this corresponds to a 5 percent earnings disadvantage relative to other displaced workers who are reemployed within the calendar year following displacement, while it is between 13 and 20 percent in relative terms in Germany.

CONCLUSION

In conclusion, the labor markets of France and Germany, although different along certain dimensions, seem to provide roughly similar outcomes for displaced workers. One reason for these similarities may be similar institutional regulations, like employment protection offered by labor law. Our analysis is purely descriptive and we have not attempted to attribute findings, and differences from the North American literature, to differences in institutional regulations. This is a promising avenue for future research.

Notes

1. See, for example, Bonnal and Fougère (1993, 1996) for France, and Hunt (1995) for Germany.
2. Note that our age selection criteria are designed to eliminate retirement as a destination after separation from one's employer.
3. See Fallick (1996) for a survey.

4. French labor law distinguishes between layoffs for economic reasons and layoffs for personal reasons, such as inadequate performance or misconduct.
5. There are special considerations for large companies that lay off at least 10 people over a 3-month period without passing the 10-people-in-30-day limit, but these will not be treated here.
6. The links between the unemployment benefits schedules and eligibility requirements are quite complicated. What is presented here is a short synopsis of the important points of the unemployment insurance law prior to the substantial reforms that took place in 1996.
7. A worker can qualify by satisfying any one of these criteria: a) 122 days or 676 hours of work over the 8 months preceding the end of the labor contract; b) 192 days or 1,014 hours of work over the 12 months preceding the end of the labor contract; c) 243 days or 1,352 hours of work over the 12 months preceding the end of the labor contract; d) 426 days or 2,366 hours of work over the 24 months preceding the end of the labor contract; or 821 days or 4,563 hours of work over the 36 months preceding the end of the labor contract. The end of the labor contract is defined as the last day of the notice period, regardless of whether this was bought off or not. Workers who become unemployed due to the closure of their plant are not required to satisfy criterion "a." The levels and duration of benefits vary according to the criterion satisfied, with the most difficult criterion, "e," providing the highest benefits. Criterion "e" entitles the worker to higher and longer benefits than "b."
8. Note that the eligibility rules for unemployment insurance give the worker the incentive to declare all separations as involuntary, while the administrative procedures described above give the firm the incentive to declare separations as voluntary. This conflict of interest often introduces a bargaining situation in the case where the employer intends to lay off a small number of workers. The firm can make side payments to the worker such that the worker declares the separation as voluntary (if asked) and does not apply for unemployment benefits. Anecdotal evidence suggests that this is a relatively frequent phenomenon.
9. Note that, upon expiration of unemployment benefits, individuals may be eligible for the Minimum Insertion Allowance (Revenu minimum d'insertion, or RMI). The RMI is a means-tested income support that has conditions and levels not directly linked to unemployment duration, previous wages, or labor market histories.
10. See Margolis (1993) for a detailed discussion of the institutional context surrounding contract extension in France, as well as an analysis of the implications of contract extension for wage setting and firm participation in employers' associations.
11. See Bughin (1985).
12. The inflation threshold was removed in 1970 with the reform that converted the SMIG into the SMIC.
13. For a detailed analysis of the minimum wage in France, see Abowd, Kramarz, Margolis, and Philippon (2000).

14. It has been complemented by the *Arbeitsschutzbereinigungsgesetz* (1969), the *Betriebsverfassungsgesetz* (1972), and the *Gesetz zur Anderung des KSchG* (1978), among others.
15. The differential treatment of blue- and white-collar workers was abolished in October 1993. We report here the regulations that were in force up to 1993, since our data covers the period up to 1990.
16. If an unemployed person fulfills the above criteria, the minimum period of eligibility is 156 days. Depending on the duration of contribution payments and the age of the applicant, this period can be extended to up to 832 days (see Kittner 1995, p. 192, for details).
17. An exhaustive DADS data set file does exist for use primarily by the tax authorities, but we were only given access to the 1/25 sample.
18. Note that these data include self-employed workers who pay themselves salaries. Self-employed workers who act as pure residual claimants will not be included. Unfortunately, the data do not allow us to separate self-employed wage earners from other wage earners.
19. Our earnings data are available as 8-byte numeric variables and are subject to neither top nor bottom coding. All labor earnings are reported.
20. See Abowd, Finer, Kramarz, and Roux (1997) for details. Given that our analysis sample begins in 1984 and that we consider seniority as a categorical variable for which the largest category is more than 10 years, our results are robust to most estimation error in the job start date due to the imputation for the left-censored spells.
21. For individuals for whom EDP data are not available, we use a multinomial logit to impute the probability that the individual had each of the educational degrees possible. See the data appendix of Abowd, Kramarz, Margolis, and Philippon (1999) for more details.
22. From 1988–1992 (1990 excluded), INSEE introduced two variables distinguishing whether the observation corresponded to a plant that had ceased to exist as an "economic" or "administrative" entity. The main difference between these variables is that firms occasionally continue to exist "administratively," but with zero workers, after their "economic" death. The manner by which mergers and acquisitions affect the plant identifier in our data is rather involved. Unfortunately, these data have serious inconsistencies, as individuals whose observations correspond to the economic or administrative death of their plant in the year t are just as likely to still be employed by the plant, and receiving a salary, in the year $t + 1$ as they are to have separated from the plant. Thus we do not consider these variables informative for the analysis of worker displacements.
23. Our approach to defining displacements is based on a combination of firm account data and payroll data. An alternative approach, such as considering separations that occur simultaneously with large reductions in firm employment as displacements (see Jacobson, LaLonde, and Sullivan 1993), is not feasible with our data, as firm employment is not available for all employees at all dates.

24. The SUSE data used here are a sample of enterprises in France with differential sampling probabilities based on reporting requirements which vary with employment (the largest firms appear with probability 1). Depending on the size of the firm and the type of accounts it sends to the relevant regulating and tax authorities, information may be available on a detailed balance sheet, income statement, and flow-of-funds statement. The smaller enterprises are not required to provide as much detailed information. Here we use the presence of *any* information on the firm as a sign of its continued existence. Therefore, we do not lose firms when they pass below the threshold for providing detailed accounts.
25. For separations in years prior to 1996, the firm clearly continues to exist, as workers employed by it are observed. For 1996, we are unable to determine whether the firm will disappear in 1997. These observations could theoretically be considered displacements, but given our eventual sample selection restrictions (see below), the question of how to classify these observations is moot.
26. The requirement that there be at least three observed employees means that, in expectation, the corresponding firm has at least 75 employees. It prevents us from arbitrarily classifying all departures from small firms as false firm deaths. On the other hand, it may cause us to miss all false firm deaths among the smallest firms in our sample. Unfortunately, given that we only have access to the 1/25 sample of employment, we cannot improve upon the treatment for small firms beyond the SUSE sampling scheme. SUSE data are available from financial reports that are mandatory for firms with total sales of at least 500,000 F per year (or at least 150,000 F per year for firms in service industries) and are optional for all others.
27. We are grateful to Peter Kuhn for suggesting this algorithm.
28. We consider the year preceding the year of firm death since, with SUSE data at least, we do not know the precise date within the year at which the firm ceased operations. Furthermore, a firm whose fiscal year ends after June 30 of the year $t + 1$ will have year $t + 1$ SUSE information, even if operations ceased in year t.
29. Results based on the more strict definition of displacement, considering only those separations occurring within one year of firm disappearance, are available upon request. A table indicative of the importance of the definitional differences can be found in Appendix B.
30. There exist other data sources that allow us to identify layoffs at the plant level and to classify them by type (economic or personal reasons). However, these data do not allow us to tell *which* workers are among those laid off, and they are subject to an even more restrictive sampling scheme than the SUSE data. One possible avenue for future research might assign a probability that a separation corresponds to a layoff for economic reasons, as opposed to relying on a simple indicator variable to denote that reason for each separation.
31. Margolis (1999) and Margolis (2000) treat both men and women.
32. Because of the complex interplay between youth employment-promotion schemes (for which eligibility ends at 25 years of age) and the minimum wage in France (see Abowd, Kramarz, Lemieux, and Margolis 2000), we begin considering individuals after they become 26 years old.

33. Note that this does not mean that there will be no workers with seniority of less than four years in our data. In particular, for the earnings-change models, we use postseparation information during which workers who have experienced a separation will typically have less than four years of seniority.
34. This latter constraint eliminates 15.2 percent of the individuals from the DADS and 16.7 percent of the individual-year combinations that satisfy our eligibility criterion (26- to 50-year-old men with at least four years of seniority in some job in 1984). In particular, 32.7 percent of the yearly observations corresponding to workers whose first separation was a displacement, and 28.6 percent of the yearly observations of workers whose first separation was for other reasons, are eliminated due to the restriction against simultaneous job holding. This may bias our results. Similar models that allow for simultaneous job holding are estimated in Margolis (1999, 2000).
35. Note that the entire, nonselected sample was used in the determination of firm "death" dates.
36. In order to give a more accurate picture of the incidence of worker displacement, we consider all separations in our sample. Considering only first separations would severely underestimate the incidence of worker displacement in the later years of our sample.
37. The duration analyses are based on data with one observation per individual, corresponding to the first separation observed in our sample window.
38. As our data do not allow us to measure revenues from non-labor-market sources, our earnings measure is available only for years in which labor market earnings are strictly positive.
39. It should be noted, however, that using such a measure can obscure the role of part-time employment on earnings (Farber 1999). Margolis (1999) shows how conclusions concerning earnings movements are sensitive to the earnings measure, in particular by comparing log(annual earnings) with log(daily earnings) measures.
40. Accordingly, the sample is left-truncated and right-censored. The truncation refers to the lowest level of earnings for which social security contributions are obligatory; the right-censoring refers to the highest level of earnings subject to contributions.
41. While we observe separations of workers at the exact date of occurrence, information on plant size is measured at a fixed date each year. Plant size refers to employment in June of the relevant year. Accordingly, the time of closure cannot be exactly dated.
42. Recall that we are looking only at permanent separations in this chapter and that individuals who spend less than a full calendar year on temporary layoff are not therefore considered as separators.
43. The discussion that follows supposes that the separations attributed to 1989 were more or less evenly distributed between 1989 and 1990.

44. Recall that we are using separations in the two calendar years preceding the calendar year in which the firm identified disappears as our criterion for distinguishing displacements from other separations.
45. Women in France are guaranteed eight weeks of maternity leave by law, of which two are indented to be taken before childbirth and six after. However, collective agreements often extend the durations of available maternity leave, sometimes to 16 weeks or more. Furthermore, the employment relation is not interrupted because of maternity leave, and the woman is guaranteed a comparable position to the one she left upon returning from maternity leave.
46. These results concerning incidence of displacement are comparable to the studies cited by Fallick (1996), who noted that job seniority was negatively related to the incidence of displacement in the United States.
47. The fact that the share of displacements in total separations is lower for 50- to 55-year-olds than for 35- to 40-year-olds suggests that the phenomenon generating the additional separations is not necessarily linked to firm closure.
48. Appendix G presents the results of a similar estimation, but there the reference group is only those workers who remain continuously employed with the same employer throughout the 1984–1989 sample window.
49. Our distinction between displaced and separated workers refers to the reason for the first separation after being in continuous employment between 1980 and 1984.
50. Recall that separation status refers to the first separation only.
51. In France, we treat all spells that do not end before December 31, 1989, as censored.
52. Informal discussions with ASSEDIC administrators suggest that, in 1998 at least, approximately one-third of individuals drawing unemployment insurance exhausted their benefits. These figures are roughly consistent with the survivor function measured a decade earlier and shown in Figure 5.1.
53. The estimated Kaplan-Meier hazards underlying Figure 5.1 are roughly linear and decreasing in the log of the hazard rate, which suggests that a Weibull-distributed baseline hazard is the most appropriate parametric specification. Semiparametric (Cox) models were not estimable under the material constraints (memory allocation and CPU time) imposed by INSEE.
54. Note that, since the parameter estimates refer to the proportionality factor in the hazard function, a positive coefficient means that higher levels of the corresponding variable are associated with higher values of the hazard function and thus shorter expected non-employment durations.
55. Benefit payments are proportional to the most recent earnings prior to separation.
56. Jacobson, LaLonde, and Sullivan (1993), on the other hand, supposed that workers not in employment after separation had zero earnings and kept these workers in the sample for the calculation of their average earnings changes.
57. Note that the earnings change for other separators combines individuals who left their jobs for better outside offers with workers who were fired for cause and workers who were laid off from firms that did not shut down within the following two calendar years.

58. One might ask why displaced workers did not leave earlier if they were going to have such large earnings gains associated with changing employers. There are several possible explanations. First, the employment-protection legislation provided them with job security with their previous employer that they stood to lose if they changed earlier. The prospect of imminent firm closure reduced the value of this nonwage component of job-specific utility, however, thus making outside offers relatively more attractive. A second possible explanation is that the offer arrival rate for on-the-job search may be lower than that for off-the-job search (or search during the notice period). In this case, workers whose first separation was a displacement may simply not have received another offer prior to their separation. A third explanation is that 1988 was a good year for the French economy, with 3.95 percent GDP growth, relative to an average of 1.51 percent over the 1984–1987 period (BLS Macroeconomic Statistics, http://stats.bls.gov/flsdata.htm). As such, there may have been better outside offers in 1988 than in earlier years. Finally, since postdisplacement wages are only measured for reemployed workers, the sample of workers contributing to the 1986 and 1988 averages are not the same. In particular, the set of workers employed in 1988 may not be representative of all workers displaced in 1987.
59. Our estimation strategy resembles that of Jacobson, LaLonde, and Sullivan (1993).
60. For France, the reference year is five years prior to separation. For Germany (see Table 5.13), it is the year immediately preceding separation.
61. See Margolis (1999) for estimates of this model using log(total annual earnings) as the dependent variable. Margolis (2000) estimated a similar model but with individual fixed effects.
62. Note that, for a given coefficient β on a regressor x in Tables 5.12–5.14, _log(y) = βx. To calculate the *percentage* change in y induced by x, i.e., $(y_{t+1} - y_t)/y_t$, one typically makes use of the approximation $\log(1 + x) = x$. This approximation is not valid when x is far from zero, and thus the coefficients are not directly interpretable as percentage changes in the dependent variable. For this reason, we have used the exact formula, i.e., $(y_{t+1} - y_t)/y_t = \exp(\beta) - 1$, in the discussion of these tables.
63 See Margolis (1999) for further analyses in this direction.
64. Abowd et al. (1999) show that the firm-specific component of earnings is negatively related to the probability of firm survival on the same DADS and SUSE data, but the estimates are relatively imprecise.
65. See Margolis (1996) for a detailed analysis of returns to seniority in France.
66. Margolis (2000) estimated a similar specification with individual fixed effects on a data set that does not eliminate individuals with simultaneous job holding and found that the size of the postseparation decline in average daily earnings was reduced, but not eliminated. One alternative strategy, as used by Jacobson, LaLonde, and Sullivan (1993), might be to include all workers in the postseparation period, but to attribute zero earnings to workers who have yet to find jobs.

67. A word of warning is necessary when comparing our results for incidence. The figures for France refer to the number of individuals who experience a type of separation per year, while the numbers for Germany refer to the number of individuals whose first separation in a seven-year period is of a given type. Thus, the figures are not directly comparable; nevertheless, we attempt to draw some conclusions below.
68. Given that the Displaced Worker Supplements are survey based, they may be subject to measurement error as a result of individuals misreporting firings for cause as layoffs.
69. As a comparison, Swaim and Podgursky (1991) found that the rate of exit from non-employment among displaced workers decreased with seniority in the United States.

Table 5.1 Incidence of Permanent Separations of Long-Tenure Workers by Year in France

Year[a]	Total observations	Total separations	Total displacements	Other separations	Separations in total (%)	Displaced in total (%)
Men						
1984	99,479	8,309	2,821	5,584	8.35	2.84
1985	95,842	8,620	3,487	5,244	8.99	3.64
1986	93,009	8,730	3,365	5,478	9.39	3.62
1987	91,458	10,517	3,633	7,000	11.63	4.02
1988	86,479	8,439	3,557	5,006	9.73	4.10
1989	85,317	15,459	6,349	9,380	18.12	7.44
Σ	550,854	60,074	23,212	37,649	10.91	4.21
Women						
1984	57,595	5,274	2,142	3,172	9.16	3.72
1985	54,588	5,113	2,044	3,119	9.37	3.74
1986	52,267	5,275	2,245	3,069	10.09	4.30
1987	50,226	5,094	1,895	3,242	10.14	3.77
1988	48,699	4,790	1,888	2,961	9.84	3.88
1989	47,465	8,184	3,301	5,010	17.24	6.95
Σ	310,840	33,730	13,515	20,573	10.85	4.35

NOTE: Long tenure = four or more years.

[a] Multiple observations in the same year are aggregated to the unique individual-year level.

SOURCE: Authors' calculations from DADS data.

Table 5.2 Incidence of Permanent Separation by Previous Seniority and Age in France in 1984

Group (years)	Total observations	Total separations[a]	Total displacements	Other separations	Separations in total (%)	Displaced in total (%)	Displaced in separations (%)
4 ≤ Seniority < 6	19,920	2,488	728	1,760	12.49	3.65	29.26
6 ≤ Seniority < 8	24,026	2,235	753	1,482	9.30	3.13	33.69
8 ≤ Seniority <10	2,791	259	124	135	9.28	4.44	47.88
≤ 10 Seniority	52,742	3,327	1,163	2,164	6.31	2.21	34.96
Σ	99,479	8,309	2,768	5,541	8.35	2.78	33.31
25 ≤ Age < 30	11,963	1,135	406	752	9.49	3.39	35.77
30 ≤ Age <35	26,154	2,267	765	1,523	8.67	2.92	33.75
35 ≤ Age < 40	19,431	1,553	539	1,034	7.99	2.77	34.71
40 ≤ Age <45	20,400	1,560	528	1,043	7.65	2.59	33.85
45 ≤ Age < 50	14,322	1,112	351	774	7.76	2.45	31.56
50 ≤ Age < 55	7,209	682	232	458	9.46	3.22	34.02
Σ	99,479	8,309	2,821	5,584	8.35	2.84	33.95

NOTE: Multiple observations in the same year are aggregated to the unique individual-year level. Numbers refer to the 1984 data year.

[a] Of these individuals, 96 experienced both displacements and other separations in 1984. Only the first separation is counted in the displacements and other separations columns in the top half of the table, as the second separations are (by design) from low-seniority jobs.

SOURCE: Authors' calculations from DADS data.

Table 5.3 Probit Models of Incidence of Separation, Total and by Type of Separation Relative to All Alternative States for France in 1984

Variable	Displacements		Other separations		All separations	
Age	–0.0048	(0.0136)	–0.0077	(0.0108)	–0.0065	(0.0096)
Age^2/100	0.0081	(0.0177)	0.0146	(0.0139)	0.0126	(0.0124)
4 ≤ Seniority < 6	0.1400***	(0.0224)	0.3563***	(0.0178)	0.3236***	(0.0155)
6 ≤ Seniority <8	0.1016***	(0.0215)	0.1849***	(0.0170)	0.1784***	(0.0150)
8 ≤ Seniority < 10	0.1378***	(0.0463)	0.0194	(0.0436)	0.0884**	(0.0362)
Elementary school	–0.0895	(0.0689)	–0.0047	(0.0550)	–0.0326	(0.0487)
Junior high school	0.0918	(0.1020)	0.0185	(0.0852)	0.0584	(0.0743)
High school	0.1011	(0.1262)	0.1022	(0.1013)	0.0783	(0.0912)
Basic vocational school	–0.0748	(0.0658)	–0.1150**	(0.0541)	–0.1113**	(0.0474)
Advanced vocational school	–0.2412**	(0.1184)	–0.0812	(0.0846)	–0.1472*	(0.0767)
Undergraduate	0.1072	(0.1185)	0.1829**	(0.0911)	0.1787**	(0.0821)
Graduate school and grande école	–0.0696	(0.1114)	0.3318***	(0.0772)	0.2452***	(0.0711)
Constant	–2.2219***	(0.2755)	–1.6680***	(0.2144)	–1.5684***	(0.1911)
No. of obs.	99,479		99,479		99,479	
Log likelilhood	–12,251		–20,886		–27,552	

NOTE: Standard errors are in parentheses. Estimates include data from 1984 only, aggregated to one observation per individual. All models also include controls for previous seniority, sector (15 categories) and skill level (3 categories). Reference groups: No educational certification and 10 or more years of seniority. Models estimate probability of specified type of separation relative to all alternative situations. *** = Statistically significant at the 1% level; ** = statistically signiticant at the 5% level; * = statistically significant at the 10% level..

Table 5.4 Breakdown of Separations by Type and Seniority for Germany

Variable	Continuously employed	Total	Other separations	Displacements	Displaced (%) In separations	Displaced (%) In total
4 ≤ Seniority < 6	5,246	4,285	3,596	689	16.07	7.23
6 ≤ Seniority < 8	4,505	3,009	2,395	614	20.40	8.17
8 ≤ Seniority < 10	8,539	4,913	3,806	1,107	22.53	8.23
10 ≤ Seniority	14,304	3,999	3,136	863	21.58	4.72
Σ	32,594	16,206	12,933	3,273	20.19	6.71
25 ≤ Age < 30	4,066	2,686	2,214	472	17.57	6.99
30 ≤ Age < 40	10,746	5,921	4,795	1,126	19.01	6.76
40 ≤ Age < 50	14,830	6,243	4,870	1,373	21.99	6.52
50 ≤ Age	2,952	1,356	1,054	302	22.27	7.01
Σ	32,594	16,206	12,933	3,273	20.19	6.71

NOTE: Seniority and age refer to 1984.
SOURCE: Authors' calculations from IAB data.

Table 5.5 Probability of Displacement or Separation between 1984 and 1990 in Germany—Marginal Effects

Variable	Displacements		Other separations	
Age/100	0.005	(0.020)	–0.238***	(0.030)
5 ≤ Seniority <7	0.003	(0.004)	–0.039***	(0.006)
7 ≤ Seniority <9	–0.014***	(0.003)	–0.088***	(0.005)
9 ≤ Seniority	–0.035***	(0.003)	–0.153***	(0.005)
Apprentice, no high school	0.008***	(0.003)	–0.006	(0.005)
No apprentice, high school	–0.023	(0.019)	0.052	(0.032)
Apprentice, high school	0.016	(0.015)	0.046**	(0.020)
Polytechnic	–0.028***	(0.007)	0.061***	(0.012)
University	–0.018**	(0.009)	0.141***	(0.014)
Education unknown	0.026***	(0.008)	0.053***	(0.011)
Sector				
2: Energy	–0.085***	(0.001)	–0.189	(0.014)
3: Mining	–0.062***	(0.005)	0.119***	(0.031)
4: Manufacturing	–0.146	(0.012)	–0.092***	(0.022)
5: Construction	–0.038***	(0.007)	–0.001	(0.023)
6: Distributional services	–0.063***	(0.006)	–0.004	(0.023)
7: Industry services	–0.078***	(0.003)	–0.055**	(0.021)
8: Consumer services	–0.069***	(0.003)	–0.081***	(0.024)
9: Public services	–0.101***	(0.003)	–0.112***	(0.019)
No. of obs.	36,689		44,402	
Probability	0.086		0.244	

NOTE: Standard errors are in parentheses. All estimations refer to 1983. Excluded categories: agricultural sector, no apprenticeship, no high school and 3 ≤ seniority <5. Comparison group: continuously employed in same plant, 1984–1990. *** = Statistically significant at the 1% level; ** = statistically significant at the 5% level.

SOURCE: Authors' calculations from IAB data.

Table 5.6 Non-Employment Spells after First Separation by Seniority in France

	All separations[a]		Displacements[b]		Other separations[c]	
Seniority level	Number	Non-empl. spell (%)[d]	Number	Non-empl. spell (%)[e]	Number	Non-empl. spell (%)[f]
4 ≤ Seniority < 6	1,699	85.40	437	79.63	1,262	87.40
6 ≤ Seniority < 8	2,912	84.38	802	81.92	2,110	85.31
8 ≤ Seniority <10	2,685	83.99	762	82.94	1,923	84.40
10 ≤ Seniority	8,998	79.06	2,406	74.44	6,592	80.75
Σ	16,294	81.48	4,407	77.79	11,887	82.86

NOTE: Statistics include only first separations and impose the retirement constraint (see text).

[a] Total number of separations, by seniority.

[b] Number of displacements.

[c] Number of other separations.

[d] Percentage of non-employment spells in total.

[e] Percentage of displacements that are followed by a positive-duration non-employment spell.

[f] Percentage of other separations that are followed by a positive-duration non-employment spell.

SOURCE: Authors' calculations from DADS data.

Table 5.7 Weibull Proportional Hazard Models for Return to Work for France

Variable	All separations		Separated for unknown reason		Displaced	
Constant	–1.4272***	(0.2757)	–1.5000***	(0.3018)	0.3903	(205.6546)
6 ≤ Seniority < 8	–0.4538***	(0.1306)	–0.4079***	(0.1429)	–0.5210***	(0.1772)
8 ≤ Seniority < 10	–0.4928***	(0.1389)	–0.4261***	(0.1528)	–0.5817***	(0.1858)
10 ≤ Seniority	–0.4807***	(0.1276)	–0.4106***	(0.1398)	–0.5827***	(0.1719)
Firm closure	0.2081**	(0.1049)	n.a.[a]	—	n.a.	—
Age	0.0080	(0.0286)	0.0064	(0.0317)	0.0102	(0.0382)
Elementary school	0.2461	(0.2101)	0.3020	(0.2333)	0.1395	(0.2776)
Junior high school	0.2906	(0.2570)	0.4343	(0.2743)	–0.0313	(0.3860)
High school	0.6020**	(0.2685)	0.6739**	(0.2967)	0.5216	(0.3601)
Basic vocational school	0.3829*	(0.2042)	0.5054**	(0.2287)	0.1283	(0.2670)
Advanced vocational school	0.4219*	(0.2530)	0.5048*	(0.2708)	0.2810	(0.3744)
Undergraduate	1.0114***	(0.2611)	1.4623***	(0.2940)	0.1666	(0.3535)
Graduate school and grande école	0.6371***	(0.2459)	0.6628**	(0.2679)	0.5379	(0.3411)
1985	–0.0187	(0.1192)	–0.0825	(0.1307)	0.1043	(0.1633)
1986	0.1601	(0.1267)	0.0811	(0.1381)	0.3163*	(0.1746)
1987	0.2202*	(0.1302)	0.1505	(0.1422)	0.3519**	(0.1782)
1988	0.1938	(0.1395)	0.1367	(0.1529)	0.2986	(0.1897)

1989	0.2968**	(0.1462)	0.1606	(0.1613)	0.5577***	(0.1984)
Weibull shape parameter	0.4335		0.4311		0.4464	
No. of obs.	13,838		10,136		3,702	
No. of failures	8,350		5,698		2,652	
Log likelihood	–25,938		–18,134		–7,701	

NOTE: Standard errors are in parentheses. Right censoring occurs when the individual is not reemployed by December 31, 1989. All models include controls for sector of preseparation firm (15 categories) and skill level (3 categories). Reference groups: 1984, 4–6 years of seniority, and no educational certification. *** = Statistically significant at the 1% level; ** = statistically significant at the 5% level; * = statistically significant at the 10% level.

[a] n.a. = not applicable.

SOURCE: Authors' calculations from DADS data.

Table 5.8 Non-Employment Spells after Separation by Seniority in Germany

	All separations[a]		Displacements[b]		Other separations[c]	
Seniority level	Number	Non-empl. spell (%)[d]	Number	Non-empl. spell (%)[e]	Number	Non-empl. spell (%)[f]
$4 \leq$ Seniority < 6	1,749	54.94	281	51.60	1,468	55.58
$6 \leq$ Seniority < 8	2,422	50.28	458	46.28	1,964	51.22
$8 \leq$ Seniority < 10	3,977	52.07	863	44.38	3,114	54.30
$10 \leq$ Seniority	8,043	46.15	16,721	33.01	6,371	49.59
Σ	16,191	49.16	3,274	39.46	12,917	51.62

[a] Total number of separations, by seniority.
[b] Number of displacements.
[c] Number of separations.
[d] Percentage of non-employment spells in total.
[e] Percentage of displacements that are followed by positive-duration non-employment spells.
[f] Percentage of separations that are followed by positive-duration non-employment spells.
SOURCE: Authors' calculations from IAB data.

Table 5.9 Cox Models for Return to Work for Germany

Variable	All separations		Separated for unknown reason		Displaced	
Age/100	–3.1258***	(0.2257)	–3.5590***	(0.2599)	–1.8075***	(0.4644)
6 ≤ Seniority < 8	0.0310	(0.0571)	0.0293	(0.0641)	0.0801	(0.1286)
8 ≤ Seniority < 10	0.0641	(0.0532)	0.0340	(0.0602)	0.2053*	(0.1178)
10 ≤ Seniority	–0.0217	(0.0617)	–0.1062	(0.0703)	0.2880**	(0.1324)
Closure	0.4035***	(0.0388)	n.a.[a]	—	n.a.	—
Apprentice, no high school	0.3749***	(0.0407)	0.4084***	(0.046)	0.2669***	(0.0826)
No apprentice, high school	0.1485	(0.3041)	0.1886	(0.3367)	–0.0092	(0.7159)
Apprentice, high school	0.0099	(0.1709)	0.3215	(0.1936)	–0.6717*	(0.3636)
Polytechnic	0.1972	(0.1309)	0.3311**	(0.1421)	–0.2354	(0.3427)
University	0.0879	(0.1276)	0.1994	(0.1302)	–1.8720*	(1.0043)
Education unknown	0.0524	(0.0721)	0.0764	(0.0842)	–0.0361	(0.1404)
1985	0.1230***	(0.0486)	0.1528***	(0.0565)	0.0886	(0.0967)
1986	0.2224***	(0.0549)	0.2278***	(0.0629)	0.2249**	(0.1143)
1987	0.1694***	(0.0621)	0.2408***	(0.0709)	–0.0342	(0.1305)
1988	0.1709***	(0.0696)	0.2146***	(0.0796)	0.0635	(0.1438)
1989	0.1533**	(0.0784)	0.2347***	(0.0884)	–0.0739	(0.1734)
1990	–0.0167	(0.1027)	–0.0879	(0.1171)	0.6807**	(0.2101)

(continued)

Table 5.9 (continued)

Variable	All separations	Separated for unknown reason	Displaced
No. of obs.	5,019	3,998	1,021
No. of failures	3,720	2,813	907
Log likelihood	–28,924	–21,269	–5,558

NOTE: Standard errors are in parentheses. Right censoring occurs when the individual is not reemployed by December 1990. Reference group: no apprenticeship, no high school. *** = Statistically significant at the 1% level; ** = statistically significant at the 5% level; * = statistically significant at the 10% level.

[a] n.a. = not applicable.

SOURCE: Authors' calculations from IAB data.

Table 5.10 Two-Period Earnings Growth by Seniority at Date of First Separation in France

	Continuously employed		All displaced		Slow displaced[a]		Other separations		Slow other separations[a]	
Group	%Δw	Obs.	%Δw	Obs.	%Δw	Obs.	%Δw	Obs.	%Δw	Obs.
4≤Seniority<6	4.70	13,712	16.62	825	–9.34	175	10.43	1,521	–12.02	349
6 ≤ Seniority < 8	4.38	35,453	12.22	1,642	1.48	213	8.91	2,180	–25.92	531
8≤Seniority<10	3.55	31,659	13.51	1,375	–3.67	154	10.05	1,464	–11.04	238
10 ≤ Seniority	2.58	138,298	9.87	4,708	–6.07	441	3.37	4,194	–23.56	556
Σ	3.15	219,122	11.88	8,550	–4.64	983	6.85	9,359	–20.12	1,674

NOTE: Data correspond to one observation per individual per year.

[a] "Slow" refers to individuals who were not reemployed in the calendar year following the separation.

SOURCE: Authors' calculations from DADS data.

Table 5.11 Two-Period Log Earnings Growth, by Seniority at Date of First Separation for Germany

Group / Seniority	Displaced		Displaced I[a]		Displaced II[b]		Separated		Separated I[c]		Cont. employed	
	%Δw	No. obs.	%Δw	No. obs.	%Δw	No. obs.	%Δw	No. obs.	%Δw	No. obs.	%Δw	No. obs.
4 ≤ Seniority < 6	2.44	242	–20.43	15	0.83	89	4.58	1,048	–8.21	102	3.50	12,603
6 ≤ Seniority < 8	5.74	397	7.04	22	2.60	111	4.31	1,422	–12.72	107	3.98	22,305
8 ≤ Seniority < 10	1.93	737	–3.42	41	–2.10	190	2.94	1,979	–13.07	135	4.82	50,482
10 ≤ Seniority	2.36	1,288	–15.45	34	–3.57	254	2.46	3,273	–23.66	113	3.14	167,374
Σ	2.75	2,665	–7.29	112	–1.46	644	3.21	7,730	–14.24	458	4.64	255,331

[a] Workers who have not found a job in the year after displacement.
[b] Workers who experience a non-employment spell of at least one week after displacement.
SOURCE: Authors' calculations.

Table 5.12 Log Average Real Daily Earnings Regressions for France

Variable	Displacements		Other separations	
Separated[a]	–0.0917***	(0.0068)	–0.0553***	(0.0060)
Sep-4[b]	–0.0042	(0.0084)	–0.0035	(0.0075)
Sep-3	–0.0121	(0.0080)	–0.0230***	(0.0069)
Sep-2	–0.0124	(0.0077)	–0.0256***	(0.0067)
Sep-1	–0.0281***	(0.0075)	–0.0520***	(0.0066)
Perm[c]	–0.0479***	(0.0109)	–0.1061***	(0.0069)
Sep1	0.1265***	(0.0080)	0.1349***	(0.0073)
Sep2	0.0377***	(0.0082)	0.0255***	(0.0075)
Sep3	0.0196**	(0.0086)	–0.0137*	(0.0077)
Sep4	–0.0049	(0.0094)	–0.0187**	(0.0083)
Sep5	–0.0250**	(0.0115)	–0.0162*	(0.0098)
Age	0.0465***	(0.0010)	0.0472***	(0.0010)
Age^2/100	–0.0440***	(0.0012)	–0.0448***	(0.0012)
1985	–0.0004	(0.0022)	–0.0006	(0.0022)
1986	0.0081***	(0.0022)	0.0106***	(0.0022)
1987	–0.0081***	(0.0022)	–0.0050**	(0.0023)
1988	–0.0045*	(0.0023)	–0.0044*	(0.0023)
1989	0.0016	(0.0023)	–0.0025	(0.0024)
Elementary school	0.0553***	(0.0053)	0.0439***	(0.0055)
Junior high school	0.2207***	(0.0080)	0.2151***	(0.0082)
High school	0.3447***	(0.0096)	0.3533***	(0.0100)
Basic vocational school	0.1357***	(0.0051)	0.1180***	(0.0053)
Advanced vocational school	0.2807***	(0.0075)	0.2677***	(0.0077)
Undergraduate	0.4108***	(0.0092)	0.4018***	(0.0093)
Graduate school and grande école	1.0866***	(0.0081)	1.0687***	(0.0081)
Constant	–2.8427***	(0.0205)	–2.8827***	(0.0210)

(continued)

Table 5.12 (continued)

Variable	Displacements	Other separations
No. of obs.	402,174	433,627
R^2	0.3608	0.3339

NOTE: Standard errors are in parentheses. Reference groups = 1984 and no educational certification. *** = Statistically significant at the 1% level; ** = statistically significant at the 5% level; * = statistically significant at the 10% level.

[a] Separated = 1 for all observations corresponding to individuals who separate at some point between 1984 and 1989.

[b] The Sep_i variables equal 1 in the *i*th year before or after separation.

[c] Perm = 1 for observations after separation if time between the two jobs exceeded one year.

SOURCE: Authors' calculations from DADS data.

Table 5.13 Earnings Regressions for Censored Regression Models for Germany: Displaced Workers Only

Variable	All		Non-employment spell[a]	
Sep_{-6}[b]	–0.0029	(0.0222)	–0.0403	(0.0691)
Sep_{-5}	0.0023	(0.0142)	–0.0586	(0.0390)
Sep_{-4}	0.0275***	(0.0113)	0.0231	(0.0282)
Sep_{-3}	0.0156	(0.0098)	0.0217	(0.0227)
Sep_{-2}	0.0062	(0.0088)	0.0052	(0.0196)
Perm[c]	–0.2159***	(0.0170)	–0.1310***	(0.0191)
Sep_1	–0.0161**	(0.0080)	–0.0414***	(0.0176)
Sep_2	–0.0222***	(0.0086)	–0.0207	(0.0190)
Sep_3	–0.0246***	(0.0093)	–0.0015	(0.0207)
Sep_4	–0.0121	(0.0103)	0.0280	(0.0225)
Sep_5	–0.0103	(0.0118)	0.0415*	(0.0250)
Sep_6	–0.0280	(0.0156)	0.0411	(0.0317)
Age	6.2292***	(0.3114)	5.4975***	(0.6326)
$Age^2/100$	–6.9903***	(0.3771)	–6.3207***	(0.7638)
1985	0.0002	(0.0086)	–0.0097	(0.0185)
1986	0.0355***	(0.0090)	0.0308	(0.0196)
1987	0.0733***	(0.0095)	0.0561***	(0.0209)
1988	0.1045***	(0.0100)	0.0654***	(0.0223)
1989	0.1140***	(0.0106)	0.0560***	(0.0234)
1990	0.1165***	(0.0113)	0.0647***	(0.0251)
Apprentice, no high school	0.1892***	(0.0056)	0.1722***	(0.0108)
No apprentice, high school	0.4315	—	0.3151***	(0.1262)
Apprentice, high school	0.3751***	(0.0222)	0.1775***	(0.0512)
Polytechnic	0.6356***	(0.0194)	0.4961***	(0.0611)
University	0.6990***	(0.0231)	0.7647***	(0.0813)
Education unknown	0.0893***	(0.0095)	0.0602***	(0.0183)
Constant	2.8313***	(0.0630)	2.9633***	(0.1275)

(continued)

Table 5.13 (continued)

Variable	All	Non-employment spell[a]
No. of obs.	19,018	4,995
Pseudo R^2	0.295	0.176

NOTE: Standard errors are in parentheses. Base education group = no apprentice, no high school degree. *** = Statistically significant at the 1% level; ** = statistically significant at the 5% level; * = statistically significant at the 10% level.

[a] Spell = at least six days after separation.

[b] Perm = 1 for observations after separation if time between the two jobs exceeded one year.

[c] The Sep_i variables equal 1 in the ith year after separation.

SOURCE: Authors' calculations from DADS data.

Table 5.14 Earnings Regressions for Censored Regression Models for Germany

Variable	Displaced		Separated	
Sep_{-6}	–0.118***	(0.0177)	0.020***	(0.0089)
Sep_{-5}	–0.107***	(0.0107)	0.014***	(0.0059)
Sep_{-4}	–0.084***	(0.0082)	0.008*	(0.0047)
Sep_{-3}	–0.095***	(0.0068)	–0.002	(0.0040)
Sep_{-2}	–0.105***	(0.0058)	–0.007	(0.0034)
Sep_{-1}	–0.112***	(0.0050)	–0.021***	(0.0029)
Perm[a]	–0.217***	(0.0150)	–0.289***	(0.0074)
Sep_1[b]	–0.121***	(0.0045)	–0.047***	(0.0027)
Sep_2	–0.125***	(0.0049)	–0.040***	(0.0030)
Sep_3	–0.124***	(0.0054)	–0.041***	(0.0033)
Sep_4	–0.110***	(0.0061)	–0.034***	(0.0037)
Sep_5	–0.101***	(0.0074)	–0.040***	(0.0045)
Sep_6	–0.110***	(0.0108)	–0.050***	(0.0063)
Age	0.051***	(0.0007)	0.055***	(0.0006)
$Age^2/100$	–0.055***	(0.0008)	–0.060***	(0.0008)
1985	0.015***	(0.0019)	0.016***	(0.0018)
1986	0.053***	(0.0019)	0.055***	(0.0018)
1987	0.080 ***	(0.0019)	0.083***	(0.0018)
1988	0.116***	(0.0019)	0.122***	(0.0018)
1989	0.111 ***	(0.0019)	0.117***	(0.0018)
1990	0.100***	(0.0019)	0.104***	(0.0019)
Apprentice, no high school	0.175***	(0.0012)	0.184***	(0.0012)
No apprentice, high school	0.330***	(0.0081)	0.341***	(0.0075)
Apprentice, high school	0.408***	(0.0050)	0.434***	(0.0045)
Polytechnic	0.549***	(0.0031)	0.571***	(0.0029)
University	0.604***	(0.0038)	0.625***	(0.0033)
Education unknown	0.080***	(0.0026)	0.082***	(0.0025)

(continued)

Table 5.14 (continued)

Variable	Displaced		Separated	
Constant	3.143***	(0.0150)	3.045***	(0.0140)
No. of obs.	267,044		323,916	
Pseudo R^2	0.4950		0.4255	

NOTE: Standard errors are in parentheses. Base education group = no apprentice, no high school degree. *** = Statistically significant at the 1% level; * = statistically significant at the 10% level.

[a] Perm = 1 for observations after separation if time between the two jobs exceeded one year.

[b] The Sep_i variables equal 1 in the ith year after separation.

SOURCE: Authors' calculations.

Appendix A

Correction for False Firm Deaths in France

Suppose we observe n_1 workers associated with firm j_1 in the last available year for the firm (prior to 1996), and a share p_{1k} were observed the following year in firm j_k, $k \neq 1$. Using p_{1k} as an estimator of $\tilde{p}_{1k}$, the true share of workers moving from firm j_1 to firm j_k, we take a normal approximation to the underlying binomial distribution under which the standard error of p_{1k} is $\sigma_{1k} = \sqrt{\frac{p_{1k}(1-p_{1k})}{n_1}}$. Thus, if for any k, $k \neq 1$, $p_{1k} + 2\sigma_{1k} \geq 0.5$, we cannot reject the [illegible]hat at least 50 percent of the firm's workforce moved together to the same successor firm ($\tilde{p}_{1k} \geq 0.5$) at the 95 percent confidence level. If this is the case for any $k \neq 1$, we consider only separations to firms for which we can reject $\tilde{p}_{1k'} \geq 0.5$, i.e., for which $p_{1k'} + 2\sigma_{1k'} < 0.5$, to be real separations. All of these are classified as separations for reasons other than displacement, since there is at least one possible successor firm to j_1. All changes in firm identifier for individuals moving to firm k'' with $p_{1k''} + 2\sigma_{1k''} \geq 0.5$ are considered to be false firm deaths, and are not coded as separations.[1] In the event that the test statistic is less than 0.5 for all k, $k \neq 1$, we maintain the estimated firm-death date. This procedure leads us to reclassify 26 percent of our estimated firm deaths in France as false firm deaths.

Appendix Note

1. We nevertheless restart the seniority counter at zero the year following the false firm death. This is because the individuals moving to a new firm identifier in this manner are "new employees" for the successor firm, despite their experience with the predecessor firm.

Appendix B

Definitions of Displacement

Table 5.B1 Type of Closures for France and Germany

Country: year	Total separations	Closure within 1 yr.		Closure within 2 yr.		Contraction by 40%	
		No.	%	No.	%	No.	%
France[a]							
1984	8,309	2,498	30.06	2,821	33.95	n.d.[b]	—
1985	8,620	3,159	36.65	3,487	40.45	n.d.	—
1986	8,730	2,993	34.28	3,365	38.55	n.d.	—
1987	10,517	3,072	29.21	3,633	34.54	n.d.	—
1988	8,439	3,238	38.37	3,557	42.15	n.d.	—
1989	15,459	5,622	36.37	6,349	41.07	n.d.	—
Σ	60,074	20,582	34.26	23,212	38.64	n.d.	—
Germany							
1984	3,181	432	13.58	637	20.02	1,101	34.64
1985	2,777	423	15.23	625	22.50	1,097	39.50
1986	2,464	402	16.31	530	21.50	955	38.75
1987	2,030	323	15.91	460	22.66	774	38.12
1988	1,821	294	16.14	420	23.06	729	40.03
1989	2,117	263	12.42	375	17.71	755	35.66
1990	1,805	227	12.57	227	12.57	5.70	31.57
Σ	16,191	2,364	14.59	3,274	20.21	5,981	36.93

[a] For France, multiple observations in the same year are aggregated to the unique individual-year level.

[b] n.d. = no data available.

SOURCE: Authors' calculations from DADS and IAB data.

Appendix C

Impact of Retirement Constraint in France

Figure 5.C1 Impact of Retirement Constraint by Age at First Separation for France

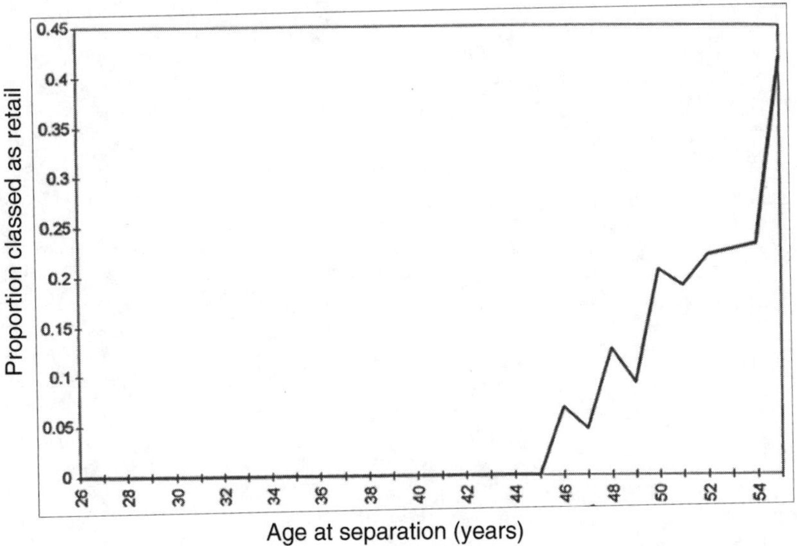

Appendix D

Descriptive Statistics for France

Table 5.D1 Sample Statistics for 1984 for France

Variable	Continuously employed 1984–89		First separation: displacement		First separation: other reason	
Age	37.82	(6.93)	37.65	(7.20)	38.26	(7.37)
Log (average daily earnings)[a]	–1.65	(0.45)	–1.81	(0.50)	–1.73	(0.57)
4 ≤ Seniority < 6	0.17		0.22		0.26	
6 ≤ Seniority < 8	0.23		0.25		0.26	
8 ≤ Seniority <10	0.03		0.04		0.03	
10 ≤ Seniority	0.58		0.48		0.46	
No educational certification	0.20		0.20		0.20	
Elementary school	0.26		0.26		0.26	
Junior high school	0.06		0.06		0.06	
High school	0.04		0.04		0.04	
Basic vocational school	0.29		0.30		0.29	
Advanced vocational school	0.06		0.06		0.06	
Undergraduate university	0.04		0.04		0.04	
Graduate school and grande école	0.05		0.05		0.05	
No. of obs.	54,918		16,876		27,685	

NOTE: Standard deviations are in parentheses. Table constructed with one observation per person per year.

[a] In thousands of 1980 francs.

SOURCE: Authors' calculations from DADS data.

Appendix E

Treatment of Censoring in Germany

Values for Germany appear in Table 5.E1. There are 16,195 first separations between 1984 and 1990. Of those, 4,242 do not return to the labor force within the observation period, and 2,943 do not claim benefits. In the subsample of workers who are displaced (according to definition 2 above), only 8 percent do not claim benefits after separation and do not return into the sample.

Table 5.E1 Separation and Censoring in Germany

Group	No.	Percent
First separations, 1984–90	16,195	100.00
Return to work	11,953	73.81
Do not return to work	4,242	26.19
Claim benefits	1,299	30.62
Do not claim benefits	2,943	69.38

Appendix F

Descriptive Statistics for Germany

Table 5.F1 Sample Statistics for 1984 for Germany

Variable	Continuously employed 1984–90		First separation: displacement		First separation: other reason	
Age	39.42	(7.30)	39.10	(7.30)	37.59	(7.40)
Daily wage[a]	85.01	(21.07)	77.15	(21.07)	83.15	(21.88)
Log of daily wage	4.41	(0.30)	4.30	(0.30)	4.38	(0.27)
4 ≤ Seniority < 6	15.89	—	18.74	—	26.52	—
6 ≤ Seniority < 8	13.79	—	17.24	—	17.47	—
8 ≤ Seniority < 10	25.76	—	29.13	—	25.23	—
10 ≤ Seniority	44.47	—	26.90	—	23.81	—
No apprentice, no high school	19.55	—	18.41	—	17.21	—
Apprentice, no high school	68.72	—	71.22	—	66.85	—
No apprentice, high school	0.37	—	0.26	—	0.47	—
Apprentice, high school	1.05	—	0.96	—	1.44	—
Polytechnic	3.53	—	1.49	—	4.46	—
University	2.63	—	1.03	—	4.46	—
Education unknown	4.10	—	6.59	—	5.09	—

Plant size, 1982	3,086	(8,376)	160	(394)	1,653	(5,003)
Plant size, 1982 (Median)	369	—	34	—	173	—
Sector						
1: Primary	0.59	—	3.72	—	1.83	—
2: Energy	2.59	—	0.39	—	0.98	—
3: Mining	1.08	—	1.39	—	1.86	—
4: Manufacturing	54.40	—	42.45	—	46.37	—
5: Construction	7.95	—	21.41	—	11.60	—
6: Distributional services	13.09	—	20.61	—	19.18	—
7: Industry services	6.08	—	4.52	—	6.79	—
8: Consumer services	1.24	—	1.03	—	1.38	—
9: Public services	12.93	—	4.42	—	9.97	—
No. of obs.	32,235		3,003		10,266	

NOTE: Standard deviations are in parentheses.
[a] In German Marks (deflated to 1975 prices).

Appendix G

Probit Models for the Incidence of Displacement Using the Continuously Employed as the Reference Group in France

Table 5.G1 Probit Models of Incidence of Separation by Type Relative to Continuously Employed in France in 1984

Variable	Displacements		Other separations	
Age	–0.0104	(0.0145)	–0.0090	(0.0113)
$Age^2/100$	0.0184	(0.0188)	0.0165	(0.0145)
4 ≤ Seniority < 6	0.2268***	(0.0240)	0.3764***	(0.0181)
6 ≤ Seniority < 8	0.1453***	(0.0227)	0.1989***	(0.0177)
8 ≤ Seniority < 10	0.1529***	(0.0489)	0.0414	(0.0462)
Elementary school	–0.1076	(0.0728)	0.0112	(0.0578)
Junior high school	0.0989	(0.1072)	0.0273	(0.0886)
High school	0.1504	(0.1303)	0.0940	(0.1076)
Basic vocational school	–0.1130	(0.0697)	–0.1009*	(0.0569)
Advanced vocational school	–0.2434*	(0.1244)	–0.0669	(0.0877)
Undergraduate	0.1933	(0.1216)	0.2030**	(0.0940)
Graduate school and grande école	0.0065	(0.1165)	0.3766***	(0.0802)
Constant	–2.0991***	(0.2920)	–1.6256***	(0.2243)
No. of obs.	71,794		82,603	
Log likelihood	–11,264.46		–19,432.70	

NOTE: Standard errors are in parentheses. Estimates include data from 1984 only, aggregated to one observation per individual. All models also include controls for sector (15 categories) and skill level (3 categories). Reference groups: no educational certification and 10 or more years of seniority. Models estimate the probability of specified type of separation relative to workers who were continuously employed with the same firm throughout the sample window (1984–1989). *** = Statistically significant at the 1% level; ** = statistically significant at the 5% level; * = statistically significant at the 10% level.

SOURCE: Authors' calculations from DADS data.

Appendix H

Weibull Proportional Hazard Model for Germany

Table 5.H1 Weibull Proportional Hazard Models for Germany

Variable	All separations		Other separations		Displacements	
Age	–3.2793***	(0.2255)	–3.7131***	(0.2597)	–1.9628***	(0.4639)
6 ≤ Seniority < 8	0.0248	(0.0570)	0.0228	(0.0641)	0.0664	(0.1284)
8 ≤ Seniority < 10	0.0633	(0.0531)	0.0293	(0.0602)	0.2250**	(0.1177)
10 ≤ Seniority	–0.0232	(0.0617)	–0.1118	(0.0704)	0.3081***	(0.1321)
Displacement	0.4250***	(0.0387)	—	—	—	—
Apprentice, no high school	0.4008***	(0.0407)	0.4332***	(0.0468)	0.3000***	(0.0826)
No apprentice, high school	0.2073	(0.3041)	0.2422	(0.3367)	0.0591	(0.7156)
Apprentice, high school	0.0200	(0.1710)	0.3562*	(0.1935)	–0.7274**	(0.3639)
Polytechnic	0.2319*	(0.1309)	0.3627***	(0.1421)	–0.2392	(0.3426)
University	0.0909	(0.1276)	0.2074	(0.1302)	–1.9875**	(1.0042)
Education unknown	0.0522	(0.0721)	0.0748	(0.0842)	–0.0251	(0.1404)
1985	0.1383***	(0.0485)	0.1707***	(0.0564)	0.0949	(0.0963)
1986	0.2598***	(0.0547)	0.2658***	(0.0626)	0.2745***	(0.1137)
1987	0.2319***	(0.0619)	0.3066***	(0.0706)	0.0180	(0.1302)
1988	0.2537***	(0.0694)	0.2971***	(0.0794)	0.1344	(0.1437)
1989	0.2703***	(0.0781)	0.3438***	(0.0879)	0.0447	(0.1732)
1990	0.0950	(0.1026)	0.0222	(0.1170)	0.7691***	(0.2106)

Constant	−2.3947***	(0.1054)	−2.1522***	(0.1184)	−2.8565***	(0.2349)
Weibull shape parameter	0.51		0.49		0.56	
No. of obs.	5,019		3,998		1,021	
No. of failures	3,720		2,813		907	
Log likelihood	−9666.48		−7531.57		−2087.78	

NOTE: Standard errors are in parentheses. Right censoring occurs when the individual is not reemployed by December 1990. *** = Statistically significant at the 1% level; ** = statistically significant at the 5% level; * = statistically significant at the 10% level.

Appendix I

Estimates Comparing Different Definitions of Displacement for Germany

Table 5.I1 Constrained Earnings Regressions for Germany: Displaced Workers

Variable	Within 1 year		Within 2 years		40 Shrinkage	
Perm[a]	–0.2087***	(0.0220)	–0.2161***	(0.0169)	–0.2318***	(0.0123)
Sep_1[b]	–0.0233***	(0.0075)	–0.0228***	(0.0062)	–0.0331***	(0.0045)
Sep_2	–0.0333***	(0.0083)	–0.0291***	(0.0069)	–0.0410***	(0.0050)
Sep_3	–0.0353***	(0.0094)	–0.0307***	(0.0078)	–0.0435***	(0.0056)
Sep_4	–0.0286***	(0.0106)	–0.0189***	(0.0088)	–0.0360***	(0.0063)
Sep_5	–0.0339***	(0.0127)	–0.0162	(0.0104)	–0.0437***	(0.0075)
Sep_6	–0.0499***	(0.0176)	–0.0343**	(0.0144)	–0.0576***	(0.0105)
Age	6.3572***	(0.3513)	6.1706***	(0.2909)	5.8927***	(0.2112)
$Age^2/100$	–7.1835***	(0.4260)	–6.9319***	(0.3529)	–6.4522***	(0.2561)
1985	–0.0065	(0.0091)	–0.0007	(0.0076)	0.0042	(0.0055)
1986	0.0351***	(0.0093)	0.0389***	(0.0078)	0.0437***	(0.0056)
1987	0.0720***	(0.0096)	0.0710***	(0.0081)	0.0769***	(0.0058)
1988	0.1064***	(0.0100)	0.1065***	(0.0084)	0.1114***	(0.0060)
1989	0.1183***	(0.0105)	0.1133***	(0.0088)	0.1204***	(0.0063)
1990	0.1259***	(0.0114)	0.1167***	(0.0096)	0.1204***	(0.0068)
Apprentice, no high school	0.1816***	(0.0064)	0.1883***	(0.0052)	0.2041***	(0.0038)
No apprentice, high school	0.3962***	(0.0510)	0.4260***	(0.0442)	0.3774***	(0.0314)

Apprentice, high school	0.3247***	(0.0267)	0.3799***	(0 .0211)	0.4318***	(0.0147)
Polytechnic	0.6629***	(0.0222)	0.6363***	(0.0181)	0.6263***	(0.0098)
University	0.6635***	(0.0258)	0.6933***	(0.0216)	0.6787***	(0.0120)
Education unknown	0.0952***	(0.0109)	0.0918	(0.0089)	0.1097***	(0.0065)
Constant	2.8071***	(0.0709)	2.8521***	(0.0586)	2.9082***	(0.0427)
No. of obs.	15,346		21,519		39,669	
Pseudo R^2	0.2743		0.2980		0.3618	

NOTE: Standard errors are in parentheses. Base education group = no apprentice, no high school degree. *** = Statistically significant at the 1% level; ** = statistically significant at the 5% level.

[a] Perm = 1 for observations after separation if time between the two jobs exceeded one year.

[b] Sep_i variables equal 1 in the *i*th year before or after separation.

References

Abowd, John M., Francis Kramarz, Thomas Lemieux, and David N. Margolis. 2000. "Minimum Wages and Youth Employment in France and the United States." In *Youth Employment and Joblessness in Advanced Countries,* David B. Blanchflower and Richard B. Freeman, eds. Chicago: National Bureau for Economic Research, pp. 427–472.

Abowd, John M., Francis Kramarz, David N. Margolis, and Thomas Philippon. 2000. *Minimum Wages and Employment in France and the United States.* Working paper, Centre de Recherche en Economie et Statistique and Laboratoire de Microeconomie Appliquée, Paris, France, August.

———. 1999. "High Wage Workers and High Wage Firms." *Econometrica* 67(2): 251–333.

Abowd, John M., Hampton S.C. Finer, Francis Kramarz, and Sébastien Roux. 1997. "Job and Wage Mobility: An Analysis of the Dynamics of Employment Durations Using Matched Employee and Employer Data from the U.S. and France." Paper presented at NBER Summer Institute, Labor Studies group, held July 21–25, Cambridge, Massachusetts.

Bender, S., J. Hilzendegen, G. Rohwer, and H. Rudolph. 1996. *Die IAB-Beschäftigtenstichprobe 1975–1990.* Beitrab, Nürnberg: Institut für Arbeitsmarktund Berufsforschung, p. 197.

Bonnal, Liliane, and Denis Fougère. 1993. "Estimating the Structural Effect of Unemployment Benefits on Job Search Costs." Working paper, CREST.

———. 1996. "Estimating the Structural Effects of Unemployment Benefits and the Minimum Wage Level on Unemployment Durations." Working paper, CREST, July.

Büchtemann, C.F. 1990. "Kündigungsschutz als Beschäftigungshemmniss?" *Mitteilungen aus des Arbeitsmarkt- und Berufsforschung* 23: 394–410.

Bughin, Evelyne. 1985. "La Négociation Salariale de Branche en 1984." *Travail et Emploi* 24(June): 51–59.

Buttler, F., W. Brandes, E. Dorndorf, W. Gaum, and U. Walwei. 1992. "Flexibility and Job Security in the Federal Republic of Germany." Technical Report 1, Working paper, SAMF.

Dustmann, Christian, and Arthur VanSoest. 1997. "Wage Structures in the Private and Public Sectors in West Germany." *Fiscal Studies* 18: 225–247.

Fallick, Bruce C. 1996. "A Review of the Recent Empirical Literature on Displaced Workers." *Industrial and Labor Relations Review* 50(1): 5–16.

Farber, Henry S. 1977. "The Changing Face of Job Loss in the United States, 1981–1995." *Brookings Papers: Microeconomics*, pp. 129–142.

———. 1999. "Alternative and Part-Time Employment Arrangements as a Response to Job Loss." Working paper 7002, NBER, Cambridge, Massachusetts.

Gibbons, Robert, and Lawrence F. Katz. 1991. "Layoffs and Lemons." *Journal of Labor Economics* 9(4): 351–380.

Herberger, L., and B. Becker. 1983. "Sozialverischerungspflichtige Beschäftigte." *Der Beschäftigtenstatistik um im Mikrozensus, Wirtschaft und Statistik,* pp. 290–304.

Hunt, Jennifer. 1995. "The Effect of Unemployment Compensation on Unemployment Duration in Germany." *Journal of Labor Economics* 13(1): 88–120.

Jacobson, Louis S., Robert J. LaLonde, and Daniel G. Sullivan. 1993. "Earnings Losses of Displaced Workers." *American Economic Review* 83(4): 685–709.

Kittner, M. 1995. *Arbeits- und Sozialordnung*. Köln: Bund Verlag.

Lefebvre, Francis. 1996. *Social 1996, Droit du Travail et Sécurité Sociale.* Mementos Pratiques, Levallois, France: Editions Francis Lefebvre.

Margolis, David N. 1993. "Compensation Practices and Government Policies in Western European Labor Markets." Ph.D. dissertation, Cornell University, Ithaca, New York.

———. 1996. "Cohort Effects and Returns to Seniority in France." *Annales d'Economie et de Statistique* 41/42: 443–464.

———. 1999. "Part-Year Employment, Slow Reemployment and Earnings Losses: The Case of Worker Displacement in France." In *The Creation and Analysis of Linked Employer-Employee Data*, James Spletzer, Jules Theeuwes, John Haltiwanger, Julia Lane, and Kenneth Troske, eds. Amsterdam: North Holland, pp. 375–416.

———. 2000. "Worker Displacement in France." Photocopy, Working paper no. 2000-01, LAMIA and CREST, Paris, France.

Rogowski, Ralf, and Klaus Schömann. 1996. "Legal Regulation and Flexibility of Employment Contracts." In *International Handbook of Labour Market Policy and Evaluation,* Jacqueline O'Reilly, Gunther Schmid, and Klaus Schömann, eds. Cheltenham, U.K.: Edward Elgar.

Schmidt, Christoph M. 1994. "Relative Wage Effects of German Unions." Working paper no. 918, CEPR.

Seitchik, Adam. 1991. "Who Are Displaced Workers?" In *Job Displacement: Consequences and Implications for Policy,* John T. Addison, ed. Detroit, Michigan: Wayne State University Press.

Stevens, Ann Huff. 1997. "Persistent Effects of Job Displacement: The Importance of Multiple Job Losses." *Journal of Labor Economics* 15(1): 165–188.

Swaim, Paul, and Michael Podgursky. 1991. "Displacement and Unemployment." In *Job Displacement: Consequences and Implications for Policy,* John T. Addison, ed. Detroit: Wayne State University Press.

6
Employment Protection and the Consequences for Displaced Workers

A Comparison of Belgium and Denmark

Karsten Albæk
University of Copenhagen

Marc Van Audenrode
Université Laval

Martin Browning
University of Copenhagen

INTRODUCTION

Belgium and Denmark offer marked contrasts in many of their labor market institutions. Belgium has long been considered by many as exemplifying the economic problem known as Eurosclerosis. Indeed, Belgium did have (and to some extent still has) almost all of the negative institutional characteristics often associated with poor economic performance: high job protection, rigid wages, and generous unemployment insurance compensation. Denmark, on the other hand, has long been considered as an example of a country that has successfully achieved a good balance between social protection and economic growth. Below we shall discuss the differences between the two countries in detail, but in Table 6.1 we present some of the features of the two labor markets along with those of a selection of other countries, to provide some context. These rankings are taken from the World Economic Forum's 1997 global competitiveness report.[1] The table gives the rankings (for 5 out of 53 countries) for various labor market indicators. In each case a lower ranking (closer to 1) means "more advantageous for employers" (or, as conventionally seen, as bad for workers). Of particular note is the fact that Belgium consistently has high scores, indicating "negative" institutional characteristics. On the other hand, Denmark is much more mixed. For example, it is seen as having generous unemployment insurance (UI) provisions but it also has the lowest impediments to hiring and firing (lower even than Singapore or Hong Kong).

Belgium and Denmark are both small open economies whose primary trading partner is Germany. They also both have a relatively generous social safety net. The major difference between their labor markets is the higher firing costs in Belgium. Thus it is very tempting to compare the outcomes of workers in the two countries who are displaced from a long-tenure job to identify how these outcomes differ and whether they can be attributed to the differences in firing provisions. This comparison is made even more attractive by the availability of two comparable administrative data sets describing the Belgian and Danish labor markets. In this work, we will use these data sets to compare worker displacement and worker adjustment to displacement in Belgium and Denmark.

LABOR MARKET INSTITUTIONS

Employment Protection

As in the United States, Belgian law recognizes the basic principle of employment at will. Thus, with a few exceptions (for example, union activity and pregnancy) employers rarely have to demonstrate just cause when dismissing an employee. Unlike the United States, however, laying off workers can be very costly in Belgium due to significant legislated notice periods and severance payments, especially in the case of white-collar workers. In Belgium, the required advance-notice period for blue-collar workers is four weeks for workers with fewer than 20 years of service, and eight weeks for those with more than 20 years. Low-wage white-collar workers are given three months of notice plus three months for every five completed years of seniority.[2] For high-wage white-collar workers, these are lower bounds. The actual period of notice has to be set in agreement between the employer and the employee. When no accord can be reached, the length of notice is set by the labor courts. According to Blanpain (1994), the length of notice courts grant to these high-paid employees is a function of age, specialization, tenure, and wage. These lengths can go as high as 36 months. Of course, these restrictions do not apply during trial periods (generally two weeks for blue-collar workers, but up to six months for white-collar workers). It is worth noting that during the period considered here, protections were sharply reduced for some categories of white-collar workers. In addition to notice, Belgian workers (both blue- and white-collar workers) are given large severance payments in case of plant closings. These payments amount to roughly one month of salary per year of seniority, plus some additional compensation for high-wage and older workers. Mass layoffs also require some severance pay, although much less generous than plant closings.

In contrast to this, the Danish industrial relations system is characterized by a small amount of interference from the state, which includes some very limited employment-protection legislation. There are two major provisions in the legislation, which are both about advance notice. The first provision, which is limited to white-collar workers, requires that advance notice be given. The length depends on the tenure of the worker, with a maximum length of six months. This set of rules was enacted in 1938. The second set of provisions encompasses the different rules about mass layoffs enacted by the European Union (EU). The Danish legislation has followed the minimum required by these EU rules, which have undergone some changes since Denmark joined the EU in 1973. The restrictions on the behavior of the employers are moderate: they have to submit a notice to the regional labor market board and they have to go into negotiations with their employees before the layoff can be enacted. Other than this, general rules about employment protection are absent from the Danish labor market. Thus there is a complete absence of severance pay, unless it has been agreed upon in a voluntary contract between the employer and the single employee. Such agreements are relatively uncommon. Just as in Belgium, procedures for dismissal are also absent; that is, employers are not required to act "fairly" or in a "socially responsible" way. It should be noted, however, that there are some provisions for specific groups in the labor market; these include, for example, pregnant workers, and workers on maternity leave, and persons elected by their fellow workers as representatives for negotiations with the employer. These provisions do not apply in the case of mass layoffs, however.

Employment-protection provisions also play a close-to-negligible role in Danish unions' collective agreements. With few exceptions, Danish collective agreements do not include such employment-protection provisions as advance notice and severance or redundancy pay. One of the reasons for this absence can be traced back to the formation of the Danish collective bargaining system. As in most other countries, Danish employers tried to avoid recognizing the right of workers to organize and bargain collectively. After a four-month nationwide general lockout in 1899, the Confederation of Danish Employers conceded. In return for recognition the trade unions granted the employers the "right to manage" in the "general agreement" between the two organizations, which was the main outcome of the conflict. The interpretation of "right to manage" is the (nearly) unlimited formal right of the employers to decide which workers to hire and which workers to fire.

Wage Setting

Union membership is very high in Belgium, and coverage rates are even higher. All firms with 25 or more employees are *de facto* unionized, since they are required to have an elected works council, and only union members can be elected to these councils. Nonunionized firms are covered by any relevant contract that has been extended. Inside firms, workers can choose not to be union members. Those who do so won't pay dues, but they will still be covered by all the relevant agreements. They cannot be candidates to the works councils, but they can vote. Finally, two or more unions can coexist and compete for membership inside the firm.

Wage bargaining in Belgium has a pyramidal structure, in which contracts can be bargained at the national, industry, and firm level. Agreements struck at a higher level immediately become lower bounds for bargaining at lower levels. These of course limit downward real-wage flexibility at the firm level, especially given the fact that as a general rule, Belgian wages are automatically indexed. The main feature of the structure of the Belgian pattern of wage bargaining pertinent to our study is the portability of seniority. Workers changing jobs between firms within the same bargaining unit (often an industry) keep their accrued seniority. This considerably limits a worker's ability to accept a wage cut, even if he or she is willing to do so.

As in Belgium, the Danish labor market is heavily unionized, with 80–90 percent of Danish workers being members of trade unions. The share of workers covered by collective agreements is not known; recent figures of as low as 50 percent have been suggested, although a more likely figure is about 75 percent.[3]

For the time period considered below, centralized negotiations in the private sector took place every second year between the Confederation of Unions, which represents both skilled and unskilled workers, and the Confederation of Employers. For wages the negotiations establish a minimum wage level, so that in more decentralized negotiations afterwards (at the plant level, for example) lower wage levels cannot be agreed to. Other items in the centralized wage negotiations are provisions about holidays, working hours, and overtime. Bargaining can also occur at several lower levels, including between single employers and shop-stewards, and can cover a wider range of issues.

Interference by the state in the bargaining process is limited to the centralized level and, then, only to instances where agreement has not been reached. The state does not extend contracts between employers and unions to employers who are not covered by collective agreements. There are no formal minimum wage laws in Denmark. This implies that despite the fact that the Danish system at face value looks very unionized and centralized, there are loopholes with respect to the acceptance of wage reductions.

Unemployment Insurance Provisions

The Belgian system of unemployment insurance is said to be one of the most generous in the world (Burda 1988). As a general rule, benefits do not expire in Belgium. They are reduced, however, after both one and two years of unemployment. In fact, a closer look at the

Belgian UI system indicates that it hardly qualifies as an insurance system. First, students can qualify for benefits even if they have never been employed. Second, and more importantly, benefits are means tested. The official replacement rate is 60 percent of the lost wage during the first year of unemployment and 40 percent after that. But, practically, these rates are meaningless. Many UI recipients receive compensation based entirely on family status and income. Thus "heads" of households receive a flat amount which can be higher than 60 percent of their lost wages, while the benefits of most other workers are limited by a cap and are often below 60 percent of their lost wages. Third, while there is a search requirement attached to UI benefits, this requirement is hardly ever enforced.

At the beginning of this century the Danish state began to subsidize the unemployment insurance system run by trade unions, who had set up special UI funds for this task. Since a reform of the system in about 1970, the UI funds no longer bear the marginal burden of expenditures for unemployment benefit. Each person pays a fixed fee in order to be a member of the UI system and the Danish state covers the remaining part of the expenditures. The UI funds are, in principle, separate administrative units, but in practice there is a close connection between the unions and the UI funds. The funds are closely regulated by the state, however, with respect to benefit levels, entitlements, and so on. One of the duties resting on the UI funds is to test that unemployed members actually search for a job. The general impression is that there is considerable variation across UI funds with respect to the efficiency with which this task is carried out.

Eligibility for unemployment benefit in Denmark is limited to persons who are members of an unemployment insurance fund. About 80 percent of Danish private sector workers are members of a UI fund. In order to become a member, workers have to fulfill a requirement of work experience. In the 1980s, six months of work within one year was required. However, persons who graduate from schools aiming at a particular trade or as skilled workers in an apprenticeship system also have a right to become members of a fund.

Concerning benefit levels, the Danish UI system is closer to a true insurance scheme than the Belgian one in that it does not have a means test for benefits. At the same time, however, it also has many features (such as the absence of differentiation with respect to risk) that reduce the insurance element. It is considered generous compared to most other countries, both with respect to the level and duration of benefits. The maximum amount in unemployment benefit is 90 percent of the previous wage, but this is obtained only by workers with low previous wage levels. At the beginning of the 1980s, the benefit level was capped at about the average wage level for workers in the private sector. Since that time, this maximum has been eroded considerably so that now the average replacement ratio is about 65 percent. Thus, Danish workers with high wage levels have a replacement ratio that is somewhat lower than in many other countries. Formally, there is a maximum duration period, but until the beginning of the 1990s unemployed workers could become eligible for continued benefits by participating in a public employment scheme. This implied that the duration period was practically unlimited.

Although the administration of UI funds is in the hands of individual trade unions, there is also a government labor exchange system that is directly responsible for matching unemployed workers and vacancies. When a firm notifies the labor exchange of a vacancy, the latter is required to identify a suitable unemployed worker and send him or her for an interview. If the worker is offered the job and refuses, the labor exchange is required to contact the UI fund and the worker loses benefits for five weeks. This is the formal procedure, but the unions also take an active role in finding jobs.

Overall, it is extremely difficult to make cross-country comparisons of the "harshness" of the pressure unemployed are exposed to from authorities, labor unions, or social norms in society. Within Scandinavia, however, there is no doubt that the Danish system is more easygoing than the Swedish and the Norwegian systems. This applies both with respect to the formal rules and to the way workers are assigned to jobs. One of the reasons is that trade unions in the other Scandinavian countries are organized as industrial unions, while the Danish ones are organized according to trade or education. Thus, the Danish system is somewhat more hesitant with respect to the demand that the unemployed search for jobs for which they have not been educated.

DATA

In this chapter, the aim of our procedures with respect to data selection and definition of variables is to come as close as possible to similar definitions for Belgium and Denmark, so that the results for the two countries are as comparable as possible. When it is possible or desirable we adopt the definitions in Jacobson, LaLonde, and Sullivan (1993), which is the main study on displaced workers using administrative data for the United States. This implies that the results in this study are to a certain extent comparable to the results for the United States as presented in the study by Jacobson, LaLonde, and Sullivan. In some instances we could come close to their study for one of our countries, but not for the other. In such cases we have chosen to select the sample to maximize comparability between Belgium and Denmark. A detailed description of the underlying data sets and our selection of extracts therefrom, with a discussion of a broad range of comparability issues between countries, is provided in the appendix to this chapter. In what follows we provide a broad overview of the main data issues relevant to understanding and interpreting our empirical results.

The Data Sets

For Belgium, we use administrative data from the Belgian social security system. All Belgian workers, with the exception of tenured employees of the federal government, are included in that database. The data provide one record per employee per employer per year, plus information about potential spells of unemployment. In these records, we directly observe the age and gender of the worker, the wage, the number of days worked, and a broad occupational classification (either blue-collar or white-collar). From these records, it is possible to reconstruct employee and firm histories and a (censored) measure of tenure. We do not, however, directly observe the reasons for separation from a job. Nor do we observe any family characteristics, so that we cannot reconstruct UI benefit entitlements. In our computations for both countries, public sector jobs will be excluded (although workers who are displaced from a private firm and find a job in the public sector will be included).

The Danish data are based on the fact that all Danish residents have a personal number. A very wide variety of transactions are recorded against these personal numbers. These data are then centralized and collated by Danmarks Statistiks and are available for research purposes (subject to very stringent controls to maintain confidentiality). Thus, in principle, it is possible to track all adult Danish residents from 1980 to 1994 (the latest year for which information is available) and to analyze a wide variety of behavior. Moreover, individuals can be linked to one another to form households and they can also be linked to the plants at which they work, which can also be followed over time. Thus there is considerable scope for research into the labor market encompassing demographic and plant information. In this study we take a subsample of workers in private firms and follow them from 1980 to 1991. Unfortunately, although the initial sample size is reasonably large (37,319 workers), we are left with only a few workers in specific strata, which somewhat limits the precision of some of the analysis. For example, the restriction to high-tenure workers leaves only 15,860 workers and the number of these displaced in our chosen reference year is only 547!

In both countries we focus on displacements that occurred in one particular "reference year," close to the end of the data series available to us. Reference years were chosen to allow us to follow workers for up to three years after displacement, and (by following workers before displacement) to construct (left-censored) tenure measures for as long as possible before displacement. Our reference years are 1983 for Belgium and 1988 for Denmark. Aside from timing, the only other major difference between the two data sets is the fact that the Belgian data are firm-based, while the Danish are plant-based. A second (minor) difference is that all point-in-time wage and employment variables for Belgium are defined for the end of the year, whereas they are defined for mid November for Denmark.

Defining Displacement

We will label as "displaced" all the workers who separate from a firm (or plant) where employment has been reduced by 30 percent or more during the reference year and which had more than five employees before this reduction in employment. In the sample used below, multiple job holders are always excluded and workers having less than three years tenure at the time of displacement are usually excluded. We have also constructed two comparison groups. The first one is made up of workers with at least three years' tenure who continued to be employed at the end of the displacing year in firms (plants, for Denmark) which displaced workers. The second comparison group is made up of workers with at least three years' tenure employed at other plants or firms. The exception to the three-year-tenure rule occurs when we compute displacement rates. Thus the analysis of the postdisplacement outcomes below includes only workers with three years or more of tenure and excludes multiple-job holders. This study of outcomes will look at displaced workers' histories up to three years after their job loss.

Firm or Plant Identification and "False Death"

Sometimes, firms or plants disappear from the Belgian and Danish data. According to the above definition, these firms will be treated as displacing all their workers as they shrink to a size of zero (or "die"). One potential problem with this is the possibility that firms may disappear from the data not because they close, but because they are acquired by another firm or are involved in some other kind of reorganization that does not involve laying off the workforce. Given differences in the nature of the data available to us, we deal with this "false deaths" problem in somewhat different ways in the two countries under study.

In Belgium, firms are identified by a unique taxpayer number that can survive change in ownership. A firm ID number will change only if the firm disappears as a corporation and all its debts have been paid in full; the ID will not change if the corporation is taken over. Given the nature of Belgian industrial organization (big holding companies holding shares in many corporations), corporations rarely disappear. Mergers do happen though, and they are probably more rare than in the United States. Some firms also die and revive under different names. To control for these possibilities we proceeded as follows: vanishing firms where at least 70 percent of the workers were reemployed (at any firm) in the next year, and where 70 percent of those rehired were rehired in a single firm, were not considered to be displacing firms.[4]

In Denmark, an establishment is considered (by Danmarks Statistiks) to be continuing from one year to the next if any one of the following four criteria is satisfied: there are the same owner and same industry; there are the same owner and largely the same employees; there are the same employees and the same industry; or there are the same employees and the same address. More precisely, "same industry" means the same ISIC code at the 5-digit level. "Same employees," in the second case, means that at least 30 percent of the first plant's employees remain at the plant or make up at least 30 percent of the second-year employees. "Same employees," in the third and fourth cases, means that at least 30 percent of the first group of employees remain at the plant *and* make up at least 30 percent of the second-year employees.[5]

Even with such a classification scheme, it remains possible, of course, to categorize workers as "displaced" even though we would not consider them as being genuinely displaced. This can happen if some of the workers at one plant are taken over by another plant. Our database contains variables to take this situation into account. In shrinking but continuing plants, sometimes a group of two or more workers leave the "main" plant and move to a second plant together. Danmarks Statistiks calls such plants "spinoffs." In such situations we classify workers remaining in the main plant as not being displaced, but those moving into the spinoffs as displaced. Among plants that disappear completely from the data, a plant is considered to be "taken over" by a new plant if at least two of its workers are employed in the new plant *and* these workers constitute at least 30 percent of the workforce in the closed plant. Workers involved in such "takeovers" are not treated as displaced workers in our analysis (they are placed in the category "other workers").

RESULTS

Who Is Displaced?

To put our results into context, we first examine some aggregate statistics for Belgium and Denmark for the two years before and after our reference years, which are 1983 for Belgium and 1988 for Denmark. These statistics are presented in Table 6.2. In the period before the reference year, Belgium was suffering a recession and unemployment grew quite quickly (from 7.8 percent to 11.7 percent). In contrast, the prereference years in Denmark were relatively healthy, although the economy declined in the reference year. The postreference-year experiences are much more similar, except that average manufacturing wages declined in Belgium but not in Denmark. In both countries unemployment increased a little in the postreference period even though there was modest real growth. We take these statistics to indicate that the postreference-year macro environment in the two countries was similar and is unlikely to account for any large differences in outcomes that we observe below.

In Table 6.3 we present the incidence of displacement in Belgium and Denmark (for all private sector workers). Although there are some significant differences, the most striking feature of this table is that long-tenure workers (those with three or more years with the firm or plant) are just as likely to be displaced in Denmark as in Belgium (3.45 percent and 3.41 percent, respectively). This comes as something of a surprise since, as we have seen, Belgium has very stringent layoff rules and Denmark has very weak ones. The major difference between the two countries is that short-tenure workers in Denmark are more likely to be displaced and Danish workers (short-tenure and long-tenure) are much more likely to be displaced from a shrinking firm than from a dying one. There are two possible explanations for this last result. It may reflect the fact that in Belgium it is more difficult for firms that continue in business to lay off workers, or it may be that Danish plants are less likely to go out of business, perhaps because they are larger. With the data at hand we are unable to distinguish between these alternatives.

In Table 6.4 we present some of the characteristics of displaced workers. Since our primary focus is on long-tenure workers, we present results only for workers who had at least three years of tenure at the plant or firm where they worked in the sample period. We also break down the sample by whether the firm closed down or not. Finally, we present the same statistics for workers who continued in "shrinking" firms and for those who were not in firms that displaced workers ("other workers"). Comparing the latter to the displaced sample, we see that displaced workers in Belgium tend to have slightly lower tenure (but remember that all the workers here have at least three years' tenure); to have lower wages; to be more likely to be blue-collar; and to work for smaller firms than "other workers." It is also clear that women are more likely to be displaced. There are similar differentials for firm size, tenure, and being blue-collar in Denmark, but the differences in wages and gender composition are much smaller there.

Finally we present an analysis of the characteristics of the displaced using a simple probit for being displaced (see Table 6.5); note that here we include all workers, not just the long-tenure ones. The first column provides a comparison with "all nondisplaced workers" and the second is a comparison with those who remain in displacing firms. In Belgium in the first comparison, the categories more likely to be displaced are: male, blue-collar, lower wage, and low tenure. Controlling for tenure, workers in all age groups over 20 are more likely to be displaced than teens, but there is no apparent age difference in displacement rates between the ages of 20 and 59. Workers over 60 appear to be at somewhat greater risk than workers with similar tenure under 60. The results for the comparison with those in displacing firms are somewhat different. In particular, the tenure effects are now stronger (with workers with less than one year of tenure being much more likely to be displaced than other workers). Despite the differences in sign, the age effects are similar (note that the comparisons are with the "under twenty" group so that the change in sign tells us something only about this group). In Denmark, the probabilities of being displaced are quite similar to those for the "other" comparisons in Belgium. Thus the first columns of Tables 6.4 and 6.5 give a similar picture in comparisons of who is displaced in the two countries except that for the comparison with "nondisplaced" workers, the Danish results do not show any significant differences in the tenure effects. All in all, there are only relatively minor differences between the personal characteristics of workers who are displaced in Belgium and Denmark. The main differences seen in Table 6.4—in the proportion who are white-collar workers and the firm size—reflect differences found in the "other worker" sample. As we shall see below, there are quite sharp differences in the postdisplacement experiences for workers in the two countries and the results presented in Tables 6.4 and 6.5 suggest that these differences in outcomes are unlikely to be due to the sample composition of the displaced groups.

Postdisplacement Employment Outcomes

In Table 6.6 we present some statistics on the unemployment outcomes after displacement (once again, only for long-tenure workers). Specifically, this gives details of how many months of unemployment displaced workers experience in the three years after their displacement. It is most important to note that these statistics give information on (registered) unemployment after displacement and *not* non-employment. Thus, someone who withdraws from the labor force after displacement or remains in the labor force but does not register as unemployed would not be included in the "unemployed" here. These results reveal some extraordinary differences between Belgium and Denmark and are quite different from experiences in other countries. First, almost two-thirds of displaced Danish workers experience no interruption in employment (or unemployment in the subsequent three years) as against one-third for Belgium. The latter figure is more in line with the international experience, so one immediate worry is that the Danish figure is incorrect. One possibility is that in the Danish sample we are misclassifying workers and our displaced sample actually includes some workers who found employment in other plants within the same firm. Although we cannot completely rule this out, as we have documented in the data section above we have gone to great lengths to ensure that we are not making such an error. We also note that the proportion of all workers in Denmark who experience some unemployment in our reference year is 23 percent. This is in line with aggregate statistics that are compiled from different sources, leading us to believe that our calculations are not seriously biased.

Turning to workers who do experience some unemployment, we see that Danish workers are unemployed for an average of five months but Belgian workers have average spells of 15 months (but note that any spell is truncated above at 36 months). Now it is the Belgian results that are out of line with the wider international experience. To investigate these differences, we also present selected quantiles of spell lengths in the lower portion of Table 6.6. From these we see that Danish workers either move out of unemployment relatively quickly (more than 50 percent of those exiting unemployment do so within about two months) or tend to stay for long spells. In contrast, the majority of workers who become unemployed in Belgium tend to have long spells—less than one-half of them have left unemployment after one year.

Combining the probability of having any unemployment and the mean spell length, we see that a Belgian displaced worker has an expected unemployment spell of about 10 months as against 6 weeks for a Danish worker. What could account for such large differences? Here we list some possibilities, informally. The first is that there is a difference in definitions. The definitions of unemployment in our two samples are not exactly the same, but they are so close that it is not credible that the differences in outcomes are attributable to this. A second possibility is that there are differences in sample composition, that is, that the composition of the displaced worker groups are very different in the two countries. As we saw in Table 6.4, however, the two samples appear to have similar personal characteristics so that it is unlikely that it is this that accounts for the differences in unemployment outcomes. A third possibility is that the differences are due to differences in notice provisions. As discussed in the institutions section, workers in Belgium generally receive more advance notice of closures and mass layoffs than workers in Denmark. Conventional search models would then suggest the converse of what we observe. Similar remarks apply to a fourth possibility, namely, that the differences in outcomes can be attributed to differences in UI systems. Both Denmark and Belgium are usually regarded as having very generous UI systems (see, for example, Table 6.1 above) but, as discussed in the institutions section, this is something of an illusion for Belgium. In fact, an unemployed worker in Denmark is more likely to receive high benefits than a comparable worker in Belgium. This is because Belgian benefits are means tested so that married workers with an employed spouse do not receive much. Given this, we regard it as extremely unlikely that the differences in unemployment outcomes in Belgium and Denmark are due to differences in the UI system. Indeed, we can go further and question whether the "generosity" of the UI system in Belgium "causes" the observed long unemployment spells, given that the UI system in Denmark is at least as generous and unemployment spells are much shorter. This is clearly work for the future but we note here that this conclusion—that the long spells in Belgium are unlikely to be solely the result of the UI system—highlights the virtue of making cross-country comparisons.

A fifth possibility is that the payment of severance pay to long-tenure workers in Belgium facilitates longer unemployment spells there. Certain aspects of the results presented here are consistent with this—for example, the longer duration for the longest-tenure workers (see upcoming discussion of Table 6.8). Moreover, this effect is absent for Denmark where severance pay is not usually given. This is certainly an explanation that deserves closer inspection. Since the data at hand do not report severance pay, we cannot follow this through here. A sixth possible explanation for the differences between the two countries is the different cyclical effects in the two countries. As discussed above, however, Belgium and Denmark experienced fairly similar cyclical conditions after the reference year; it is difficult to believe that such small differences could lead to such large differences in outcomes. Yet another alternative (number seven) is that because the UI system in Denmark is administered by the unions they have more incentive, or more ability, to find displaced workers new jobs. With respect to this hypothesis it is sufficient to note that although the unions administer UI payments they have no direct financial incentive to move workers from unemployment to a new job. It thus seems unlikely that unions' incentives explain the difference between the countries.

An eighth alternative is that labor-demand conditions differ significantly between the two countries. Although the cyclical conditions in the countries are similar, it is still possible that there could be permanently lower arrival rates of job offers in Belgium. In a conventional search model this would lead to longer unemployment durations. This would also be consistent with the major difference in employers' firing flexibility between the two countries: high firing costs in Belgium lead to employers being less willing to hire and, consequently, to longer unemployment durations. If this explanation is to be consistent with the roughly equal unemployment rates in the two countries (see Table 6.2), then it means that flows into unemployment must be much higher in Denmark. Given that displacement rates in Denmark are not dramatically higher than in Belgium (see Table 6.3), the bulk of Danish unemployment has to be the result of something other than displacement; for example a higher quit rate. We cannot check this with the data at hand, but this is clearly a promising avenue of future research.

Finally, it could be that the differences arise because Danish wages are less rigid downwards. The aggregate figures on wage growth given in Table 6.2, however, suggest that, if anything, the converse is the case. These show that the average wage in Belgium declined in the year after the sample year but Danish wages did not. On the other hand, these aggregate changes may be masking changes for displaced workers in Denmark who take a job. Thus we need to look at what happened to the earnings and wages of reemployed displaced workers. We shall do this shortly. For now we anticipate those results and state that we do not believe that the very large differences in unemployment outcomes are attributable to a greater propensity for unemployed Danish workers to accept lower wages.

To complement the unemployment statistics of the previous table, we present reemployment rates at annual intervals after the displacement in Table 6.7. These largely confirm the analysis above—Belgian displaced workers have much lower subsequent reemployment rates than Danish displaced workers, particularly in the year after the displacement. One additional interesting feature in Table 6.7 is that Belgian workers who were in a shrinking firm in the reference year but were not displaced are significantly less likely to be employed in later years than "other" workers. This is not the case for Denmark—the employment rates for "other" workers and workers who stayed with shrinking firms are almost identical. Once again, the likeliest explanation for this is the difference in firing costs: Danish firms adjust more quickly to negative demand shocks and are less likely to experience persistent downsizing.

We end the analysis of reemployment with a regression analysis of the determinants of reemployment. Coefficients from comparable Cox partial likelihood models of unemployment durations in both countries are presented in Table 6.8. These coefficients give the (assumed proportional) impacts of different characteristics on the probability of being reemployed. In Denmark we can draw no firm conclusions regarding the determinants of reemployment, due to the small sample size. In Belgium, reemployment is significantly more likely for men, for white-collar workers, high-wage workers, young workers, and (controlling for age) high-tenure workers. As was discussed in Chapter

2 of this volume, this positive effect of tenure may reflect the greater advance notice and other reemployment assistance provided to senior workers under Belgium's strict system of employment protection law.

Postdisplacement Wages and Earnings

We turn now to earnings and wages for those who find a job. We present statistics on earnings in the years after displacement in Table 6.9; once again these are for long-tenure workers. The preparation of these figures makes them somewhat different from those presented for the United States by Jacobson, LaLonde, and Sullivan (1993). In the latter study the possibility of out-of-state migration (with consequent attrition from the sample) meant that Jacobson, LaLonde, and Sullivan had to condition on having some positive earnings in all of the comparison years after the displacement. In our analysis we condition only on being in employment at the end of the relevant year (actually, in November for Denmark—see the appendix for more details). In the top panels of Table 6.9 we present average earnings in the year, conditional on our employment condition, so these are comparable to those given by Jacobson, LaLonde, and Sullivan. These averages are not for the same people in each year so that employment change, wage changes, and selection are all confounded. In the lower panel we present mean log differences in annual earnings as compared to the displacement year so that the comparison in any year is with the same workers in the reference year (year 0). The most obvious feature of the lower panels is the very large drop for displaced workers in Belgium in the year after displacement. This reflects the fact that Belgian displaced workers are more likely than Danish displaced workers to have only part-year employment in the year after, even if they are back in work one year later. There is also a strong decline in year two for Belgian "nondisplaced workers at displacing firms." This mirrors the persistence in displacement seen in Table 6.7. Comparing the results for the two countries, we see that for Denmark even "other workers" record a small loss in earnings (of 1.5 percent) over the three years while displaced workers have a larger loss of 8.3 percent. Thus, Danish displaced workers seem to have a medium run earnings loss of about 6.8 percent as compared to "other workers." In Belgium, however, three-year earnings losses are actually smaller for displaced workers than for "other workers." Indeed, Belgian workers who were not displaced ("other workers") experienced an earnings loss of 7.6 percent in the year after the reference year. This is consistent with the macro evidence on wage and employment changes in year one given in Table 6.2.

In Table 6.10, we present average wage levels and log wage changes. Once again, we concentrate on the latter. For wages the perverse effect noted for earnings for Belgium disappears. Now both Danish and Belgian workers show a decline relative to "other" workers. The order of the decline for Denmark is similar to that of earnings (a relative loss of 6.4 percent as against a relative loss of 6.8 percent for earnings). This suggests that all of the relative medium run negative impacts on earnings for Danish workers are driven by wage losses and not employment changes. In contrast, Belgian displaced workers suffered a relative wage loss of 3.7 percent as against a relative earnings gain of 6 percent. It is important in interpreting these results to keep in mind that we are always conditioning on being back in work at the end of the relevant year. For the reasons discussed above, this probably does not matter much for Denmark but in Belgium those who have found a job after one year are the exception rather than the rule. The finding that displaced Belgian workers who are reemployed are doing relatively better than those who were not displaced seems very likely to be a selection effect.

We finish our analysis in Table 6.11 with a regression of the wage loss for those who are reemployed within two years of the displacement. For both countries the coefficient on the lagged wage is significantly less than 1 so that higher wage workers lose relatively more. Moreover, this effect is more pronounced for Denmark, suggesting that higher wage workers in Denmark do a good deal worse; this is consistent with the earlier analysis suggesting that Danish workers go back to work much more quickly and suffer some wage loss as a consequence. There is no significant effect of age for workers aged between 20 and 60 but workers aged over 60 who choose to go back to work suffer very large falls: 14 percent for Belgium and 28 percent for Denmark. Both countries also show much larger wage losses for women (15 percent for women relative to men for Belgium and 17 percent for Denmark). Given that the reemployment probabilities seem to be lower for women than for men (see Table 6.8), this is clearly an important area for future research. One other notable feature is that postdisplacement wage losses do not seem to be correlated with tenure (given the selection on having at least three years of tenure).

CONCLUSIONS

We have compared the displacement experience in two countries—Belgium and Denmark—that share some common features in their labor market institutions but that also display significant differences. In particular, both have what are thought to be generous UI systems, but firing costs in Belgium are high relative to other countries whereas firing costs in Denmark are very low by international standards. We found that displaced workers in Denmark are more likely to be displaced from a firm that continues in existence than are displaced Belgian workers. This is consistent with the fact that firing costs are much higher for Belgian firms and that, consequently, they are less likely to shed workers if they stay in business. Apart from this we did not find significant differences in the predisplacement characteristics of displaced workers in the two countries. When we compared postdisplacement outcomes we found very significant differences in employment outcomes but only relatively minor ones in wage losses for those who are reemployed. Belgian workers have an expected unemployment spell of ten months while Danish workers have an expected spell of only six weeks. We reviewed a number of possible explanations for this difference. In particular, we rejected the proposition that the longer Belgian spells are due to the UI system since the Danish UI system is even more likely to induce long unemployment spells. We concluded that of all of the explanations we examined, only one is likely to be the cause of the longer spells, namely, that there are permanent differences in the demand side and Belgian workers face a much lower arrival rate of job offers. This lower propensity to hire by Belgian firms is consistent with the differences in firing costs.

Notes

Van Audenrode carried out the analysis on the Belgian data and Albæk and Browning the analysis on the Danish data. This work was supported in part by an EU grant. We thank Martin Junge for his excellent research assistance and Peter Kuhn and conference participants for very helpful comments on an earlier draft.

1. World Economic Forum rankings are based on a combination of objective information and employers' subjective rankings of the difficulty of making employment adjustments. See World Economic Forum 1997.
2. The threshold between low and high wages is set by decree and indexed.
3. Using a survey of private sector employees, Scheuer (1997) found that only 52 percent of the respondents answered that they were covered by a collective agreement. This figure is low compared to other information, including a more recent survey of about 2,000 firms with more than ten employees conducted by Statistics Denmark. In this survey, 69 percent of firms indicated that a majority of their employees were covered by collective agreements. When weighted by the number of employees in the firms, these responses suggest that 83 percent of the workers in firms with more than ten employees are employed in firms where the majority of workers are covered by collective agreements. However, the coverage among firms with less than ten employees is probably considerably below that for larger firms (the coverage among firms with 10–19 employees was 63 percent). Given that about 20 percent of Danish workers work in plants with fewer than ten employees and the 63 percent applies to firms with fewer than ten workers, then we get an average coverage of 79 percent. This figure is an upper bound. If we assume 50 percent coverage for firms with fewer than ten employees then we have an overall coverage of 76 percent. On the basis of these calculations, an estimate of 75 percent coverage of collective agreements among private sector employees seems reasonable.
4. A dying firm from which fewer than 70 percent of its workers failed to become reemployed would automatically be considered a displacing firm according to our 30 percent employment-reduction criterion above.
5. Although our data contain only a small sample of workers, it is important to note that the counts on which these definitions of continuity are based were generated by Danmarks Statistiks from the full population of employees at all plants. Thus we avoid the sampling and inference problem confronted by Bender et al. in their analysis of the French data in this volume.

Table 6.1 Labor Market Characteristics (Ranking out of 53 countries)

Country	Flexible hiring and firing	Low legislative restrictions on firing	Unemployment Insurance "meanness"
Belgium	39	46	52
Canada	10	11	24
Denmark	1	10	46
U.K.	8	5	10
U.S.A.	7	8	5

SOURCE: World Economic Forum (1997).

Table 6.2 Macroeconomic Environment in Belgium and Denmark

	Time to displacement year				
Characteristic	–2	–1	0	1	2
Year					
Belgium	1981	1982	1983	1984	1985
Denmark	1986	1987	1988	1989	1990
Real GDP growth rate					
Belgium	–1.4	1.5	–0.1	1.3	2.1
Denmark	3.6	0.3	1.2	0.6	1.4
Employment growth rate					
Belgium	–0.1	–2.0	–1.3	–1.1	0.0
Denmark	2.6	0.5	–0.6	–0.5	0.0
Unemployment rate					
Belgium	7.8	10.0	11.7	12.9	12.9
Denmark	7.9	7.9	8.7	9.5	9.7
Inflation					
Belgium	7.6	8.7	7.7	6.3	5.2
Denmark	3.3	4.0	4.5	4.6	2.6
Growth in real manufacturing wages					
Belgium	1.4	–1.4	–1.7	–2.1	1.4
Denmark	1.5	0.4	2.0	0.3	1.8

Table 6.3 Incidence of Displacement among Private Sector Workers in Belgium and Denmark (%)

Group of workers	Total	Firms shrinking	Firms dying
Belgium			
All displaced	4.78	2.67	2.11
≥ 3 yr. tenure	3.41	1.80	1.61
Denmark			
All displaced	6.61	4.96	1.65
≥ 3 yr. tenure	3.45	2.84	0.61

SOURCE: Authors' calculations.

Table 6.4 Characteristics of Displaced Workers with Tenure of at least Three Years in Belgium and Denmark

	Belgium		Denmark	
Group	Mean	Std. error	Mean	Std. error
All displaced workers				
Proportion men	0.68	0.002	0.68	0.02
Proportion white-collar	0.36	0.002	0.48	0.021
Age (yr.)	38.66	0.056	41.1	0.49
Tenure (yr.)	5.09	0.006	5.77	0.088
Proportion with more than 6 yr. tenure	0.56	0.002	0.56	0.496
Proportion displaced because of closure	0.48	0.002	0.18	0.016
Average daily wage lost job (BF or DKr)	1942	6.77	128.8	2.7
Average size of firm (no. of workers)	23.37	0.82	45.7	5.39
Number of observations	42,255	n.a.[a]	547	n.a.
Displaced workers in dying firms				
Proportion men	0.656	0.003	0.667	0.049
Proportion white-collar	0.332	0.003	0.563	0.051
Age (yr.)	37.95	0.080	40.4	1.18
Tenure (yr.)	5.104	0.008	5.57	0.212
Proportion with more than 6 yr. tenure	0.567	0.003	0.479	0.051
Proportion displaced because of closure	1.000	n.a.	1.00	n.a.
Average daily wage lost job (BF or DKr)	1.865	8.87	125.3	6.14
Average size of firm (no. of workers)	20.330	1.242	27.3	4.40
Number of observations	20,294	n.a.	96	n.a.
Displaced workers in shrinking firms				
Proportion men	0.707	0.003	0.683	0.022
Proportion white-collar	0.393	0.003	0.457	0.023
Age (yr.)	39.32	0.079	41.2	0.540
Tenure (yr.)	5.082	0.008	5.81	0.097
Proportion with more than 6 yr. tenure	0.555	0.003	0.528	0.023
Proportion displaced because of closure	0	n.a.	0	n.a.
Average daily wage lost job (BF or DKr)	2,014	10.10	129.6	3.01
Average size of firm (no. of workers)	24.824	1.057	50.8	6.77
Number of observations	21,961	n.a.	451	n.a.

Group	Belgium		Denmark	
	Mean	Std. error	Mean	Std. error
Nondisplaced workers in displacing firms				
Proportion men	0.704	0.002	0.660	0.019
Proportion white-collar	0.369	0.002	0.544	0.020
Age (yr.)	39.746	0.057	40.7	.4400
Tenure (yr.)	5.772	0.008	5.68	0.084
Proportion with more than 6 yr. tenure	0.542	0.003	0.497	0.020
Proportion displaced because of closure	n.a.	n.a.	n.a.	n.a.
Average daily wage lost job (BF or DKr)	2,053	8.54	127.4	2.03
Average size of firm (no. of workers)	24.824	1.057	69.5	11.03
Number of observations	39,231	n.a.	608	n.a.
Other workers				
Proportion men	0.732	0.000	0.668	0.004
Proportion white-collar	0.454	0.000	0.542	0.004
Age (yr.)	39.288	0.010	41.0	0.087
Tenure (yr.)	5.386	0.001	6.14	0.017
Proportion with more than 6 yr. tenure	0.703	0.000	0.608	0.004
Proportion displaced because of closure	n.a.	n.a.	n.a.	n.a.
Average daily wage lost job (BF or DKr)	2,294	1.35	131.2	.499
Average size of firm (no. of workers)	49.120	1.548	66.7	2.03
Number of observations	1,104,004	n.a.	14,705	n.a.

[a] n.a. = Not applicable.

SOURCE: Authors' calculations.

Table 6.5 Factors Affecting the Probability of being Displaced, Compared with Nondisplaced Workers in Belgium[a] and Denmark[b]

	Belgium relative to		Denmark relative to	
Worker group	All workers	Workers in displacing plants or firms	All workers	Workers in displacing plants or firms
Male	0.043 (.004)	–0.008 (0.009)	0.025 (0.023)	0.171 (0.048)
White-collar	–0.122 (0.003)	–0.014 (0.008)	–0.176 (0.022)	–0.213 (0.047)
log(wage)	–0.291 (0.004)	–0.066 (0.009)	–0.117 (0.025)	–0.206 (0.054)
Aged 20–29[c]	0.153 (0.008)	–0.133 (0.024)	–0.112 (0.037)	–0.104 (0.080)
Aged 30–39	0.161 (0.008)	–0.270 (0.024)	–0.137 (0.041)	–0.188 (0.088)
Aged 40–49	0.161 (0.008)	–0.304 (0.025)	–0.119 (0.042)	–0.236 (0.090)
Aged 50–59	0.172 (0.009)	–0.304 (0.025)	–0.135 (0.048)	–0.344 (0.098)
Aged 60 or over	0.250 (0.013)	–0.245 (0.032)	0.044 (0.093)	–0.160 (0.185)
Tenure of 1 yr.[d]	0.128 (0.005)	–5.95 (0.062)	–0.234 (0.029)	–0.279 (0.061)
Tenure of 2 yr.	0.017 (0.007)	–6.16 (0.063)	–0.333 (0.036)	–0.414 (0.074)
Tenure of 3 yr.	–0.051 (0.007)	–6.13 (0.063)	–0.473 (0.046)	–0.539 (0.092)
Tenure of 4 yr.	–0.020 (0.007)	–6.02 (0.064)	–0.445 (0.051)	–0.463 (0.102)
Tenure of 5 yr.	–0.033 (0.008)	–6.09 (0.064)	–0.470 (0.063)	–0.407 (0.126)
Tenure of 6 yr.+	–0.209 (0.005)	–6.16 (0.063)	–0.594 (0.033)	–0.340 (0.069)
Pseudo R^2	0.026	0.106	0.045	0.044
Sample size	1,861,806	142,275	37,319	3,494

NOTE: Standard errors are in parentheses.

[a] For Belgium, probit analysis of being displaced during 1983 (dependent variable = 1 if displaced).

[b] For Denmark, probit analysis of being displaced during 1988 (dependent variable = 1 if displaced).

[c] Omitted age is "less than 20."

[d] Omitted tenure is "less than one year."

Table 6.6 Unemployment for Long-Tenure Displaced Workers in the Three Years after Displacement

	Belgium	Denmark
Proportion of displaced workers with some unemployment	0.65 (0.002)	0.31 (0.020)
Mean number of months unemployed[a]	15.22 (0.068)	5.31 (0.585)
Percentile		
5	0.69	0.15
10	1.38	0.24
25	4.16	0.89
50	13.86	2.09
75	25.40	5.33
90	32.10	16.73
95	33.49	25.48

NOTE: Standard errors are in parentheses. Does not include non-employment spells that are not registered as unemployment.

[a] Maximum is set to 36 months.

SOURCE: Authors' calculations.

Table 6.7 Reemployment[a] after Displacement in Belgium and Denmark (Share of workers employed)

	Years after displacement			
Group	0	1	2	3
Belgium				
Displaced workers	1	0.370 (0.002)	0.583 (0.002)	0.664 (0.002)
Nondisplaced workers at displacing firms	1	1	0.712 (0.002)	0.785 (0.002)
Other workers	1	0.930 (0.000)	0.871 (0.000)	0.892 (0.000)
Denmark				
Displaced workers	1	0.718 (0.019)	0.750 (0.019)	0.746 (0.019)
Nondisplaced workers at displacing firms	1	1	0.911 (0.012)	0.859 (0.014)
Other workers	1	0.957 (0.002)	0.918 (0.002)	0.879 (0.003)

NOTE: Standard errors are in parentheses.

[a] Proportion employed at the end of the year (Belgium) or in November of the year (Denmark).

SOURCE: Authors' calculations.

Table 6.8 Duration Analysis of Reemployment for Long-Tenure Workers in Belgium and Denmark

Group of workers	Belgium	Denmark
Male	0.095 (0.014)	0.117 (0.202)
White-collar	0.142 (0.013)	–0.325 (0.193)
Log(wage)	0.192 (0.015)	0.221 (0.412)
Aged 20 to 29[a]	–0.090 (0.057)	–0.315 (1.082)
Aged 30 to 39	–0.200 (0.057)	–0.234 (1.094)
Aged 40 to 49	–0.417 (0.058)	–0.366 (1.108)
Aged 50 to 59	–0.941 (0.059)	–0.577 (1.105)
Aged 60 or over	–1.686 (0.075)	–0.709 (1.226)
Tenure of 4 yrs.[b]	–0.019 (0.020)	–0.282 (0.298)
Tenure of 5 yrs.	0.106 (0.021)	0.615 (0.364)
Tenure of 6+ yrs.	0.137 (0.017)	0.163 (0.230)
Sample size	42,223	135

NOTE: Standard errors are in parentheses. Cox non-parametric estimation of reemployment hazard, compared to all nondisplaced workers, workers with three or more years of tenure only.

[a] Omitted age is "less than 20."

[b] Omitted tenure is "three years."

Table 6.9 Average Annual Earnings and Earnings Growth for Long-Tenure Workers by Years after Displacement

Panel	–1 yr.	0	1 yr.	2 yr.	3 yr.
A. Average earning level of workers					
Belgium (1981 BF)[a]					
Displaced	397,783 (1,114)[b]	327,101 (1,354)	366,496 (1,516)	370,934 (1,548)	n.d.[c]
Nondisplaced	402,002 (1,157)	394,304 (1,390)	323,612 (1,435)	350,049 (1,575)	n.d.
Other	498,963 (245)	489,596 (313)	491,471 (321)	484,745 (330)	n.d.
Denmark (1988 DKr)[d]					
Displaced	185,375 (5,003)	169,031 (4,687)	174,887 (5,017)	170,386 (5,199)	n.d.
Nondisplaced	194,045 (4,350)	189,703 (4,388)	181,627 (4,333)	179,697 (4,118)	n.d.
Other	201,811 (840)	197,817 (865)	197,601 (899)	196,941 (931)	n.d.
B. Earnings growth of workers[e]					
Belgium (1981 BF)[a]					
Displaced	n.d.	n.d.	–0.393 (0.004)[f]	–0.094 (0.004)	–0.026 (0.004)
Nondisplaced	n.d.	n.d.	–0.044 (0.002)	–0.387 (0.004)	–0.091 (0.004)
Other	n.d.	n.d.	–0.076 (0.000)	–0.064 (0.000)	–0.086 (0.000)
Denmark (1988 DKr)[c]					
Displaced	n.d.	n.d.	–0.060 (0.018)	–0.049 (0.025)	–0.083 (0.030)
Nondisplaced	n.d.	n.d.	–0.031 (0.010)	–0.044 (0.012)	–0.062 (0.015)
Other	n.d.	n.d.	–0.013 (0.002)	–0.015 (0.003)	–0.015 (0.003)

[a] BF = Belgian francs. Sample selection = wage rate positive at end of relevant year.
[b] Earnings growth for long-tenure workers is in parentheses.
[c] n.d. = No data available.
[d] DKr = Danish kroner. Sample selection = wage rate positive in November of relevant year.
[e] Growth is measured by $\log(\text{Earnings}_t) - \log(\text{Earnings}_0)$.
[f] Standard errors are in parentheses.
SOURCE: Authors' calculations.

Table 6.10 Average Wages and Wage Growth for Long-Tenure Workers

	Years after displacement				
Panel	–1	0	1	2	3
A. Average wage level of workers					
Belgium (1981 BF)[a]					
Displaced	1,870 (6.52)[c]	1,776 (7.75)	2,012 (5.36)	2,077 (5.49)	n.d.[b]
Nondisplaced	1,824 (7.61)	1,882 (4.414)	1,773 (5.83)	1,716 (6.60)	n.d.
Other	2,124 (0.92)	2,122 (1.24)	2,102 (1.16)	2,082 (1.63)	n.d.
Denmark (1988 DKr)[d]					
Displaced	129 (2.70)	134 (3.97)	133 (3.82)	134 (3.46)	n.d.
Nondisplaced	127 (2.03)	129 (2.94)	132 (2.23)	133 (2.31)	n.d.
Other	131 (0.50)	133 (0.61)	139 (0.61)	142 (0.57)	n.d.
B. Wage growth of workers[e]					
Belgium					
Displaced			–0.038 (0.002)[f]	–0.065 (0.002)	–0.088 (0.002)
Nondisplaced			0.008 (0.002)	–0.038 (0.002)	–0.076 (0.002)
Other			–0.018 (0.000)	–0.032 (0.000)	–0.051 (0.000)
Denmark					
Displaced			–0.032 (0.021)	–0.015 (0.020)	0.001 (0.021)
Nondisplaced			0.004 (0.008)	0.023 (0.010)	0.031 (0.11)
Other			0.008 (0.002)	0.049 (0.002)	0.065 (0.002)

[a]Daily wage rates in 1981 Belgian francs. Sample selection: wage rate positive at end of the relevant year.
[b] n.d. = no data available.
[c] Wage growth for long-tenure workers is in parentheses.
[d] Hourly wage rates in 1988 Danish kroner. Sample selection: wage rate positive in November of the relevant year.
[e] Wage growth is measured as $\log(\text{Wage}_t) - \log(\text{Wage}_0)$.
[f] Standard errors are in parentheses.
SOURCE: Authors' calculations.

Table 6.11 Regression Analysis of Wages in Subsequent Job

Variable	Belgium	Denmark
Log wage on lost job	0.587 (0.005)	0.382 (0.054)
20 < Age ≤30	–0.022 (0.016)	0.595 (0.133)
30 < Age ≤ 40	–0.006 (0.016)	0.611 (0.134)
40 < Age ≤50	–0.020 (0.016)	0.614 (0.135)
50 < Age ≤60	–0.016 (0.016)	0.498 (0.137)
Age > 60	–0.159 (0.022)	0.332 (0.215)
Male	0.148 (0.004)	0.174 (0.043)
White-collar	0.167 (0.004)	0.073 (0.041)
Tenure = 4 yr.	0.003 (0.006)	–0.062 (0.059)
Tenure = 5 yr.	–0.010 (0.006)	–0.099 (0.068)
Tenure = 6 yr. or more	–0.003 (0.005)	–0.051 (0.049)
Lost job firm dead	0.033 (0.003)	0.027 (0.048)
Size of lost job firm	0.001 (0.001)	0.008 (0.014)
Adjusted R^2	0.60	0.26
Sample size	27,567	408

NOTE: Standard errors are in parentheses. OLS for wage in a new job in Belgium in 1985 (two years after a displacement in 1983) and in Denmark in 1990 (two years after displacement in 1988). Controls for region and occupation are included.
SOURCE: Authors' calculations.

Appendix
Data Selection and Definitions

EMPLOYER SIDE

Plants or Firms

For the Belgian data set the unit is firms, but for the Danish data set it is plants. However, the Danish data set contains a variable that indicates if a worker transfers from one plant to another in the same firm. These workers are not considered displaced workers in this study; they are placed in the control groups (the group of stayers or nondisplaced workers in displacing plants). Nevertheless, the difference between firm unit and plant unit is probably the major problem in this study with respect to comparability between the two countries.

The Jacobson, Lalonde, and Sullivan (1993) study (hereinafter called "JLS") appears to analyze firms. JLS (p. 706) stated that the basic statistics are based on "Pennsylvania Unemployment Insurance (UI) tax reports and the state ES202 data on firms' employment." The issue is perhaps not quite clear, however, since they have no explicit discussion about plants or firms as units. JLS (p. 687) mentioned "firm" but it also mentioned "geographical location." Both a plant and a single-plant firm have a "geographical location," while this term is not unambiguous for a multi-plant firm, either.

Size Reduction of Plants or Firms

In our study workers are considered displaced if they separate from a firm (Belgium) or plant (Denmark) which experiences a 30 percent reduction in the workforce from one year to the next. This 30 percent rule will produce more displaced workers when applied to plants than when applied to firms. In general one would expect that it is more serious to separate from a downsizing firm than from a downsizing plant, as firms can reallocate the separated workers to another of their plants. These reallocated workers are not considered displaced in our Danish data set, however, as mentioned.

The JLS study also applied a 30 percent downsizing threshold, but they did not apply this rule to year-to-year changes in employment. Instead they applied the following definitions: ". . . separators whose firms' employment in the year following their departure was 30 percent or more below their maximum level during the late 1970s" (JLS, p. 688).

Size of Plant or Firm (Cutoff Point)

In this study we eliminate firms (Belgium) and plants (Denmark) with five or fewer employees. This cutoff point is applied to one particular year. The main reason for the comparatively small cutoff point is that a higher one would reduce the sample size of displaced workers for Denmark to too low a level. The JLS study had a cutoff point of 50 employees in one particular year, 1979 (p. 688).

Identity of Establishments (False Death Problem)

In Belgium, firms are identified by a unique taxpayer number that can survive a change in ownership. A firm ID number will change only if the firm disappears as a corporation and all its debts have been paid in full. It will not change if the corporation is taken over. Given the nature of Belgian industrial organization (big holding companies holding shares in many corporations), corporations rarely disappear. Mergers do happen, however, although they are probably more rare than in the United States. Some firms also die and revive under a different name. To control for that possibility we proceeded as follows: dying firms from which at least 70 percent of the workers were rehired (so as not to meet our criteria for being called a displacing firm) and 70 percent of those rehired were rehired in a single firm were not considered to be displacing firms.

For Denmark, the IDA database[1] considers an establishment as continuing if just one of the following four criteria is satisfied: 1) same owner and same industry, 2) same owner and same employees, 3) same employees and same industry, or 4) same employees and same address. More precisely, "same industry" means the same ISIC code at the five digit level, and "same employees" (in case 2) means that either at least 30 percent of the earlier employees remain at the plant or these employees make up at least 30 percent of the second-year employees, while "same employees" (in case 3 and 4) means that at least 30 percent of the earlier employees remain at the plant *and* they make up at least 30 percent of the second-year employees. Moreover, a reduction in the workforce in a plant could also take place when one would not consider the workers as genuinely displaced. This could be the case if a share of the workers at a plant were taken over by another plant. The IDA database contains variables to take this situation into account. For continuing plants, these plants are considered "non-identical" if at least two workers find employment in another plant. The creators of the IDA database called these workers "spin offs." A second such situation would concern closed plants which are considered "taken over" by another plant if the other plant employs at least two of the earlier workers *and* these workers constitute at least 30 percent of the workforce in the closed plant. The creators of the IDA database called these workers "take overs." For the present purpose, to ensure maximum comparability between Belgium and Denmark, the following rules apply: The "spin offs" are considered displaced workers (although "spin offs" within a firm are not). The "take overs" are not considered displaced workers (they are placed in the category "other workers").

For the U.S. case, JLS stated p. 707: ". . . [it is] important to account for cases in which a firm's employer identification number (EIN) changes from one period to the next, . . ." and "In cases of mergers and divestitures that occurred during the sample period, we treated the separate parts as a single firm, even in years when they were legally distinct."

Public Sector Exclusion

The present study considers displacement only from the private sector. The analysis of displacement from the public sector is problematic in both the Belgian and Danish cases. The Belgian data set contains no observations for some of their public sector employees. The present version of the Danish IDA database contains considerable measurement errors with respect to plant size. Therefore public sector employees are excluded from the initial state of analysis. If a worker displaced from the private sector gets a job in the public sector, the observation is kept in the sample and the subsequent wage rate in the public sector job enters into the calculations.

In the JLS study, there was no explicit discussion of this topic. Perhaps U.S. economists are supposed to know if the public sector is included in "ES202 data on firms' employment."

EMPLOYEE SIDE

Multiple Jobholders, Identification of Main Employer, Timing during the Year

For the identification of a worker's main employer in Denmark, the IDA definition is used. This means that employed workers at one particular date in the middle of November are assigned to the plant from which they received their main earnings. For Belgium, the employer that comes closest to an employment relationship in November is used: in most cases this amounts to the last employment relationship during the calendar year.

The JLS study allowed only one employer-employee relationship within a year, that where there was the "greatest amount of earnings during the year" (p. 707).

Multiple Jobholders, More Than One Employment Relationship by the End of the Year

For Belgium, those workers who have two jobs at the time of displacement and fulfill the tenure condition of three or more years of employment in *both* of them are deleted from the sample. For Denmark, IDA contains an indication of "side employment" besides the main job (the one with the highest earnings) in November. There is no tenure variable for these "side jobs." Displaced workers with "side jobs" are retained in the calculations.

Wages

For Belgium, wages are wage income per day. In calculating this figure the numerator is the wage income during the year in the firm and the denominator is the number of days employed in the firm. For Denmark, wages are wage income per hour. In calculating this figure the numerator is the wage income during the year in the plant and the denominator is the number of estimated hours employed in the plant. The assessment of the number of hours worked is based on weekly contributions to a pension scheme, for which the size of the contribution depends on the number of working hours. There are some measurement errors contained in the IDA data on the number of hours worked.

The JLS study did not consider wages.

Earnings, Annual

For both Belgium and Denmark we consider wage earnings during the calendar year, including the wage income from all plants or firms in which the worker has been employed. Nominal earnings are deflated by the consumer price index in the two countries (this index is also used for deflating wages). We select workers with positive wage rates. In the Danish case we have wage rates only for workers who are employed at the November date when workers are assigned labor market status including plant affiliation. These workers are the ones that are included in Table 6.10, the table describing the development of wages after displacement (that is the only possibility for Denmark since we do not have wage rates for workers who are not employed at the November date). The figures used in such an earnings table are the early earnings (wage income) from all employers (not only the employer at the November date). Such an earnings table ensures comparability with the table over wage losses since the drop in earnings can be decomposed into a wage loss and a drop in hours. Precisely the same individuals figure in the wage table and the earnings table. This means, however, that we exclude many workers who have positive earnings during the year, but who are not employed at the November date. Such workers might be unemployed most of the year and have just a small number of working hours placed somewhere during the year, but not at the November date.

We also include displaced workers who do not have a positive wage rate. In the previous procedure we included only those workers who were fortunate enough to have a positive wage rate after displacement. The conjecture must be that those workers who do not have positive wage rates fare worse with respect to early earnings (or income). To the extent that there is a difference in the transition rates into other states than employment between the displaced workers and the control group, the above selection will underestimate the drop in yearly earnings as a consequence of displacement. A minimal extension of the sample in the previous procedure is to include workers who have positive yearly earnings in each of the years after displacement. This would be a sample selection where we come as close to the JLS selection scheme as we can with the databases at hand. A further procedure would be to extend the sample to workers who have positive earnings in just one of the years after displacement.

Tenure Condition

In some cases we consider only displaced workers with three or more years of tenure at the year of separation. In the Danish data set we run into sample-size problems if the tenure condition is set higher. The Danish tenure variable is plant tenure while the Belgian one is firm tenure.

In the JLS study the tenure condition was higher—". . . workers who had six or more years of tenure by the beginning of 1980" (p. 689).

Migration and Commuting from the Area of Interest

In the JLS study for Pennsylvania migration and commuting presented a potentially severe problem. The solution applied by JLS is (p. 689): ". . . we have eliminated from our sample the approximately 25 percent of high-tenured separators who subsequently never have positive earnings in our data," and "Finally, to reduce biases due to sample attrition, we required that every worker receive some wage or salary earnings during each calendar year."

For Belgium and Denmark this is probably not a major problem, as the amount of commuting and immigration to other countries is limited compared to other states in the United States.

Reemployment

In the Danish data set a worker is considered reemployed if the worker has a job the next November, when each Danish resident is assigned a particular labor market status. For Belgium an employment and labor market status is constructed for each worker by the end of the year. This construction should come as close to the IDA definition as possible.

In the JLS study (p. 689) workers were considered reemployed if the wage income is positive each calendar year.

Comparison Groups (for Income and Wage Losses)

For Belgium and Denmark we select employees in one particular year, and comparison groups are found among these workers. Workers who enter employment in subsequent years are excluded from the analysis. The main comparison groups to the displaced workers considered in this study are all other workers and nondisplaced workers in displacing establishments.

The JLS study considered different variants of control groups. JLS (p. 690) considered "separators," which must be all workers leaving a firm. The separators were divided in "non-mass layoffs" and "mass layoffs" (the displaced workers according to the different selection criteria). The rest of the workers were labeled "stayers."

OTHER ISSUES

Years, Sample Period

For Belgium the sample period is 1978 to 1985. Dismissal is considered from 1983 to 1984. This makes it possible to trace the effect of displacement two years after its occurrence. The maximum length of tenure in the Belgian data is six years. For Denmark the sample period is 1980 to 1991. Dismissal is considered from 1988 to 1989. Calculations on the consequences two years after displacement are possible. The maximum length of tenure in the Danish data for the year 1988 is eight years.

In the JLS study, the sample period was 1974 through 1986. The observation unit was quarterly, and the data are quarterly observations, although some of the conditioning was performed on a yearly basis.

Aggregate Economic Conditions

For Belgium and Denmark, the years of displacement were moderate to severe with respect to economic activity.

For the JLS study, the conditions were unusually severe in Pennsylvania.

Unemployment

For Belgium, there is information on the number of days unemployment benefit has been paid out. There is also information on the number of days of employment. For Denmark there is information on a quarterly basis on the share of the normal working time when unemployment benefits have been paid out. For both Belgium and Denmark we calculate the length of the unemployment spell after displacement before the entrance into a new job. The unit of measurement is months.

References

Burda, M.W. 1988. "Unemployment in Europe." *Economic Policy* 7: 391–426.

Blanpain, R. 1994. "Employment Security Laws in Belgium." In *Employment Security: Law and Practice in Belgium, Bulgaria, France, Germany, Great Britain, Italy, Japan and the European Communities*, R. Blanpain and T. Hanami, eds. Leuven (Belgium): Peeters Press, pp. 67–88.

Jacobson, Louis, Robert LaLonde, and Daniel Sullivan. 1993. "Earnings Losses of Displaced Workers." *American Economic Review* 83(4): 685–709.

Scheuer, Steen. 1997. *Arbejdstid og overenskomst.* Copenhagen: Nytfra Samfunds-videnskaberne.

World Economic Forum. 1997. *The Global Competitiveness Report.* Geneva, Switzerland.

The Authors

Jaap H. Abbring is a fellow of the Royal Netherlands Academy of Arts and Sciences at the Department of Economics, Free University Amsterdam.

Masahiro Abe is associate professor on the Faculty of Economics at Dokkyo University and a faculty fellow, Research Institute of Economy, Trade and Industry (RIETI), Tokyo, Japan.

Karsten Albaek is an associate professor at the University of Copenhagen.

Stefan Bender is a senior researcher in the Regional Labour Market Research and Analytical Statistics section of the Institute for Employment Research, Nuremberg.

Jeff Borland is an associate professor of economics at the University of Melbourne, where he has held a full-time teaching position since 1988. He is also currently a visiting fellow at the Centre for Economic Policy Research at Australian National University.

Martin Browning is a professor at the University of Copenhagen.

Christian Dustmann is a reader of economics at University College London, a research fellow at DEPR and IZA, and a research associate at the Institute for Fiscal Studies.

Pieter A. Gautier is an assistant professor at the Department of Economics, Erasmus University Rotterdam, and is also affiliated with the Tinbergen Institute.

Paul Gregg is a reader in the economics department at the University of Bristol. He has research associations with the CMPO at Bristol and the Centre for Economic Performance at the LSE, and he is a member of the Council of Economic Advisers at H.M. Treasury.

Yoshio Higuchi is a professor on the Faculty of Business and Commerce, Keio University, and a faculty fellow, Research Institute of Economy, Trade and Industry (RIETI), Tokyo, Japan.

Genevieve Knight is a research fellow at the Policy Studies Institute.

Peter J. Kuhn is a professor of economics at the University of California, Santa Barbara, and is co-editor of the journal *Labour Economics*.

David Margolis is a researcher at CNRS. He is affiliated with TEAM-Universiti Paris 1 Panthion-Sorbonne, CREST, and IZA.

Costis Meghir is a professor of economics at University College London, deputy research director of the Institute for Fiscal Studies, and a research fellow at CEPR.

Masao Nakamura is a professor on the Faculty of Commerce and Business Administration, Konwakai Professor of Japanese Research, and director of the Centre for Japanese Research at the University of British Columbia, Canada.

Christopher J. Ruhm is the Jefferson-Pilot Excellence Professor of Economics at the University of North Carolina at Greensboro and a research associate at the National Bureau of Economic Research.

Arthur Sweetman is an assistant professor in the School of Policy Studies, Queeen's University, Ontario, Canada.

Marc Van Audenrode is a professor at the Université Laval.

Gerard J. van den Berg is a professor of economics at the Free University Amsterdam and is also affiliated with the Tinbergen Institute, IFAU Uppsala, the Centre of Economic Policy Research (CEPR), the Institute for the Study of Labour (IZA), and CREST (Paris).

A. Gijsbert C. van Lomwel is a senior researcher at the CentER Applied Research, Tilburg University.

Jan C. van Ours is a professor of labor economics at Tilburg University and is also affiliated with CentER, CEPR, IZA, and OSA.

Jonathan Wadsworth is a lecturer at Royal Holloway, University of London.

Cited Author Index

The italic letters *f*, *n*, and *t* following a page number indicate that the cited name is within a figure, note, or table, respectively, on that page.

Subject Index

The italic letters *f*, *n*, and *t* following a page number indicate that the subject information is within a figure, note, or table, respectively, on that page.

About the Institute

The W.E. Upjohn Institute for Employment Research is a nonprofit research organization devoted to finding and promoting solutions to employment-related problems at the national, state, and local levels. It is an activity of the W.E. Upjohn Unemployment Trustee Corporation, which was established in 1932 to administer a fund set aside by the late Dr. W.E. Upjohn, founder of The Upjohn Company, to seek ways to counteract the loss of employment income during economic downturns.

The Institute is funded largely by income from the W.E. Upjohn Unemployment Trust, supplemented by outside grants, contracts, and sales of publications. Activities of the Institute comprise the following elements: 1) a research program conducted by a resident staff of professional social scientists; 2) a competitive grant program, which expands and complements the internal research program by providing financial support to researchers outside the Institute; 3) a publications program, which provides the major vehicle for disseminating the research of staff and grantees, as well as other selected works in the field; and 4) an Employment Management Services division, which manages most of the publicly funded employment and training programs in the local area.

The broad objectives of the Institute's research, grant, and publication programs are to 1) promote scholarship and experimentation on issues of public and private employment and unemployment policy, and 2) make knowledge and scholarship relevant and useful to policymakers in their pursuit of solutions to employment and unemployment problems.

Current areas of concentration for these programs include causes, consequences, and measures to alleviate unemployment; social insurance and income maintenance programs; compensation; workforce quality; work arrangements; family labor issues; labor-management relations; and regional economic development and local labor markets.

Lewis & Clark College - Watzek Library
3 5209 00708 9424